SAP PRESS e-books

Print or e-book, Kindle or iPad, workplace or airplane: Choose where and how to read your SAP PRESS books! You can now get all our titles as e-books, too:

▸ By download and online access
▸ For all popular devices
▸ And, of course, DRM-free

Convinced? Then go to **www.sap-press.com** and get your e-book today.

Project Management with SAP® Project System

 PRESS

SAP PRESS is a joint initiative of SAP and Galileo Press. The know-how offered by SAP specialists combined with the expertise of the Galileo Press publishing house offers the reader expert books in the field. SAP PRESS features first-hand information and expert advice, and provides useful skills for professional decision-making.

SAP PRESS offers a variety of books on technical and business-related topics for the SAP user. For further information, please visit our website: *www.sap-press.com*.

Kieron Dowling
Project Builder in SAP Project System—Practical Guide
2015, approx. 325 pp., hardcover
ISBN 978-1-4932-1209-5

Ian Ryan, Birgit Starmanns
Product Costing and Manufacturing with SAP
2015, approx. 600 pp., hardcover
ISBN 978-1-4932-1188-3

Jawad Akhtar
Production Planning and Control with SAP ERP
2013, 1033 pp., hardcover
ISBN 978-1-59229-868-6

Janet Salmon
Controlling with SAP—Practical Guide (2nd edition)
2014, 700 pp., hardcover
ISBN 978-1-4932-1012-1

Mario Franz

Project Management with SAP® Project System

Bonn • Boston

Galileo Press is named after the Italian physicist, mathematician, and philosopher Galileo Galilei (1564–1642). He is known as one of the founders of modern science and an advocate of our contemporary, heliocentric worldview. His words *Eppur si muove* (And yet it moves) have become legendary. The Galileo Press logo depicts Jupiter orbited by the four Galilean moons, which were discovered by Galileo in 1610.

Editor Sarah Frazier
Acquisitions Editor Emily Nicholls
German Edition Editor Kerstin Billen
Translation Lemoine International, Inc., Salt Lake City, UT
Copyeditor Melinda Rankin
Cover Design Eva Schmücker, Graham Geary
Photo Credit Shutterstock.com/135575027/© Flegere
Layout Design Vera Brauner
Production Graham Geary
Typesetting SatzPro, Krefeld (Germany)
Printed and bound in the United States of America, on paper from sustainable sources

ISBN 978-1-4932-1006-0
© 2015 by Galileo Press Inc., Boston (MA)
4th edition 2015
4th German edition published 2014 by Galileo Press, Bonn, Germany

Library of Congress Cataloging-in-Publication Data
Franz, Mario.
[Projektmanagement mit SAP Projektsystem. English]
Project management with SAP project system / Mario Franz. -- 4th edition.
pages cm
Includes index.
ISBN 978-1-4932-1006-0 (print : alk. paper) -- ISBN 1-4932-1006-8 (print : alk. paper) --
ISBN 978-1-4932-1007-7 (ebook) -- ISBN 978-1-4932-1008-4 (print and ebook : alk. paper)
1. SAP R/3. 2. Project management. 3. Project management--Computer programs. I. Title.
HF5548.4.R2F7313 2014
658.4'04028553--dc23
2014039972

Contents at a Glance

Dear Reader,

Overwhelmed. It's a feeling we've all had and would soon like to forget. As an editor, juggling one, two, or even three books a month can make me want to hide under the covers of life and hibernate into next spring. Prioritizing, time management, project management—these become more than just words when big work tasks are looming—they become lifelines. That's what SAP Project System and this book are—your lifeline.

Providing the necessary insights needed for mastering the basics, author Mario Franz demonstrates how to carry out the essential project steps and phases through SAP Project System. Back and better than ever, this fourth edition offers updated screenshots, an expanded index, information on the new SAP Commercial Project Management tool, details on new SAP Fiore-based apps, and much more. From development to invoicing, with this book you'll learn how to improve your business processes, while maintaining your time and sanity.

We at SAP PRESS want to hear from you! What did you think about the fourth edition of *Project Management with SAP Project System*? Your comments and suggestions are the most useful tools to help us make our books the best they can be. We encourage you to visit our website at *www.sap-press.com* and share your feedback.

Thank you for purchasing a book from SAP PRESS!

Sarah Frazier
Editor, SAP PRESS

Galileo Press
Boston, MA

sarah.frazier@galileo-press.com
www.sap-press.com

Contents

5   Period-End Closing 373

6 Reporting 447

7 Integration Scenarios with Other Project Management Tools 513

Introduction

Due to the pressure of implementing projects successfully within increasingly shorter periods and under continuously rising costs, project management methods and tools are becoming more important in the industry and in the public sector. Projects range from smaller cost and investment projects, to development or plant maintenance projects, to large-scale projects in plant engineering, construction, and mechanical engineering.

An abundance of project management software products are available that project managers can use for support in planning and implementing their projects. Many companies also use programs they have developed by themselves for individual aspects of project planning and implementation; however, only a few project management tools can map the entire lifecycle of a project completely and uniformly. A lack of integration options frequently results in project data, such as cost information or time data, needing to be entered several times. Therefore, most project management tools suffer from inaccurate project data and restricted transparency of project-related information and documents.

To avoid these problems, companies that already use an SAP Enterprise Resource Planning (ERP) system, such as an R/3, Enterprise, or ERP Core Component (ECC) system, are now increasingly using SAP Project System to manage their projects and therefore benefit from the close integration of SAP Project System with Accounting, Materials Management, Sales, Production, Human Resources, and so on. Since the early stages of SAP Project System in the R/2 system, the range of functions of SAP Project System, and the integration options available, has continued to grow. At the same time, usability has increased considerably. The experiences and requirements of companies from different branches have been incorporated into the development of SAP Project System.

Because SAP Project System offers functions for managing almost all types of projects (and often in different ways, depending on the requirements), most companies that use SAP Project System only use a small portion of the available functions. Frequently, companies initially only use a few of the SAP Project System tools (for example, to control their project costs) and then gradually use other options.

Objective of this Book

The objective of this book is to explain the main functions and integration scenarios of SAP Project System. We will discuss business processes that can be mapped using SAP Project System and also highlight the required settings for doing this and for Customizing in SAP Project System. References to customer enhancements (user exits) and Business Add-Ins (BAdIs) or to notes addressing modifications indicate additional customizing options of SAP Project System. Although this book is written with SAP ERP 6.0 Enhancement Package 6 in mind, most of the functions are also available in earlier releases. Therefore, this book can also be used by readers who, for example, use an Enterprise release or SAP ERP 6.0 without any enhancement package. Functions that are provided in various enhancement packages or functions that require the use of the SAP HANA platform will be specifically mentioned in the text.

The range of SAP Project System functions can be used across different project types and industries. This book therefore describes the functions of SAP Project System in the most general sense possible, without restricting itself to specific uses or to individual project types. Nevertheless, you will note that often only explicit examples and specific screenshots can truly clarify functions and contexts. In these cases, the book uses an Internet Demo and Evaluation System (IDES) scenario of an engineer-to-order production of elevators. If you have the opportunity to use IDES data, you can reproduce the specified examples in your own SAP system.

Target Audience

This book is intended for readers who require detailed knowledge of the different settings options of SAP Project System for the purpose of system implementation. These users could include consultants or persons responsible for SAP Project System implementation or people who want to broaden or refresh their knowledge, such as project managers, Competence Center employees, or key users of a company. However, this book is also for readers who are interested in getting an overview of the functions and concepts of SAP Project System, such as decision makers in a company who are responsible for deciding to implement SAP Project System.

As a general prerequisite for using this book, you as the reader must have basic business knowledge and be familiar with project management methods. Due to its integration with various other SAP components, a basic knowledge of these SAP components is also required to understand many of the functions and processes of SAP Project System. SAP Project System does not contain any organizational units of its own, for example, but instead uses organizational units of Financial Accounting, Production, Purchasing, Sales and Distribution, and so on. Therefore, readers with only a modicum of SAP knowledge should, if necessary, use the SAP Glossary and SAP Library that are available for free at *help.sap.com*.

Structure of the Book

The structure of this book reflects the individual phases of managing a project using SAP Project System. **Chapter 1** first describes how you can map your projects in the SAP system using suitable structures. These structures, and their master data, form the basis for all other planning and execution steps.

With this structuring, you set the course for other planning and execution functions using the profiles and control indicators covered in this chapter. If you want to use this book as an initial introduction to project management with SAP Project System, skip the details about these profiles and indicators when you first read the book.

Chapter 2 deals with the various functions of SAP Project System available for planning the logistical and relevant accounting aspects of your projects. For many projects (in particular, cost or investment projects), budgeting takes place in the approval phase. **Chapter 3** describes the functions of SAP Project System available for budgeting. **Chapter 4** discusses typical processes that can be mapped in the SAP system as part of the execution phase of projects following approval and the resulting quantity and value flows. The wide range of integration options of SAP Project System with other SAP components is also addressed in this chapter. Additional procedures, such as calculating overhead costs or project settlement, are carried out periodically. **Chapter 5** covers the periodic procedures available in SAP Project System for the planned and actual data of your projects.

A key aspect of project management is the analysis of all project-related data. The reporting functions of SAP Project System that support you in every phase of your project management process are introduced in **Chapter 6**. Finally, **Chapter 7** discusses the possible integration of SAP Project System with Microsoft Project, Primavera, SAP Portfolio and Project Management, and SAP Commercial Project Management.

The most important database tables of SAP Project System and a list of Business Application Programming Interfaces (BAPIs) available for developing your own interfaces and process steps are listed in the **Appendix**. Furthermore, in the Appendix you can find an overview of the reuse and query views that are currently provided in SAP HANA Live to define you own evaluations. The Appendix additionally contains tables listing the transaction codes and menu paths of the most important transactions and Customizing activities mentioned in the text.

How to Use this Book

To make it easier for you to use this book, we have included special symbols to indicate information that might be particularly important to you.

[!] This icon refers to specifics that you should consider. It also warns you about frequent errors or problems that can occur.

[+] This icon highlights tips that provide further information on the current topic. It flags tips that will make your work easier.

[◉] Text passages highlighted with this icon summarize thematic relationships at a glance.

In SAP Project System, structuring projects is the basis for all subsequent project management steps. Therefore, selecting the right structures and an efficient structuring process are critical when managing your projects.

1   Structures and Master Data

A prerequisite of project management using SAP Project System is the mapping of projects in the SAP system via appropriate structures. These structures form the basis for planning, entering, and analyzing all data that is relevant to a project. For this purpose, SAP Project System provides two structures: *work breakdown structures* (WBS) and *networks*. These two structures differ in the way they enable you to structure projects and in the functions provided for them in the SAP system. For example, if you need a hierarchical budget management function for a project, then you would want to use a work breakdown structure. If you also want to perform capacity requirements planning for the same project, then you would have to use networks as well.

Work breakdown structures and networks

We begin this chapter with a description of the basic differences between work breakdown structures and networks and the authorization concept of SAP Project System, which was already enhanced for Enhancement Package (EHP) 3. Then we will discuss the essential master data of the two structures and milestones, documentation options, and Customizing activities that are necessary in a structuring process. Statuses play a major role in controlling projects. We will show you the functions that statuses are responsible for in SAP Project System and how you can define your own statuses. We will also introduce you to the transactions and tools you can use for structuring purposes and for processing master data. You will learn how to use versions of SAP Project System to document the progress of a project and for what-if scenario analyses. Finally, we'll describe the different steps and necessary prerequisites for archiving and deleting project structures.

1.1 Basic Principles

Depending on your specific requirements, you may only be able to map a project via a work breakdown structure, or only by using networks, or a combination of both.

Structuring options

Figure 1.1 illustrates the different structuring options. The symbols used for the different structure objects in the figure correspond to the symbols used in the SAP system to represent those objects. The following sections describe the basic differences between the different structuring options.

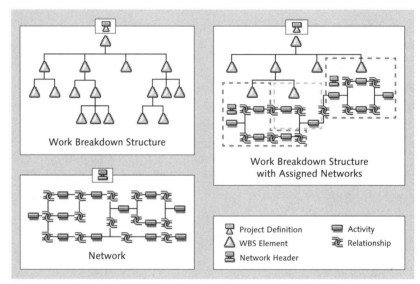

Figure 1.1 Usage Options of Work Breakdown Structures (WBS) and Networks to Structure Projects

1.1.1 Overview of Project Structures

Work breakdown structure

Work breakdown structures enable you to map the structure of a project in the SAP system. This is done via WBS elements that are located at different levels and that structure the project hierarchically (see Figure 1.2). An advantage of a hierarchical structure is that within the structure, data can be inherited or distributed in the top-down direction, and it can be aggregated or summarized in the bottom-up direction.

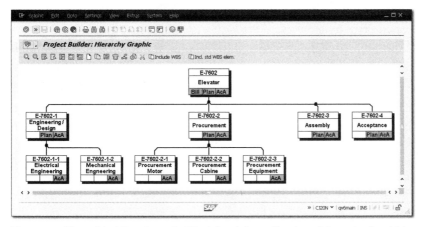

Figure 1.2 Hierarchical Structure of a Work Breakdown Structure (Hierarchy Graphic)

You can use WBS elements to structure your projects (for example, based on phases, functions, or organizational aspects) at the individual level. There is no universal recommendation with regard to how you should structure a project using a work breakdown structure. Instead, the selection of appropriate structures depends on many different aspects and should be carefully thought out before a project starts. Section 1.2 has some general tips on how you can structure projects using a work breakdown structure.

The following list provides an overview of important functions of work breakdown structures in the SAP system:

Functions of work breakdown structures

- ▶ Planning and entering dates
- ▶ Cost planning and account assignment of documents
- ▶ Planning and invoicing revenues
- ▶ Planning and monitoring payment flows
- ▶ Hierarchical budget management
- ▶ Material stock management
- ▶ Various period-end closing tasks
- ▶ Monitoring a project's progress
- ▶ Aggregated data analysis

Because of their functional scope, work breakdown structures that are not assigned to networks are typically used to map projects that focus on controlling aspects and therefore require fewer logistical functions. These kinds of projects usually involve overhead cost or investment projects. Work breakdown structures are also frequently used in real life due to their controlling functions, and actual project management tasks are performed using other project management tools (see Chapter 7). Work breakdown structures are also used, for example, instead of internal orders, because a WBS enables you to carry out hierarchical project controlling activities. For example, you can distribute a budget to individual parts of a project within a work breakdown structure. This is not possible if you use internal orders.

Network   You can use one or several networks to map the flow of a project or of parts of a project in the SAP system. To do this, you need networks that are linked to each other via *relationships* (see Figure 1.3).

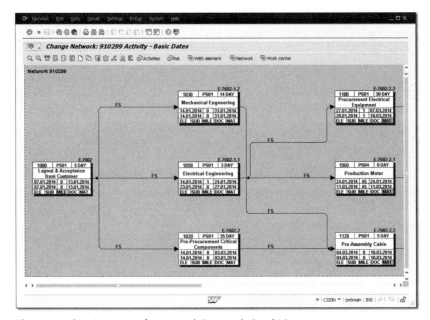

Figure 1.3 Flow Structure of a Network (Network Graphic)

The relationship between two activities defines the logical sequence of the activities (predecessor-successor relationship) and their time-based interdependencies. You can also map project flows across different networks by linking activities of different networks to each other. An essential advantage of the network technique is that SAP systems can automatically determine planned dates for each activity and the entire network on the basis of the duration of individual activities and their chronological sequence. In addition, the system can also determine floats and time-critical activities.

The following list provides an overview of important functions of networks in the SAP system:

Functions of networks

- Scheduling
- Resource planning
- Confirmation of work
- External procurement of services
- Material requirements planning, procurement, and delivery
- Network costing
- Various period-end closing tasks
- Monitoring a project's progress

Because of their functionality, networks are predominantly used to map projects in which logistical functions, such as automatic time scheduling, resource planning, or the procurement of materials, are required. You can use networks independently of or in conjunction with a WBS.

To utilize the functions and benefits of work breakdown structures and networks at the same time, you can assign network activities to WBS elements. A WBS element can be assigned several activities (even from different networks, if required); however, an activity can only be assigned to a maximum of one WBS element. Once you have assigned activities to WBS elements, you can exchange data between the work breakdown structure and the activities. For example, activities can inherit statuses from the WBS elements they are assigned to. Conversely, you can total up project activity dates to the WBS elements or check funds allotted to activities against the budget of the WBS elements. In reporting, you can obtain an aggregated analysis of the data of assigned activities at the level of WBS elements.

Work breakdown structures and networks

Operative and
standard
structures,
versions

In general, the structures available in SAP Project System are divided into *operative structures* (work breakdown structure and network), *standard structures* (standard work breakdown structure and standard network), and *versions* (project version and simulation version).

Although you can use the operative structures for planning and carrying out your projects (that is, for operational project management), the standard structures merely serve as templates for the creation of operative structures or of parts of those structures. Versions can be used to record the status of a project at a specific point in time or at a certain stage in the system. In addition, you can use versions to test changes that are implemented retroactively before including them in your operative project.

1.1.2 Access Control Lists

SAP Project System uses the general authorization concept of the SAP ERP Enterprise Core Component (ECC) system, which is based on authorization objects and authorization profiles.[1] However, because this authorization concept only indirectly allows assigning authorizations for individual objects or parts of a project, SAP developed access control lists in EHP 3. These lists provide the option to directly assign object-specific authorizations in operative projects.

Access control list

Access control lists describe which user, user group, or organizational units should have administrative, change, or display authorizations or even no authorization at all for a specific object (see Figure 1.4). Provided you have activated the respective option in Customizing, you can enter separate access control lists for all operative structure objects (with the exception of appended objects, such as milestones or material components), which facilitates the assignment of object-specific authorizations considerably. If required, you can also enable the inheritance of authorizations in access control lists via Customizing. To specify that an

---

1 You can find more details about the general authorization concept in the SAP ECC system in the book *Authorizations in SAP Software: Design and Configuration* (SAP PRESS, 2010). In addition, SAP Notes 554415 and 522426 provide useful tips about general authorizations in SAP Project System.

authorization is supposed to be inherited, you must set the corresponding flag in the access control list.

Figure 1.4 Sample Access Control List for Assigning Object-Specific Authorizations

Transaction CNACLD enables you to view the authorizations of a project that have been assigned via access control lists. In addition, you can use that transaction to delete all access control lists of a project, either completely or with the exception of administrative authorizations. Once you have deleted an access control list in its entirety, the RPSACL_MIGRATE program allows you to reactivate it or to activate an access control list retroactively for a specific project.

Access Control Lists and General Authorizations	[+]
Note that access control lists merely represent an option to further detail general authorizations. Thus, to have authorizations for an object, a user must have the general authorizations and be authorized via the access control list of that object.	

1.2   Work Breakdown Structure

You can subdivide a project into different parts by using the WBS elements of a work breakdown structure. You can further subdivide those parts until you have reached the required level of detail. Technically, you can use any number of WBS elements at each level; however, for performance reasons, a work breakdown structure should not contain more than 10,000 WBS elements.[2]

Size of work breakdown structures

A work breakdown structure should map all relevant aspects of a project to enable comprehensive planning and analysis of a project in the SAP

---

2 You can find more detailed information on the size of work breakdown structures in SAP Note 206264.

system. The tasks of the different project parts, particularly the individual WBS elements, should be defined clearly and unambiguously, and they should be time-dependent and feasible. Furthermore, the tasks should contain criteria that enable you to analyze their progress, which is important for analyzing the progress of the entire project.

Methods of structuring Let's take a brief look at a sample elevator project to demonstrate some possible ways of structuring a work breakdown structure at a specific level:

▸ **Phase-based structuring**
This type of structuring could involves the following WBS elements: *engineering*, *procurement*, or *assembly*. Phase-based structuring is particularly well-suited for time scheduling and a step-by-step execution of project parts.

▸ **Function-based structuring**
This structuring method could comprise WBS elements for individual assemblies of the elevator, such as *motor*, *elevator shaft*, or *elevator cabin*. If you use project stocks (see Chapter 2, Section 2.3.2), then those elements enable you to keep separate stocks for the different assemblies.

▸ **Structuring based on organizational aspects**
If this type of structuring is used, individual structures could contain single WBS elements for *Sales and Distribution*, *Purchasing*, or *Production*, or they could be separated by responsible cost centers. With regard to reporting, this type of structuring allows the direct evaluation of cost portions for the different organizational units.

Shown previously, Figure 1.2 illustrates the structure of the elevator project, which is used as a real-life example here. We used phase-based structuring for level 2, whereas the structuring type we chose for level 3 is based on functional aspects. The example shows that you can choose different structuring logics for different levels. Note, however, that you should not vary the structuring types at a single level within the work breakdown structure.

When structuring your projects, you should pay also attention to the following question: "Based on which aspects do you want to analyze the data in reporting?" You can use different project views and the project summarization function in reporting to include alternative evaluation hierarchies in your analysis (see Chapter 6).

The required level of detail in cost planning and budgeting can provide you with additional information about how many hierarchy levels you may need. You should also consider which structuring option might be the most appropriate one if you want to settle the project costs at a later stage or carry out a results analysis (see Chapter 5).

Alternative Structuring Options	[+]
Avoid creating too many hierarchy levels and WBS elements. For example, if you want to use WBS elements to track dates or events and not for controlling purposes, you can also work with milestones or progress tracking (see Chapter 4, Section 4.7.3).	

1.2.1 Structure and Master Data

A work breakdown structure consists of WBS elements that are located at different levels to map the hierarchical structure of a project. Each work breakdown structure is based on a *project definition* that serves as a framework for the project and contains parameters that control the properties of the entire project. Furthermore, the project definition contains default values that are passed on to newly created WBS elements. However, it is the WBS elements that actually contain the cost, revenue, budget, and scheduling data. The project definition is not a separate controlling object in the SAP system.

Assignment of WBS Elements	[!]
Each WBS element is uniquely assigned to a project definition. This assignment cannot be changed; that is, you cannot reassign a WBS element that is based on a specific project definition to another project definition.	

Project Definition

If you create a project in SAP Project System by using one of the transactions described in Section 1.7, you must first create a project definition (see Figure 1.5). Some processes require you to first create a WBS

Identification

element. The project definition is then created automatically when you save the WBS element. Note that once you have saved a WBS element this element can never exist without an associated project definition.

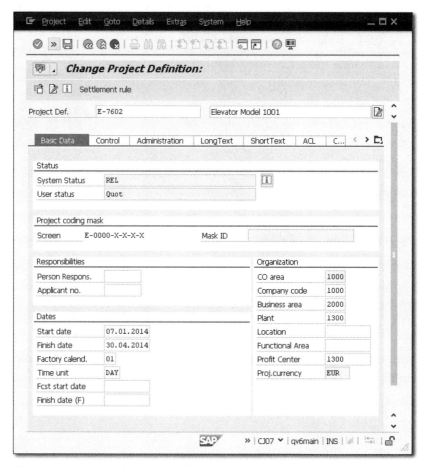

Figure 1.5 Basic Data of a Project Definition

During the creation process, you must specify a unique identification for the project definition, which may consist of a maximum of 24 characters. You can also search for an available identification. You can control the structure of the identification via coding masks (see Section 1.2.2).

In addition to the identification, you also specify a *short text* as a description for your project. If necessary, you can also enter a descriptive *long text*. Depending on the scheduling settings (see Chapter 2, Section 2.1), you must specify a start or end date for your projects; otherwise, the system will propose using the current date. You can always change the dates later during the date planning process.

Short and long text

When creating the project definition, you must always specify a *project profile*. The project profile contains control data and default values for the project. You can store all additional mandatory fields of the project definition as default values in the project profile, so it is usually sufficient to specify the identification and the project profile when creating the project definition. You cannot change the project profile of a project at a later stage. Project profiles can be created for different project types in the Customizing section of SAP Project System (see Section 1.2.2).

Project profile

You must assign your project to a controlling area at the project definition level. The assignment to a controlling area is mandatory. It can be proposed via the project profile and cannot be changed after you have saved your project for the first time.

Organizational assignments

Assignment to the Controlling Area

The assignment of a project to a controlling area via the project definition is unique. For this reason, a work breakdown structure cannot comprise several controlling areas.

[!]

Although the COMPANY CODE and PROJECT CURRENCY fields are also mandatory, the entries you store in the project definition are merely default values for the WBS elements. Therefore, the assignment to a company code can be changed for each individual WBS element.

The PROJECT CURRENCY field has the following purpose: All currency-based data of your projects is managed in three different currencies—the controlling area currency, the transaction currency (that is, the currency of the respective business transactions), and the project or object currency if this is explicitly permitted for the controlling area.

Object currency

The conversion of currency-based data then occurs automatically when the data is entered and on the basis of the latest exchange rates defined in Customizing.

You can choose the object currency for each WBS element separately, provided you use only one company code in your controlling area. If you cover several company codes in cost accounting, then the object currency is automatically derived from the local currency of each company code and cannot be changed manually.

The assignments to other organizational units within FI (business area, profit center) and logistics (plant, location) that you can enter in the project definition serve as default values for the WBS elements of the project. However, you should note that the BUSINESS AREA field is also mandatory if business area balance sheets are maintained.

You can also store a *responsible person* for your project in the project definition and an *applicant* (see Section 1.2.2). These entries are automatically adopted as default values when you create a WBS element.

Partner determination procedure

If you want to enter additional personal data or partner information for purely informational purposes, you can enter a *partner determination procedure* in the project definition (see Section 1.2.2). Once you have specified the partner determination procedure, the system displays an additional tab for the project definition (and all assigned WBS elements) in which you can enter additional responsible persons, personnel numbers, SAP users, or even suppliers and customer IDs, depending on the definition of the partner determination procedure. You can even navigate into the detailed views of all of those entries. The reporting section provides a separate report for analyzing this partner data.

In addition to the partner determination procedure, you can also define the planning profile, budget profile (see Chapter 2, Section 2.4 and Chapter 3, Section 3.1), and simulation profile (see Section 1.9.2) in the project definition. All other profiles contained in the CONTROL DATA tab of the project definition are default values for the WBS elements of the project.

Another important setting to be made at the project-definition level involves the project stock indicators. Chapter 2, Section 2.3.2 has details about this setting. However, you should note that you can no longer modify the settings as to whether you want to allow a valuated project stock once you have saved the project definition.

Project stock

The SALES PRICING fields are only relevant if you want to carry out sales pricing exclusively on the basis of your project data—that is, without any relation to a customer inquiry (see Chapter 2, Section 2.5.4).

You can control the presentation of the project definition fields using *field selection* (see Section 1.8.1). Additional project definition fields can be implemented by using a customer enhancement.

As of EHP 3, the system provides two additional important functions at the project definition level: the assignment of authorizations using access control lists and the definition of grouping indicators. If you define grouping indicators in a project in the form of a free text, then you can use these indicators later in assigned networks to summarize procurement-relevant items (material, external activities, and services) of the project in a suitable way (see Chapter 2, Section 2.2.4).

Grouping indicator

WBS Elements

Figure 1.6 shows the detail screen of a WBS element. Like the project definition, a WBS element also contains a unique external identification that consists of a maximum of 24 characters and can be controlled through a coding mask. Because the project definition and WBS elements involve different objects, a WBS element can have the same identification as the project definition. Internally, the system assigns another unique number to the WBS element, which allows you to modify the external identification at a later stage. However, you cannot modify the external identification at a later point in time if you have distributed the work breakdown structure to other systems via Application Link Enabling (ALE), or if the status of a WBS element does not allow for a modification. In addition to the unique identification and the short text as a description, you can also specify a *short identification*.

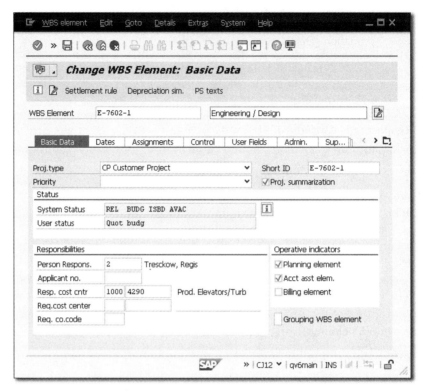

Figure 1.6 Basic Data of a WBS Element

Short identification

You can use short identifications to save space for displaying the WBS elements in tabular displays or in hierarchical cost planning or budgeting. You can either assign a short identification of your choice manually or use the MASK ID field in the project definition screen to derive the short ID of the WBS elements from their IDs.

Organizational assignment

You can integrate a WBS element into your company structure by assigning it to organizational units in accounting and logistics. Most of the organizational units can be proposed using the project profile or project definition, and, if required, you can modify each WBS element separately; however, you should note that those changes must comply with your existing company structure.

Cross-Company Code Projects [+]

In an international project, you can store different company codes in different WBS elements. However, all of these company codes must be assigned to the controlling area you have specified in the project definition.

The company code, object currency, object class, and—if business area accounting is carried out—even the business area are mandatory fields at the level of WBS elements and can no longer be modified once the planned or actual values have been entered.

The WBS elements contain numerous control profiles and indicators. We will describe the control indicators in the following sections, and the profiles will be discussed in Chapter 5, Section 5.3, Section 5.4, Section 5.6, and Section 5.9.

The basic data of a WBS element contains three operative indicators: PLANNING ELEMENT, ACCOUNT ASSIGNMENT ELEMENT, and BILLING ELEMENT. You can use these indicators to define the controlling properties of the WBS element.

Operative indicators

WBS elements you want to plan costs for manually must be marked as planning elements. If you use the appropriate settings in the planning profile of the project (see Chapter 2, Section 2.4), you can even ensure that manual cost planning on a WBS element is only possible if this indicator is set. Creating planned costs by rolling up planned values of subordinate WBS elements or orders is possible regardless of the PLANNING ELEMENT indicator.

Planning elements

The ACCOUNT ASSIGNMENT ELEMENT indicator determines whether you can assign orders to the WBS element (in particular, activities and networks). It also controls whether you can assign any documents to the WBS element that result in actual or commitment postings to the WBS element. If you don't set this indicator for a WBS element, for example, you cannot assign a purchase requisition or invoice to this WBS element. You can also store this indicator as a default value for all WBS elements in the project profile.

Account assignment elements

If you want to base revenue planning on a WBS element and post actual revenues to the WBS element at a later stage, then you must mark the

Billing elements

WBS element as a billing element. Refer to Chapter 5, Section 5.6 and Section 5.9 for information on how to set this indicator.

You can define any combination of those indicators for a WBS element, regardless of the element's hierarchy level. Shown previously, Figure 1.2 shows an example of the operative indicators of a project. The example shown there allows for manual cost planning only on WBS elements of levels 1 and 2. However, the display of actual costs can be more detailed, because the account assignment of documents can also be carried out for WBS elements at level 3. In addition, the highest-level WBS element is also responsible for planning and implementing revenues.

Statistical WBS elements

Another indicator that's also used for defining the controlling properties of a WBS element is the STATISTICAL flag. If you set this indicator for a WBS element (you can also set it as a default value for all WBS elements in the project profile), then the actual costs are only updated statistically for this WBS element under value type 11 (STATISTICAL ACTUAL) instead of value type 4 (ACTUAL). This means that when you assign documents to a statistical WBS element you must specify the WBS element as an account assignment recipient and a "real" account assignment object that serves as a recipient of actual costs. If that element is always a specific cost center, then you can store this cost center as a default account assignment in the detail screen of the statistical WBS element.

There are different ways to use statistical WBS elements and statistical projects. Some companies use statistical projects for purely hierarchical analyses. In that case, operational controlling is still carried out at the level of cost centers, internal orders, or cost objects, for example.

Statistical budget monitoring

Another typical usage of statistical WBS elements consists of indirect budgeting and availability control (see Chapter 3, Section 3.1.5) of objects in the SAP system that otherwise are not assigned a budget. For example, in asset accounting you cannot assign budgets to assets. This means that you cannot use availability control to control direct capitalizations of the asset to automatically avoid exceeding specific threshold values. But, you can achieve this aim by entering a statistical WBS element as an account assignment for investment in the master record of the asset. In addition, the corresponding balance sheet accounts must be defined as statistical cost elements and must contain a field status definition that allows for additional account assignment to a WBS element. Moreover, you must activate WBS elements as account assignment objects in asset accounting.

Once the WBS element has been budgeted and the availability control has been activated for the project, each posting to the asset is accompanied by a statistical account assignment on the WBS element. This means that the statistical actual costs are automatically validated against the budget of the WBS element.

[!]

Restrictions for Statistical WBS Elements

Note that not all accounting functions are available for statistical WBS elements. For example, you cannot carry out any overhead application based on the statistical actual costs; neither can you perform any settlement of the statistical actual costs. Although statistical WBS elements can be used for calculating interest, the interest itself must be updated in a real account assignment object (see Chapter 5, Section 5.5).

The INTEGRATED PLANNING indicator refers to a specific function that allows you to pass planned activity inputs of a project as scheduled activities to cost center accounting. Chapter 2, Section 2.4.3 and Section 2.4.6 provide more detailed information on integrated planning.

Integrated planning

You can use the PROJECT SUMMARIZATION indicator in the basic data of a WBS element to control how the WBS element should be treated in an analysis (typically cross-project) using custom evaluation hierarchies (see Chapter 6, Section 6.4). In the project profile, you can store this indicator as a default value for all WBS elements, only for account assignment elements, or only for the billing elements. If you don't use project summarization, then the indicator has no other specific function.

Project summarization

The GROUPING WBS ELEMENT indicator marks a WBS element as relevant for the grouping of requirements and stocks of material components that are maintained in individual requirements inventory. The indicator can be set either manually for selected WBS elements or automatically for the highest-level WBS element provided that automatic requirements grouping has previously been set in the project definition. Chapter 2, Section 2.3.2 contains further details on the possible attributes this

Grouping WBS elements

indicator can have and on additional prerequisites of requirements grouping.

Detail screens are available for each WBS element for date planning and entering actual dates. In addition, a separate detail screen is available for each WBS element to determine the progress of a project.

Project type, priority A lot of fields in the WBS elements are pure information fields that don't contain any control functionality. For example, in Customizing you can define attributes for the fields PROJECT TYPE, PRIORITY, SCALE, or INVESTMENT REASON and store these attributes separately for each WBS element. In addition, the EQUIPMENT and FUNCTIONAL AREA fields in the ASSIGNMENTS detail screen are also used for purely informational purposes; that is, you can analyze all those fields in Reporting, use them to build groups or for filtering purposes in reports, or employ them as selection criteria when selecting objects to be analyzed.

User fields Usually, each company has its own requirements regarding information fields in WBS elements that are supposed to be analyzed along with master data fields in Reporting. For this purpose, each WBS element contains the USER FIELDS detail screen (see Figure 1.7), which provides the following fields:

- Two fields for 20 alphanumeric characters each
- Two fields for 10 alphanumeric characters each
- Two date fields
- Two numeric fields for measurement units
- Two numeric fields for currencies
- Two indicators

You can use the field key (see Section 1.2.2) to control the assignment of names to the fields in the detail screen. The field key, in turn, can be proposed via the project profile. For example, instead of using the default name, FIELD 1, you can store the name, MODEL SERIES, for the first alphanumeric field in the Customizing section of the field key. Using a customer-specific extension would then enable you to implement a validation of the entries. By default, it is not possible to implement an input help for the alphanumeric fields.

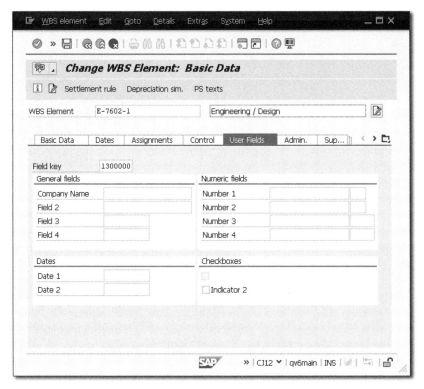

Figure 1.7 User Fields of a WBS Element

If the number of available user fields does not meet your requirements, then you can use a customized extension to define additional fields for WBS elements. Those additional fields are typically displayed in a separate detail screen.

Detail screen

> **Using the Field Key**   **[!]**
>
> When working with user fields, you should note that you can set the field key individually for each WBS element; however, this may lead to confusion in Reporting. For example, if you use two different field keys in your project, one of which contains the name MODEL SERIES for the first alphanumeric field, whereas the other one contains the name COLOR for the same field, then the field values are displayed in the same report column in Reporting, regardless of the fact that WBS elements with the first field key contain information on

> model series, whereas the WBS elements with the other field key contain color information.
>
> For this reason, you should either use a uniform field key within a project or use the field key as a selection criterion in your evaluations.

If necessary, you can log changes to master data as *change documents* and evaluate those documents at a later stage. As is the case with the project definition, the FIELD SELECTION option in Customizing allows you to control which fields of the WBS elements you want to hide, display, use for data input, highlight in a specific color, or define as mandatory (see Section 1.8.1).

Further tabs You can activate various other tabs for WBS elements according to your requirements. Depending on your Customizing settings, you can use, for example, additional tabs for integration scenarios—for example, in Integrated Product and Process Engineering (iPPE), Joint Venture Accounting, depreciation simulations in Asset Accounting, or in Funds Management. As of EHP 3, you can also display tabs for the definition of access control lists or for statistical key figure planning.

1.2.2 Structure Customizing of the Work Breakdown Structure

Figure 1.8 shows the different activities in structure Customizing of operative work breakdown structures. Before you can create a WBS, you must create at least one project profile here. Prior to the initial creation of a WBS, you should also consider defining coding masks. Using coding masks is not mandatory, but it has many advantages. You can only create or modify coding masks at a later stage—with many restrictions.

Depending on your specific requirements, you must specify various settings in structure Customizing of operative work breakdown structures in addition to defining project profiles and coding masks. The following sections briefly describe the individual Customizing activities involved. The Implementation Guide (IMG) of the SAP system also contains detailed documentation for each of these Customizing activities.

Figure 1.8 Structure Customizing of Work Breakdown Structures

Project Profile

When creating a project, you must always specify a project profile that has been previously defined for the respective project type in Transaction OPSA. The project profile contains values and profiles that can be used as default values for project definitions or WBS elements during the creation phase. Depending on the field selection and status of the object, those values and profiles can be modified—for example, with regard to the project type, organizational units, and so on. In addition, the project profile contains *referenced fields* (see Figure 1.9).

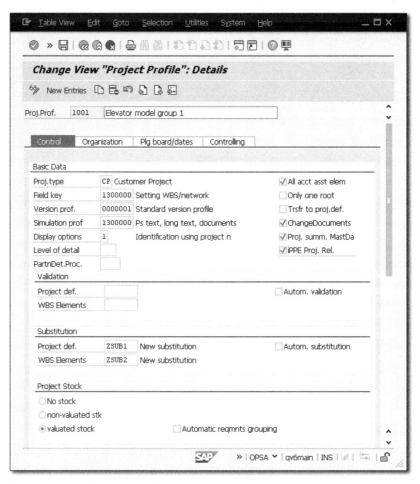

Figure 1.9 Sample Project Profile

Referenced
fields

Referenced fields define properties of your project without being displayed or editable in the work breakdown structure.

The ONLY ONE ROOT indicator controls whether one or several WBS elements are allowed at level 1 of the work breakdown structure. If you set this indicator and try to save two or more WBS elements at the highest level, then the system will output an error message and you will have to change the hierarchical structure before you can save the project.

The project profile contains two indicators that are relevant for writing change documents:

Change documents

- The indicator for changes to master data
- The indicator for status changes

Besides activating the respective indicator, you must meet another requirement to write change documents—namely, a status must explicitly allow the business operation CREATE CHANGE DOCUMENT (see Section 1.6).

The PROJECT SUMMARIZATION VIA MASTER DATA (PROJ. SUM. MASTDA) indicator is only relevant if you want to use the project summarization function for your analyses (see Chapter 6, Section 6.4). This indicator enables you to decide whether you want to carry out the summarization process based on the master data or based on a classification of the WBS elements. Particularly with regard to system performance, you should summarize on the basis of master data characteristics. In the project profile, you can mark billing elements, account assignment elements, or all WBS elements of the project as relevant for inheriting master data during project summarization.

Project summarization

The VERSION PROFILE is responsible for the automatic creation of project versions on the basis of their statuses. It is referenced via the project profile.

Project versions

If you specify SUBSTITUTIONS and VALIDATIONS and set the AUTOMATIC (that is, AUTOM. VALIDATION or AUTOM. SUBSTITUTION) indicator, then you can make sure that logics for setting and checking field values, which you personally have defined, are processed during the save process (see Section 1.8.4 and Section 1.8.5).

The specification of STATUS PROFILES (see Section 1.6) for project definitions and WBS elements is only a default value for the respective objects. However, you can no longer modify a status profile in the object if it is used to directly set a user status. In that case, the entry of a status profile in the project profile has a referencing character as well. Because the retroactive entry of status profiles in the objects is rather complex and cannot be done via mass changes, you should store your custom schemas in the project profile right from the start.

Graphical display You can call a graphical display of WBS element data in hierarchical arrangement via the processing transactions (see Section 1.7) or by using the transactions for cost planning, time scheduling, and budgeting. The graphical presentation of the data is controlled by the GRAPHICS PROFILES that you must store for various purposes in the project profile. If required, you can define your own graphics profiles, but usually the default profiles will suffice.

If you set the IPPE PROJ. REL. indicator, then the system displays an additional tab for WBS elements, which allows for integration with iPPE (see Chapter 2, Section 2.3.1).

Settlement rules If you enter a STRATEGY in the CONTROLLING tab of the project profile, you can automatically generate the settlement rules for WBS elements. Chapter 5, Section 5.9 provides a detailed description of how to define strategies and how to derive settlement rules.

If you want to use access control lists to assign object-specific authorizations, set the ACL WITHOUT INHERITANCE or ACL WITH INHERITANCE indicator in the project profile.

Coding Masks

To enable employees in different departments to use project structures easily in their daily work, it is useful to agree on certain conventions regarding the identification of WBS objects—for example, identifying on the basis of the type and usage of projects. To do this, you can define coding masks to control the external identification of project definitions and WBS elements in Customizing.

Defining coding masks You can define coding masks on the basis of *keys* in Customizing activity DEFINE PROJECT CODING MASK (OPSJ). A coding mask contains sections for the external identifications. These *sections* are separated by special characters. A section consists either of numbers that are represented by zero characters in the coding mask or of alphanumeric characters that are represented by X characters in the mask. You can store a descriptive text for each coding mask in Customizing and use *lock indicators* to control whether the key and the associated mask can be used for operative or standard work breakdown structures.

In the following sections, we will demonstrate the definition of coding masks on the basis of our IDES example, the elevator projects. All elevator projects in the IDES Company begin with the letter "E." For this reason, the coding mask shown in Figure 1.10 was defined in Customizing for the key "E" even before the first elevator project was created. Each identification of project definitions and WBS elements that begins with an "E" is now based on the convention that the "E" key must be followed by a hyphen as a special character, which, in turn, is followed by a section containing a maximum of four characters that may only consist of numbers. If a letter is entered in the first section, then the system outputs an error message.

Sample definition

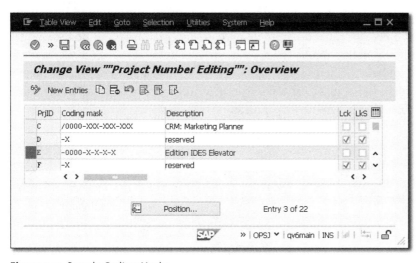

Figure 1.10 Sample Coding Masks

In the IDES Company, the first section is used for the sequential numbering of projects. The system supports this in that it provides the option to search for the next available number.

If a longer ID must be assigned to WBS elements, then the numerical section must be followed by a second hyphen, which is followed by a one-digit section that may contain an alphanumeric character, and so on. When entering the identification, you can usually omit the special characters because the system automatically inserts them after you've pressed the ⌷Enter⌷ key. However, the external identification is stored without special characters in the database table of the WBS elements. SAP Note 536471 provides further information on coding masks.

Lock indicators

Because a lock indicator is set neither for operative nor for standard structures in the example, we can create both operative projects and standard work breakdown structures with identifications for the key "E."

> **[!]** **Restrictions for the Creation of Coding Masks**
>
> Note that you can only create a coding mask for a key as long as no object exists for that key.

You should consider using coding masks when you first implement SAP Project System and before you create the first project. If necessary, you should define masks for keys as early as possible—even if you want to use them at a later stage—and lock those coding masks. You can further detail those masks at a later point in time and release them for usage (that is, remove the lock indicators).

> **[!]** **Restrictions for Changing Coding Masks**
>
> Coding masks that are already used by objects can only be modified to a certain extent. The only two possible options to change coding masks retroactively consist of adding alphanumeric sections and converting a numeric section into an alphanumeric one of identical length.

When you create or change coding masks, the system carries out several checks; however, not all of the steps involved in those checks are carried out when you transport Customizing settings to coding masks. For this reason, we recommend that you don't transport coding masks; instead, you should create them manually in the respective systems.

Defining special characters

To define coding masks in Customizing, you must first enter several settings in Customizing activity DEFINE SPECIAL CHARACTERS FOR PROJECTS (OPSK; see Figure 1.11). Here, first define the length of the keys for the coding masks. Note that the maximum length for a key is five (numeric or alphanumeric) characters. For example, if you enter "3" in the respective field, then you can only use keys of a maximum of three characters when defining the coding masks. If you want the keys to be exactly

three-characters long and no shorter, then you must also set the STRUC-
TURE LENGTH (SL) indicator.

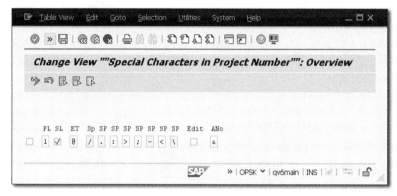

Figure 1.11 Examples of Special Characters

You can simplify the tabular creation of WBS elements by entering any character in the ENTRY TOOL (ET) field. Instead of always having to enter the complete ID for a new WBS element, which can be prone to errors when you use long IDs, you can simply enter the entry tool character for the part of the ID that is identical to the object on the higher level. When the data is confirmed by pressing Enter , the system replaces the character with the identification of the higher-level object.

Input help

In the eight SPECIAL CHARACTER fields, you must store the characters you want to use as separators between two sections when defining the coding masks.

Special characters

By setting the EDIT indicator, you can ensure that project definitions and WBS elements can only be created with identifications that are controlled by coding masks that aren't locked. For example, if you haven't defined a coding mask for the key "Z," then you can't create any projects that begin with "Z" when the EDIT indicator is set.

If you enter a character of your choice in the AUTOMATIC NUMBER ASSIGNMENT (ANo) field when creating a WBS element from the template area, then the system will automatically propose an ID for that WBS element (see Section 1.7.1). If the system cannot automatically propose a number, then it will assign a temporary number that begins with the character you have previously entered in the ANo field.

Project Type and Priority

The definition of project types and priorities merely consists of a key and a description. You can enter project types and priorities in the basic data of WBS elements. They are usually used for purely informational purposes, but you can also use them as selection criteria in Reporting. You can store default values for the project type and priority in the project profile.

Partner Determination Procedure

Defining partner roles

The definition of partner determination procedures consists of three Customizing activities. First, create the identifications and names for the roles you want to assign to projects at a later stage and link the IDs and names with the partner number types provided.

[+] **Roles**

The term *role* is used in different contexts here. The roles defined here are not related to the roles that are used to assign authorizations or to the roles that are defined in SAP Portfolio and Project Management (SAP PPM), for example.

For example, if you want to store the sold-to party as additional information in customer projects, you must create a SOLD-TO PARTY role and link this role to the CUSTOMER type. This allows you to specify a customer number for the SOLD-TO PARTY role and to view the data of the corresponding customer master record in the project.

Language-dependent conversion

In the second Customizing activity, you can translate the name of the roles into other languages. Depending on the logon language, the system will then output the corresponding name.

Defining partner determination procedures

The final step consists of summarizing the roles you want to be available for selection in your project into a partner determination procedure. When doing so, you can define for each role whether it must be specified in any case, whether an entry for a role can be modified at a later stage, and whether it should be possible to enter several values for a role. You can store a partner determination procedure as the default value in the project profile.

Applicants and Responsible Persons

You can use Transactions OPS6 and OPS7 to create possible responsible persons and applicants for project definitions and WBS elements. The definition of applicants and responsible persons consists of an ID that may contain a maximum of eight characters and the name of the corresponding person. You must make these entries manually; you don't need any data from Human Resources (HR) for this process.

In addition, you can assign the corresponding SAP users to responsible persons. This type of entry is relevant if you want to notify the user automatically via email in case of budget overruns (see Chapter 3, Section 3.1.5).

Field Key

You can use field keys to control the names of user fields (see Figure 1.7). Data can only be entered into the fields for which you have stored a name in the field key definition. For the two quantity fields of the user fields, you can create a link to the parameters to use the quantities in formulas at a later stage (see Chapter 2, Section 2.3.1). You can enter a default value for the field key in the project profile.

1.2.3 Standard Work Breakdown Structures

A standard work breakdown structure consists of a *standard project definition* and *standard WBS elements* , and it can be used as a template for live projects. You can create standard work breakdown structures by using Transaction CJ91. You must also have a reference to a project profile. You can also use other standard work breakdown structures or even operative projects as templates.

A standard work breakdown structure may already contain important master data. Standard WBS elements can be assigned milestones (see Section 1.4) or PS texts (see Section 1.5.1); however, you cannot store any planning data, such as date information, planned costs or revenues, and settlement rules, in the standard WBS. Moreover, you cannot assign document info records in a standard WBS.

Master data

Furthermore, you cannot set any statuses for the standard WBS elements; however, you can store the status profiles for the operative project definition and WBS elements in the standard project definition.

In addition, there are three different system statuses available at the level of the standard project definition:

▸ **Created (Standard WBS)**
The system issues a warning message if you want to use the standard work breakdown structure as a template in this initial status.

▸ **Released (Standard WBS)**
You can use the standard work breakdown structure as a template without any restrictions. Note that you cannot undo this status.

▸ **Closed (Standard WBS)**
You cannot copy the standard work breakdown structure.

[◉] **Work Breakdown Structures**

You can use the WBS elements of a work breakdown structure to map a project hierarchically in the SAP system. All WBS elements of a work breakdown structure are uniquely assigned to a project definition.

You can also store data for informational purposes and control profiles and indicators in the master data of those project elements. Standard work breakdown structures can be used as templates for actual projects. Before you can create work breakdown structures, you must define a project profile in the Customizing section of SAP Project System. It is useful to also define coding masks in Customizing that enable you to control the identification of the project elements.

1.3 Network

You can use networks to map the flow of different project activities as activities and relationships in the system. In particular, networks enable you to use various logistical integrations with Materials Management (MM), Production, Plant Maintenance, Purchasing, Capacity Requirements Planning, and Time Scheduling.

Networks should not exceed a size of approximately 500 activities, because you usually only store one responsible person per network.

This person is referred to as the MRP controller. Another reason for keeping the aforementioned size can be found in the lock logic of networks. Whenever a network object is edited or confirmed, for example, the entire network is locked. The bigger your networks and the higher the number of possible confirmations, the greater the risk that the network gets locked for editing.

1.3.1 Structure and Master Data

A network consists of a *network header* and *activities*. The activities can be linked to each other via *relationships*. *Activity elements* allow you to further detail or complement activities.

You can enter the identification of a WBS element in the header of a network and in the activities and activity elements to create an assignment to a work breakdown structure. Based on this assignment, you can then exchange data between the network objects and the respective WBS elements.

As of EHP 3, you can use access control lists to define object-specific authorizations for network headers, activities, and activity elements if required.

Each network contains a unique ID that consists of a maximum of 12 characters. Depending on the Customizing settings, either you must enter this ID manually when creating the network or the ID is automatically assigned by the system. For networks assigned to a WBS element, you can also derive the ID from the ID of the WBS element via a customer enhancement.

Identification

Technically, networks are implemented as orders, so some of their functions will probably remind you of production, maintenance, or service orders and, to a certain extent, even of internal orders. In the SAP system, the different orders are distinguished by firmly defined *order categories*. Networks represent order category 20.

Orders

The properties of orders are specified within the individual order categories through *order types* that must be defined in the Customizing section of the respective application. In the context of networks, these order types are referred to as *network types*. Depending on the network type and the plant in the header of the network, you can define additional network properties in the Customizing section of SAP Project System (see Section 1.3.2).

Network Header

A network header acts as a framework for the various objects of a network. The network header contains control profiles and indicators, and default values for the different network objects (see Figure 1.12).

Figure 1.12 Control Data of a Network Header

When creating a network header (see Section 1.7), you must enter a Network profile, a Network type, and a Plant. Note that you can also specify the network type and the plant via the network profile. The plant is used to identify the associated company code and controlling area.

The plant is also forwarded as a default value to the activities of the network from which it can be modified, provided that the new plant belongs to the same controlling area of the network header. Other data included in the network header, such as the Business Area, the Profit Center (in the Assignments tab), and the Res./Purc. Req. indicator are also used as default values for the activities of the network.

In addition to specifying the MRP controller in the network header, you must also enter various settings regarding time scheduling, capacity requirements planning, and costing. Those settings are described in greater detail in Chapter 2, Section 2.1.2, Section 2.2.1, and Section 2.4.6.

You can use the Execution Factor field to multiply quantity data in the activities, activity elements, and the assigned material components. If you use an integer as an execution factor and store it in the network header, then the system automatically multiplies the duration, work, costs, and quantities of activities, and the associated activity elements and material components by that factor. However, you should note that only those activities that you have explicitly marked for this multiplication process are taken into account.

Execution factor

Activities

In the context of networks, we must differentiate from among the following four activity types:

- Internally processed activities
- Externally processed activities
- Services
- Costs

Each activity type is defined by the *control key* of the activity (see Section 1.3.2). You can use the name, long texts, or assigned PS texts and documents (see Section 1.5) to further specify the purpose of each individual activity.

Within the network, each activity contains a unique identification that consists of four characters so that the activity can be uniquely identified in conjunction with the network ID. When you create a new activity, the system automatically proposes an ID for the new activity, which is based on the highest previous activity number within the network and on the activity increment specified in the network profile.

Internally processed activities

An internally processed activity—control key PS01 is available by default for this activity type—can be used for planning and entering a service that is rendered by capacities (for example, people or machines) of your own company. Figure 1.13 shows for the elevator example an internally processed activity, which is used to map a first layout of the elevator in the network.

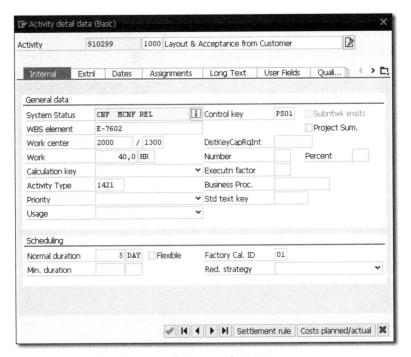

Figure 1.13 Example of an Internally Processed Activity

The Normal Duration field enables you to plan the length of time to be considered in time scheduling for rendering the internal service. If you want to plan costs and capacity requirements for the internal service, then you must specify a Work Center (see Chapter 2, Section 2.2.1) that is supposed to render the respective service. In addition, you must enter the amount of work in the Work field.

If, for an internally processed activity, a fixed reference exists between the planned work and its duration, then you can use the Calculation Key field to ensure, for example, that the duration is calculated on the basis of the planned work of the activity and the amount of time that the work center is used. If you use the Number and Percent fields, you can also specify how many different capacities should be considered and at what percentage during the calculation. Conversely, you can also calculate the amount of work required on the basis of the duration of the activity. A possible third alternative to using the calculation key is to manually specify the planned amount of work and its duration. Based on these aforementioned entries, the system then calculates the number of different capacities required. As of EHP 3, you can also initially derive the value of the Work field from a statistical key figure that you have planned for the activity (see Chapter 2, Section 2.4.8).

Calculation key

An externally processed activity—for which you can use control key PS02 by default—enables you to plan and procure a service that is supposed to be provided by an external resource. You can specify the service to be procured either manually, by using long texts, PS texts, or assigned documents, or by specifying appropriate Info Records or Outline Agreements from Purchasing. Figure 1.14 shows an example of an externally processed activity that is used to procure an external construction service within the network.

Externally processed activities

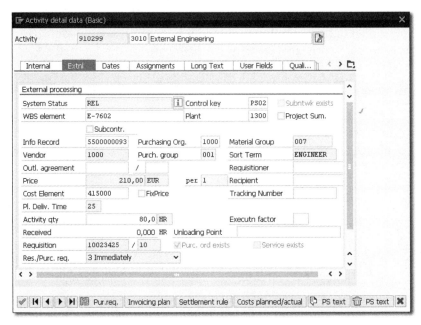

Figure 1.14 Example of an Externally Processed Activity

Res./Purc. Req. indicator

Based on your entries regarding the external service, the PLANNED DELIVERY TIME, the ACTIVITY QUANTITY, the MATERIAL GROUP, and the responsible PURCHASING ORGANIZATION and PURCHASING GROUP, the system can create a purchase requisition. This process depends on the RES./PURC. REQ. indicator:

- IMMEDIATELY—that is, automatically the next time the network is saved
- FROM RELEASE of the activity and the subsequent save process
- NEVER automatically but at any time during the save process once you have manually set the indicator from NEVER to IMMEDIATELY

Services

Like an externally processed activity, you can use a service activity (default control key PS05) to plan and procure external services through Purchasing (see Figure 1.15). Whereas external processing allows you to procure only one specified service, a service activity enables you to plan and procure several services and to enter data for services that has not yet been specified in detail.

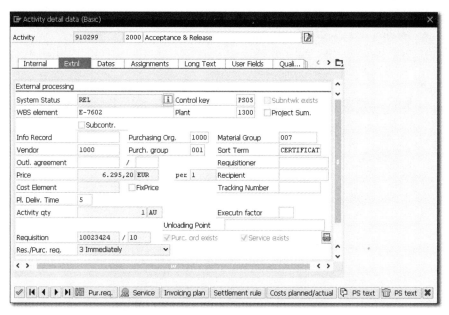

Figure 1.15 Example of a Service Activity

To do this, you must create *service specifications* when creating a service activity. These specifications could be structured as a table containing information on SERVICE MASTER RECORDS, or SAMPLE or STANDARD SERVICE SPECIFICATIONS that refer to planned services. If necessary, the table could also be hierarchically structured (see Chapter 2, Section 2.2.5). In addition, you must specify a VALUE LIMIT for unplanned services, that is, for services that cannot yet be exactly specified. This limit must not be exceeded by the supplier during *service entry* when the values of unplanned services are entered (see Chapter 4, Section 4.4.2).

Service specifications

As is the case with an externally processed activity, you can use the RES./ PURC. REQ. indicator to control exactly when a purchase requisition should be created on the basis of the data of a service activity. The purchase requisition is then processed further using the functions of the service area in Purchasing.

Cost activities can be used for planning and for the account assignment of costs that are not generated by internal services, the procurement of external services through Purchasing, or the consumption of materials.

Cost activity

The types of costs involved in cost activities are usually travel costs and other primary costs. By default, control key PS03 is provided for cost activities. Figure 1.16 shows an example of a cost activity that maps insurance costs within the network.

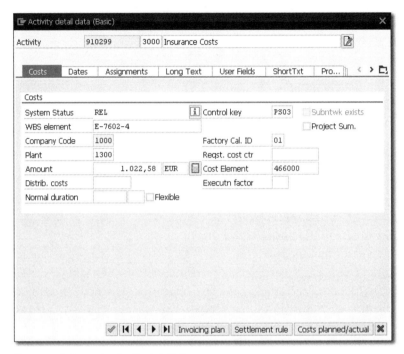

Figure 1.16 Example of a Cost Activity

Cost activities provide various options to plan these types of costs. The easiest way to plan for a type of cost is to specify an AMOUNT and a COST ELEMENT. In contrast to that, you can carry out unit costing or use invoicing plans to store more detailed information (see Chapter 2, Section 2.4.6).

If you want to distribute the costs across several periods, you can enter a duration in a cost activity and—if you don't want an equal distribution across the entire duration—a DISTRIBUTION KEY (see Chapter 2, Section 2.2.1).

Relationships

Relationships allow you to define the sequence of activities. When creating a relationship between two activities, you must define which activity is the *predecessor* and which activity is the *successor*. This way, you can specify the logical sequence. In addition, you must specify the type of relationship, based on which the system determines the chronological sequence of predecessor and successor in the context of time scheduling.

The following types of relationships exist:

Analyzing relationships

▸ **FS (Finish-start relationship)**
The successor begins once the predecessor has finished.

▸ **SS (Start-start relationship)**
The successor begins at the same time as the predecessor or once the predecessor has started.

▸ **FF (Finish-finish relationship)**
The successor ends at the same time as the predecessor, or once the predecessor has ended.

▸ **SF (Start-finish relationship)**
The predecessor begins once the successor has finished.

If you enter a positive time interval in a relationship during time scheduling, then you can ensure that the time interval is kept between the activities. Conversely, a negative time interval means that in a finish-start relationship, for example, the activities can overlap by this time interval.

Time interval

You can enter the time intervals as absolute values, such as a number of days, or as a percentage based on the duration of the predecessor or successor. If you want the time intervals to refer exclusively to workdays or the operating time of capacities, then you must also enter a factory calendar or work center in the relationship.

You can create relationships for activities in a tabular view. In addition, you can use the *connection mode* in the network graphic and Project Planning Board to create relationships graphically. Moreover, the Project Planning Board allows you to simply select activities and use the

CONNECT SELECTED ACTIVITIES icon to automatically create finish-start relationships between those activities in the order in which they are listed in the table.

You can also create relationships between activities of different networks and therefore map interdependencies between the networks. The networks that are connected by relationships in such a way may also belong to different projects. Relationships between activities of different networks are also referred to as *external relationships*.

Activity Elements

There are four different types of activity elements:

- Internal elements for planning and entering performances of capacities of your own company
- External elements for planning and procuring external services
- Service elements for planning and procuring external services using service specifications
- Costs elements for planning and assigning additional primary costs to accounts

As is the case with an activity, an activity element enables you to plan the costs and capacity requirements for internal services, to plan and trigger the procurement of external services through Purchasing, and to plan additional costs. All of those operations depend on the control key that defines the type of activity element. An activity element is identified by a unique number within the network. Figure 1.17 shows an example of a costs type activity element.

However, in contrast to an activity, an activity element doesn't contain any relationships and is therefore not relevant for time scheduling. An activity element must be firmly assigned to an activity so that it adopts the dates that pertain to the activity. Note that you can specify time intervals to define that the activity element starts later or finishes earlier than the superordinate activity. However, the planned period of an activity element must always be within the limits of the planned period of an activity.

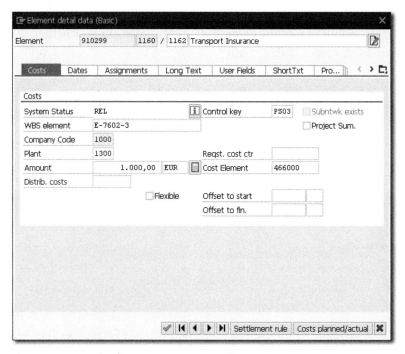

Figure 1.17 Example of a Costs-Type Activity Element

Another difference between activity elements and activities is that you cannot assign any additional objects—particularly PS texts, documents, milestones, or material components—to activity elements.

By using activity elements instead of activities, you can keep a clear structure of the network and the time scheduling component of the network. The following two examples of the elevator project will demonstrate the advantage of using activity elements instead of activities:

Examples of activity elements

▸ **Example 1: Delivery**
The delivery of elevator components is mapped by the internally processed activity, DELIVERY. For the transport, you want to plan additional insurance costs. To do that, you use a costs element called TRANSPORT INSURANCE, which you assign to the DELIVERY activity. Due to the fixed date assignments between the activity and the activity element, the planned costs of the costs element automatically lie within the scheduled delivery period.

▸ **Example 2: Assembly**

The assembly of an elevator component is carried out by several work centers; a part of this service is rendered by an external supplier. Because the different kinds of work are carried out simultaneously, and thus a detailed flow plan of the individual activities is not needed, you should use activity elements instead of individual activities for each work center and each external service. This means that you must create an activity with a planned duration for the entire assembly of the component, including the required relationships. Then you have to assign an activity element to this activity for each work center that is involved and for the required external procurements.

Subnetworks

Subnetworks are networks that are linked to an activity of another network via an assignment at the network header level. Thus, subnetworks can be used to further specify the superordinate activity.

Data exchange When assigning a network to a superordinate activity, the system passes activity dates to the subnetwork header. In addition, the subnetwork can carry out the assignment of the activity to WBS elements, organizational data, and the relationships of the activity in the subnetwork. During the assignment of a subnetwork, the SUBNTWK EXISTS indicator is set in the superordinate activity, and the control key of the activity changes (see Section 1.3.2). You can also assign several subnetworks to an activity. Furthermore, you can assign subnetworks to the activities of a subnetwork. Instead of creating subnetworks manually, you can also use milestone functions to automatically create networks based on standard networks and simultaneously assign the networks as subnetworks to activities (see Section 1.4.2). The example described in the following sections will demonstrate a possible way of using subnetworks.

Example of subnetworks At an early planning stage of the elevator project, you want to define a network to roughly map the flow of individual project activities. You can use the network right away to plan dates, costs, and capacity requirements for planning, construction, and assembly of the elevator.

In the context of the detailed project planning, you then want to create new, detailed networks—especially for construction and assembly.

These networks are assigned separate responsible persons, and the network headers are assigned to the CONSTRUCTION and ASSEMBLY activities of your first network. The system passes the dates of the activities and the assignment to the work breakdown structure of the elevator project to the two subnetworks.

To avoid the duplication of planned costs and capacity requirements for the construction and assembly for your project in Reporting, you will have needed to define in Customizing that the control keys of superordinate activities are automatically modified in such a way that they are no longer relevant for costing and the calculation of capacity requirements.

The persons responsible for the subnetworks can then process the subnetworks and add more details without locking the superordinate network. If basic dates of the project or parts of the project must be shifted, then you can use overall network scheduling to simultaneously recalculate the dates of the superordinate network and of the subnetworks (see Chapter 2, Section 2.1.2).

Plant Maintenance and Service Ordersas Subnetworks

You can also assign plant maintenance and service orders as subnetworks to activities of a network to define the sequence of the orders and schedule their execution periods. Moreover, you can use the network or project in extensive plant maintenance activities for planning all preparatory measures, for planning the required materials and resources, and for progress monitoring. If at the same time you assign these orders to WBS elements as well, you can also use the project for managing the budget of the plant maintenance activities, which allows you to check the planned costs of the orders against the available budget (see Chapter 3, Section 3.1.5).

The process of assigning plant maintenance and service orders to network activities or WBS elements occurs in the header of the respective orders. As of EHP 2, you can use the ORDER ASSIGNMENT TO PROJECT function (Transaction ADPMPS) either via drag-and-drop or automatically (see Figure 1.18). The REF. ELEMENT PM/PS field allows you to activate automatic assignments in network activities and order headers or

Assigning orders to the project

their templates. If you select a project or network and orders in the ORDER ASSIGNMENT TO PROJECT function and automatic assignment is triggered, then the WBS elements or network activities are assigned all of the selected orders that have the same reference element. You can define reference elements in Customizing for plant maintenance.

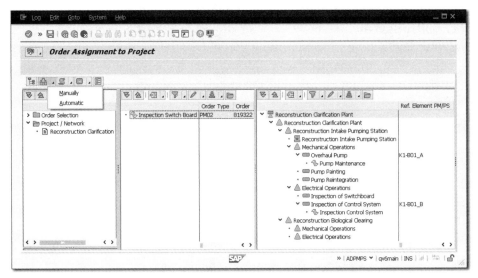

Figure 1.18 Assigning Plant Maintenance Orders to Projects Using Transaction ADPMPS

Maintenance Event Builder

You can call the ORDER ASSIGNMENT TO PROJECT function either directly or via the MAINTENANCE EVENT BUILDER (Transaction WPS1), which provides additional functions for a revision-specific planning of plant maintenance activities and allows for linking projects or networks to revisions, for example.[3]

1.3.2 Customizing the Structure of the Network

Before you can create operative networks in the SAP system, you must configure several settings in the Customizing section of SAP Project Sys-

---

3 For further information on Maintenance Event Builder, for details on the Order Assignment to Project function, and for general information on the planning and execution of maintenance activities with SAP, you can refer to *Plant Maintenance with SAP—Practical Guide*, 3rd edition, by Karl Liebstückel (SAP PRESS, 2014).

tem. In addition to settings in the Customizing structure that are described in the following sections, you must define *scheduling* and *confirmation parameters* and enter the necessary settings to carry out *material availability checks*. These Customizing activities are described in more detail in Chapter 2, Section 2.1.2 and Section 2.3.3, and Chapter 4, Section 4.3.

Network Type

In the first step, define a network type in Transaction OPSC (see Figure 1.19) and assign this network type to a number range.

Internal and external number assignments

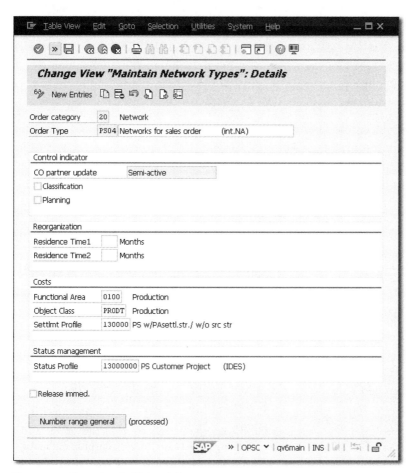

Figure 1.19 Example of a Network Type

When defining the number ranges for all order types (Transaction CO82), you must also define whether you want the number to be automatically assigned by the system or whether it should be manually assigned by the user (internal or external number assignment).

[+] **Network and Order Types**

Because networks are technically implemented as orders in the SAP system, the Customizing section of SAP Project System often uses the generic term *order type* as a synonym for the term *network type*.

Furthermore, you can store default values for the FUNCTIONAL AREA, the OBJECT CLASS, the SETTLEMENT PROFILE (SETTLMT PROFILE) of network objects, and the STATUS PROFILE of a user (see Section 1.6). If you activate the RELEASE IMMED. indicator, you can make sure that all network objects are assigned the status RELEASED as their initial status, which means that you can enter actual data in the network immediately after you have created the network.

Planning networks Besides control settings that are used for classification and archiving purposes (RESIDENCE TIMES; see Section 1.10), you can use the PLANNING indicator to determine whether the planned values of the network should be validated against the budget of assigned WBS elements during an active availability check (see Chapter 3, Section 3.1.5).

Networks whose planned costs are not included in the availability check are referred to as *planning networks*. Planning networks are particularly relevant for projects that utilize a non-valuated project stock (see Chapter 2, Section 2.3.2) because, contrary to regular networks, planning networks can display planned costs for material components that are stored in the non-valuated project stock.

Network Type Parameters

Once you have defined a network type, you must define the network type parameters for a combination of the PLANT and the NETWORK TYPE in Transaction OPUV (see Figure 1.20). In addition to the default values for the REDUCTION STRATEGY (RED. STRATEGY; see Chapter 2, Section 2.1.2), the planned and actual COSTING VARIANTS (CSTGVARIANTPLAN), and the time of PLAN COST CALCULATION (PLAN COST CALC.), the network type parameters are the only assigned referenced control settings.

Figure 1.20 Example of Network Type Parameters

These settings comprise parameters for generating settlement rules (see Chapter 5, Section 5.9), for writing change documents when master data and statuses are changed (CHANGE DOCUMENT indicator), for automatic determination of alternative bills of materials, and for indicators for external procurement processes (see Chapter 4, Section 4.4).

The specification of a change profile is only relevant if you use the variant configuration of networks (see Section 1.8.6). In this case, the change profile that you can define via Transaction OPSG determines how retroactive changes to the configuration should be handled once a network has been released.

The ACTVTYACCTASGN. indicator enables you to define whether you want to use *header account assignment* or *activity account assignment* for networks of this combination of plant and network type.

If you use header account assignment for a network, all planned and actual costs and commitments are stored at the level of the network header. This method does not allow for a more detailed evaluation of costs at the level of activities. The use of header account assignment for networks is necessary if you want to assign networks without work breakdown structures to sales order items.

[!]

Activity Account Assignment for Networks with Header Account Assignment

If you use header account assignment for networks in combination with work breakdown structures, then you should not assign the activities of these networks to different WBS elements. Because the cost information is displayed in aggregated form only in WBS elements that have been assigned the network headers, assigning activities of these networks to different WBS elements could prove to be very confusing when analyzing the costs.

If you use activity account assignment for networks, then the activities and activity elements represent separate account assignment objects. All cost-related information can be analyzed separately in the individual activities and activity elements. Unlike networks that are based on header account assignments, networks for which you use activity account assignments allow you to assign the activities to different WBS elements without any problems. You cannot use header account assignment and activity account assignment in parallel for the same network. Furthermore, you cannot retroactively change this property of a network.

The plant-dependent definition of the network type parameters enables you to define different parameters to use networks in different plants if that is necessary. The network type parameters you define are determined on the basis of the plant and network type you have specified in the network header during the creation of a network.

Network Profile

To create a network, you also need a network profile that you can define using Transaction OPUU (see Figure 1.21). In the network profile, you can enter various default values for the fields and the presentation of network headers, activities, activity elements, relationships, and material components.

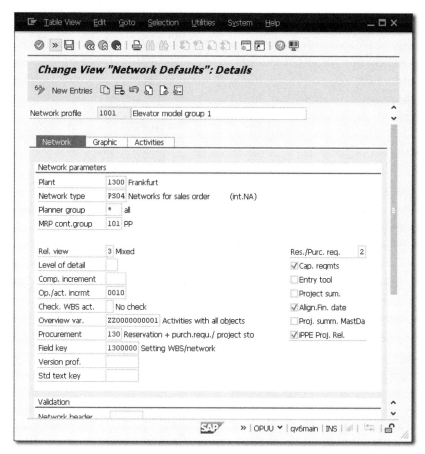

Figure 1.21 Sample Network Profile

Defining default values

In particular, you can already store default values for the plant, the network type, and the MRP controller of the network in a network profile so that you only need to specify a network profile when creating a network. If you haven't defined any MRP controllers in Production yet or if you want other MRP controllers to be responsible for the networks, then you must first define MRP controllers for your networks in Customizing.

As is the case in the project profiles of the work breakdown structures, in the network profile you can configure the settings for creating project versions (see Section 1.9.1), for using substitutions and validations (see Section 1.8.4 and Section 1.8.5), for aggregating and graphically displaying networks, and for using access control lists.

In addition, you can enter various default values for activities and activity elements in the network profile depending on the type of activities and activity elements used. In particular, you can store default values for the respective control keys of the activities and activity elements.

Material forecasting

To enter material forecasting values in internally processed activities, you must specify a cost element for the forecast costs of material forecasting in the network profile. Those *material forecasting values* enable you to enter planned costs for materials at an early planning stage without having to explicitly assign materials to the respective activity. If you assign material components to the activity at a later stage, then the share of the material forecasting value in the planned costs is automatically reduced by the planned value of the assigned components. In this way, duplication of the planned costs is avoided.

Control Key

The standard version of the application already contains control keys for the different activity types, but if necessary you can also create your own control keys using Transaction OPSU (see Figure 1.22). The fields GEN. COSTS ACT., SERVICE, and EXT. PROCESSING allow you to define the type in each control key.

The COST, determine capacity requirements (DET. CAP. REQ.), and SCHEDULING indicators in the control key are used to control whether you want to determine planned costs, calculate capacity requirements, or include a scheduling-relevant duration for a specific activity. For example, if you don't set the SCHEDULING indicator, then the system will always use the duration 0 in time scheduling, regardless of the activity dates. The SCHED. EXT. OP. indicator enables you to specify for the two activity types, EXTERNAL PROCESSING and SERVICE, whether the planned delivery time of the activity or the NORMAL DURATION field in the INTERNAL tab should be used for scheduling the activity.

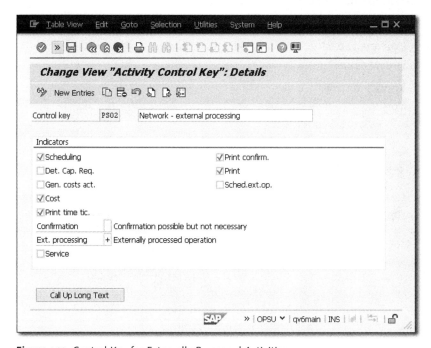

Figure 1.22 Control Key for Externally Processed Activities

If you set the CONFIRMATION indicator, then you can define whether an activity must be confirmed before you can close it, whether confirmations are permitted but not required, or whether the entry of confirmations is not possible for activities with this control key.

To print shop papers (that is, *completion confirmation slips* or *time tickets*) for an activity, you must permit the printout by setting the respective indicators in the control key. Furthermore, you must first define the *print control* in the structure Customizing section of the networks.

Shop papers

Finally, you must specify the number of shop papers to be printed and the printer in the operative network activities.

Subnetwork Parameters

If you want to use a subnetwork, you must enter two settings in the Sub-NETWORK PARAMETERS. These settings depend on the network type of the superordinate network being used and on the network type (or order type in the case of plant maintenance or service orders):

- **Specify the control key**
  You must specify the control key that must be set automatically for the superordinate activity once a subnetwork has been assigned.

- **Specify dates**
  You must specify the dates you want to pass from the activity to the subnetwork header.

In addition, you can define priorities and field keys for user fields in the Customizing section of operative networks. This process is similar to customizing the work breakdown structures (see Section 1.2.2).

[!] | **Necessary Customizing for Networks**

Before you can create operative networks, you must first define scheduling parameters, confirmation parameters, and—if materials are used in the network—the material availability check in the Customizing section of SAP Project System in addition to the structure Customizing settings.

These settings are described in more detail in Chapter 2, Section 2.1.2 and Section 2.3.3, and Chapter 4, Section 4.3.

1.3.3   Standard Networks

Structure of standard networks

A standard network consists of a *standard network header* and *standard network activities* , and you can use it as a template for operative networks. You can create standard networks using Transaction CN01. By defining an assignment to standard WBS elements in the header of the standard network and of the standard network activities, you can use both standard structures together as templates (see Section 1.7).

As in an operative network, you can use the four different activity types for structuring purposes in a standard network and create relationships between the activities of the standard network and the activities of other standard networks. You can also use activity elements and milestones to further specify the standard network activities. If you want to document the activities of a standard network, then you can use long texts and PS texts, but not document info records.

Unlike networks, standard networks are technically not implemented as orders in the SAP system but as plans (comparable to the routings that can be used as templates for production orders). For this reason, several essential differences exist between operative networks and standard networks:

Differences from operative networks

- ▸ To create standard networks, you need *standard network profiles* that you must have previously defined in the Customizing section for standard networks in SAP Project System. Standard network profiles contain data that is similar to the data contained in network profiles for operative networks (see Section 1.3.2).

- ▸ When creating a standard network, you can use another standard network as a template, but you can't use an operative network for this purpose.

- ▸ A standard network can be identified by an eight-digit key that is based on specific number range intervals for standard networks and an alternative number. This means that you can create different structures for a standard network key, each of which can be distinguished by a different alternative.

- ▸ You can only specify statuses in the header of the standard network; however, note that you must first create those statuses in the Customizing section of standard networks. When doing so, you can use a specific indicator to control whether you want the system to issue a warning message when the standard network is used as a template.

| Networks | [◉] |

A network consists of a network header and activities that can be linked to each other via relationships to map the flow of different tasks within a project. Depending on the activity type, you can store different data related to planning and controlling in that activity. Activity elements and subnetworks are simply different methods of detailing activities. You can create standard networks to use them as templates for operative networks. Before you can create networks, you must establish various settings in the Customizing section of SAP Project System.

1.4 Milestones

In SAP Project System, milestones can be used to map events of particular importance, such as the completion of critical project stages. For this reason, you can store a descriptive short text in a milestone and, if necessary, a long text and the planned date on which the milestone will probably be reached. This information is complemented by data on the milestone's purpose or function. You can document the achievement of a milestone by an actual date. Unlike in some other project management tools, in SAP Project System milestones don't control time scheduling for WBS elements and activities.

You can create any number of milestones for WBS elements or activities in operative structures and in standard structures. When doing so, the system automatically assigns a unique ID number to each milestone.

Standard milestones and milestone groups

If you want to use milestones that are similar to each other on a regular basis, then you can create *standard milestones* as templates via Transaction CN11. Moreover, you can assign several milestones as *milestone groups* to one object. To do this, you must first define the relevant milestone groups in Customizing of SAP Project System (Transaction OPT6) and then assign the standard milestones to those milestone groups.

Depending on whether you want to assign milestones to a WBS element or to an activity, you can use different methods of usage.

1.4.1 Milestones Assigned to WBS Elements

Figure 1.23 shows the detail screen of a milestone that is assigned to a WBS element. You can use milestones that have been assigned to a WBS element for purely informational purposes. The reports in the structure info system enable you to analyze the milestone data separately by their usage. *Exceptions* allow you to highlight (in color) those milestones in Reporting for which the planned dates have already passed.

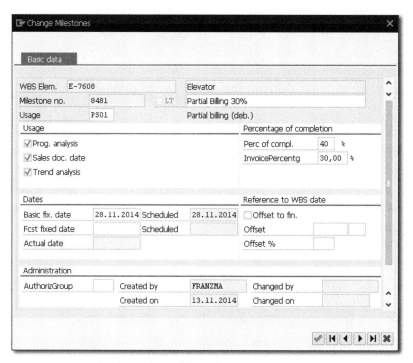

Figure 1.23 Example of a Work Breakdown Structure Milestone

When you create billing plans for WBS elements or sales order items (see Chapter 2, Section 2.5.3) or when you create invoicing plans for activities (see Chapter 2, Section 2.4.6), you can use the dates and the planned percentage of the milestones for which the SALES DOC. DATE indicator has been set. When the milestone dates change, the dates in the billing and invoicing plans change automatically as well. The USAGE field of the milestone enables you to enter further details of revenue and cost planning. The technique of transferring milestone dates to sales documents is also used in milestone billing (see Chapter 4, Section 4.6.1).

Billing and invoicing plans

If you use project versions (see Section 1.9.1) and set the TREND ANALY-SIS indicator for a milestone, then you can analyze retroactive changes to

Milestone trend and progress analysis

milestone dates either in a table or graphically at a later stage via *milestone trend analysis* (see Chapter 4, Section 4.7.1).

The planned date and planned percentage in the COMPLETION field in the milestone can be used to determine planned percentages of completion (see Chapter 4, Section 4.7.2) if you set the PROG. ANALYSIS indicator. If you enter an actual date in the milestone, then you can also use the percentage of completion as an actual percentage of completion.

Milestone dates — You can either specify the planned date of a milestone that is assigned to a WBS element as a FIXED DATE or derive it based on the scheduled date of the WBS element. This date is determined in the time scheduling process for the work breakdown structure (see Chapter 2, Section 2.1) either on the basis of the activities assigned or — if you don't use any networks — on the basis of the planned dates of the WBS element. In this context, you can specify whether you want the milestone date to refer to the start date or to the finish date. In addition, you can specify an absolute or percentage time interval (based on the duration of the WBS element). If you use a time reference for the WBS element, then changing the scheduled WBS element date will automatically change the milestone date as well, whereas a fixed date is not affected by date changes in the WBS element.

To document that a milestone of a WBS element has been reached, you must manually enter an actual date into the milestone. You cannot derive that actual date from the actual dates of the WBS element.

1.4.2 Milestones Assigned to Activities

You can use milestones that are assigned to activities in the same way as those that are assigned to WBS elements (see Section 1.4.1).

Milestone functions — However, milestones assigned to activities provide the following additional milestone functions that can be used in any combination (see Figure 1.24):

▶ RELEASE FOLLOWING ACTIVITIES
This function releases all activities that are linked as direct successors to the activity via relationships.

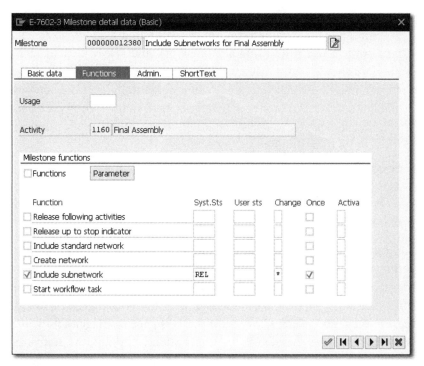

Figure 1.24 Functions of Activity Milestones

▶ RELEASE UP TO STOP INDICATOR
This function releases all subsequent activities; however, the automatic release process stops when it reaches activities that have been assigned a release stop indicator. A release stop indicator is an activity milestone for which the RELEASE STOP IND. flag has been set.

▶ INCLUDE STANDARD NETWORK
This function enables you to automatically include new activities. You must use the parameters of this function to store the standard network that is supposed to be used as a template and to store the predecessor and successor of the new activities.

▶ CREATE NETWORK
This function creates a new network. To do this, the standard network you enter in the parameters for this function is used as a template.

▶ INCLUDE SUBNETWORK
You must use the parameters of this function to define which activity you want to detail by using a subnetwork and also which standard network should be used as a template for the subnetwork. When you trigger this function, the system will automatically create a network and link this network to the activity specified. In this context, a dialog window allows you to decide whether you want the relationships of the activity to be adopted by the subnetwork.

▶ START WORKFLOW TASK
This function triggers a workflow that you must specify in the parameters for this function. Note that prior to this you must define the workflow.

You can use the fields provided for each function in the milestone to define whether a function should be used and, if so, when it should be triggered. A milestone function can start automatically if the milestone contains an actual date and the status of the activity changes or if one of these two events occurs. If you use a status change to trigger a function, you must also specify whether setting a status, undoing the status, or both status changes should be relevant. In addition, you must define which status combinations should be relevant. Finally, you can use the ONCE indicator to specify whether you permit multiple triggering of the function or whether you don't want the function to be executed more than once.

Milestone dates
As with milestones that are assigned to WBS elements, you can enter the planned dates of activity milestones either manually (fixed dates) or by referencing the dates contained in the activity.

You can either enter the actual dates of activity milestones manually or derive them from the actual dates contained in activity confirmations (see Chapter 4, Section 4.3).

Usage
You can define usages in the Customizing section of the milestones and store those *usages* in milestones that are assigned to WBS elements or activities. On the one hand, a usage serves as a sorting and/or filtering criterion in the context of analyses; on the other hand, you can store specific control settings in a usage.

If you enter a billing/invoicing rule in the usage, that rule can be transferred to the billing and invoicing plans along with the date and percentage of a milestone. This way, the usage of a milestone enables you to control, for example, whether a down payment, a partial invoice, or a final invoice is due on the milestone date (see Chapter 2, Section 2.5).

By setting the No Dialog indicator, you can hide dialog windows that are only used for informational purposes when triggering a milestone function.

1.5 Documents

You can use long texts to describe objects in greater detail and assign those long texts to all structure objects of SAP Project System: project definitions, WBS elements, network headers, activities, activity elements, and milestones. The short text of an object corresponds to the first 40 characters of the first line of the long text. As of EHP 3, you can also activate multiple language support for various object types in Customizing, which enables you to save short and long texts in different languages. The system automatically displays the short and long texts in your logon language. If no text has previously been entered in your logon language, then the system uses the text of a language you can select (master language). The entry of short texts in multiple languages occurs in a new tab.

Short and long texts

However, note that you cannot simply copy texts from one object to another. Moreover, short and long texts don't support any status or version management. For this reason, SAP Project System allows you to use *PS texts* or *documents from document management.*

Generic Object Services	[+]
In addition, you can assign any documents to projects by using the generic object services. However, this type of assignment is not explicitly displayed in the editing or reporting transactions of SAP Project System.	

1.5.1   PS Texts

You can create PS texts using either Transaction CN04 or various other editing transactions of project structures and assign those texts to WBS elements or activities. The SAP Mail System can also be used to send PS texts to other SAP users. A PS text can be identified on the basis of the PS text type, name, format, and language of the PS text; PS texts are stored in the SAP database. The text type serves as a sorting criterion for your PS texts. You must define appropriate text types for PS texts in the Customizing section of SAP Project System.

PS text formats   You can use the SAPscript format as the text format or choose one of the following formats: DOC, RTF, PPT, and XLS. Depending on the format you choose, you can also use the corresponding user interface for creating the PS texts. For example, if you want to create a PS text in DOC format, you can do that in Microsoft Word. This means that you can also include existing MS Word documents or use them as templates.

PS texts can be created in different languages. The LANGUAGE field in the identification of the PS texts will enable you to distinguish the texts at a later stage. The system automatically provides you with the existing PS texts in your logon language. If no PS text is available in your logon language, then the system displays a dialog in which you can select a PS text.

You can use PS texts as templates for other PS texts or create references between the texts. If you reference a PS text that has been assigned to a specific object in another object, which may even be located in a different project, then changes to the PS text assigned to the former object will also occur in the PS text assigned to the other object.

1.5.2   Integration with Document Management

You can assign *document info records* of SAP Document Management to operative WBS elements and activities and thus directly access the original documents that are managed by the document info records while editing project transactions.

Depending on the settings in the document management system, you can use virtually any document format in projects. The original documents don't need to be saved in the SAP database and can be stored on separate document servers. In addition, you can use functions such as *status management*, *versioning*, or *classification* for documents. Once you've created an assignment to an existing document info record, you can directly navigate to that record from your projects.

Documents

In addition, you can use the editing functions for projects to create new document info records and check in original documents. At the same time, you can create a link to a WBS element or activity. The Internet service CNW4 enables you to access project documents through the Internet without having to install an SAP GUI on your machine.

Restrictions for Document Info Records	[+]
Note that you cannot assign any document info records to standard work breakdown structures and standard networks.	

1.6 Status

Project definitions, WBS elements, network headers, activities, and activity elements contain statuses. Statuses document the state of an object and therefore serve as information or selection criterion for evaluations. They also define which business transactions are currently possible for the respective object.

Using statuses

There is a general distinction between *system statuses*, statuses that are predefined in the system, and *user statuses*, statuses that you can define in the Customizing section of SAP Project System and then summarize in a user status profile.

The four-digit short forms of up to seven system and user statuses each are displayed in the basic data of the objects. The detail screens of the statuses contain all active system statuses for the respective object and all user statuses that have been defined within the status profile, including their short forms and short texts (see Figure 1.25).

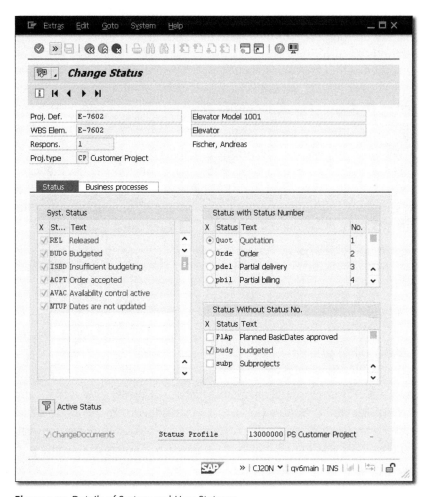

Figure 1.25 Details of System and User Statuses

The detail screen of the statuses also tells you which business processes the current combination of system and user statuses will permit, which ones are forbidden, and which business processes are only permitted with a warning. The *transaction analysis* provides information about which statuses are responsible for each situation.

To carry out a business process, there must be at least one active status that permits the process, and no status that prohibits the process or permits it only with a warning can be active at the same time. A warning is issued for a business process when there is at least one active status that permits the process with a warning and when no status is active that prohibits the process.

| Interaction of Statuses | [+] |

As soon as there is one active status that prohibits the business process—regardless of whether it is a system or a user status—the process cannot be carried out.

Statuses can be automatically set by the system based on different business processes (such as budgeting or entering actual dates), activated by inheritance, or manually assigned by the user.

The following list contains some important system statuses for work breakdown structures that you can set manually:

System status

- **CRTD (Created)**
  Initial status that allows all planning activities and structure changes but not the entry of actual dates or actual costs.

- **REL (Released)**
  Status that allows the entry of actual data. This status is automatically passed on to subordinate project elements and cannot be reset.

- **PREL (Partially released)**
  This status is automatically assigned by the system when a subordinate object is released. For WBS elements, this status allows the entry of actual start dates.

- **TECO (Technically completed)**
  This status is automatically passed on. It does not allow any planning activities, but it does permit the account assignment of costs and revenues. This status deletes capacity requirements and controls the transfer of assets under construction to completed assets within the scope of the settlement for investment projects (see Chapter 5, Section 5.9).

- **CLSD (Closed)**
  This status prohibits not only planning activities but also postings of actual costs. It also deactivates assets under construction. The status is automatically passed on. Resetting this status leads to the TECO status.

- **DLFL (Deletion flag)**
  This status prohibits virtually all business processes and is a prerequisite if you want to archive and delete projects at a later stage. The status can be inherited and reset.

- **FNBL (Final billing)**
  This status can be set for billing elements and cannot be inherited. It prohibits additional billing processes, but allows you to post costs.

In addition to the preceding list, you can manually set various system statuses—for instance, to lock cost planning or time scheduling processes or even for the account assignment of documents.

User status profile   To enhance the functionality of system statuses, you can define your own statuses, which are referred to as *user statuses*. To do that, you must first create an ID and a name for a user status profile in Customizing Transaction OK02, and then assign those object types to the profile for which you want to use the user status profile. Last, you must define user statuses for the status profile. Figure 1.26 shows an example of a user status profile.

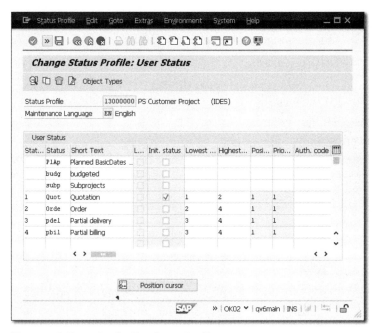

Figure 1.26 Example of a User Status Profile

User statuses can be divided into statuses with and without *status numbers*. You can define a sequence for statuses that have a status number. This means that you can set those statuses in the defined sequence (but you should carefully read the [F1] help for the LOWEST and HIGHEST STATUS NUMBER fields). Note that only one status with a status number can be active for an object.

Conversely, you can set any number of user statuses without status numbers. The POSITION and PRIORITY fields enable you to define which user status is displayed in its short form in the basic data of the objects.

The user statuses that are supposed to be set during the creation of an object or during the assignment of the user status profile must be marked as INITIAL. By assigning authorization keys to user statuses, you can assign explicit authorizations for setting and resetting user statuses.

Authorizations for Business Transactions Using Statuses **[+]**

If you allow for a user status to be automatically set as a follow-up action of a business process, then you can use authorization object B_USERST_T to indirectly assign the authorization for the business process (for example, the release) through the authorization key.

Next actions and influences

The detail screen of each status enables you to define *influences* and *next actions* for the respective status. You can use the indicators of the NEXT ACTION columns to define whether you want the user status to be set automatically through a business transaction or whether you want it to be reset. The indicators of the INFLUENCE columns allow you to define which business transactions are allowed by the user status and which ones are allowed with warning, prohibited, or not influenced at all.

You can store user status profiles as default values in project profiles and network types and in standard project definitions. However, once a user status of the user status profile has been active in an object you cannot enter any other user status profile in that object.

Status combination codes

The statuses of project objects are stored in a different database table in the SAP system than their master data. Therefore, if you use statuses as selection criteria in Reporting, then the system must read multiple database tables for the purpose of object selection, which can affect your system's performance, particularly when you select many objects. As of EHP 3, you can copy a combination of active statuses of an object as a so-called status combination code into the object master data and use the status combination code as selection criteria in Reporting; this increases the system performance during object selection.

You can enter specific settings for the status combination codes in the Customizing section of SAP Project System. There are 14 predefined combination codes available for system status combinations. For user statuses, you can define your own combination codes and assign combinations from user statuses. If multiple status combination codes are available for a specific object, then the priority of the combination code determines which combination code will be included in the master data of the object.

The `STATUS_COMB_UPDATE` program enables you to trigger a global identification process for status combination codes and to adopt these codes in the master data of the respective objects. Then the status combination codes are updated every time the status of a project object changes.

1.7 Editing Functions

Using templates
You can create operative project structures either manually or based on templates. For example, you can use standard work breakdown structures, standard networks, and other operative project structures and simulation versions as templates (see Section 1.9.2).

When you create a WBS using a template, the system automatically aligns the first section of the identification with the identification of the new project. You can add a customized extension that enables you to align multiple sections of the identification. If you only use parts of the template, then you must carry out the alignment of the identification yourself by using the REPLACE function.

If you want to create projects that consist of a WBS and a network using templates, the following two methods are available:

▸ **Create project with a template**
If you use this function and set the WITH ACTIVITIES indicator, then

you can control whether you want to copy the networks that have been assigned to the template as well.

▸ **Create network with a template**
If you use this method, then you must first create a network using a template. If the network or standard network you use as a template is assigned to a WBS or standard WBS, then the system will propose that you also create a new operative work breakdown structure on the basis of a template when you save the new network. This function is typically used for variant configurations with networks (see Section 1.8.6) and for assembly processing (see Section 1.8.7).

Even when editing operative structures, you can always use templates to extend your project structures. The process of creating new project parts by using templates is referred to as *inclusion*.

Including project parts

SAP Project System provides various transactions for creating, changing, and displaying operative project structures, such as the *Project Builder*, the *Project Planning Board*, or the *special maintenance functions*. As of EHP 4, you can use the *Project Editor* to display and change large project structures. You don't need to decide on using only one transaction to edit your projects. For example, you can create projects in the Project Builder and edit them later in the Project Planning Board or Project Editor.

1.7.1   Project Builder

You can use the Project Builder (Transaction CJ20N) to create, modify, and display project structures. Because of its structure and functions, the Project Builder is well suited for structuring projects. You don't need to make any additional settings in Customizing if you want to use the Project Builder. The user-specific options of the Project Builder enable you, for example, to define which objects may be edited in the Project Builder, or how many hierarchy levels of a project should be opened when you launch a project in the Project Builder (see Figure 1.27). As of EHP 6, the two options EXCLUDE MATERIAL MASTER DATA and EXCLUDE PURCHASE ORDER HISTORY are also available. By setting these indicators, you can improve the performance for opening and editing networks with a large number of material components and purchase requisitions.

Creating, displaying, and changing project structures

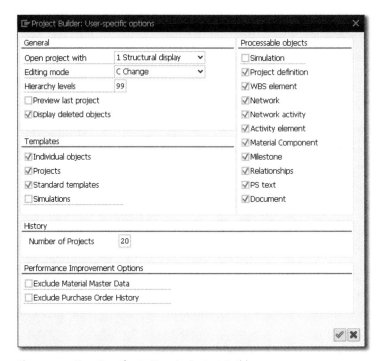

Figure 1.27 User-Specific Options in Project Builder

Customer Enhancements Possible

You can use a customer enhancement to use these performance improvement options for other transactions. Note, however, that selecting the EXCLUDE PURCHASE ORDER HISTORY option results in fields about the goods receipt quantity or existing purchase orders no longer being displayed in the network.

Worklist The user interface of the Project Builder consists of three areas (see Figure 1.28). The WORKLIST on the lower left hand side always contains the last five projects you have worked on. However, you can also include other projects or parts of projects in the WORKLIST folders via right-clicking. If you want to edit a project that's contained in the WORKLIST, you can simply double-click on the relevant project.

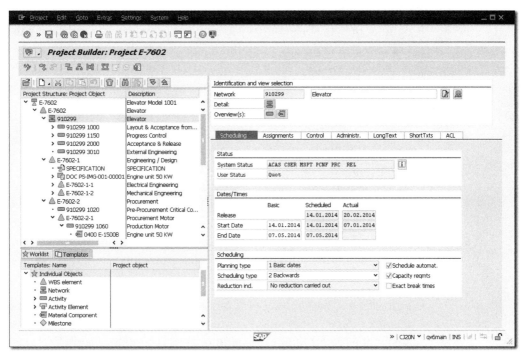

Figure 1.28 Editing a Project in the Project Builder

Once you've opened a project for editing, the structure of the project is displayed in the structure tree in the upper left. At the same time, the system switches from the WORKLIST to the TEMPLATES area in the lower left. You can insert objects from the templates area, such as new WBS elements or activities, into the structure of the project either by double-clicking on the objects or via drag-and-drop.

Templates area

Depending on the settings of the Project Builder, the structure tree displays the project definition, WBS elements, network headers, activities, activity elements, milestones, PS texts, documents, and assigned material components of a project, including its IDs and descriptions. By right-clicking on the structure tree heading, you can change the order in which the IDs and description are displayed. You can change the project structure via drag-and-drop or by right-clicking—for instance, to modify the WBS hierarchy or to create or include new objects. The structure tree also allows you to navigate within the project structure.

Structure tree

85

Preview area

If you set the PREVIEW LAST PROJECT indicator in the Project Builder options, then the project that you last worked on will be displayed in the PREVIEW area in the structure tree. When you double-click on the project in the PREVIEW area, the project opens and can be edited while the system immediately navigates to the last object you had worked on.

Work area

The area on the right in the Project Builder—the *work area*—displays data of the object that you have selected in the structure tree. The upper part of the work area displays the ID and description of the object selected in the structure tree. You can use the icons on top of the work area to toggle between the detail screen of the object, a tabular list of objects of the same type, and a table that lists assigned objects. By right-clicking in the detail screen of an object, you can navigate, for example, to the settlement rule of an object, to the billing and invoicing plans, or so on. As of EHP 3, you can also save changes temporarily in the Project Builder.

From the Project Builder, you can go directly to the Project Planning Board, to Easy Cost Planning, or to the sales pricings that you have created in the Project Builder. In addition, you can call the *hierarchy graphic* or—if you have selected a network object—the *network graphic*.

Hierarchy Graphic

Displaying work breakdown structures

The hierarchy graphic displays the hierarchical structure of the WBS as a graphic (as shown previously in Figure 1.2). Depending on the graphics profile stored in the project profile of the project and on your selection under WBS ELEMENT DISPLAY, the system can display different data for each WBS element. By default, a hierarchy graphic that you call from within an editing transaction displays the IDs, descriptions, and operative indicators of the WBS elements.

You can change operative indicators by clicking on them or by calling the detail screen of a WBS element. You can also create new WBS elements in the hierarchy graphic—either with or without using a template—and you can even delete WBS elements, provided this is permitted.

The CONNECTION MODE enables you to define the hierarchical relationship between two WBS elements by drawing a connection line from the upper-level WBS element to the lower-level one. The CUT function allows you to delete the hierarchical connection lines of a WBS element.

Connection mode of the hierarchy graphic

If you use large work breakdown structures, then you can show a *navigation area* in which you can select the project parts you want to display. The VERTICALLY FROM LEVEL function allows you to define that—from a specific level—you no longer want to display WBS elements horizontally but vertically.

Navigation area

Network Graphic

The network graphic provides a graphical display of the activities of one or several networks (see Figure 1.3). In this context, the system arranges the display of activities in accordance with their logical sequence. However, you can change this order via drag-and-drop. In addition, you can group the activities based on the work centers used or on the WBS elements to which they are assigned. As in the hierarchy graphic, you can also show a navigation area if you use large network structures.

Displaying networks

Depending on the graphics profile stored in the network profile and on your selection under DISPLAY ACTIVITIES, the network graphic can display the IDs, descriptions, control keys, duration, planned dates, and floats of the activities. In addition, specific indicators used in the extended display of the activities allow you to determine which objects have been assigned to an activity.

Time-critical activities (with an overall float smaller than or equal to zero) are highlighted in red in the network graphic, white partially confirmed activities are displayed with a single strikethrough, and confirmed ones are displayed with a double strikethrough (see Chapter 2, Section 2.1.2 and Chapter 4, Section 4.3).

For the display of relationships, you can choose between a time-dependent presentation and a finish-start presentation. If you choose the *finish-start relationship* presentation, then the relationships are always displayed as connection lines between the finish of the predecessor and the start of the successor, regardless of the relationship type. Contrary to

Displaying relationships

this, the time-dependent presentation displays a start-start relationship—for example, as a connection between the start of the predecessor and the start of the successor. The type and, if necessary, fixed time interval of a relationship are displayed in the graphical presentation of the relationship.

You can navigate to the detail screen of an activity or relationship by double-clicking on it. Moreover, you can create and delete activities and relationships in the network graphic.

Connection mode of the network graphic

To create relationships in the network graphic, you must draw a connection line between the predecessor and the successor in the connection mode of the network graphic. To create a finish-start relationship, you must connect the finish of the predecessor with the start of the successor, to create a finish-finish relationship you must connect the finish of the predecessor with the finish of the successor, and so on.

Loop analysis

The LOOP ANALYSIS function of the network graphic enables you to highlight relationships that lead to a cyclical sequence of activities in specific colors. Networks with a loop cannot be scheduled.

You can also print out the hierarchy and network graphics of a project. When doing so, you can include additional graphics, such as a company logo, in the graphic as well.

1.7.2 Project Planning Board

Transactions CJ27, CJ2B, and CJ2C of the Project Planning Board enable you to create, modify, and display work breakdown structures and assigned networks. To open a project in the Project Planning Board, you must specify a *planning board profile*, provided the project profile does not propose any. The planning board profile controls the display and functions of the Project Planning Board.

The user interface of the Project Planning Board is based on an interactive SAP bar chart in which you can display data related to the project definition, WBS elements, activities, activity elements, and milestones, both as a table and in a diagram (see Figure 1.29). The planning board profile defines which of the aforementioned object types and which table fields are displayed. Note that you can change this setting in the Project Planning Board.

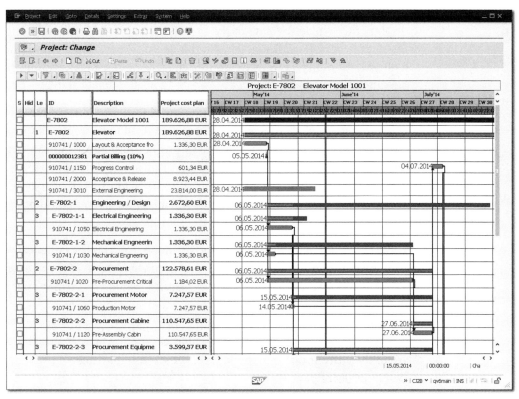

Figure 1.29 Editing a Project in the Project Planning Board

Filtering, sorting, and grouping functions also enable you to define which objects should be displayed in which order. Moreover, you can use the HIGHLIGHT OBJECTS function to highlight those project elements that have been assigned documents, for example, or that contain specific properties.

Table section

From the menu of the Project Planning Board, you can also navigate to the assignment of PS texts and documents. Call the detail screen of a network header by clicking on the corresponding icon. A separate overview of assigned material components is available in the Project Planning Board. When a TEMPLATES area is displayed, you can create new objects

89

for a project by double-clicking on a template or dragging and dropping it to a project.

Diagram section

The graphical area of the Project Planning Board—the *diagram section*—displays the scheduling data of the objects displayed in the form of different time bars. In addition, dates and different master data fields of the objects can be displayed to the left or right, above or below, and even directly on the time bars.

Planning board assistant

The graphical presentation of the different objects in the table section, and particularly in the diagram section, is controlled by a graphics profile that's stored in the planning board profile. However, you can customize the presentation using the PLANNING BOARD ASSISTANT in the Project Planning Board. A preview area in the planning board assistant allows you to view how your changes will affect the presentation of the objects.

Periods displayed

The overall period displayed in the diagram section is referred to as the *evaluation period*. The evaluation period consists of a *pre-evaluation period*, a *planning period*, and a *post-evaluation period*. To further clarify these periods, you can display each of them in a different scale. For example, you can choose a greater scale for project stages that are in the past or the distant future than you would choose for project stages that are in the current planning period, for which you may need a presentation in terms of days.

Timescale assistant

You can control the size and layout of the evaluation period and the presentation of the timescale (color layout, display of the day of week or date, etc.) via subprofiles of the planning board profile; however, you can customize them using the OPTIONS and the TIMESCALE ASSISTANT. You can edit an object in the Project Planning Board in a table or in the detail screen, for example, by double-clicking on the object in the table or diagram section.

If necessary, you can change scheduled dates graphically by moving, extending, or shortening the respective time bars. Relationships between activities can be created as tables in the Project Planning Board, graphically in the connection mode, or by using the CONNECT SELECTED ACTIVITIES function. If you use this function, the system automatically creates finish-start relationships for all selected activities in the order in which the activities are listed in the table section.

Besides the date overview described previously, you can show additional overviews for selected objects. All of the overviews consist of a table section and a graphical area. For those overviews, you can use a field selection to define which fields should be displayed in the table section. Furthermore, the context menu enables you to open a legend of the objects displayed and additional functions. The following additional overviews are available in the Project Planning Board:

Additional overviews of the Project Planning Board

- ▶ **Component overview**
  The graphical section of this overview displays requirement dates and, if needed, delivery and goods movement dates for assigned material components. You can navigate to the detail screen of a material component by double-clicking on it.

- ▶ **Cost overview**
  The graphical section displays planned costs and, if available, planned and actual revenues of WBS elements as a totals curve.

- ▶ **Capacity overview**
  This overview compares the available capacity of work centers assigned to activities with the (total) capacity requirement for different periods as a bar chart or histogram. You can display the work centers by double-clicking on them.

- ▶ **Plant maintenance overview**
  The graphical section of this overview displays the dates of plant maintenance orders that you have assigned as subnetworks to activities.

Other functions that can be called through the Project Planning Board include the following:

- ▶ Hierarchy graphic and network graphic
- ▶ Planning boards for capacity leveling
- ▶ Workforce planning
- ▶ Milestone trend analysis

▸ Cost and capacity reports

▸ Overview of direct predecessors and successors of an activity

User-specific
changes

When exiting the Project Planning Board, you can save the changes to the Project Planning Board that you made using the planning board and timescale assistants and the field selection, and some changes to the options of the Project Planning Board. This way, you can utilize those changes the next time you open a project in the Project Planning Board. The UNDO USER SETTINGS function enables you to delete the changes. As of EHP 3, you can save user-specific zoom factors and a user-specific separation between the table and graphical areas.

[+]

Deleting User-Specific Settings

You can use Report RSAPFCJGR to simultaneously reset user-specific settings for multiple users in the Project Planning Board.

Planning Board Profile

The standard version of the program already contains planning board profiles and subprofiles that are needed for the Project Planning Board. However, you can also define your own planning board profiles in the Customizing section of SAP Project System (see Figure 1.30).

Profiles of the
Project Planning
Board

In a planning board profile, you must specify the field selection for the date overview and the other overviews of the Project Planning Board. The graphics profile in the planning board profile is used to define the presentation of the objects in the table and graphical sections. To create new graphics profiles, you can use the planning board assistant in the same way as you did in the Project Planning Board. Other subprofiles of the Project Planning Board include the following:

▸ **Time profile**
This profile determines the beginning and end of the evaluation and planning periods. This means that pre-evaluation and post-evaluation periods are defined automatically.

▸ **Scale profile**
This profile enables you to define the scale to be used for the planning period and for the pre-evaluation and post-evaluation periods.

▶ **Timescale profile**
This profile defines the presentation of the different timescales (such as annual, monthly, or daily period splits), and it determines which timescales should be displayed with which scales.

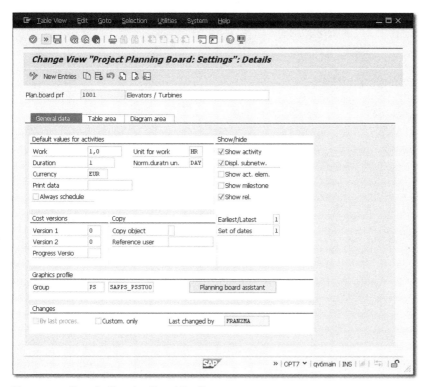

Figure 1.30 Sample Planning Board Profile

Furthermore, a planning board profile allows you to specify which objects, dates, and floats and which data should be displayed with the different time bars. You should also note that to display cost and progress data you need to define the corresponding CO versions in the planning board profile.

1.7.3 Special Maintenance Functions

The menu for special maintenance functions in SAP Project System provides transactions that enable you to create, change, and display work

Transactions

breakdown structures (Transactions CJ01, CJ02, CJ03), networks (Transactions CN21, CN22, CN23), and work breakdown structures with networks assigned (Transactions CJ2D, CJ20, CJ2A). Figure 1.31 shows, for example, how you use structure planning (Transaction CJ20) to edit a project.

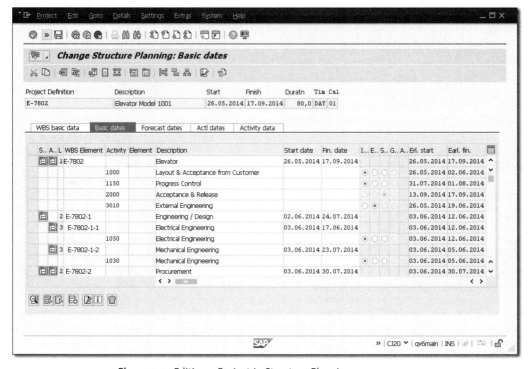

Figure 1.31 Editing a Project in Structure Planning

All of the preceding transactions allow you to toggle between the detail screen of the project definition or network header and the table views of WBS elements or activities. Conversely, you can navigate from a table view into the detail screen of an object. The menu also enables you to call lists of assigned objects, such as PS texts, documents, or milestones.

You can also call the hierarchy and network graphics from the special maintenance functions and navigate to planning board displays.

You don't need to enter any additional Customizing settings to use the special maintenance functions. You can simply define the presentation

of objects in table views and graphics and functions for capacity requirements planning in the relevant settings of the project or network profiles.

Transactions CJ06, CJ07, CJ08, CJ11, CJ12, and CJ13 allow you to create, change, or display individual project definitions or WBS elements.
When creating a new WBS element using Transaction CJ11, you must
either create an assignment to an existing project definition or create a
new project definition when saving the WBS element. That new project
definition must then be filled with the data of the WBS element. To create a new project definition, use a project profile in which the TRANSFER
TO PROJECT DEFINITION indicator has been set.

In live projects, the special maintenance functions are typically used by
users who don't need more than a simple table option to edit project
structures and who regard the Project Builder or the Project Planning
Board as too complex.

1.7.4   Project Editor

As of EHP 4 and further enhanced in EHP 6, the Project Editor (Transaction PSHLP20) is available, which has been developed specifically for the
performance-optimized editing of master data in very large and complex
project structures.

*Editing large
projects*

The editing interface of the Project Editor resembles that of the Project
Builder; however, it does not provide its entire functionality. For example, the Project Editor does not support the hierarchy graphic or network graphic. Moreover, it is not possible to add, reassign, or delete
objects and change material components with the Project Editor. Nevertheless, the Project Editor provides various functions that avoid performance and lock problems of the other editing functions and are further
detailed in the following sections.

In contrast to all other editing transactions in SAP Project System, the
Project Editor enables you to select the data to be edited in *data sets* in
its initial screen (see Figure 1.32). Data sets represent groups of data
defined by SAP.

Data sets

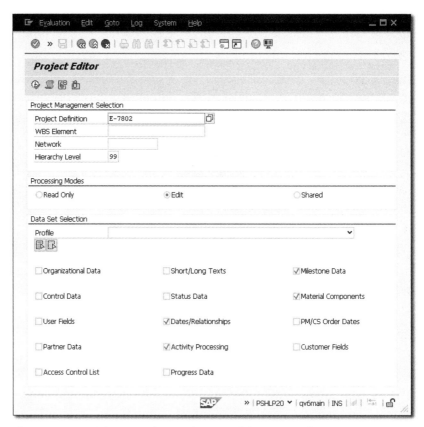

Figure 1.32 Data Selection in the Initial Screen of the Project Editor

For example, the CONTROL DATA data set contains all control data, whereas the DATES/RELATIONSHIP data set contains date information. At first, only the data sets you select in the initial screen are made available for editing in the Project Editor (see Figure 1.33). If necessary, however, you can always load additional data sets in the Project Editor.

Selection profile Instead of selecting data sets manually, you can also select a selection profile and store this profile as a default value in your user parameters. The selection profile automatically proposes a selection of data sets in the initial screen of the Project Editor. You can define selection profiles in the Customizing section of SAP Project System.

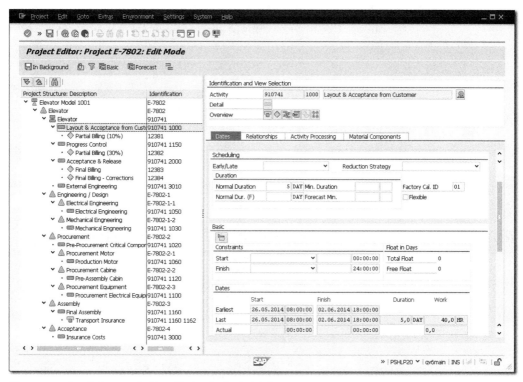

Figure 1.33 Detail Screen of a Data Set in the Project Editor

Regardless of the selection of data sets, you can also use the Project Editor to edit assigned documents and settlement rules if necessary.

In addition to the common edit modes, READ ONLY and EDIT, you can use a customer enhancement to release the SHARED mode for the Project Editor (Figure 1.32). If you use this module, the selected project elements are locked only when they are saved, not when they are opened or changed.

Shared mode

Shared Mode   **[!]**

This mode enables multiple users to change projects or networks in parallel without the system outputting information or warning messages. You should use appropriate selection profiles or authorizations to ensure that the individual users process separate data sets or different activities of a network, for example.

Drafts Instead of making changes directly to an operative project or network, you can use the Project Editor to create one or several *drafts* of the project, drafts of project parts, or of individual networks. You can then edit these drafts in the Project Editor and retransfer them into the operative project later on.

You can create drafts directly in the initial screen of the Project Editor via the CREATE DRAFT icon or, when processing a project, by using the SAVE AS A DRAFT function. The Draft Workbench (Transaction PSHLP30) enables you to compare drafts, compare them with the data of the operative project (see Figure 1.34), or delete drafts. Drafts also allow you to simulate changes to projects without locking the operative projects.

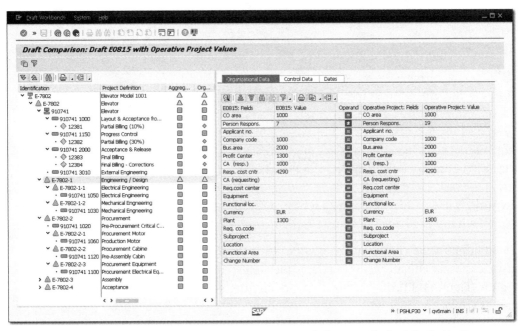

Figure 1.34 Comparing Operative Data with the Data of a Draft in the Draft Workbench

Background saving In addition to directly saving changes to the project elements or saving changes as drafts, the Project Editor provides the BACKGROUND SAVING function. In this case, changes are saved in a background job. If errors occur during this process—for example, due to locks—then the system automatically saves a draft and informs the user. In a log, the user can then analyze the errors and open the draft.

Log entries can be deleted manually by users or administrators or automatically—depending on the number of entries or on how long the entries exist in the system. For this purpose, the appropriate settings must be made in Customizing and a regular background job for the deletion must be scheduled.

You can also use the Project Editor to schedule projects (see Chapter 2, Section 2.1.3). It provides, for example, functions for loop analyses, for scheduling comparisons, and for exception selections as well as a general overview of the dates of the various project elements or a simple Gantt chart presentation of dates. If maintenance or service orders are assigned to network activities of a project as subnetworks, then you can display their order headers in the Project Editor and, for example, schedule them together with the project.

Order dates

You can further optimize the time required for loading large structures in the Project Editor by means of a cache concept. For this reason, an administrator can load projects into a cache by means of the Administrator Workbench (Transaction PSHLP90). If you open the projects for editing in the Project Editor at a later stage, then the data is read directly from the cache. If the projects have not previously been loaded into the cache or if the data in the cache has not been updated, then the Project Editor automatically reads the data from the normal database tables.

Project cache

Project Cache and Performance	**[!]**
Note that the project cache does not always accelerate the data loading process in the Project Editor. Therefore, it should be tested in advance.	

Further features of the Project Editor include the following:

▶ **Object filter**
To keep the number of objects to be displayed as small as possible, you can define a user-specific filter.

▶ **Table overviews based on SAP List Viewer (ALV)**
In these tabular overviews, you can sort, filter, print, or define your own layouts.

- **Selective mass update**
  This function allows you to change fields of several objects in the tabular overviews in parallel.
- **Browsing in tabular overviews**
  In the tabular overviews, you can switch between a presentation by page and an overall presentation of all records. Because the Project Editor only loads data if necessary, the presentation by page provides shorter loading times for very large structures.
- **Enhancement options**
  There are various enhancement options for the Project Editor—for example, for hiding fields or functions depending on the user requirements or for integrating additional functions in the tabular overviews.

[!]

Restrictions of the Project Editor

Note that the Project Editor contains various functional restrictions. For example, you cannot create new structure elements for projects in the Project Editor. The documentation and SAP Notes 1607785, 1607856, and 1607861 provide further information on these restrictions.

Project Worklist

You can also navigate to the project editing function of the Project Editor via the Project Worklist (Transaction PSHLP10). The Project Worklist displays user-specific lists of projects, WBS elements, and networks, which you can use to open the objects in the Project Editor (see Figure 1.35).

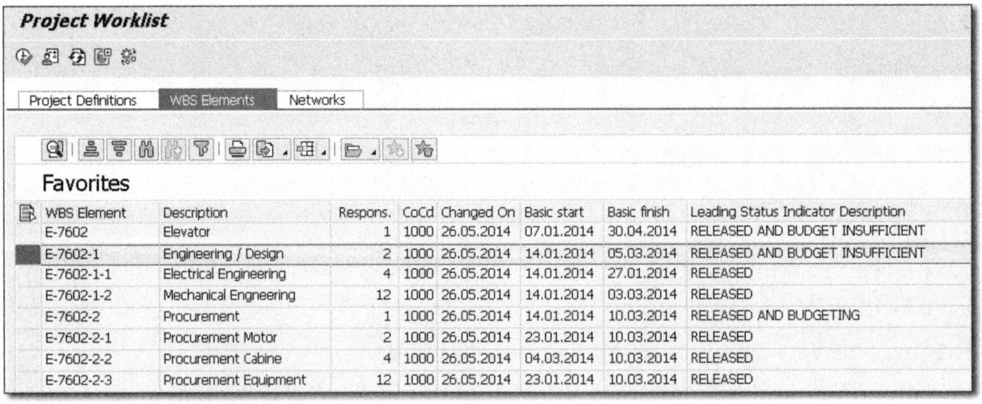

WBS Element	Description	Respons.	CoCd	Changed On	Basic start	Basic finish	Leading Status Indicator Description
E-7602	Elevator	1	1000	26.05.2014	07.01.2014	30.04.2014	RELEASED AND BUDGET INSUFFICIENT
E-7602-1	Engineering / Design	2	1000	26.05.2014	14.01.2014	05.03.2014	RELEASED AND BUDGET INSUFFICIENT
E-7602-1-1	Electrical Engineering	4	1000	26.05.2014	14.01.2014	27.01.2014	RELEASED
E-7602-1-2	Mechanical Engneering	12	1000	26.05.2014	14.01.2014	03.03.2014	RELEASED
E-7602-2	Procurement	1	1000	26.05.2014	14.01.2014	10.03.2014	RELEASED AND BUDGETING
E-7602-2-1	Procurement Motor	2	1000	26.05.2014	23.01.2014	10.03.2014	RELEASED
E-7602-2-2	Procurement Cabine	4	1000	26.05.2014	04.03.2014	10.03.2014	RELEASED
E-7602-2-3	Procurement Equipment	12	1000	26.05.2014	23.01.2014	10.03.2014	RELEASED

Figure 1.35 Favorites List of WBS Elements in the Project Worklist

You can switch between the lists, which are automatically populated based on your access control authorizations, your FAVORITES, or your last objects used. As of EHP 6, you can also use the Project Worklist to open objects in the Project Builder or—with a customer enhancement—in other editing transactions.

1.7.5   Editing Customer Projects

Especially for customer projects in the service sector, where the SAP professional service solutions are used, a Web Dynpro-based editing interface is available as of EHP 5 for work breakdown structures (see Figure 1.36).

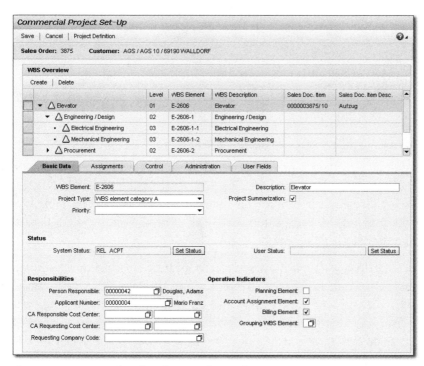

Figure 1.36 User Interface for Editing Professional Service Customer Projects

A typical usage scenario for this interface is as follows:

Web Dynpro interface

A user creates a sales order using the corresponding Web Dynpro sales interfaces. When the order is saved, the system automatically creates a work breakdown structure and links it to the sales document (see Section 1.8.7). After having saved the sales document, the user directly opens the new editing interface for the created work breakdown structure via the SAVE AND FOLLOW UP function—for example, to adapt organizational data or change statuses. If required, the user can also create new WBS elements or delete elements that are no longer needed from the structure (as of EHP 6). The WBS overview here is used for navigation within the structure and as an overview of the linked sales document items for each WBS element.

In this scenario, the user may use an integrated uniform, Web Dynpro-based work environment without having to navigate to SAP GUI transactions.

[+] **Limited Range of Functions**

Note that the interface for editing customer projects has a limited range of functions and, for example, cannot be used for editing WBS element dates, documents, settlement rules, or progress data.

1.7.6 Mobile Applications—SAP Fiori

As of 2014, you can use transactional SAP Fiori apps to perform specific tasks in SAP Project System. The SAP Fiori user interface is HTML5-based and supports various end devices, such as desktop PCs, tablets, or smartphones; the apps automatically adapt to the respective ratios and specifics of the given end device.

Transactional apps Transactional SAP Fiori apps typically address an individual user role and task. Compared to SAP GUI-based and Web Dynpro-based transactions, they provide a very lightweight user interface that allows users to perform tasks on mobile end devices when traveling, on construction sites, or on-site at the customer's location, for example. Figure 1.37 shows a sample app for changing WBS element statuses.

In this app, you first select the object to be changed via a list of WBS elements that can be restricted via a search option and grouped by projects as needed. For these WBS elements, you can view the respective active system and user statuses in the corresponding tabs. You can now set a new status or undo a status. In this context, the same rules as for changing statuses in SAP transactions apply. For example, specific system statuses are inherited automatically, whereas for user statuses you can decide on inheritance rules yourself.

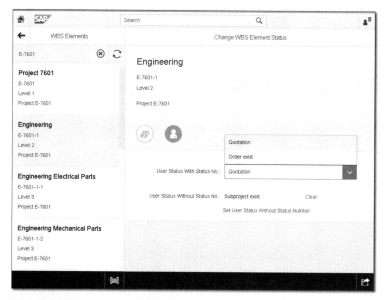

Figure 1.37 Transactional SAP Fiori App for Changing WBS Element Statuses

If you use SAP Jam for project collaboration scenarios, then you can use the transactional apps of SAP Project System to directly share information on an object or comments with other users in an SAP Jam group or discuss them in SAP Jam.

SAP Jam integration

Currently, you can use the following transactional apps for SAP Project System:

- Change WBS Element Status
- Change Network Activity Status
- Confirm Project Milestone
- Confirm Network Activity

An app is executed via the SAP Fiori Launchpad (see Figure 1.38), which in turn is initiated via a browser. You can select the individual apps from

SAP Fiori Launchpad

a catalog and arrange them in a user-specific manner in the Launchpad using tiles. By defining groups, you can structure the arrangement of tiles in the Launchpad according to your requirements. Besides transactional apps, you can also place analytical SAP Fiori apps as tiles in you Launchpad. Chapter 6, Section 6.5 discusses the analytical SAP Fiori apps of the SAP Project System.

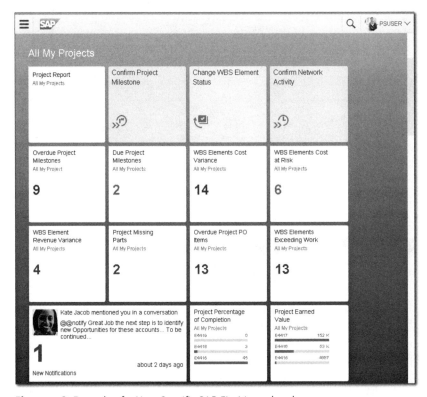

Figure 1.38 Example of a User-Specific SAP Fiori Launchpad

SAP Fiori search and fact sheets SAP Fiori search (see Figure 1.39) is another Launchpad function via which you can search for apps in the Launchpad and particularly for business objects within SAP Business Suite. You can navigate to the fact sheet of a business object by using the search result.

A fact sheet comprises the most important data of the object concerned and its context information. Figure 1.40 shows an example of a WBS element fact sheet.

Figure 1.39 Example of SAP Fiori Search Results

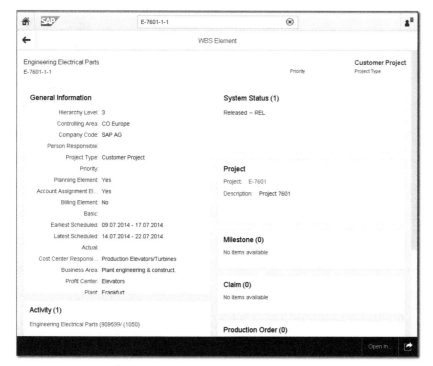

Figure 1.40 WBS Element Fact Sheet

Besides the name and identification of the business object, the header of a fact sheet can provide additional important information, such as the priority and project type of the WBS element, as shown in Figure 1.40. You can find critical selected data on the object in the GENERAL INFOR-MATION area. The other areas show linked objects. From the fact sheet, you may navigate to further details of the object or linked objects, or you can call transactional apps or SAP ERP transactions.

From the technical point of view, the SAP Fiori search is based on SAP NetWeaver Embedded Search and various search models. In SAP Note 1861013, you can find a list of search models that are provided by SAP by default.

[+] | **SAP Fiori App Types and SAP HANA**

Besides the transactional and analytical apps, the fact sheets represent a third SAP Fiori app type. In contrast to transactional SAP Fiori apps, fact sheets and SAP Fiori search require the use of an SAP HANA database. The analytical SAP Fiori apps require the use of SAP HANA. Different from the SAP Fiori search, however, analytical apps also support *sidecar approaches*, in which SAP HANA is implemented in parallel to the existing database and data is replicated to the SAP HANA database virtually in real time.

1.8 Tools for Optimized Master Data Maintenance

You can employ various tools in SAP Project System to keep the creation and modification of project structures as simple as possible for its users. These tools allow you to customize the user interface in various ways to avoid the possibility of users entering incorrect entries and to increase the end users' general acceptance of the different editing transactions. You can also automate the maintenance of master data where necessary to make it as efficient as possible.

1.8.1 Field Selection

Field properties
The field selections in structure Customizing of SAP Project System enable you to manipulate fields in project definitions, WBS elements,

network headers, activities, and activity elements. You can use a field selection to mark the properties of fields in the following way:

▶ **Ready for input**
Data that is contained in this type of field can be modified, provided this is not forbidden by a specific status.

▶ **Displayed**
Data contained in this type of field is visible but cannot be modified in tables or in the detail screen. However, note that you can still change display fields via mass changes or via a substitution.

▶ **Hidden**
Fields of this type are not displayed.

▶ **Required field**
You must enter data in this type of field before you can save the respective object.

▶ **Highlighted**
The values of these fields are displayed in a different color than the values of the other fields.

Thus, you can use field selections—in accordance with the requirements of your projects—to completely hide fields that aren't needed, to display fields that are intended to be filled with data only via the template or default values in Customizing, or to force certain entries to be made during the creation of an object.

Although you can define a client-wide field selection, you usually combine field selections with influencing values, such as the project or network profiles or the network type. For example, you can select and control different fields for different project types.

1.8.2 Flexible Detail Screens and Table Controls

Flexible detail screens enable you to control the distribution of the fields to different tabs for WBS elements and activities. By default, each tab displays exactly one detail screen, including the corresponding data. For example, the DATES tab contains the DATES detail screen, including all date fields.

Flexible detail screens

The LAYOUT DETAIL SCREENS function allows you to define your own tabs and to integrate up to five detail screens in any sequence in each tab. When doing so, you can define the name of each tab and, if required, select an icon that is supposed to be displayed in conjunction with the name. The FIRST TAB PAGE indicator can be used to define which tab should be displayed first when the object is opened. Figure 1.41 shows a sample definition of a tab.

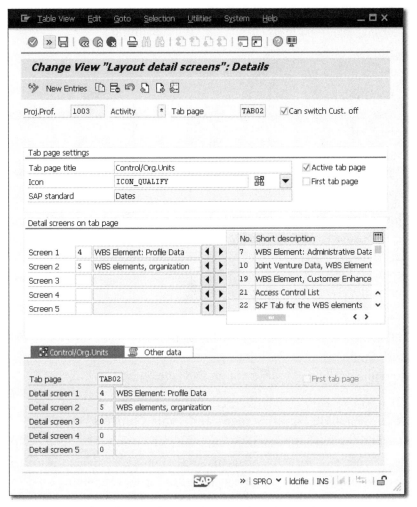

Figure 1.41 Sample Definition of a WBS Element Tab in Customizing

You can either define tabs for all users in the Customizing section of SAP Project System or for individual users in the editing transactions. You can define tabs in Customizing based on the project or network profile and the activity type (CREATE, CHANGE, DISPLAY, or ALL ACTIVITIES). The CAN SWITCH CUST. OFF indicator allows you to define whether users can switch between the tabs defined in Customizing and the standard tabs.

Authorized users can also create tabs when editing WBS elements or activities on the basis of the respective project profile or network profile. When doing so, you can manually create new tabs, use the standard tabs, or use those that have been defined in Customizing as templates. The definition of those tabs can be used temporarily or stored for each user individually.

The presentation of all project structure objects in tables is made possible by *table controls* in the editing transactions, with the exception of the Project Planning Board and the Project Editor. Table controls allow you to modify the column width and the order of the columns displayed by dragging and dropping. The changes you make can then be saved as variants for each user. **Table controls**

When opening a table at a later stage, you can then select a variant that you have defined so that you can display the columns according to your requirements. If you select a variant as the default setting, then the table is automatically displayed on the basis of that variant.

You can use the administrator settings to apply the table control settings to all users. The administrator settings also enable you to hide complete columns and to define the number of fixed columns—that is, columns that should always be displayed regardless of where you scroll within your table.

1.8.3 Mass Change

If you want to change the field contents of multiple objects simultaneously, then you can use the MASS CHANGE function in SAP Project System. The following objects can be changed via a mass change: **Objects for mass changes**

- Project definitions
- WBS elements
- Network headers
- Activities and activity elements
- Milestones
- Relationships

The object types you use will determine which fields can be changed by using the MASS CHANGE function. Usually, you can only change the master data fields of objects in a mass change; however, in WBS elements, you can also change planned dates, and you can set the RELEASED status for activities—but you cannot change settlement rules or status profiles using a mass change.

If you want to change objects of a single project, then you can call the MASS CHANGE function from within the Project Builder, the Project Planning Board, or the structure planning. If you want to change objects of multiple projects simultaneously, then you can trigger the mass change of those projects via the structure information system or using Transaction CNMASS. This transaction also allows you to schedule the execution of the mass change as a background job.

If field values are changed using the mass change, then the system performs the same checks as in a manual change. In particular, this means that you need to be authorized to change an object in order to change the data of that object via the mass change.

Mass change process

In order to carry out a mass change directly, you must start the MASS CHANGE function and select the objects to be changed. Then you must select the fields you want to change and enter the new field value. If necessary, you can use the previous field value as an additional filtering criterion for the changes. For numerical fields, you can also define formulas that calculate the new values on the basis of the original field values.

You can test your changes prior to executing and saving mass changes to objects. In addition, you can use Transaction CNMASS to save a log of the changes that have been implemented and analyze that log at any time using Transaction CNMASSPROT.

Mass Changes Cannot Be Reversed **[!]**

Note that you cannot simply cancel a mass change; that is, you cannot undo it. If necessary, you must manually correct changes to field values that have been implemented by incorrect mass changes.

To obtain a higher degree of control when performing mass changes to multiple objects, you can carry out a tabular mass change instead of the direct mass change via Transaction CNMASS (see Figure 1.42).

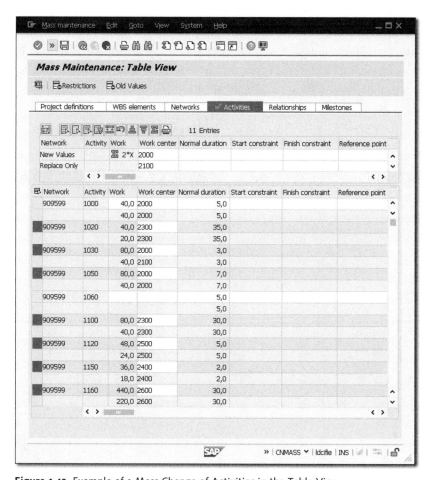

Figure 1.42 Example of a Mass Change of Activities in the Table View

Tabular mass change After selecting the objects and fields in a tabular mass change, the system first displays a list of selected objects in which you can use a filtering function to manually exclude objects from the mass change. In addition, you can also display the previous field values in this view, then carry out a mass change, and finally compare the new values with the old ones. Not until you have saved the changes can you undo the changes made in the tabular mass change.

1.8.4 Substitution

Substitutions enable you to automatically change master data fields of project definitions, WBS elements, network headers, and activities in accordance to conditions that you have defined. Figure 1.43 shows an example of the definition of a substitution. This substitution automatically sets the responsible cost center (RESP. COST CNTR) 4290 for those WBS elements into which responsible persons with the numbers 1 through 20 have been entered.

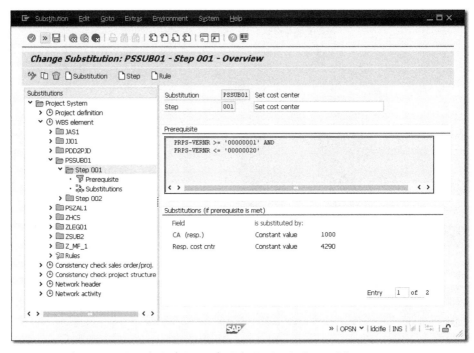

Figure 1.43 Sample Definition of a Substitution in Customizing

You must define substitutions in the structure Customizing section of work breakdown structures or networks. When creating a substitution, you must specify the object type for which you want to use the substitution and assign an ID and a description to the substitution. Then you must create one or more steps within the substitution. For each step, you can choose which fields must be changed and which prerequisites must be fulfilled in order for a change to be made.

Defining substitutions

To define prerequisites, you can use the master data of the respective object and general system data, such as client, date, or user name, as parameters; for WBS elements, you can use the data of superordinate objects as parameters. You can then use relational operands in an editor to match those parameters to fixed values or to other field values. A traffic light icon indicates whether the prerequisite you have defined is complete.

Only if this prerequisite is fulfilled during the execution of the substitution for an object will the field values be replaced. If the prerequisite is not fulfilled, the system performs the next step of the substitution.

When defining the field value substitution of a substitution step, you can either use fixed values for the fields to be changed or you can use the values of other fields.

You can trigger a substitution manually or have the system execute it automatically when objects are saved. A manual substitution can be carried out from within all editing transactions. To do this, you must first select the objects to be processed and then choose the SUBSTITUTION function. The system then displays a dialog in which you can select the substitution you want to execute. Once you have selected the substitution, the system displays a log that lists the changes that have been made.

Performing a substitution

For project definitions and WBS elements, you can avoid the window for selecting the substitution by entering a substitution for project definitions or WBS elements in the project profile.

To have the system automatically perform a substitution during a save process, you must store the relevant substitution in the project profile either for project definitions or for WBS elements and set the AUTOMAT.

SUBSTITUTION indicator. To enable the automatic substitution function for networks, you only need to enter the relevant substitution in the network profile.

[+] **Performing Substitutions for Several Projects**

A common method for triggering an automatic substitution for multiple projects simultaneously is to carry out a mass change of a non-required field in those projects. The automatic substitutions are then processed when the mass change is saved.

1.8.5 Validation

Validations enable you to carry out self-defined checks for master data fields of project definitions, WBS elements, network headers, and activities. The result of a validation can consist of informational messages, warnings, or even error messages. Note that if an error message occurs you cannot save the respective object.

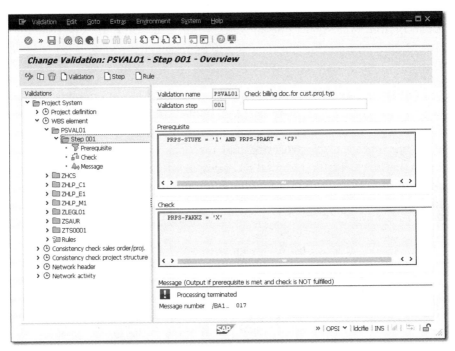

Figure 1.44 Sample Definition of a Validation in Customizing

For example, you can use validations to ensure that projects, which contain a specific project profile, always begin with the same key, or you can validate the consistency of IDs within the project structure. Figure 1.44 shows an example of a validation that ensures that level 1 WBS elements, which belong to the project type CUSTOMER PROJECT (CP), are marked as billing documents.

Like substitutions, you must define validations in structure Customizing of SAP Project System. A validation can comprise several steps, each of which performs a separate check. For each step, you must define a PREREQUISITE, a CHECK, and a corresponding MESSAGE. The check will be performed only if an object fulfills the prerequisite. If the condition of the check is fulfilled, then the system issues a message; otherwise, the validation step for the object in question will terminate.

Defining validations

The definition of prerequisites and checks occurs in the same way as the definition of prerequisites in substitutions (see Section 1.8.4). When defining the message, you must first specify whether the message type is INFORMATION, a WARNING, an ERROR, or a TERMINATION. Then, create a message text for a message number and assign the text to the message. Within the message, you can define fields as variables (for example, the identification of the object) and include the corresponding field values in your message text.

As is the case with substitutions, you can trigger the execution of validations either manually or automatically during the save process. To enable automatic validations of project definitions or WBS elements, you must enter the relevant validation in the project profile and set the indicator for automatic validation. For network headers and activities, you must store the validations in the network profile only.

Running validations

If both substitutions and validations are executed during a save process, then the substitution steps are carried out step-by-step first, followed by the validation steps.

1.8.6 Variant Configurations with Projects

We will now describe the use of variant configurations in project structures on the basis of the IDES example: the engineer-to-order production of elevators. Then we will discuss the necessary prerequisites that must be fulfilled.

Example of a variant configuration

The IDES company produces different elevator types in different sizes and variants. In the context of engineer-to-order production, each elevator variant requires different material components and activities. Standard structures are used as the template for the creation of the required project structures. Instead of defining a separate standard network—including the required material components and activities and a separate WBS as a template for each potential variant—the company only uses one standard network that can be configured in different ways.

Characteristic value assignment

The configurable standard network contains material components and activities for all possible variants of the different elevator types.

If the configurable standard network is used as a template for an operative network, then the respective elevator variant must first be specified via a *characteristic value assignment* (elevator type, size, variant, and so on; see Figure 1.45). Based on the characteristic value assignment and the *object dependencies* in the activities of the standard network and bill of material (BOM) items (that is, the material components), the system copies only those activities and components that are actually required for the variant. If, during the save process for the configured operative network, a WBS based on a template is created as well, then the system only copies those WBS elements that are assigned at least one operative activity, including their superordinate WBS elements. This way, the WBS is configured "indirectly," because WBS elements cannot contain any object dependencies.

Characteristics and classes

To use the variant configuration with project structures, you must first define *characteristics* in the central logistical functions. These characteristics may include the elevator type, the size of the elevator, and so on and can be defined using Transaction CT04. When doing so, you must specify, among other things, the input format, possible characteristic values, and, if necessary, a default value for each characteristic value. You can then summarize the characteristics into *classes* (Transaction CL02) so that you can define which of the characteristics should be displayed during the characteristic value assignment process. Note, the classes must belong to a class type that allows variant configuration (by default, this is class type 300).

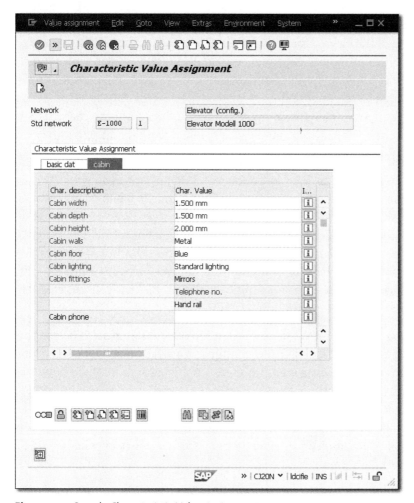

Figure 1.45 Sample Characteristic Value Assignment

You can define the necessary object dependencies either directly during the maintenance of standard network activities (*local object dependencies*) or centrally using Transaction CU01 (*global object dependencies*). Global object dependencies can be used multiple times in different standard networks or BOMs. Note, however, that you cannot modify them there.

Object dependencies

The object dependency type SELECTION CONDITION is used to determine whether an object should be copied. The dependency editor that uses a specific syntax (see SAP documentation) is available for the definition of conditions within such an object dependency (for example, "Should the sides of the elevator be made of glass?"). If the condition you define and assign as an object dependency to a BOM item or standard network activity is met in the characteristic value assignment, then the object will be copied. You can use the object dependency type PROCEDURE to derive field values of material components or activities from the characteristic value assignment (for example, the planned work for an activity).

Standard structures and configuration profile

Finally, you must define the standard structures you want to use as templates (see Section 1.2.3 and Section 1.3.3) and link them with the class of characteristics. The standard structures must contain activities, relationships, material components, and, if necessary, WBS elements for all possible variants. The necessary object dependencies must be assigned to the relevant standard network activities and BOM items. You can link the standard structures, or rather, the standard network, with the class of characteristics by using a *configuration profile* that you can create in Transaction CU41 in SAP Project System.

Change profile

If you want changes to the characteristic value assignment to be possible after you have released the configured operative network, then you must define a *change profile* in the Customizing section of the networks and assign this profile to the respective network type. Depending on the respective statuses, you can use the overall change profile—for example, to control whether the object changes that are necessary for the new variant should result in error messages or warnings or whether single changes are even permitted.

In addition, you can use standard workflows in variant configurations—for example, to inform the MRP controller of the network about retroactive changes and to enable the controller to decide whether those changes should be implemented.

If you use configurable subnetworks for structuring purposes, then the characteristic value assignment is passed on from the superordinate network, provided its templates have been assigned to the same class. Finally, you can also combine variant configurations with assembly processing. In this case, you can carry out the characteristic value assignment directly in the relevant sales document.

1.8.7 Assembly Processing

The concept of *assembly processing* describes a process in which the creation of a sales document item involves the simultaneous creation of an operative network and, if required, of an operative WBS. The process also involves the exchange of scheduling, quantity, and controlling data between the sales document item and the project.

Time scheduling for the network is directly carried out in the sales document on the basis of a customer's desired delivery date and the quantity that is transferred to the network as an execution factor. The system then proposes the calculated finish date of the network as the date for the complete delivery of the item in the sales document. At the same time, the system calculates the network and transfers the calculated costs to the sales document item, in which they can be used for pricing purposes in accordance with the pricing procedure used.

Data exchange

If the project contains milestones that are marked as relevant to sales documents, then the dates and billing data of those milestones can also be automatically included in the billing plan of the item.

If an operative WBS is generated when the sales document is saved, then the sales document item can be automatically assigned to a WBS element.

The link between the sales document item and the network allows you to use the schedule lines of the item to navigate directly to the network display or, conversely, to navigate directly to the sales document item display via the network header. Furthermore, you can transfer retroactive changes to the sales document directly to the project and vice versa.

If you use a sales document that contains multiple items, then you can also create a separate operative network for each item through assembly processing. If, in that case, the corresponding standard networks are already linked to each other via relationships, then those external relationships can also be automatically created for the operative networks. The time scheduling process for all networks of the sales document is carried out simultaneously using overall network scheduling (see Chapter 2, Section 2.1.2).

You can only create one WBS per sales document by using assembly processing. If you set the SD/PS ASSIGNMENT indicator in the project definition of the standard WBS, then the system will create a separate hierarchy within the project for each sales document item including a separate WBS element at level 1. Note that coding masks are required for using the SD/PS assignment. You must ensure that the ONLY ONE ROOT indicator is not set in the project profile.

The identification of a project that is created in the context of assembly processing is automatically derived from the sales document ID. If you have defined a coding mask for the identification of the standard WBS, then the ID of the operative project consists of the key of the mask and the sales document number, which is copied into the first section of the project ID. If the first section of the coding mask is shorter than the sales document ID, then the system will only copy the last digits of the ID. Therefore, you should ensure that the first section of the respective coding masks is long enough. In case of an SD/PS assignment, the item number is also copied to the second section of the WBS element ID. If you don't use any coding masks, then the project will have the same ID as the sales document.

Using assembly processing makes sense whenever you want to process customer projects that always contain identical structures and shouldn't be created until a requirement has been generated in sales and distribution (caused by a request, a quotation, or a sales order), when you want to automate the creation of the project structures and the exchange of data between SAP Project System and the sales and distribution department.

The following list contains the prerequisites that must be fulfilled if you want to use assembly processing:

▸ **Standard structures**
   You must create a standard network and—if a WBS is required as well—a standard WBS that can be used as templates for the operative project structures.

▶ **Material master record settings**

You need a material master record whose ITEM CATEGORY GROUP (sales view SALESORG 2) or STRATEGY GROUP (MRP VIEW 3) references a requirements class for assembly processing with networks.

▶ **Assignment between material and standard network**

Optionally, you can assign the material to a standard network. If you don't create this assignment now, then you can do so later when creating the sales document item.

▶ **Customizing settings**

In Customizing, you must enter the relevant settings that enable the system to determine an appropriate requirements class based on the sales document type and the material master record data.

The following sections describe the prerequisites in greater detail. When you create a sales document and enter a material number into an item, the system performs a *requirements type determination* in the background. The requirements type can be determined in two different ways.

Requirements type determination

On the one hand, the system can use the STRATEGY GROUP in the material master record to determine a primary strategy, which, in turn, is used to determine a requirements type. If the material master record does not contain a strategy group, then the system tries to determine a strategy group based on the MRP group of the material. If the material master record doesn't contain an MRP group either, then the system tries to derive the MRP group on the basis of the material type.

On the other hand, the system can use the ITEM CATEGORY GROUP of the material and the DOCUMENT TYPE of the sales document to determine, among other things, an item category that defines the basic properties of the sales document item and that also references a requirements type. Finally, the setting in Customizing activity CONTROL OF REQUIREMENTS TYPE DETERMINATION for the combination of the item category group and, if available, the MRP type of the material (MRP VIEW 1) determines which of the two requirements types should be used.

The requirements type, in turn, is uniquely assigned to a requirements class. The requirements class (Transaction OVZG) ultimately controls the

Requirements class for assembly processing

procurement of the material (see Figure 1.46). For assembly processing, the following fields are relevant in this context:

▶ ASSEMBLY TYPE and ORDER TYPE
  The ASSEMBLY TYPE allows you to define whether you want to carry out assembly processing using networks. The ORDER TYPE defines the network type of the automatically created operative network.

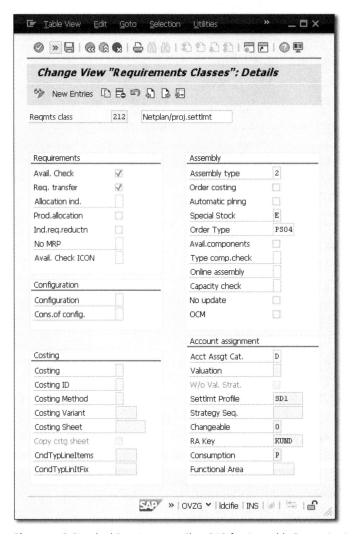

Figure 1.46 Standard Requirements Class 212 for Assembly Processing Using Networks

▶ REQUIREMENTS TRANSFER and AVAILABILITY

These indicators must be set if you want to exchange scheduling and quantity data between the sales document item and the network.

▶ ACCOUNT ASSIGNMENT CATEGORY

The ACCOUNT ASSIGNMENT CATEGORY in the requirement class refers to the CONSUMPTION POSTING and SPECIAL STOCK indicators to control the value flows in assembly processing and the inventory management of the finished material.

▶ NO MRP

Because the network is used for procuring the finished material in assembly processing, you can use the NO MRP indicator to define that no MRP should be carried out for this material.

You can find all of the necessary Customizing settings for account assignment categories, requirements classes, and especially for the requirements type determination in the material Customizing section of SAP Project System under CONTROL OF SALES-ORDER-RELATED PRODUCTION. By default, you can use Requirements Type KMPN and Requirements Class 212 for assembly processing.

Requirements Class 212 and MRP Relevance	**[+]**
Note that Requirements Class 212 does not prohibit any MRP process for the material. To avoid MRP, you must customize the requirements class, define a new requirements class, or deactivate MRP via the material master record of the respective material.	

If you use assembly processing without work breakdown structures, you can use the standard account assignment category E that provides for value and inventory management at the sales-document-item level. If, in assembly processing, a WBS is generated in addition to the network, then value management must occur at the project level. Depending on the stock you want to use for the finished material (see Chapter 2, Section 2.3.2), you can use the standard account assignment categories Q (project stock) or D (sales order stock).

Possible account assignment categories

To enable the system to automatically determine an appropriate template for the operative project structures during assembly processing, you must assign the material number to a standard network. The

Network parameters from sales order

assignment of the standard network to a standard WBS then also enables the system to automatically determine the template for the operative WBS.

In SAP Project System, you must use Transaction CN08 to assign a material number to a standard network (see Figure 1.47). If necessary, you can define this assignment on the basis of the network type. In addition, you can also specify during the assignment process whether you want external relationships to be created automatically, which MRP controller is responsible for the operative network, and to which WBS element you want to assign the sales document item.

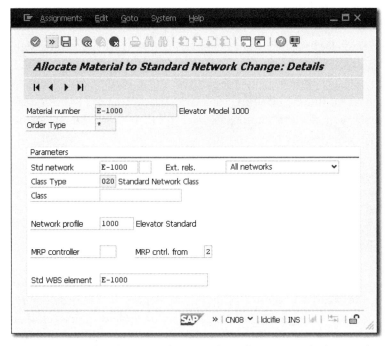

Figure 1.47 Sample Assignment of a Material Number to a Standard Network in Transaction CN08

Assembly processing without networks

As of EHP 5, for customer projects in the service sector, where the SAP professional service solutions are used, you can have the system generate projects when saving sales documents without having to use networks. You can make the necessary settings in Transaction CN08CI. Here, depending on the material number, sales document type, and sales organization, you define which standard WBS is supposed to be used as the template for a new customer project (see Figure 1.48).

A customer enhancement enables you to implement an alternative logic for the determination of the template. In addition, there are also customer enhancements to derive the ID and other master data of the new project from the sales document. You can use the user interface for customer projects (see Section 1.7.5) to modify the automatically generated project directly after the creation of a sales document without having to change the user interface.

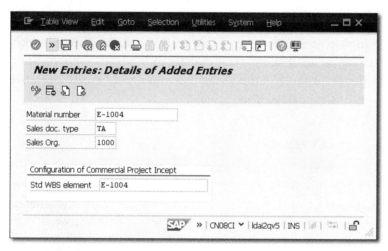

Figure 1.48 Sample Assignment of a Material Number to a Standard WBS in Transaction CN08CI

1.9   Versions

SAP Project System distinguishes three types of versions that can be used for different purposes:

Version types

▸ **CO versions**

You can use CO versions in the context of project planning to save several different cost and revenue plans for one object and to evaluate those plans separately or compare them with each other. You can use the values of CO versions for different evaluations in accounting. Moreover, CO versions can be used for specific purposes, such as progress analyses or for cost forecasts in SAP Project System (see Chapter 4, Section 4.7.2 and Chapter 5, Section 5.8). In addition to using the term *CO version*, you can also use *planning version* or just *version*.

▸ **Project versions**
Project versions are used to capture the state of a project at a specific point in time or for a certain system status to document the project flow. Project versions are a prerequisite for a milestone trend analysis (see Chapter 4, Section 4.7.1).

▸ **Simulation versions**
You can use simulation versions to test different project structures, planning activities, changes to the structure, or plans of projects without having to implement actual changes in the operative structures. After that, you can use the simulation versions to create operative projects or to update existing projects.

1.9.1 Project Versions

Project versions are "snapshots" of project data. You can create project versions at specific moments and therefore document the progress of your projects over time. Furthermore, you can automatically generate different versions of objects when specific status changes occur.

Version key | When creating project versions, you must always specify a *version key*. This means that the objects contained in project versions can be identified based on the combination of the operative ID and the version key. *Version groups* allow you to summarize versions that contain objects of the same type.

[!]
> **Project Versions and Milestone Trend Analysis**
>
> Only if you mark a project version as being relevant to milestone trend analysis will you be able to use its data for this purpose.

Time-dependent project versions | You can carry out a time-dependent creation of project versions either by using the structure information system (Transaction CN41) or directly via Transaction CN72. To do so, you must use the relevant selection screen and database profile to define which objects and which data of those objects should be copied to the project version. Transaction CN72 also allows you to schedule a background job to automatically create new project versions at regular intervals.

Alternatively, you can create time-dependent project versions for individual work breakdown structures or networks by using the special maintenance Transactions CJ02 or CN22, respectively. In this context, the *version profile* (see Figure 1.49) defines which data of the objects should be copied to the project version.

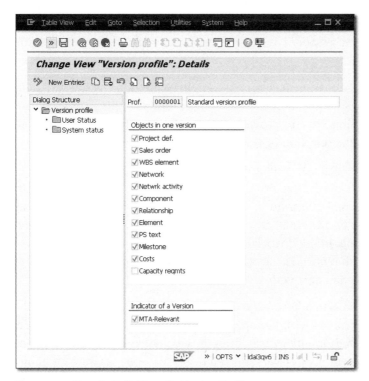

Figure 1.49 Sample Definition of a Version Profile

To enable the automatic creation of project versions based on the status of the objects, you must first create a version profile in the Customizing section of SAP Project System (Transaction OPTS) and assign this version profile to the project profile or network profile in question. The version profile defines whether the object is relevant to the milestone trend analysis and which data should be copied to the project version.

Status-dependent project versions

In addition, the version profile determines for which status changes a project version should be created and the corresponding version key and description to be used. The status change can refer to both the system status and the user status.

For example, if you define that the project version with version description RELEASED must be used when an object is released, then the system will write a copy of an object to the project version every time an object is released. If you release parts of projects at different times, then the project version will be complemented step by step with the newly released objects. What this means is that status-dependent project versions don't necessarily have to reflect the state of a project at a specific point in time.

Evaluating project versions

You can evaluate project versions in the structure information system of SAP Project System and by using hierarchy reports of the financials project information system, provided the database profile or report definition allows the selection of version data (see Chapter 6, Section 6.1).

For example, you can compare individual lines of data of multiple project versions or operative projects with each other in the structure information system. Furthermore, you can use version-dependent exceptions to highlight (in different colors) differences between version data and operative data. In the financials project information system, you can use the standard report PROJECT VERSION COMPARISON: ACTUAL/PLAN to compare version data with actual data.

Deleting project versions

Project versions that have been created automatically on the basis of the status are archived with the operative project structures and can therefore be deleted simultaneously from the database (see Section 1.10). For time-dependent project versions, you can carry out separate archiving and deletion sessions. However, you can also delete project versions manually at any time using the structure overview (Transaction CN41).

1.9.2 Simulation Versions

Simulation versions enable you to carry out what-if analyses for project structures. You can create simulation versions without an existing operative project (for example, during the quotation phase), and you can generate simulation versions by *transferring* operative projects or other simulation versions.

A simulation version can be identified by a combination of the project ID and a version key. Thus, if required, you can simultaneously create, edit, and compare multiple simulation versions for one project identification, versions which are independent of each other. You can use *input templates* in the Customizing section of SAP Project System to define which version keys can be assigned to simulation versions (Transaction OPUS).

To manually create and edit simulation versions, you can either use the Project Builder (provided that simulation versions are marked as changeable objects in their options) or Transaction CJV2, which has the editing options that are also provided in the Project Planning Board.

Editing options

If you want to plan the costs of simulation versions, then you can do that in the context of Easy Cost Planning (see Chapter 2, Section 2.4.4) and network costing (see Section 2.4.6). You can only perform revenue planning for simulation versions by using billing plans (see Section 2.5.3).

To create simulation versions via transferring operative projects or other simulation versions and retransferring them into operative projects, you must use Transaction CJV4. This transaction also allows you to test the transfers. A transfer involves all master data and planned data of work breakdown structures and networks, and the milestones and material components assigned to them. In addition, actual data of operative structures is also transferred to the simulation versions for informational purposes; however, this data is not retransferred into the operative project.

Transferring simulation versions

You can define a *simulation profile* in the Customizing section of SAP Project System and then store it in the project profile or project definition. A simulation profile enables you to define whether you want to include long texts, PS texts, or the assignment to documents in the document-management system in the transfer as well. Transaction CJV5 allows you to delete simulation versions at any time.

Every time you create a simulation version, the system generates administration data for the respective version. You can analyze this data using

Administration data

Transaction CJV6 (see Figure 1.50). In addition to this data having creation and modification information, it also contains the INACTIVE and COPIED indicators.

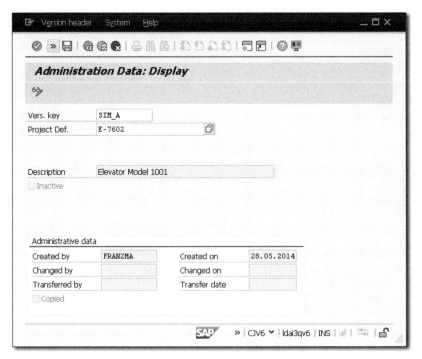

Figure 1.50 Sample Administration Data of a Simulation Version

Inactive indicator   If a simulation version is active, that is, if the INACTIVE indicator is not set, then the system issues a warning message whenever you try to modify the structure of the operative project or its planned data or master data, because those changes may impede a retransfer of the simulation version.

If you retransfer a simulation version back into the operative project, then the system automatically sets the INACTIVE indicator for all simulation versions that belong to this project. You should note that this means you can no longer edit those simulation versions. However, you can deactivate (uncheck) the INACTIVE indicator manually, although we recommend that you transfer the operative project into a new simulation version.

In addition, the simulation version that has been retransferred is automatically marked as copied so that you can use the administration data to determine which version was used for the update process. Simulation versions can be evaluated in the same way as project versions. In particular, you can use the *version comparison* function in the structure project information system—for example, to highlight deviations between the simulation version and the operative project in color.

In addition, you can also use a specific capacity report for simulation versions. This report reads the work centers of the activities of the simulation version and determines all capacity requirements of those work centers, but instead of the requirements of the operative project the report uses the requirements of the simulation version. This way, simulation versions enable you to analyze to what extent possible date and structure changes would affect the capacity utilization of the work centers in your company.

Capacity report for simulation versions

In addition to the limited cost and revenue planning options, simulation versions are subject to other restrictions. Simulation versions don't support integration with other components of the SAP system. Objects with a reference to operative objects cannot be deleted here; however, you can set the DELETION FLAG status (see Section 1.6). Apart from that, no other status changes, such as system or user status changes, are possible for simulation versions. Furthermore, you cannot archive simulation versions.

Restrictions for simulation versions

As of EHP 4, you can also use drafts for certain what-if scenarios (see Section 1.7.4). Unlike simulations, drafts can be restricted to specific data sets so that other data is not changed during the transfer. However, drafts have less function than simulations. In particular, simulated cost planning and what-if analyses of cost changes are possible only with simulation versions, not with drafts.

1.10 Archiving Project Structures

You can delete operative work breakdown structures and activities in every editing transaction. A prerequisite for this is that the status of the work breakdown structures and activities is either CREATED or RELEASED and that no documents have been assigned to them yet. However, once a document has been assigned to a WBS or network you must first archive the project structure before you can delete the data from the database.

You can delete standard structures, project versions, and simulation versions at any time without having to meet any specific requirements. If you want to archive project data without deleting the data from the database, then you can also do this without meeting any additional requirements. However, if you want to archive operative projects that have already been assigned documents and delete those projects afterward, then you must carry out specific steps, each of which must meet certain requirements:

1. When deleting operative project structures, the first step you must carry out is setting the DELETION FLAG status. A prerequisite for setting this status is that assigned orders have also been flagged for deletion. Another requirement is that no open purchase requisitions or purchase orders can exist for the project. In addition, the project balance must be zero; otherwise, the project might not be subject to settlement (see Chapter 5, Section 5.9).

   When a project is flagged for deletion, almost all business processes are forbidden; however, you should note that you can deactivate the DELETION FLAG status if required.

2. The second step involves setting a *deletion indicator* for the project structures via archiving transactions. A prerequisite for setting this indicator is that the deletion indicator is already active in assigned orders. To avoid premature deletions of networks, a certain number of months have to pass between the first two steps. This period is referred to as RESIDENCE TIME 1, and you can define it in the Customizing section of the network type.

   You can still display and evaluate projects carrying the deletion indicator in all editing and reporting transactions, but you can no longer execute any business processes for those projects.

3. The final step consists of archiving the project structures and deleting the project data from the SAP database. This is only possible for projects carrying the deletion indicator. For networks, RESIDENCE TIME 2

must have passed between the setting of the deletion indicator and the deletion process itself. This residence time must have been stored in terms of months in the network type.

You Cannot Undo Deletion Indicators	**[!]**
Note that you cannot undo the setting of the deletion indicator.	

You can carry out all of the necessary steps for archiving projects using the general archiving Transaction SARA with a reference to archiving object PS_PROJECT. Alternatively, you can use Transaction CN80 in SAP Project System, which is specifically provided for this archiving object. The archiving object PS_PROJECT enables you to archive the master data, planned data, and actual data of operative work breakdown structures and networks and of project versions. The information and programs required for writing and evaluating the archive files are linked to this archiving object.

Archiving object

Transaction CN80 enables you to carry out the different steps for archiving and deleting project structures continuously. This way, you can use selection variants to select multiple projects at the same time and, if required, to schedule the execution of the individual steps in the background. In addition, you can store a descriptive text for the archiving session in the selection variant for archiving structures.

The job monitor allows you to analyze which of the jobs for setting deletion flags or deletion indicators and for archiving or deleting projects has been carried out successfully, which of them are still active, and which have been terminated due to errors. Logs for the individual jobs provide you with additional details. The log that is created when archive files are written contains, among other things, the technical names of the archive files, their size, and the relevant database tables.

Job monitor

The administration data of Transaction CN80 allows you to analyze which archiving sessions have been completed. Traffic lights indicate which sessions have been completed successfully and which caused problems. You can view the details of an archiving session by double-clicking on it. Moreover, you can call all relevant Customizing activities related to the archiving of projects from the overview.

Administration data

Retrieval The RETRIEVAL function in Transaction CN80 enables you to evaluate the archived data at any time. Note that this is also possible if you use the reports provided by the structure and financials project information systems, given that the database profile allows the selection of archive files. As of EHP 3, you can also display archived projects in the Project Builder. SAP Project System does not allow you to copy archived project data as operative data or to use archived project structures as templates for new projects.

SAP Project System contains the additional archiving objects PS_PLAN for standard networks and CM_QMEL for claims. There are also various other archiving objects in other applications for documents and objects, which can be linked to projects. Within the scope of archiving, a customer enhancement allows you, for example, to explicitly select purchasing documents or maintenance orders via your project reference or to explicitly exclude them from selection. This way, project-related objects are immediately archived with projects or excluded from archiving as long as the projects are still used. The system does not allow you to archive simulation versions, drafts, or standard work breakdown structures.

Additional archiving functions For selected projects, the PSARCHPRECHECK program enables you to have the system display a list of objects that avoid the setting of deletion indicators or deletion flags, including message details (see Figure 1.51). If required, you can also use the list to directly navigate to the respective objects—for example, to analyze further details. This allows you to identify possible project-archiving problems at an early stage and eliminate their causes. SAP Note 1631113 provides further information on how to activate this program.

Advantages of data archiving The archiving of projects and the subsequent deletion of the project data from the SAP database have several advantages: Because you can store archive files in compressed form and on separate servers, you can significantly reduce the database load by deleting the operative data. This, in turn, increases performance and simplifies the administration of the system. Moreover, the IDs of deleted project structures are no longer included in the search helps, so you can assign them to new projects if you want to do so.

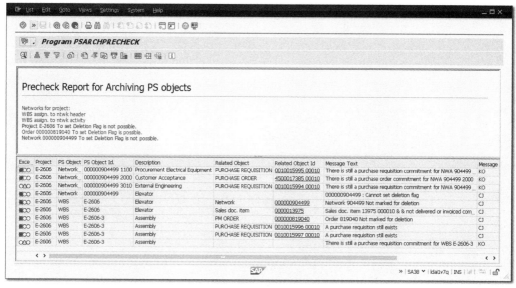

Figure 1.51 Sample Message Details in the PSARCHPRECHECK Program

It is also useful to consider archiving aspects before a project starts, especially if you use many projects or large project structures that entail a substantial growth of the data volume over time. Due to the different requirements that must be met to archive or delete projects, you should collaborate with other departments that may be involved.

1.11 Summary

In this chapter, we described the two structures, WBS and network, that can be used to map projects in the SAP system. In addition to the master data of those structures and different detailing options (for example, using milestones or documents), we discussed the Customizing activities that are necessary for creating the structures, and we introduced transactions and tools that enable you to create, edit, archive, and delete the structures. The next chapter will explain how you can plan your projects on the basis of those structures.

Using project planning, you can preview the time flow, the required resources and materials, and the expected cost and revenues for the individual project parts. It is thus an essential part of project management.

2   Planning Functions

Once you have properly mapped a project using the *work breakdown structure (WBS)* and the *network structure*, you can use various SAP Project System functions to plan the dates of the individual work packages, estimate the expected costs and revenues, and provide internal and external resources and materials on schedule before the project starts.

Depending on your requirements, there are planning functions with different levels of detail. For example, within a quotation phase or approval phase, you can create a preliminary plan of dates and costs with very little effort and add specifications later, if necessary, using other planning functions or additional structures.

Preliminary and detailed planning

In the implementation phase, the planned data is compared with actual data that is posted to the project structures by different business transactions (see Chapter 4). In the processing transactions, particularly in the reporting of SAP Project System, you can therefore make a plan/actual comparison later and then monitor the project earned value.

In this chapter, we'll first discuss the various possibilities of time scheduling in SAP Project System, which are the basis of several other planning activities. Then, we'll explain how to use networks to plan internal and external resources, and material for projects. Lastly, we'll explore the possibilities for planning costs and revenues for your projects in SAP Project System.

2.1   Date Planning

The planning of the dates of a project or parts of a project is integral to your project planning. The planning of capacity requirements (see Section 2.2.1), for example, requires prior scheduling. The cost planning via Easy Cost Planning (see Section 2.4.4) or network costing (see Section 2.4.6) is automatically aligned with the planned project dates as well.

Depending on whether you use work breakdown structures or networks for structuring your projects, different functions are available for planning dates. These are discussed separately in Section 2.1.1 and Section 2.1.2. If you use both a work breakdown structure and networks, scheduling data can be exchanged between the WBS elements and the activities, which is discussed in Section 2.1.2 as well. Section 2.1.3 then introduces the Project Editor as a sample scheduling tool.

Sets of dates   Regardless of the structures you use for mapping your projects (WBS or network), there are two separate sets of dates available for time scheduling in SAP Project System: *basic dates* and *forecast dates*. You can schedule dates in both sets of dates separately; however, you can also copy dates from one set of dates to the other as often as you like. A third set of dates is available for entering actual dates. Figure 2.1 shows the various sets of dates in the DATES detail screen of a WBS element.

Figure 2.1 Dates Detail Screen of a WBS Element

[+]   **Exclusive Functions of Basic Dates**

The calculation of capacity requirements, the requirement date of material components, or, for example, the Easy Cost Planning and the planned costs calculation using network costing are exclusively based on the basic set of dates.

Typically, the forecast set of dates is used for *baselining*; that is, fixing planned dates at a specific planning stage. To do this, you copy the basic set of dates into the forecast set of dates. Changes to dates at a later stage are made to the basic set of dates, while the dates in the forecast set of dates remain unchanged. Therefore, you can always read the current status of time scheduling in the basic set of dates while the forecast set of dates reflects your original time schedule. If you want to maintain several stages of time scheduling, you can use project versions (see Chapter 1, Section 1.9.1).

Using the forecast set of dates

The presentation of forecast dates depends on the respective transaction. The tabular presentation of structure planning contains, for example, separate tabs for the respective sets of dates (see Chapter 1, Section 1.7.3). In Project Builder, the WBS elements detail screen shows all sets of dates, while either the basic set of dates or the forecast set of dates is displayed for networks, depending on the settings. In the Project Planning Board, you determine the field selection and the options for which dates are to be listed or graphically displayed. Figure 2.2 shows the simultaneous presentation of basic and forecast dates in the Project Planning Board.

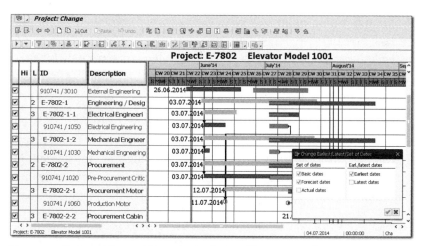

Figure 2.2 Basic and Forecast Dates in the Project Planning Board

2.1.1 Scheduling with WBS Elements

When creating a project, you can enter a planned start and end date for the project in the project definition. When you later schedule dates on the WBS elements level, the system notifies you if the WBS element dates are outside of the date range specified in the project definition. If you want, however, start and end dates of the project definition can be adapted to the dates of the WBS elements.

Dates for WBS elements can be scheduled in Project Builder in the WBS elements detail screen, in the Project Planning Board, or via the special maintenance functions, either in a tabular format or, in the Project Planning Board, in a graphical format. Optionally, you can specify both planned start and end dates, or one of the two along with a planned duration for the WBS element. The system then calculates the other date automatically.

Factory calendar   In this time scheduling, the system considers the factory calendar of the WBS element, which distinguishes workdays and non-workdays (holidays, weekends, company holidays, etc.). The entered duration in days, for example, is interpreted as the number of workdays; start or end dates on non-workdays cause system warnings. In the Project Planning Board, the maintenance and presentation of nonworking times are controlled by the NONWORKING TIME tag in the options or the planning board profile, respectively.

The standard version already contains numerous predefined factory calendars. You can also define your own factory calendars in Customizing using Transaction SCAL. Select the factory calendars separately for every WBS element, or enter them as default values in the project definition or in the project profile.

In addition to the manual maintenance of planned dates for WBS elements, there are various functions that—depending on the transaction—support you in your time scheduling tasks. Using the Project Planning Board as an example, we will explain in detail various time scheduling functions for WBS elements without assigned activities.

Shifting dates   Using the SHIFT DATES function, you can shift the planned dates of individual WBS elements, or of entire subtrees, or of your entire project. For example, if you select a WBS element and choose the SHIFT SUBTREE function, a dialog box opens in which you can either enter a new start or a new end date, depending on the WBS scheduling parameters (see Section 2.1.2). The system then shifts both the WBS element and all subordinate WBS elements accordingly.

Chronological Shifting of WBS Elements of the Same Level	[+]
Because WBS elements do *not* have relationships, the shifting of WBS elements does *not* automatically cause the planned dates of WBS elements on the same level to be shifted.	

Using the COPY TOP-DOWN function, you can copy the start and end dates of a WBS element to all hierarchically subordinate WBS elements and, if required, to the assigned activities. Existing planned dates are thereby overwritten.

Inheriting dates

Instead of inheriting dates in a top-down fashion, you can, in turn, aggregate dates within the work breakdown structure hierarchy using the EXTRAPOLATE DATES function. Using this function you have to distinguish between *bottom-up* and *strict bottom-up extrapolation*.

Projecting dates

If you run the EXTRAPOLATE DATES function for your project and the OPEN PLANNING or BOTTOM-UP planning method has been set, the date ranges of the project definition and of all WBS elements are adapted so that they span the dates of the respective subordinate WBS elements. The date ranges of higher-level objects are therefore extended, if necessary, but not reduced. This means the date range of a higher-level object can therefore be larger than that of the subordinate objects.

Bottom-up extrapolation

Figure 2.3 shows an example of the bottom-up projecting of WBS element dates. The dates of the WBS elements ELECTRICAL ENGINEERING and MECHANICAL ENGINEERING have been time-shifted and the dates have been projected to the higher-level ENGINEERING/DESIGN WBS element. The upper time bars (forecast dates) correspond to the dates before and the lower time bars (basic dates) correspond to the dates after the shifting and projecting process.

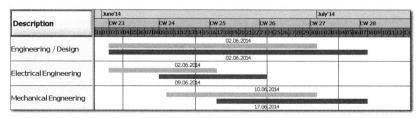

Figure 2.3 Bottom-up Extrapolation

Strict bottom-up extrapolation If you execute the EXTRAPOLATES DATES function for a project for which the STRICT BOTTOM-UP planning method has been set, the date ranges of the project definition and of all WBS elements are accurately adapted to the scheduling frameworks of the subordinate WBS elements (see Figure 2.4). The date ranges of higher-level objects are thus both extended and reduced, if necessary.

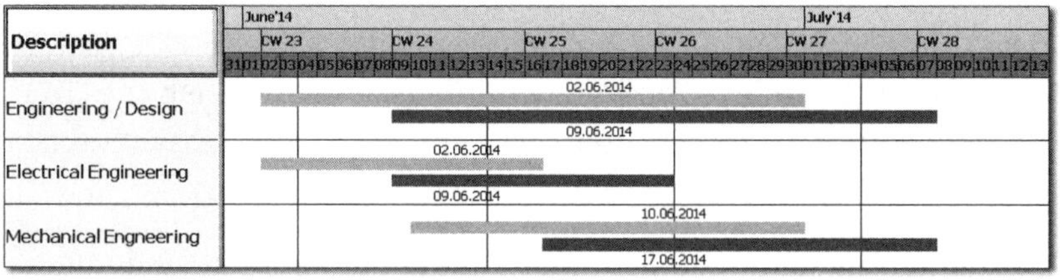

Figure 2.4 Strict Bottom-up Extrapolation

Checking dates Another function you can implement when time scheduling with WBS elements is the CHECK DATES WITHIN PROJECT STRUCTURE function. The system then highlights WBS elements in color where planned dates of the subordinate WBS elements are outside of the scheduling framework of the WBS element itself. You can therefore avoid hierarchically inconsistent time scheduling for projects.

Planning methods Using planning methods, several of the functions just mentioned can be automatically executed during the saving process, regardless of the processing transaction. The following planning methods are available:

▶ **Top-down**
When saving, the system automatically checks the dates within the project structure. If the time scheduling is not consistent, the project cannot be saved. However, no dates are automatically changed.

▶ **Bottom-up**
When saving, the system automatically changes the dates of WBS elements and project definition via bottom-up extrapolation.

▶ **Strict bottom-up**
When saving, the system automatically changes the dates of WBS elements and project definition using a strict bottom-up extrapolation.

▶ **Open planning**
The system does not automatically check or change the dates. However, you can manually trigger the CHECK DATES WITHIN PROJECT STRUCTURE or EXTRAPOLATE DATES functions.

You specify the planning method to be used separately for the basic and the forecast set of dates in the project definition. In the project profile, you can store default values for the planning methods of both sets of dates.

If you work with WBS without assigned networks, the *scheduled dates* of WBS elements, that is, their earliest and latest start and end dates (refer back to Figure 2.1), are only relevant if you use milestones, the dates of which are derived from the WBS element dates. Because the dates of milestones are exclusively derived from the scheduled dates, you must run the WBS SCHEDULING function at least once in this case. For WBS without assigned networks, the WBS scheduling only causes the planned dates to be accepted as scheduled dates.

2.1.2 Scheduling Using Networks

While you enter the planned dates of WBS elements manually or via projecting or inheritance, the planned dates of activities are automatically calculated by the system. This determination of the planned dates of networks is called *scheduling*. Depending on the transaction you used to trigger the scheduling, you use *network scheduling*, *overall network scheduling*, or *WBS scheduling*.

Planned dates

In network scheduling, only one network is scheduled. All activities of the network are selected and their dates are calculated. If you use overall network scheduling, several networks are scheduled at the same time, provided they are linked via relationships or subnetworks. All activities of these networks are then scheduled. In WBS scheduling, you select one or more WBS elements, or the entire project, and trigger the scheduling process. The system then selects only those activities for scheduling that are assigned to the selected WBS elements and calculates their dates. Before we elaborate on more differences between the various scheduling methods, we will first describe the scheduling concept, which is the same for all three methods.

[+]

Forward and Backward Scheduling

In SAP Project System, the scheduling always takes place both in a forward and backward direction.

Forward
scheduling

In *forward scheduling*, the system first determines the activities that—due to their relationships—don't have any predecessors among the selected activities. Beginning with a start date, the system calculates the earliest possible start date for these activities. Depending on the scheduling settings, the start date of forward scheduling can originate from the header of the network or from the assigned WBS elements (WBS determines the dates), or be the current date.

After the earliest start date of these activities has been determined, the system calculates the earliest possible end date of these activities using the scheduling-relevant duration. Then, the system selects the direct successors of these activities and calculates their earliest start and end dates. Each type of relationship (see Chapter 1, Section 1.3.1) determines whether the earliest start date must be after the end date of its predecessors (finish-start) or after their start date (start-start), etc.

Earliest dates

The scheduling now goes through all selected activities in a forward direction and calculates their earliest possible start and end dates. Forward scheduling results in the *earliest dates* of activities.

Backward
scheduling

In *backward scheduling*, the system first determines the activities that—due to their relationships—don't have any more successors among the selected activities. Starting from an end date—depending on the settings of the network header or the assigned WBS elements—the system now calculates the latest possible end date of these activities. Based on the scheduling-relevant duration of the activities, the latest start dates of these activities are then calculated.

The system then goes through the network in a backward direction, following the relationships, and thus successively calculates the latest possible start and end dates for all selected activities, considering their types of relationship and their durations. Backward scheduling determines the *latest dates* of activities.

Latest dates

The earliest start date and the latest end date of the network activities are forwarded to the network header as the scheduled dates. In WBS scheduling, the activity dates are also indicated in an aggregated fashion as scheduled dates at the level of the assigned WBS elements.

This logic of forward and backward scheduling requires a number of additional notes regarding the various influencing factors that are relevant to scheduling.

Without relationships, the result of scheduling in SAP Project System would not be a chronological sequence of the activities. The type of relationship determines how two activities will interact chronologically. If you specified a time interval for a relationship, this will be taken into account during scheduling. This time interval, however, is only interpreted as a minimum time interval, that is, the scheduled time interval between predecessor and successor can be longer than the time interval defined in the relationship.

Relationships in scheduling

If the activities selected for scheduling have relationships to activities that are not scheduled at the same time, these relationships are still taken into account. If relationships cannot be met, the system issues warnings that you can analyze in a scheduling log.

The calculation of the scheduling-relevant duration and the consideration of nonworking times depend on the respective activity type; however, for all activity types, the control key of the activities must permit scheduling so that a duration unequal to zero is used during the date calculation.

Scheduling-relevant duration

For internally processed activities, the scheduling-relevant duration—as long as no actual dates have been entered (see Chapter 4, Section 4.1.2)—is derived from the value of the NORMAL DURATION field or, if a work center has been stored in the activity, from an appropriate *formula* in the scheduling details of the work center. Typically, however, you will store the standard formula SAP004 in the work center, which references the value of the NORMAL DURATION field in the activity.

The Unit of the NORMAL DURATION field is relevant as well. For example, if you enter a duration of 24 hours, these hours are interpreted as working hours. If the scheduling-relevant capacity of the work center uses an operating time of eight hours per day, this results in a scheduling-relevant duration of three (working) days. If you entered a duration of one day, the system would only use one (working) day as the scheduling-relevant duration.

Nonworking times | The scheduling of internally processed activities also considers nonworking times. If you maintained a work center in the activity, the system only uses the working times of the scheduling-relevant capacity of the work center for scheduling. Start and end dates are only scheduled for working days. The differentiation between working and nonworking days originates from a factory calendar that is determined according to the following priority:

1. Factory calendar in the activity

2. Factory calendar in the work center

3. Factory calendar of the plant in the activity

For externally processed activities and service activities, the system, by default, uses the PLANNED DELIVERY TIME as the scheduling-relevant duration without differentiating between working and nonworking days. But, if you want to use a deviating duration for scheduling, you can define a control key with the SCHEDULING EXTERNAL OPERATION indicator and manually enter the scheduling-relevant duration in the NORMAL DURATION field of the INTERNAL tab.

For general costs activities, you can manually specify the scheduling-relevant duration via the NORMAL DURATION field. Using factory calendars in the costs activities, you can restrict scheduling to working days.

Reduction | If necessary, the system can automatically reduce the duration of activities if the scheduled dates are outside of the basic or forecast dates of the network header. The system can therefore automatically adapt the duration of activities to enable the network to be carried out in a given timeframe. This automatic adaptation of activity durations is called *reduction*. By specifying a minimum duration in an activity, you can ensure that a time interval that is required for processing an activity is not further reduced.

The reduction of the activity durations is performed in several successive stages. In the first stage, for example, the durations could be reduced by 10%. If this reduction is not sufficient, the originally planned durations could be reduced by 15% in a second stage, and so forth. A maximum of six stages could be implemented. After scheduling, you will find the actual number of required reduction levels in the network header.

Reduction levels

For a system to automatically reduce the duration of an activity, you must store a *reduction strategy* in the relevant activity. In the definition of a reduction strategy, for each reduction level, you specify the percentage by which the planned duration of an activity is to be reduced. Figure 2.5 shows an example of the definition of a reduction strategy in the Customizing of SAP Project System.

Reduction strategy

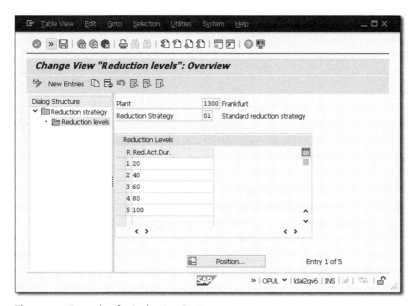

Figure 2.5 Example of a Reduction Strategy

Finally, you need to specify in the *scheduling parameters* that a reduction is to be carried out. To do this, you specify the maximum number of levels to run through. In addition, you can specify in the scheduling parameters whether all activities that have a reduction strategy are to be reduced or only those that are *time-critical*.

Copying replenishment lead times
: You can adapt the duration of an activity to the replenishment lead times of the assigned material components. Call the function TRANSFER DELIVERY TIME TO DURATION for an activity. The system then determines the longest replenishment lead time of the assigned components and uses them as the activity duration.

Scheduling constraints
: Scheduling calculates the planned earliest and latest dates of activities, and the scheduled dates of network headers and WBS elements. The corresponding fields cannot be changed manually.

Manual constraints
: However, you may want to assist in scheduling activities to, for example, define fixed dates or to consider constraints that cause activities to be feasible only within specific periods. To do this, you can specify *scheduling constraints* for activities (see Figure 2.6).

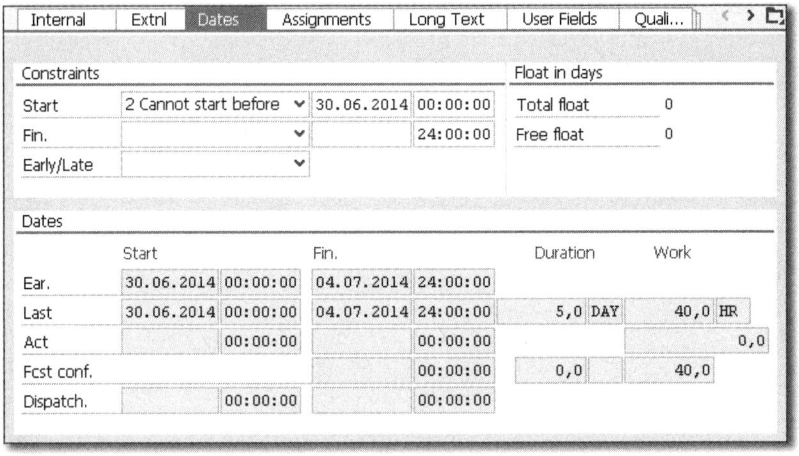

Internal	Extnl	Dates	Assignments	Long Text	User Fields	Quali...	< >

Constraints

			Float in days	
Start	2 Cannot start before ⌄	30.06.2014	00:00:00	Total float	0
Fin.	⌄		24:00:00	Free float	0
Early/Late	⌄				

Dates

	Start		Fin.		Duration	Work
Ear.	30.06.2014	00:00:00	04.07.2014	24:00:00		
Last	30.06.2014	00:00:00	04.07.2014	24:00:00	5,0 DAY	40,0 HR
Act		00:00:00		00:00:00		0,0
Fcst conf.				00:00:00	0,0	40,0
Dispatch.		00:00:00		00:00:00		

Figure 2.6 Example of a Scheduling Constraint for an Activity

Using scheduling constraints, you can either fix the earliest or latest start or end dates of activities (MUST START/FINISH ON) or restrict them via threshold values (CANNOT START/FINISH BEFORE/NO LATER). You can manually enter scheduling constraints or graphically determine them in the Project Planning Board, depending on the options or the planning board profile (see Chapter 1, Section 1.7.2). In scheduling, the various influencing factors are considered according to the following prioritization:

1. Actual dates (see Chapter 4, Section 4.1.2)

2. Scheduling constraints

3. Relationships

4. Start and end dates of the network header or the assigned WBS elements if the work breakdown structure determines dates

From the scheduled dates of the activities, the system also determines *floats* for each activity, which can be displayed in the detail screen of the activities and the network graphic, or graphically illustrated in the Project Planning Board, respectively. Regarding floats, there is a distinction between a *total float* and a *free float*.   **Floats**

The total float of an activity results from the difference between its latest and earliest dates, and therefore specifies the time interval by which you can shift an activity from its earliest date without exceeding the end date defined in the network header or—if it determines dates—of the assigned WBS element. Activities with a total float smaller than or equal to zero are regarded as *time-critical* and are highlighted in color in the network graphic and the diagram section of the Project Planning Board. In the Project Planning Board, you can use the options or even the planning board profile to control the total float starting from which activities are to be highlighted in color.   **Total float**

The free float of an activity is the interval by which you can shift the activity from its earliest date without affecting the earliest date of the succeeding activities. For two activities that are linked to each other by a finish-start relationship (without a time interval), the free float of the   **Free float** predecessor results, for example, from the difference between the earliest start date of the successor and the earliest end date of the activity itself.

"Flexible" indicator

Free floats typically result from scheduling constraints of succeeding activities, or they occur when there are parallel paths within the network where one path consumes more time than the other (see Figure 2.7). Because you can use the free float to perform activities without affecting subsequent activities with regard to scheduling, you can set the FLEXIBLE indicator for an activity to cause the earliest dates of this activity to be calculated based on the normal duration plus the free float. Consequently, the capacities have more time for performing the activity.

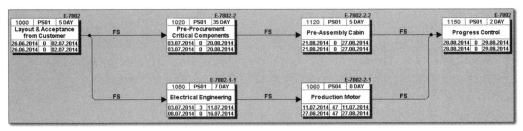

Figure 2.7 Time-Critical Activities and Floats in the Network Graphic

Dates of activity elements

You can supplement activities or add more details (see Chapter 1, Section 1.3.1) via activity elements. Because activity elements don't have a duration or relationships, they don't affect the scheduling result. Just like activities, however, activity elements have earliest and latest start and end dates. These dates are derived from the scheduled dates of the activity to which the activity elements are assigned and from the time intervals you may have entered in the activity elements.

[+] **Date Reference of Activity Elements**

The planned dates of the activity elements always fall within the activity dates. Scheduling constraints can be defined at an activity level, but not for activity elements.

For milestones you have assigned to activities, you can either manually enter *fixed dates* or establish a *time reference to the activity*. If you use a time reference, you can use appropriate indicators to specify whether the milestone date is to be taken from the earliest or latest date, and the start or the end date of the activity. Furthermore, you can specify a time interval either in absolute terms (for example, in a number of days), or in terms of percentage based on the duration of the activity. When using a time reference, every date shift of the activity directly affects the milestone date.

Dates of activity milestones

Even if you assign material components to an activity (see Section 2.3.1), you can select between a fixed requirement date for the material and a requirement date that is derived from the start or the end of the activity. The scheduling parameters control whether the date reference should refer to the earliest or the latest date of the activity. If necessary, you can also specify an absolute time interval that is considered when deriving the requirement date from the activity date.

Requirement date of material components

Network scheduling

In network scheduling, all activities of an individual network are scheduled. Whenever you call the scheduling from the specific maintenance function CN22 or from the Project Builder and Project Editor, provided you have selected a network header or a network activity in the structure tree, you trigger a network scheduling.

In network scheduling, the scheduling settings are determined from the network scheduling parameters, but can also be temporarily modified. Before you can create a network, you must have defined network scheduling parameters for the combination of the plant and the network type of the network header in the Customizing of SAP Project System (Transaction OPU6). Figure 2.8 shows an example of defining network scheduling parameters.

Network scheduling parameters

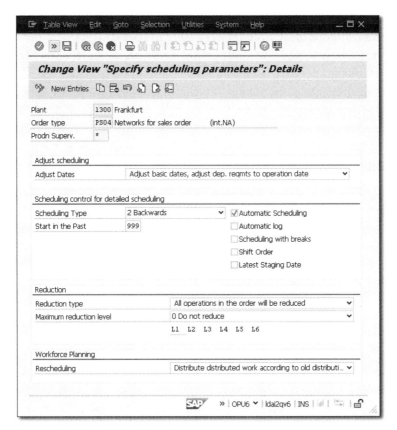

Figure 2.8 Network Scheduling Parameters

Scheduling types

In the scheduling parameters, you first store the SCHEDULING TYPE. This value is displayed at the network header level and can be changed there, if necessary. The following scheduling types are available in SAP Project System:

▶ **Forward**
The system first performs a forward and then a backward scheduling. You use forward scheduling if you know the start of the execution, but not its end date.

▶ **Backward**
The system first performs a backward and then a forward scheduling. You use backward scheduling if you know the end of the execution (for example, an agreed delivery date), but not its start date.

▸ **Current date**

Instead of start dates that lie in the past, the system uses the current date for forward scheduling. You can therefore see if the planned period for the execution is still sufficient and which floats may still be available. This also includes both forward and backward scheduling.

▸ **Only capacity requirements**

The activities use the start and end dates from the network header (or the assigned WBS elements, if they determine dates) as the earliest and latest start and end dates. Relationships or the duration of individual activities are not taken into account in this scheduling type. You can implement this scheduling type if you don't want to specify any details (yet) about the process and duration of individual activities, but want to calculate the capacity requirements for the total runtime (see Section 2.2.1).

Scheduling Type Restrictions   **[+]**

In SAP Project System, start and end dates for scheduling can be specified in the network header or the WBS elements to the day only. Scheduling types with a reference to the time of the day cannot be implemented in SAP Project System.

Using the ADJUST BASIC DATES indicator in the scheduling parameters, you control if the system accepts the scheduled dates at the network header level as basic or forecast dates. For example, if there is a fixed timeframe for the execution, enter the start and end dates manually in the network header and set the DO NOT ADJUST BASIC DATES indicator. Your dates will remain fixed during the scheduling process, and by comparing the scheduled dates, you can determine whether the timeframe is sufficient for the execution. If the scheduled dates are outside of the predefined dates, the scheduling log issues appropriate warnings.

"Adjust basic dates" indicator

However, if you only know the start date, for example, and want the system to calculate the end date and to adjust it if changes need to be made at a later stage, select the FORWARDS scheduling type, set the ADJUST BASIC DATES indicator, and manually enter a start date in the network header. Based on your start date, the system first calculates the scheduled end of the network, inserts it as the end date, and then performs the backward scheduling based on this date.

153

Start in the past The number of days you enter in the START IN THE PAST field in the scheduling parameters controls the handling of start dates that have already passed. If the system determines a start date during scheduling that is further in the past than you permitted in the START IN THE PAST field, the system issues a warning and automatically uses the current date for forward scheduling (this is called *today scheduling*).

[+] **Any Start Dates in the Past**

If you enter 999 in the START IN THE PAST field, the system permits start dates that can be anywhere in the past without performing a today scheduling.

Automatic scheduling By setting the AUTOMATIC SCHEDULING indicator in the scheduling parameters, you cause a scheduling to be performed automatically when the network is saved whenever there has been a scheduling-relevant modification to the network. The indicator is forwarded as a default value to the network header and can be changed there. At the latest, during the implementation phase of a network, it is usually recommended that you remove this indicator from the network header to avoid uncontrolled changes to capacity requirements, purchase requisitions, or reservations of material due to automatic scheduling.

Other indicators in the scheduling parameters control the output of scheduling logs in Transaction CN22, the handling of breaks in the scope of scheduling, the date reference of material components, the consideration of actual dates from partial confirmations (see Chapter 4, Section 4.3), and how later date changes affect a workforce planning (see Section 2.2.2).

Overall Network Scheduling

In overall network scheduling, all networks or orders that are linked to each other via external relationships or subnetworks are scheduled at the same time. Overall network scheduling is run automatically within the assembly processing (see Chapter 1, Section 1.8.7) or started from a sales document. You can trigger overall network scheduling in SAP Project System using Transactions CN24 or CN24N.

During overall network scheduling, the scheduling settings are determined, just like in network scheduling, from the scheduling parameters for the network type.

If you use Transaction CN24 for overall network scheduling, first specify the identification of a network and the set of dates for scheduling. Then you can make temporary changes to the scheduling settings, if necessary, or enter new start and end dates for scheduling (see Figure 2.9).

CN24 (Overall Network Scheduling)

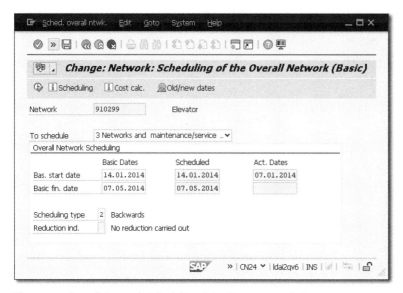

Figure 2.9 Overall Network Scheduling Using Transaction CN24

If you work with maintenance or service orders as assigned subnetworks, you can use the To Schedule field to determine whether only these orders are to be scheduled, only the networks, or both networks and assigned maintenance or service orders.

After you have performed the scheduling you can use the Old/New Dates function to compare the old dates to the newly calculated dates. Afterward, you can save the date changes of the networks or orders, respectively.

In contrast to Transaction CN24, Overall Network Scheduling with Selection Options (Transaction CN24N) enables you to influence the selection of the networks and subnetworks to be scheduled before the

CN24N

scheduling process (see Figure 2.10) and to also use a monitor for observing the dates of subnetworks.

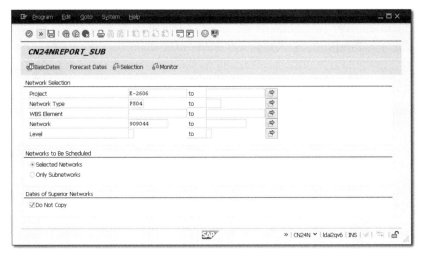

Figure 2.10 Overall Network Scheduling with Selection Options

Subnetwork Monitor

In the *Subnetwork Monitor*, both data from the selected networks and data from the assigned subnetworks are displayed in a table (see Figure 2.11). You can go to the activity or network header display by clicking on your mouse. In addition, you can enter activity confirmations in the Subnetwork Monitor or call the Project Information System: Structures (see Chapter 6, Section 6.1). Traffic lights indicate when the dates of the subnetworks are outside of the dates of the higher-level activity (CONFLICT) or don't exactly match (UPDATE REQUIRED).

Levels

To use the functions of overall network scheduling with selection options in the Customizing of SAP Project System, you need to define *levels* in addition to the scheduling parameters for the network type, and then manually assign these levels to the network types and number range intervals of the networks and subnetworks. The level definition must reflect the hierarchical arrangement of the networks and subnetworks. The levels serve as selection criteria in Transaction CN24N. A scheduling using Transaction CN24N can span a maximum of two levels. If you use more than two levels in your project structure, you have to perform scheduling successively several times.

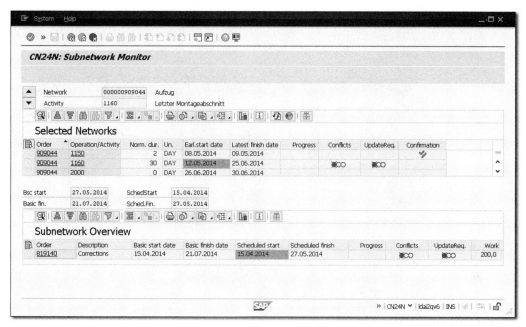

Figure 2.11 Subnetwork Monitor

Transaction CN24N is intended primarily for companies that work with a large number of multilevel subnetwork structures and that don't always want to schedule all networks and subnetworks at the same time.

WBS Scheduling

In WBS scheduling, the scheduling is started based on one or more WBS elements. In WBS scheduling, activities that are scheduled are assigned to these WBS elements. Therefore, you can schedule individual parts of a project without scheduling all activities of a network. A WBS scheduling can be started in the specific maintenance functions (Transaction CJ20 or CJ02), using project scheduling (Transaction CJ29), or in the Project Planning Board. In the Project Builder or Project Editor, you can perform a WBS scheduling if you've selected the project definition or a WBS element in the structure tree.

In WBS scheduling, the scheduling settings are determined from the control parameters for WBS scheduling, but can also be changed temporarily.

Parameters for WBS scheduling

These control parameters are grouped in a profile that you can define in the Customizing of SAP Project System (see Figure 2.12) and entered in the project profile as a default value for the project definition.

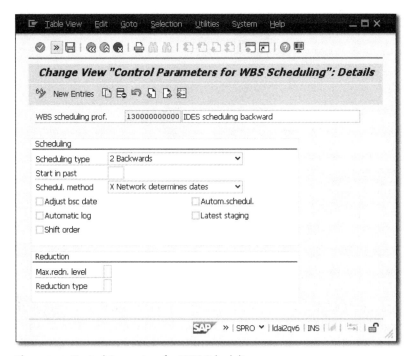

Figure 2.12 Control Parameters for WBS Scheduling

The control parameters for WBS scheduling basically contain the same settings as the parameters of network scheduling, that is, the scheduling type, an indicator for automatically scheduling at saving time, or reduction settings. If you set the ADJUST BASIC DATES in WBS scheduling, not only are the network header dates adapted to the scheduled dates, but the planned dates of the WBS elements are also derived from the scheduled dates of the assigned activities. For that reason, the planned dates of activities and WBS elements can be determined at the same time during the WBS scheduling.

Scheduling methods   In addition, the parameters for WBS scheduling include the SCHEDULING METHOD field with the following two options:

- **Network determines dates**
  The network header determines the start and end dates of scheduling.

- **WBS determines dates**
  The planned dates of the WBS element determine the start and end dates for scheduling the assigned activities.

Therefore, the idea of the WBS DETERMINES DATES scheduling method is to first make a manual time schedule at the WBS element level and to then schedule the assigned activities. The scheduling of the activities is then based on the manually planned start and end dates of the WBS elements.

In the time scheduling process using WBS elements and networks, the scheduling parameters that control the scheduling of the activities and the data exchange with the WBS elements play an important role, and the planning methods control the hierarchical exchange of planned dates between WBS elements on different levels. You can define the WBS scheduling parameters in Customizing and specify them together with the planning methods for your project. Alternatively, you can also use predefined *scheduling scenarios* with WBS elements and networks.

If you select a scheduling scenario for scheduling a project, all settings are determined via the scheduling scenario. The following scheduling scenarios are available:

Scheduling scenarios

- **Bottom-up scenario**
  Based on the basic start date of the network header (which may be anywhere in the past), a forward scheduling and then a backward scheduling are performed. The scheduled dates are used as planned dates at the network header level and the assigned WBS elements. The planned dates of the WBS elements are finally projected in a bottom-up fashion.

- **Top-down scenario**
  In this scenario, you first have to make a manual scheduling at the WBS element level. During this process, the system checks the hierarchical consistency of this time scheduling when scheduling or saving. The scheduling of the assigned activities is based on the planned dates of the WBS elements (which may be anywhere in the past).

In both scheduling scenarios, requirement dates for material are derived from the latest date of activities, and reductions are not performed. The settings of both scheduling scenarios, bottom-up and top-down, are pre-defined and cannot be changed.

If you want to use one of the two scheduling scenarios, you can store the scenario in the project definition or enter it as a default value in the project profile. However, if you want to use different settings, you need to set the SCHEDULING SCENARIO field to the FREE SCHEDULING VALUE and specify the appropriate settings manually.

2.1.3 Scheduling with the Project Editor

As of EHP 6, the Project Editor (Transaction PSHLP20), which you already know from Chapter 1, Section 1.7.4, combines scheduling functions from various transactions; for example, from the Project Builder, from the Project Planning Board, and from overall network scheduling including selection options. Therefore, it's a convenient transaction for project and network scheduling. You can use the Project Editor to schedule and analyze dates of maintenance order or service orders, which are assigned to activities of a network as subnetworks, together with the dates of the respective project elements. The Project Editor only displays the order headers of the maintenance and service order and their dates. If necessary, however, you can navigate to the order details display anytime.

Overview of the dates
In the Project Editor, you can schedule and analyze dates in object detail screens or in tabular overviews. An overall dates overview provides you with a tabular overview of the dates of all structure elements of a project (see Figure 2.13). The tabular dates overviews enable you to define exceptions, for example, to mark date conflicts using traffic lights. If necessary, you can use customer enhancements to define your own conditions for exceptions. Using additional fields for scheduling comparisons, you can analyze and highlight (in different colors) date changes.

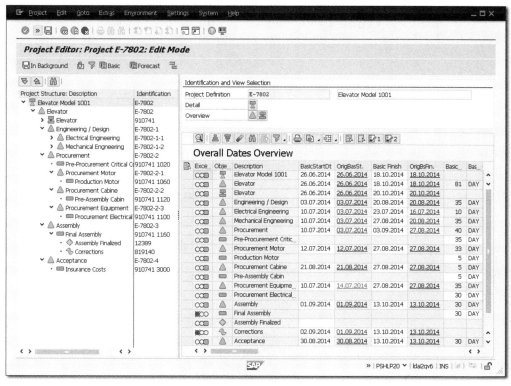

Figure 2.13 Overall Dates Overview in the Project Editor

Similar to the process in the Project Builder, depending on the selected object type, you can trigger WBS scheduling or network scheduling in the Project Editor. Assigned maintenance or service orders can be scheduled separately or together with the superordinate activities. *Loop analyses* enable you to identify and eliminate cyclical sequences of network activities that prevent scheduling. You can determine activities without predecessor or successor by defining appropriate exceptions and then create the missing relationships.

Analyzing relationships

To graphically display or print dates, you can call a Gantt chart presentation in the Project Editor (see Figure 2.14). The user settings here enable you to define, for example, which date bars and columns are supposed to be displayed and how they are supposed to be labeled. You can then save and manage these settings as variants. A print preview enables you to optimize the printouts of the Gantt charts.

Gantt chart

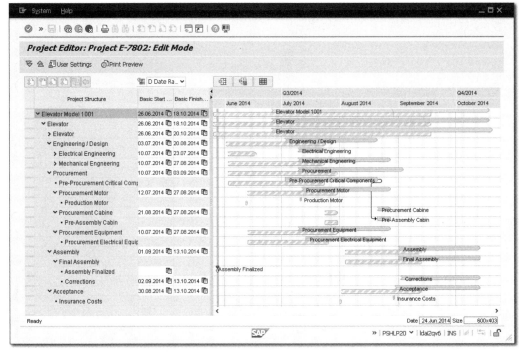

Figure 2.14 Gantt Chart Presentation in the Project Editor

[!] **Restrictions of the Gantt Chart Presentation**

Compared to the Project Planning Board, the Gantt chart presentation in the Project Editor has an extremely limited range of functions. For example, you cannot display more than two date bars per object at the same time and you cannot trigger scheduling.

Further scheduling functions of the Project Editor include:

▸ Transferring scheduled dates

▸ Projecting, inheriting, and checking dates

▸ Transferring dates from one set of dates to another

▸ Copying scheduling data of maintenance orders to superordinate activities in the form of durations or constraints

▸ Using drafts for what-if analyses

> **Date Planning** [◉]
>
> Using scheduling, you can have the system automatically calculate the planned dates of activities and assigned objects, and identify time-critical activities. If the activities are assigned to WBS elements, date information can be exchanged between the activities and the WBS elements. If necessary, you can manually schedule dates at the WBS element level. You are supported by various functions, like the projecting of dates or hierarchical consistency checks. You can use different scheduling transactions according to your requirements.

2.2   Resource Planning

If you mapped a project using only a work breakdown structure, you can plan costs for internal or external resources (see Section 2.4) and later assign activity allocations, purchase requisitions, purchase orders, goods receipts, and acceptances, for example, to WBS elements and thereby post the costs of the resource usage to the project (see Chapter 4, Section 4.2). A logistic resource planning in the sense of a capacity planning, or an automatic data exchange between the project structure and purchasing documents is only possible in SAP Project System if you also implement networks. A manual cost planning for the required resources and a manual assignment of purchasing documents at the WBS element level are not necessary when using networks.

Resource planning without networks

> **Lean Staffing for Internal and Customer Projects** [+]
>
> As of EHP 5, the SAP for Professional Services provides the Lean Staffing application, which enables you to manage employee assignments for internal and customer projects without networks, merely at the level of WBS elements. The application includes the following functions, for example:
>
> ▶ Identification and assignment of appropriate employees
>
> ▶ Integration with the CATS time sheet for easier time data recording
>
> ▶ Evaluation and forecasts of employee utilization
>
> You can find more information on these functions and the numerous Lean Staffing enhancement options in the documentation of the SAP for Professional Services solution.

The following sections deal with the functions that are available for planning resources via network activities.

2.2.1 Capacity Planning with Work Centers

When structuring your projects, you use internally processed activities or internally processed activity elements for specifying services that will be provided by internal resources; for example, machine or personnel resources. Within scheduling, the system has calculated when these services will be performed; however, the scheduling doesn't verify whether there are sufficient internal resources at the planned date. To make statements about the availability of your resources and thus the feasibility of your projects in terms of capacities, you can use the *capacity requirements planning* in SAP Project System.

Capacity requirements planning

The primary function of capacity requirements planning is to determine capacity requirements and to periodically (for example, on a weekly or daily basis) compare these requirements with the available capacity using the appropriate reports (see Chapter 6, Section 6.3.3). The available capacity is defined using work centers, while the required capacity is derived from the activity data of networks or, for example, production order or maintenance orders If you discover that the capacity requirement is higher than the available capacities during a specific period, you will need to make a *capacity leveling* to get your planning in line with the capacities.

Definition of Work Centers and Available Capacity

Work centers are organizational units in the SAP system that define where an activity can be performed and by whom. If you have already defined work centers for production or maintenance, you can use these work centers in networks as well, provided that this is permitted by the application of the work centers. If you have not yet defined any work centers in the SAP system, or if you want to use separate work centers for projects, you can create new work centers in SAP Project System (Transaction CNR1). A mandatory prerequisite for capacity requirements planning using networks is the definition and usage of work centers.

When creating a new work center, in addition to the identification and the plant of the work center, you also specify the WORK CENTER CATEGORY (see Figure 2.15). Among other things, the work center category defines the fields (FIELD SELECTION) and tabs (SCREEN SEQUENCE) to be displayed in the master record of the work center. By default, you can use the 0006 (PROJECT MANAGEMENT) work center category in SAP Project System. If required, you can define additional work center categories (Customizing Transaction OP40).

Work center category

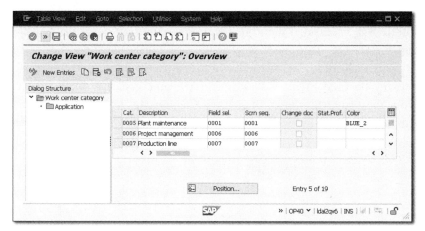

Figure 2.15 Definition of Work Center Categories

The USAGE field in the basic data of the work center determines the task list types and order categories in which the work center can be used. For a work center to be used in standard networks and particularly in operative networks, it must have a usage that is assigned to the task list type 0 (STANDARD NETWORK). If the work center is to be exclusively used for networks, you can, for example, enter the application 003 (NETWORKS ONLY) in the master record of the work center. If you want, you can use Customizing Transaction OP45 to define your own usages and assign them to the relevant task list types.

Usage

Depending on the work center category, you can make a number of settings for the time scheduling (see Section 2.1.2) and the calculation (see Section 2.4.6) of activities in the master data. For capacity requirements planning, however, the settings on the CAPACITIES tab are relevant.

Capacity categories   On this tab, you first store one or more capacity categories, for example, for persons or machines, and then define the respective available capacity. Capacity categories are defined in Customizing and specify, among other things, whether the available capacity must be defined in time units or in base or volume units, or whether, for example, you can assign persons from Human Resources (HR).

Available capacity   In the simplest case, the definition of an available capacity consists of the specification of a factory calendar for distinguishing working and nonworking days, information about the beginning, the end, and the duration of breaks of a working day, the specification of a capacity utilization rate, and the number of available individual capacities. The rate of capacity utilization describes how much of the daily working time can actually be used for production. The available capacity finally results from the productive operating time of a capacity, multiplied with the number of individual capacities (see Figure 2.16).

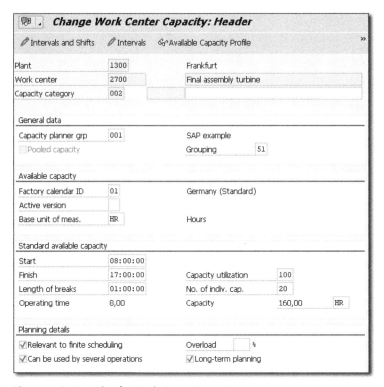

Figure 2.16 Example of a Work Center Capacity

In addition to the definition of the standard available capacity, there are several more detailed options for defining available capacities. On the one hand, you can specify time intervals and define a separate available capacity for every interval.

Thus, you can map employment relationships depending on the season, for example. On the other hand, you can define shift sequences in Customizing (Transaction OP4A) and assign them to the capacity category in the work center. Using shift sequences, you can then specify exact break times that can be considered in capacity requirements planning.

Finally, you can also define *individual capacities* and assign them to the capacity category in the work center. Using appropriate reporting settings, you can then also use the aggregated availability of the assigned individual capacities for capacity evaluations instead of the standard offer. For personnel resources, the availability of individual capacities is derived from the planned working time (Infotype 0007) that is maintained for the employees in HR.

After you have defined the available capacity, in the work center enter a formula in the FORMULA REQUIREMENTS INTERNAL PRICING field for the capacity category. The formula determines how the capacity requirements are to be calculated from the activity data. Usually, the standard formula SAP008 is entered here. Figure 2.17 illustrates the definition of this formula. The SAP_07 parameter in the SAP008 formula is linked to the WORK field in activities or activity elements.

Formula for capacity requirements

In Customizing, however, you can also define your own formulas (Transaction OP21) to consider values of other activity fields as well when calculating capacity requirements. This way you can also include user fields in formulas, for example. To do this, you must define a separate parameter for the corresponding user field and assign it to the user field in the field key definition. This parameter can then be used for the definition of a formula. In the work center, you can first test the calculation of capacity requirements using a formula before you save the work center. If you define your own formulas, however, note that the calculation of capacity requirements should always be clearly documented in the reporting.

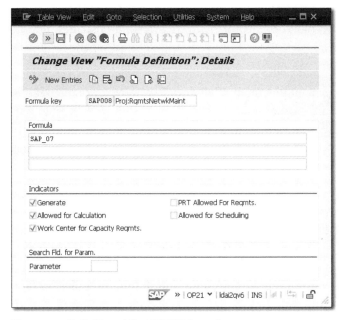

Figure 2.17 Definition of the SAP008 Formula

Distribution key   Using a distribution key in the work center, you can specify how the capacity requirements of an activity are to be distributed across the activity duration. A distribution key consists of a distribution strategy and a distribution function (see Figure 2.18).

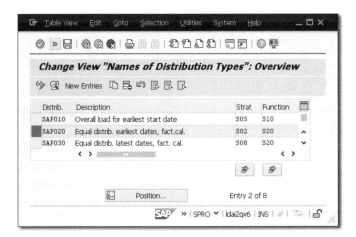

Figure 2.18 Definition of Distribution Keys

The distribution function determines—after which percentage of the activity duration—what percent of the entire capacity requirement is needed (see Figure 2.19).

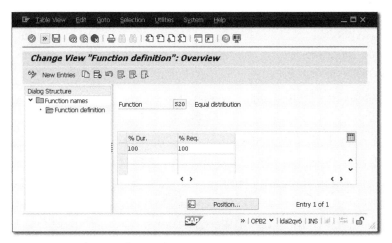

Figure 2.19 Definition of a Distribution Function

Among other things, the distribution strategy determines whether the distribution is to take place via the earliest or the latest dates of the activity (see Figure 2.20).

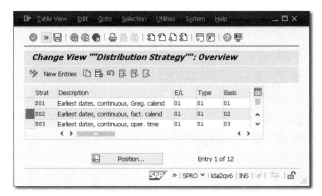

Figure 2.20 Definition of a Distribution Strategy

In the standard version, various distribution keys are already defined, such as SAP030 (EQUAL DISTRIBUTION ACROSS THE LATEST DATES) or SAP020 (EQUAL DISTRIBUTION ACROSS THE EARLIEST DATES). If you want, you can also define additional distribution keys, functions, or strategies in the Customizing of SAP Project System.

Prerequisites for Determining Capacity Requirements

To compare the available capacities shown in capacity reports with the corresponding capacities required by your projects, the network must meet various prerequisites:

- The network activities must contain the work centers and planned work.
- The control key of the activities must be identified as relevant to the determination of capacity requirements (see Chapter 1, Section 1.3.2).
- The calculation of capacity requirements must be enabled, that is, the CAPACITY REQUIREMENTS indicator must be set in the network header.

  You can remove the CAPACITY REQUIREMENTS indicator from the network header at any time if capacity requirements are no longer required for a network. This may be relevant, for example, if a project is cancelled or stopped during the implementation phase.

- After you have enabled capacity requirements, a scheduling must have been performed.

Also note that a final confirmation or setting the status to TECHNICALLY COMPLETED sets the (remaining) capacity requirement of an activity to zero (0).

[+] | **Capacity Requirements Planning for Suppliers**

If you want, you can perform your capacity requirements planning for suppliers as well, that is, using externally processed activities or service activities, if the control key permits this. To do this, you need to define a separate work center with the appropriate required capacities for the supplier, and enter the work center on the INTERNAL tab of the activity.

Determining the requirements distribution

If necessary, you can enter a distribution key in the activities just like you would in a work center. Unless the report you use for the capacity evaluation provides a dedicated distribution key, the system determines the distribution of capacity requirements according to the following strategy:

1. Distribution key of the activity

2. Distribution key of the work center

3. Equal distribution across the latest dates of the activity

After you have created the capacity requirements for a network, you can use various reports to compare the capacity requirements of the network plus the requirements of other projects or orders to the corresponding available work centers or capacities, respectively. Figure 2.21 shows the capacity overview of the Project Planning Board, which graphically illustrates the available capacities of work centers and the respective total capacity requirement using bars or histograms. Capacity overloads, that is, requirements that exceed the available capacities during a specific period, are highlighted in color. Additional detailed capacity reports are discussed in Chapter 6, Section 6.3.3.

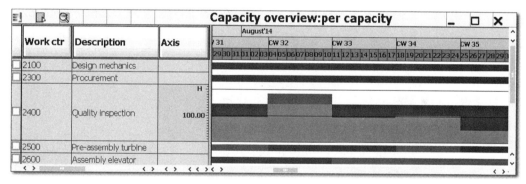

Figure 2.21 Capacity Overview of the Project Planning Board

During the implementation phase of projects, the capacity requirements are adjusted due to the completed work and forecast data from confirmations. Capacity reports therefore distinguish from among three different capacity requirements:

Planned, remaining, and actual capacity requirements

▸ **Planned capacity requirements**
The capacity requirement resulting from the planned data of the activities

▸ **Remaining capacity requirements**
The current capacity requirements resulting from the originally planned requirements, the previously confirmed services, and possibly the forecasted remaining work

▸ **Actual capacity requirements**
The service that has actually been used and has already been confirmed

[+] **Prerequisite for Actual Capacity Requirements**

In addition to the relevant settings of the extended capacity reports, it is necessary for an analysis of actual capacity requirements that the relevant work centers determine actual capacity requirements.

2.2.2 Workforce Planning

A work center can consist of several available individual capacities; however, if you perform your capacity requirements planning only at the work center level, you won't be able to specify which individual capacity of the work center will provide the respective service. Therefore, you can't create meaningful capacity evaluations for the individual capacities.

Capacity splits
For some projects, however, you must plan individual capacities—particularly as far as personnel resources are concerned—to avoid an overload of individuals or to consider employees' qualifications when planning the project, for example. To do this, you can distribute the work via capacity splits, that is, split the planned work of an activity into individual capacities. Capacity splits can be individual machines, organizational units, or positions, for example. Usually, however, the SAP Project System performs a *workforce planning*; that is, a distribution with a direct reference to the personnel numbers. The work distributed to a person can later be used as a default value for the time data recording using the cross-application time sheet (CATS) (see Chapter 4, Section 4.3.3).

Prerequisites for Workforce Planning

HR master data
A prerequisite for workforce planning is that SAP Project System is provided with various HR master data. This can either be maintained in the

system as HR mini-master records, or originate from an HR system. The minimum requirement is HR master data of the Infotypes 0001 (ORGANIZATIONAL ASSIGNMENT) and 0002 (PERSONAL DATA). If you want to consider the availability of the person or their qualifications in your planning, you will also need Infotypes 0007 (PLANNED WORKING TIME) and 0024 (QUALIFICATIONS). Another later use of the data in the timesheet also requires Infotype 0315 (DEFAULT VALUES TIME SHEET).

Prerequisites for Workforce Planning   [+]

Before you can distribute the work of an activity to individuals, you must have already determined the capacity requirements. This means you need at least one work center for workforce planning as well.

The persons to whom you want to distribute the work do not necessarily have to be assigned to that work center. Depending on the system settings, you can use the following personnel for workforce planning:

▶ Persons who are assigned to the work center of the activity

▶ Persons of a project organization

▶ Any personnel resources

There are two ways of assigning personnel to a work center: First, you can assign an organizational unit or an HR work center to the work center and therefore indirectly assign personnel. And second, you can directly assign positions or persons to the work center capacity. The benefit of the second option is that you can use the total amount of availabilities of the assigned personnel included in capacity reports as the available capacity of the work center instead of the standard availabilities.

Personnel assignment to work centers

Project organization refers to persons, positions, or organizational units that you assign to WBS elements as the default set for a later workforce planning. If you use Transaction CMP2 (Workforce Planning–Selection Project View), the system always first suggests the persons, positions, or organizational units of the project organization for your workforce planning. If you have not assigned a project organization to a WBS element, Transaction CMP2 of the system provides the project organization of the hierarchically superior WBS element for workforce planning. If you

Project organization

only want to store one project organization for the entire project, an assignment at the top project level will suffice. You can assign project organizations to WBS elements in Transaction CMP2 or in most of the processing transactions for work breakdown structures. Figure 2.22 shows an example of assigning a project organization to a WBS element.

If you want, however, you can plan personnel resources in your workforce planning that are not assigned to the work center or to your project organization. Depending on the transaction you use for workforce planning, however, you must explicitly enable this in the activity or the workforce planning profile.

Ranking lists   If you want to take into account the qualifications of the personnel while planning the workforce (for example, language skills, education, and so on), you can store a requirements profile in the individual activities that describes the qualifications required for accomplishing an activity. If you also defined the qualifications of the individual personnel resources (Transaction PPPM), the system can create a ranking list during workforce planning listing those persons who are best qualified to meet the requirements of the activity.

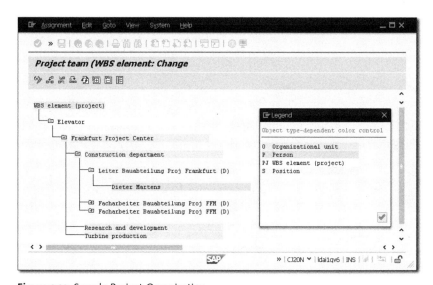

Figure 2.22 Sample Project Organization

Workforce Planning Process

There are different ways to plan a workforce. You can assign persons to an activity on the PERSON ASSIGNMENT tab and specify the date, the planned work, and the permitted duration for every split; the system then automatically distributes the requirements across the specified duration (see Figure 2.23). You can use Transactions CMP2 (Project View) or CMP3 (Work Center View) for distributing your work to persons, positions, or organizational units. You can also manually distribute the work to different days or weeks, for example, or use the graphical or tabular planning board of capacity requirements planning to include capacity splits (see Section 2.2.3).

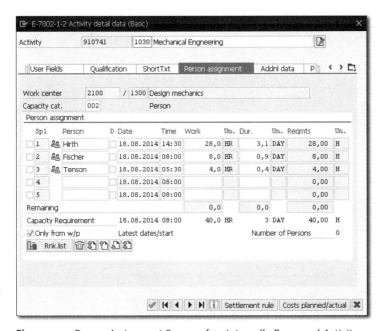

Figure 2.23 Person Assignment Screen of an Internally Processed Activity

For advanced requirements for workforce planning as needed in the context in service projects, you can use SAP Multiresource Scheduling (MRS) together with the SAP Project System networks. MRS provides expert functions, for example, the integration with geographical information systems, graphical planning boards, or the usage of advanced qualification catalogs.

Workforce
planning profile To use Transactions CMP2 and CMP3 in SAP Project System, you first need to define a workforce planning profile in Customizing (Transaction CMPC; see Figure 2.24). Among other things, the profile specifies whether it is permissible to plan resources that don't belong to the work center or to the project organization, and which periods (for example, days, weeks, or months) are to be used for planning. Here, you can also define mixed period splits to make a day-based planning for the next period, for example, but only a week-based planning for activities that are based more in the future. If you use Transaction CMP9 to evaluate your workforce planning, you can use the profile to define traffic light functions (*Exceptions*) indicating, for example, undistributed work or overloaded employees.

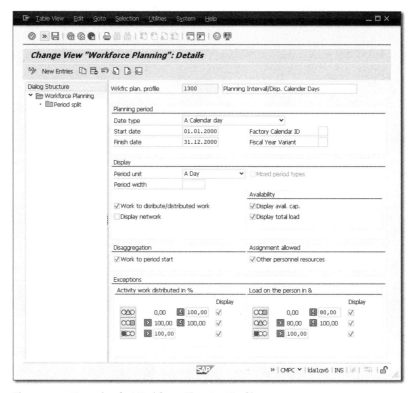

Figure 2.24 Example of a Workforce Planning Profile

CMP2
(Project View) In a workforce planning using Transaction CMP2 (Project View), you select the activities for workforce planning by specifying one or more

projects, WBS elements, or networks. You receive a list of activities for which there are capacity requirements and then can create an assignment to organizational units, positions, or personnel resources. If there is a project organization, it will be suggested for the assignment; however, you can also use the work center resources and—provided this is permitted by the profile—any other personnel resources.

Editing period specifications

However, the assignment of a resource is not sufficient for workforce planning; so in addition, you need to enter the period in which the resource is to accomplish the specified amount of the planned work of the activity. At first, the system only offers the period for distribution that covers the capacity requirements of the activity. If you want, however, you can also use different periods for workforce planning.

You can also display the availability (planned working time) or the total load of the resources for each period. The total load shows a resource's total work distribution to network activities for a specific period. Work distributions to other order categories are not taken into account.

You can also display details of the activities or show the planned distribution of the activities' capacity requirements. Figure 2.25 shows an example of workforce planning using Transaction CMP2.

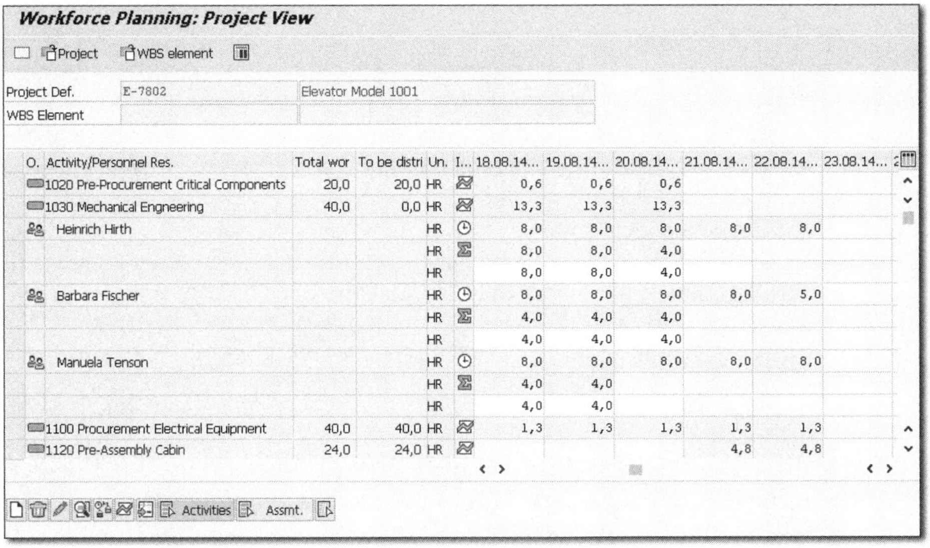

Workforce Planning: Project View

Project   WBS element

Project Def. E-7802 Elevator Model 1001

WBS Element

O. Activity/Personnel Res.	Total wor	To be distri	Un.	I...	18.08.14...	19.08.14...	20.08.14...	21.08.14...	22.08.14...	23.08.14...
1020 Pre-Procurement Critical Components	20,0	20,0	HR		0,6	0,6	0,6			
1030 Mechanical Engneering	40,0	0,0	HR		13,3	13,3	13,3			
Heinrich Hirth			HR		8,0	8,0	8,0	8,0	8,0	
			HR		8,0	8,0	4,0			
			HR		8,0	8,0	4,0			
Barbara Fischer			HR		8,0	8,0	8,0	8,0	5,0	
			HR		4,0	4,0	4,0			
			HR		4,0	4,0	4,0			
Manuela Tenson			HR		8,0	8,0	8,0	8,0	8,0	
			HR		4,0	4,0				
			HR		4,0	4,0				
1100 Procurement Electrical Equipment	40,0	40,0	HR		1,3	1,3	1,3	1,3	1,3	
1120 Pre-Assembly Cabin	24,0	24,0	HR					4,8	4,8	

Activities   Assmt.

Figure 2.25 Example of Workforce Planning from the Project View

CMP3 (Work Center View) In some companies, it is not a project manager who uses Transaction CMP2 for workforce planning; instead, the persons responsible for specific work centers do this planning. They can use Transaction CMP3 (Work Center View) to distribute work to the resources of their work center (see Figure 2.26). Resources and activities are selected by specifying one or more work centers.

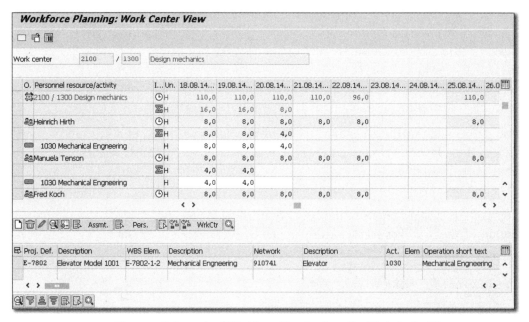

Figure 2.26 Example of Workforce Planning from the Work Center View

[!] **Network Lock for Workforce Planning from the Work Center View**

You should note that during workforce planning—from a work center view—all activities that have capacity requirements for the selected work centers in the given period are read, and that the corresponding networks are consequently locked. We therefore recommend that you use Transaction CMP3 to explicitly specify those networks as filters for which you want to distribute work.

CMP9 (Evaluation) After you have performed a workforce planning, you can evaluate it using the individual capacity reports or Transaction CMP9. In Transaction CMP9, you can use the information about projects, work centers, or personnel resources for selecting workforce planning. In the evaluation, you can use the exceptions defined in the profile to highlight overloaded resources or activities with work that has not yet been completely distributed (see Figure 2.27).

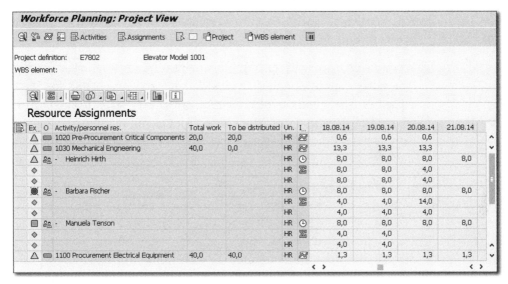

Figure 2.27 Example of an Evaluation of Workforce Planning

If activity dates are shifted after a workforce planning has been completed, the RESCHEDULING indicator in the scheduling parameters for the network type (see Section 2.1.2) decides whether the workforce planning is to be shifted as well, or distributed work outside the new activity dates is to be deleted, for example.

2.2.3 Capacity Leveling

If, during your capacity requirements planning, you find that required resources are overloaded, you will need to adjust your planning. To do so, you must perform *capacity leveling*. This can be, for example, an adjustment of the time scheduling, that is, a chronological shifting of activities or increasing their duration. Capacity leveling can also include the creation of new activities or activity elements with additional work centers or resources. If necessary, you can also change the control key of an internally processed activity, and therefore the activity category, to procure the planned work externally (see Section 2.2.4 and Section 2.2.5).

Rescheduling

Capacity planning board
In a stricter sense, however, the term *capacity leveling* refers to the usage of graphical or tabular *capacity planning boards*, that is, specific capacity requirements planning tools for a fixed chronological planning of capacity requirements. These tools are used primarily in production for planning bottleneck work centers, for example, and are rarely used in companies for project planning.

When using a capacity planning board in capacity leveling, you must first select capacities and activities that have requirements for these capacities. Then, you can plan the requirements to be performed by the planned capacity or by a different one. The planning can be done manually, where either you specify the dates for the planning or they are specified automatically (for example, the earliest or latest dates of an activity).

Scheduled status
Activities, for which you have planned the requirements by using a capacity planning board, automatically obtain the status SCHEDULED. All activity fields that are relevant to capacity requirements planning, like the planned work and duration, the work center, or the activity dates, are locked against being changed due to this status. You can only undo the planning of an activity in a capacity planning board if you shift the activity or change other capacity-relevant data.

You can use capacity planning boards both for capacity leveling of work center capacities and for scheduling individual capacities of the work centers, like personnel resources.

Graphical planning boards
Graphical planning boards (see Figure 2.28) are based on Gantt chart presentations. The graphical area displays the capacity requirements and the periods they cover, and existing scheduled capacity requirements, as individual bars on a time axis. The tabular area shows information about the capacities and the requirements sources. Manual requirement plannings for capacities can be performed via drag-and-drop. If a capacity would be overloaded due to this planning, more than permitted according to the definition of the available capacity, you are informed via error messages in a planning log that this planning is not possible.

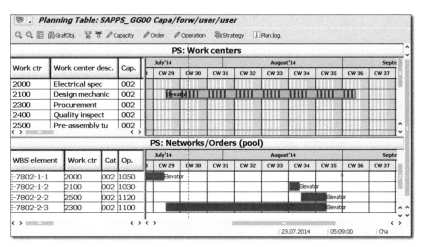

Figure 2.28 Graphical Capacity Planning Board

Tabular planning boards present capacity data and the requirements of activities, and additional data of the requirement sources in a tabular format (see Figure 2.29). In contrast to graphical planning boards, the availabilities of the capacities can be displayed for the respective periods. This enables you to detect whether the capacity will be overloaded even before the planning.

Tabular planning boards

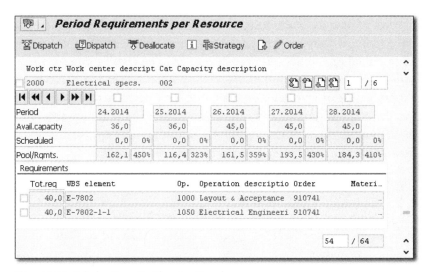

Figure 2.29 Tabular Capacity Planning Board

2.2.4 Externally Processed Activities

Often, not all services necessary for completing a project can be provided by internal company resources. Using externally processed activities (or external elements; see Chapter 1, Section 1.3.1), you can therefore plan, procure, and monitor services that are to be provided by vendors.

Specifications for external services

For a manual specification of external activities, you can use describing long texts, documents, or PS texts in SAP script format, and enter a planned quantity and a unit of measure in an activity. For a cost planning of the external procurement, you can also specify a price per unit, the relevant currency, and a cost element (see Section 2.4.6). To consider the timeframe for the later procurement of the service in the scheduling process, you can store a planned delivery time or duration (see Section 2.1.2) in the activity. You can also specify a preferred vendor.

To automatically create purchase requisitions from the activity data later, you must store a purchasing organization, a purchasing group, and the material group of the external activity in the activity. This organizational data, and the cost element, currency, and unit of measure, can be entered in the network profile (Transaction OPUU) as default values (see Chapter 1, Section 1.3.2).

Purchasing info records, outline agreements

Instead of manually entering specifications of the external activity, price, planned delivery time, material group, and so forth in the activity, as described previously, you can also refer to *purchasing info records* or *outline agreements* from purchasing. If you store an info record for external processing or an outline agreement in an externally processed activity, the activity automatically uses all necessary purchasing data from these purchasing information sources. This data—except for the quantity—can no longer be changed manually in the activity.

Automatic purchase requisitions

From the activity data, the system can automatically display a purchase requisition. Depending on the setting of the RES./PURC. REQ. field, this can be done even before the activity is released (IMMEDIATELY), automatically by setting the RELEASED (FROM RELEASE) status, or at a later stage. For the last option, first set the indicator to the NEVER value, and then change the setting to IMMEDIATELY later. The value of the RES./PURC. REQ. field can be preset via the network profile.

The purchase requisition is automatically filled with all data relevant to the purchase. The system uses the latest end date of the activity as a delivery date in the purchase requisition. You can use a customer enhancement to influence the creation of a purchase requisition from the activity data. If relevant data is changed in advance, the purchase requisition is adapted automatically. A manual change of the quantity, the material group, and the purchasing group taken from the activity is not possible in the purchase requisition.

From an externally processed activity, you can go to the display of the created purchase requisition at any time. In addition, SAP Project System also provides the PURCHASE REQUISITIONS FOR PROJECT report, which enables you to analyze or further process purchase requisitions of one or several projects in parallel (see Figure 2.30).

Displaying purchase requisitions

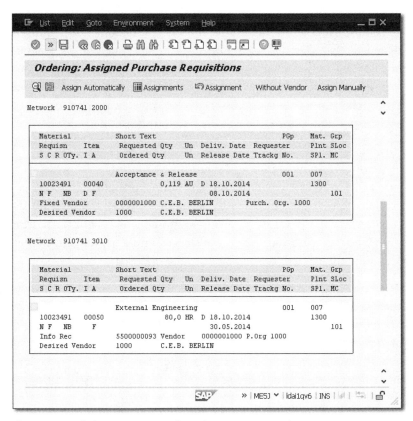

Figure 2.30 Tabular Presentation of Purchase Requisitions for a Project

The *project-oriented procurement* (ProMan) (see Chapter 4, Section 4.5.3) allows you to evaluate quantity or date information of purchase requisitions and use traffic light functions to highlight deviations from your planning.

Selecting a vendor

The automatically created purchase requisitions are also visible in purchasing and can be further processed by a responsible purchaser. Unless you referred to a purchasing info record or an outline agreement in the activity, the purchaser also selects the vendor. In purchasing, this can be achieved, for example, via a bidding process or an automatic source determination.

Commitments

If a vendor has been selected and assigned to the purchase requisition, the data of the purchase requisition can be transferred to a purchase order. The purchase order authorizes the vendor to offer the services ordered for your project, provided that external activities can later be documented via goods or invoice receipts. All purchasing documents are assigned to the activity so that not only can you analyze the planned costs, but the commitments according to the purchase requisition and purchase order, and the actual costs of the external service performed for the activity or the network, respectively. The purchasing process and the corresponding value flows are discussed in detail in Chapter 4.

Document type and account assignment category

In the Customizing section of SAP Project System (Transaction OPTT, see Figure 2.31), you define the *document type* for networks, which is to be used for creating the purchase requisition, and in the ACCT. ASSGMT. GEN. field, you specify the *account assignment category* that controls the value flows of the purchase requisition and all subsequent purchasing documents. These settings are consistently implemented for all networks and independent of the plant or network type.

In network type parameters (Transaction OPUV), you can specify per plant and network type whether a separate purchase requisition is to be created for every externally processed activity (and every service operation and every purchased part (see Section 2.3.1), or whether only one purchase requisition is to be created per network, which then has one item for every external procurement (collective purchase requisition).

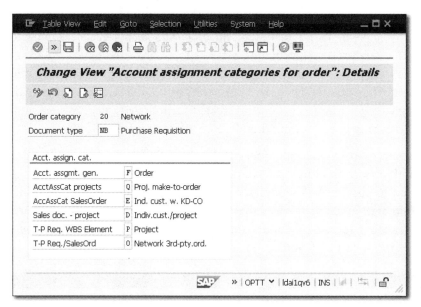

Figure 2.31 Determination of the Account Assignment Categories for Networks

As of EHP 3, you can decide how to best summarize purchase order-relevant items within a project, even across different networks, if necessary. To do that, you must activate the same grouping indicator in the COLLECTIVE PURC. REQ. field for all externally processed activities and service activities, and for every purchased part you want to aggregate. Possible grouping indicators have to be defined at the project definition level first.

If you're implementing an external purchasing system, you can specify for combinations of purchasing and material groups that purchase requisitions are transferred directly to the external purchasing system and that any further purchasing processes are performed there. You can also use a customer enhancement to determine criteria for selecting the purchase requisitions to be transferred.

External purchasing systems

2.2.5 Services

If your company's purchasing department also supports the procurement of services using service specifications and acceptances of services performed, SAP Project System provides service activities and service activity elements for planning and procuring such services. Similar to externally processed activities, services to be provided by external vendors are planned using service activities by specifying purchasing info records or outline agreements, if necessary. For service activities, purchase requisitions can then be created from activity data as well, and purchasing processes can therefore be triggered automatically.

Service specifications

Contrary to an externally processed activity that you simply use to plan and procure an individual external activity, you can use a service operation to plan several vendor services in one step and specify additional information about services that cannot yet be defined in detail. When creating a service operation, the system prompts you to create *service specifications* (see Figure 2.32).

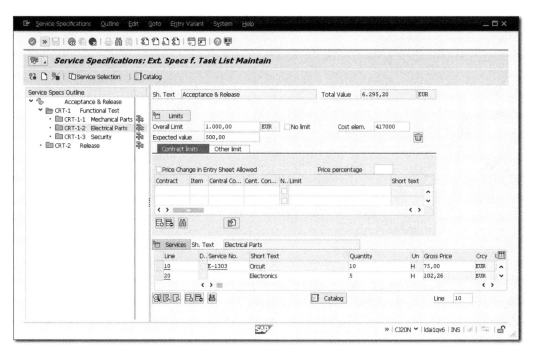

Figure 2.32 Sample Service Specifications

In service specifications, you can create a list of planned services in a hierarchical structure, if necessary. To do this, you can use *service master records* from purchasing that might already store various data of a service. Using the purchasing condition technique, prices for service master records can then be automatically determined and used for calculating the activity. You can also select services from other service specifications, for example, from existing purchasing documents or other networks or purchase orders, and copy them into your service specifications.

In purchasing, *model service specifications* can be defined that can then serve as a template for creating service specifications in the network activity. In some branches, it is common practice to specify services using standardized text modules. In purchasing, this can be mapped via *standard service catalogs*. If you refer to a standard service catalog in your service specifications, you can then plan services by selecting individual text modules.

Model service specifications and standard service catalogs

You can also call intranet or external Internet catalogs in service specifications to select services from these catalogs and transfer them to the service specifications. This is implemented via the *Open Catalogue Interface* (OCI) (see Section 2.3.1).

Catalogs

Frequently, not all services can be planned in detail before a project starts because the required services may depend on the course of the project, for example. In addition to planned services, you can also specify information about unplanned services in the service specifications. To calculate a service operation, you can store an expected value for unplanned services in the service specifications. This value and the total value of planned services add up to the planned costs of the activity.

Unplanned services

In addition, you can limit the value of unplanned services by entering a limit of values in the service specifications. If the vendor later provides services that you didn't explicitly specify in the service specifications, the value of this unplanned service is checked against the limit of values. If the value of the unplanned services exceeds the specified limit, the entered services cannot be saved.

Limit of values

Another difference between externally processed activities and service activities can be found in further purchasing management. At first, a vendor selection and the purchase order implementation take place for a purchase requisition of a service operation in purchasing as well.

External services management

While, depending on the account assignment category, a goods receipt can be posted to document services for externally processed activities, service activities always require a service entry and an acceptance of services performed. More purchasing management details for service activities are discussed in Chapter 4, Section 4.4.2.

Purchase requisitions due to service activities use the same document type and the same account assignment category as externally processed activities (Transaction OPTT). Depending on the material and purchasing group of the purchase requisition, a transfer to an external purchasing system can be performed as well. In the network profile (Transaction OPUU), you can store default values for service operations in the activity, which cover the cost type of the planned services, the material and purchasing group, and the unit of measure.

[◉]

Planning Internal and External Resources Using Networks

Using networks, you can plan internal and external resources for completing your projects. Internal resources are planned based on work centers (capacity requirements planning). If you want, however, the planning can be carried out in greater detail up to workforce planning. Using externally processed activities or activity elements, respectively, you can plan the use of external resources and trigger their procurement via purchasing.

2.3 Material Planning

The completion of many projects requires material. Within the scope of your project planning using SAP Project System, you can plan for material that is required, and its procurement, consumption, and delivery. Using the elevator project as an example, different assemblies, such as parts of the motor, cabin, or shaft, must be provided for a final assembly of the elevator. If the material is not available in stock, purchasing processes or the in-house production of the material must be triggered. If necessary, the required material needs to be delivered to the construction site or to the customer.

Using WBS elements, you can plan costs for procuring material, and assign various documents like material reservations, purchase requisitions, purchase orders, goods receipts, and issues to WBS elements. An integrated material planning where data is automatically exchanged between a project and purchasing or production, however, is only available if you use networks. In this case, a manual costs planning and the manual assignment of documents to WBS elements are no longer necessary.

2.3.1 Assigning Material Components

To plan material via networks, you must assign *material components* to the network activities. Material components are summaries of specific information, like the specification of the material (for example, by specifying a material number), the required amount and the unit of measure, the requirements date, the price per unit or, for purchased parts, the material and purchasing groups and so on (see Figure 2.33).

Material components

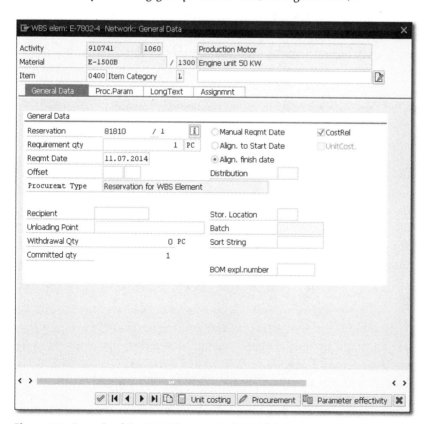

Figure 2.33 Example of the Detail Screen of a Material Component

As of EHP 3, you can also implement custom fields in a separate tab using the `BADI_MAT_CUST_SCR` BAdI and define a field selection in the Customizing of SAP Project System. You can either enter the requirements date of a material component manually as a fixed date, or it can be derived from the dates of the activity to which the component is assigned (see Section 2.1.2).

Item categories

In particular, a material component includes an *item category* that plays an important role in determining the procurement type and the stock management of the material. In SAP Project System, the main item categories used are N (non-stock item) and L (stock item).

Non-stock item

Using the item category N, you can plan the direct procurement of a material via purchasing. As with the external procurement of services via an externally processed activity (see Section 2.2.4), the system uses the component data to automatically create a purchase requisition for a non-stock item as well—depending on the RES./PURC. REQ. indicator—and thus triggers a purchasing management. If you enter a material number in the material component to specify the material, other purchasing data required for creating the purchase requisition can be transferred from the material master data. You can also plan and procure a non-stock item although there is no material master record for this material.

If the vendor delivers a non-stock item within the implementation phase of a project, it is typically documented by a *goods receipt*. When goods are received, however, a non-stock item is not posted to a stock location, that is, no stock is created. Instead, a direct consumption posting is performed by the network activity. A stock management for non-stock items is not possible; consequently, material components of the item category N cannot be managed in the plant stock or in an individual stock.

All documents—the purchase requisition, the purchase order, as well as the goods and invoice receipt of a non-stock item—are assigned to the activity. Therefore, in an activity-assigned network, you can analyze the planned, commitment, and actual costs for the procurement and the material consumption on the activity level (see Chapter 4, Section 4.5.1).

In contrast to the non-stock items, a stock management is provided for   Stock item
stock items (item category L). Moreover, stock items are not directly
procured via purchasing, but via the material requirements planning of
a company. If you assign a material component with the item category L
to an activity, you must also specify a material number so that the system can derive the control data required for the material requirements
planning from the material master record. Stock items can be managed
in the plant stock or in individual stocks.

The simplest procurement type for a stock item is the creation of a reservation. Depending on the setting of the RES./PURC. REQ. field, this can
be either IMMEDIATELY, FROM RELEASE, or NEVER, that is, never automatically but only manually after the release. The reservation is displayed in
the material requirements planning under a unique reservation number
as a requirement and the material is provided in the planned quantity on
the planned requirements date.

Reservation Numbers for Networks	[+]
The system issues one reservation number per network. The reservations of the individual material components of a network are distinguished via an up to four-digit item number within the network reservation number. Therefore, only 9999 material components can be planned per network.	

After the creation of a reservation, the responsible MRP controller needs
to trigger the procurement of the material if it is not available in stock on
the requirements date. For purchased parts, the procurement can be
affected by purchasing; for material produced in-house, the procurement can be affected by the internal company production. After the
material has been procured, it can be posted in a stock. In the last step,
a *goods issue* can be posted with a reference to the original reservation.
The goods issue documents that the material has been taken from stock
and consumed by the network activity.

Even in the project planning phase, you can use the availability check for
stock items to determine whether the material can be provided on the
requirements date (see Section 2.3.3).

Assemblies Stock items that you assign with a negative required quantity to an activity are referred to as *assemblies*. While a positive quantity represents a material requirement, the negative quantity of an assembly documents that the network provides material. From the point of view of material requirements planning, assemblies represent planned additions to a stock. You can implement assemblies if you use networks instead of production orders for producing individual materials, and if this requires multilevel production processes and you want to make the corresponding material movements as transparent as possible in the material requirements planning.

[+] **Integration with SAP Advanced Planning and Optimization (SAP APO)**

For advanced scenarios for Production Planning and Procurement Planning considering material requirements from projects, an integration with SAP Advanced Planning & Optimization (APO) can be implemented. The APO system then displays networks as projects orders. This way, material requirements from networks can be transferred to Production Planning and Procurement Planning in the APO system.

In contrast to planning in the SAP ERP system, planning in the APO system can include capacity and material availabilities at the same time. Finally, scheduling changes to project orders resulting from the planning and optimization process in the APO system are automatically transferred to the networks.[1]

Other item categories Other item categories you can implement in SAP Project System, in addition to the two item categories N and L, are T (text item), R (variable-size item), and C (planning element). Material components of the item category T are for information only and are used, for example, after a BOM explosion. Material components of the item category R provide similar procurement and stock management options as stock items. The required quantity of variable-size items, the *variable-size quantity*, is derived from sizes such as the length, width, and height of a material. Therefore, instead of manually entering an individual required quantity directly, you have to specify sizes for material components of the item

---

1 You can find a comprehensive description of project planning using SAP APO in the SAP PRESS book *Project Planning Using SAP* (Bonn, 2010; German only). Restrictions for integration with project orders is available in SAP Note 708517.

category R. You can use item category C, which has been available in SAP Project System as of EHP 3, for components that have been copied from catalogs to avoid a retroactive copying of those components in the editing transactions of the system.

Basically, the SAP system provides different options for material stock management. One possibility is the usage of the *collective stock*, an anonymous plant stock. All projects and orders requiring a material managed in a collective stock can take this material from the plant stock. A previous assignment of the stocks and stock costs to the consumers is not possible for a collective stock.

Collective and individual stocks

Another option of material stock management is the use of *individual stocks*. In this case, material stocks are explicitly managed with a reference to a sales order item (sales order stock) or a WBS element (project stock). Without a previous transfer, material managed in an individual stock can only be taken for the corresponding sales order item or the WBS element, respectively, or objects assigned to these. Depending on the system settings, the value of material in an individual stock can be reported as stock costs on the object keeping stock records (see Section 2.3.2).

After you have assigned a material component to an activity, you need to specify the *procurement type*. For stock and non-stock items, different procurement types are available. For non-stock items, you can choose between the following two procurement options (see Figure 2.34):

Procurement types for non-stock items

- **Purchase requisition for network**
  A direct procurement of the material is triggered. The material is delivered by the vendor to the company to be consumed by the activity.

- **Third-party order**
  A direct procurement is triggered as well; however, the material is not delivered by the vendor to the company, but instead it is delivered directly to a customer, to another vendor, or to any other delivery address.

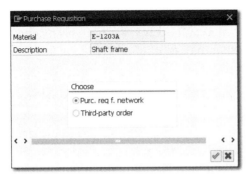

Figure 2.34 Selection of the Procurement Type for a Non-stock Item

Delivery address   If you select the THIRD-PARTY ORDER procurement type for a non-stock item, you need to specify a *delivery address* that is transferred together with the other relevant data of the material component to the purchase requisition and later to the purchase order. You can either enter the required address data manually in a delivery address, or reference an address, customer, or vendor number (see Figure 2.35).

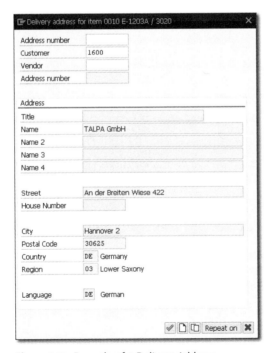

Figure 2.35 Example of a Delivery Address

The system takes the address data from the central address management, from the customer master record of SD, or from the vendor master record of the Purchasing department. If the same delivery address is used frequently for the third-party orders of a project, you can set the REPEAT ON indicator when you create the first delivery address. Note that as of EHP 3, you can also assign material components that do not explicitly have the THIRD-PARTY ORDER procurement type to delivery addresses.

The following procurement types can generally be used for stock items (see Figure 2.36), procurement types that differ only regarding stock management are listed together in the following overview:

Procurement types for stock items

▸ **Reservation for network/Reservation WBS element/Reservation sales document**
These three procurement types only create a reservation. If you use the first type, the material component is managed in the collective stock. If you use either of the other two types, the reservation references the project or the sales order stock.

▸ **Purchase requisition + Reservation WBS element/Purchase requisition + Reservation sales document**
In addition to a reservation, these two procurement types create a purchase requisition at the same time, whether or not a stock exists. You can manage the material component in the project or in the sales order stock. The purchase requisition is assigned to the object holding the stock.

▸ **Third-party requisition WBS element/Third-party requisition sales document**
A third-party order is created. Depending on which of the two types you select, the purchase requisition references the project or the sales order stock.

▸ **Preliminary purchase requisition WBS element/Preliminary purchase requisition sales document**
An advance procurement of purchased parts via purchasing is triggered with a reference to the project or sales order stock.

> ▸ **Planned independent requirements/Planned independent requirements WBS element/Planned independent requirements sales document**
> An advance procurement for material produced in-house is triggered with a reference to the plant, project, or sales order stock.

Figure 2.36 Selection of the Procurement Type for a Stock Item

Advance procurement — The preceding advance procurement types require additional explanations. For material with very long replenishment lead times, it may be necessary within the project implementation to trigger its procurement although the actual consumers (that is, an appropriate network activity or production order) do not yet exist. To do this, assign the required material as a material component with an advance procurement type to the project. Once the actual consumers exist, just reassign the material to them, but this time with a simple reservation as a procurement type. By referencing the reservation, you can ensure that the procured material is taken from stock and consumed. For more information regarding the process of advance procurements see Chapter 4, Section 4.5.1.

Relationships of procurement types — You should note that not all of the procurement types for the stock items listed earlier are always available. They can be used if the following prerequisites are met:

- To create a purchase requisition for a material component, in addition to its reservation, the material must permit external procurement (see the PROCUREMENT TYPE field of the MRP 2 view in the material master).

- To use procurement types with a reference to the plant stock, the material must permit collective stock management.

- For a procurement to be affected with a reference to a project or sales order stock, the material must permit individual stock management.

The stock management options of a material are controlled via the INDIVIDUAL/COLLECTIVE field of the MRP 4 view in the material master. For material components that you have transferred from a BOM, you can also overwrite the material master settings for procurement and stock options in the bill of materials, if necessary.

- Procurement types with a reference to the project stock are only available if the project definition allows for project stock management (see Chapter 1, Section 1.2.1 and Section 2.3.2).

- For you to select a procurement type with a reference to a sales order stock, the network header must be assigned to a sales order item. In addition, the position type must enable stock management for the sales order item.

You can specify the procurement type of a material component either manually—the system only offers the procurement types that are possible due to the settings in the material master or the BOM item, project definition, or sales order item—or you can use a *procurement indicator*.

Procurement indicators are defined in the Customizing of SAP Project System using Transaction OPS8 (see Figure 2.37). In a procurement indicator, you can specify the item category. You can also use the indicators PURCHASE REQUISITION NETWORK, 3RD PARTY, and PRELIMINARY REQUIREMENTS, and a prioritization of stock management to suggest the procurement type via a procurement indicator. The PURCHASE REQUISITION NETWORK indicator causes a reservation and a purchase requisition to be created at the same time for material components carried in project stock. By entering a procurement indicator in the network profile, you

Procurement indicators

can use this indicator as a default value for every assignment of a material component.

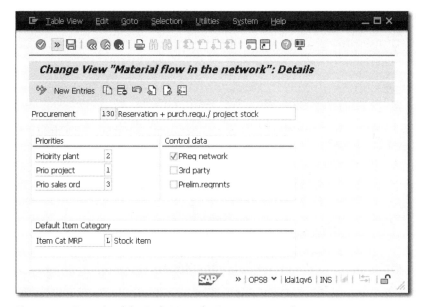

Figure 2.37 Example of the Definition of a Procurement Indicator

A manual selection of the item category and the procurement type for a material component isn't necessary if you use procurement indicators. If this is still permitted, however, you can also manually change a procurement type later.

Various options are available for the assignment of material components to network activities, which will be discussed in the following sections.

Manual Assignment

In every processing transaction for networks (except for the Project Editor), you can manually assign material components to activities, regardless of the activity category. Depending on the transaction, you can make this assignment individually, for example, via drag-and-drop from a templates area, or in a table (see Figure 2.38). If you don't work with procurement indicators, you must manually select the item category and the procurement type during this assignment. For stock items, you must also specify a material number before you can select the procurement type. If a third-party order is created later for the material component, a dialog displays where you are to specify the delivery address.

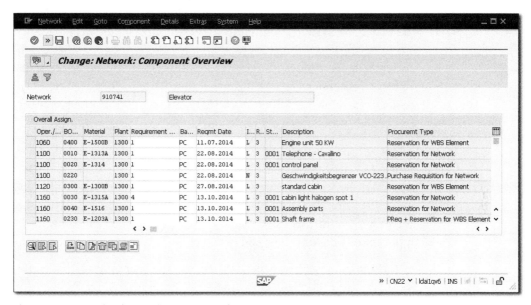

Figure 2.38 Example of a Tabular Overview of Material Components

Finally, for every material component, you enter the data necessary for planning and later procurement, unless this data is automatically transferred from the material master record or purchasing info records. In the detail screen of a material component on the PROCUREMENT PARAMETERS (PROC. PARAM) tab, you will find the relevant material master data, like the individual/collective stock or procurement indicator. This tab also shows the account assignment category, the consumption posting indicator, and the special stock indicator as well as the predefined movement type. If you want, you can go directly to the material master data display from the tabular overview of the material components.

Procurement parameters

If necessary, you can also use the OCI interface for a manual assignment of material components. Using this interface, you can employ the tabular overview of the material components of an activity to call an external catalog for selecting material. The external catalog can be a company-

OCI interface

internal intranet catalog, or a catalog of a fixed vendor that is accessible via the Internet.

After you have called a catalog and selected the material from this catalog, you can use the interface to transfer the data on the selected material to the SAP system and thereby add material components to an activity. If an appropriate material number for the catalog material can be detected in the SAP system in an appropriate mapping process, the material component can be assigned as a stock item; otherwise, it is assigned as a non-stock item. As of EHP 3, the additional item category C is available for copied components.

A prerequisite for using the OCI is that you define the external catalog and its call structure, that is, the URL and the corresponding parameters regarding user and password, for example, in Customizing, and then assign the catalog to the network. You can assign several catalogs to one network type. In this case, when you call the catalog interface in the application, a dialog opens and prompts you to select the catalog.

In Customizing, you also need to define the mapping of the catalog HTML fields to the fields of the material component in the SAP system. You might also have to specify conversions between catalog data and the field values in the SAP system. If necessary, you can also define conversion modules for determining material numbers, for example.

Material BOMs   In the SAP system, complex product structures can be mapped using bills of material. Depending on its usage, a bill of material contains a list of all materials required, for example, for the engineering, producing, or selling a product. A *material BOM* is essentially identified via the product's material number. The individual list elements for material listed in a bill of material are referred to as *BOM items* and, besides the appropriate material number, they include information about the required quantity, an item category, and other various kinds of information. Figure 2.39 shows an example of the material BOM for building the elevator.

There can also be a bill of material for the material of a BOM item (*assembly*); bills of material can be defined on multiple levels. In SAP Project System, you can use bills of material to assign BOM items as material components to network activities. This assignment can be handled manually or automated using *bill of material transfers*.

200

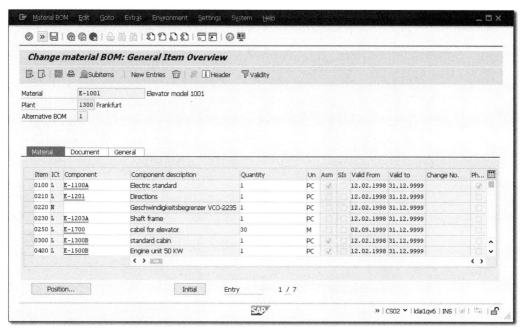

Figure 2.39 Example of a Material BOM

For a manual assignment of BOM items, call the EXPLODE BOM function in the component overview of an activity. A dialog box is then displayed in which you can specify the bill of material and the required quantity, and* where you can also determine whether the bill of material is to be exploded on one or on several levels. A list of all BOM items is then displayed, from which you can select the items to be assigned to the activity. With the assignment, the system finally receives the material number, the quantity, and the item category, for example, from the BOM items.

Bill of material (BOM) explosion

BOM Explosion and Text Items [+]

You can also first assign the BOM header material to the activity. After the BOM explosion of this component, the system automatically sets the item category T (text item) for this component. The material component is thus no longer relevant for procurement; however, the information—from which the bill of material items were assigned—is still visible.

A typical characteristic of many projects is their uniqueness. In sales and distribution projects, for example, the list of required material components can vary from one project to another due to the customer-specific requirements. Instead of creating a new bill of material and thus possibly a new material master for every project, you can define *WBS BOMs*. A WBS BOM is a bill of material that, in addition to the material number of the header material, is identified via a WBS element ID. Therefore, for the same material number, you can create different bills of material that can be distinguished by different WBS element IDs.

When creating WBS BOMs, you can use other bills of materials, for example, material or WBS BOMs, as a template (see Figure 2.40).

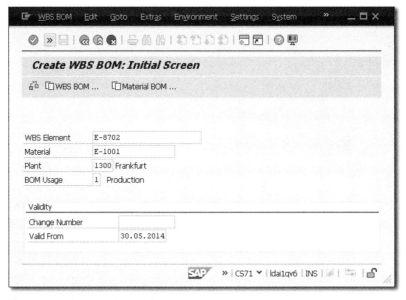

Figure 2.40 Creating a WBS BOM

Then you can adapt the WBS BOM to the requirements of the respective project by deleting items, adding new BOM items, or changing item data like the quantity, for example. You can use WBS BOMs not only for the highest level of a bill of material structure, but you can also define WBS BOMs for inferior levels as well. As with material BOMs, you can assign items from WBS BOMs to activities either manually via the BOM explosion or automatically via the bill of material transfer.

Bill of Material Transfer

Using the bill of material transfer (Transaction CN33), you can automate the assignment of BOM items to network activities. Using the bill of material transfer particularly makes sense if you need to assign a lot of material components to different activities, or if the bill of material structure might change in the course of project planning and you want to avoid a duplication of changes (on the one hand in the bill of material, on the other hand in the project).

The automated assignment of BOM items to network activities is typically performed via the REFERENCE POINT field that you can find in internally processed activities on the ASSIGNMENTS tab and in the BOM items in the BASIC DATA detail screen. If the value of the field in the BOM item is identical to the one of the activity, the bill of material transfer can automatically assign the item to the activity. *Prerequisites for the bill of material transfer*

The possible values of the REFERENCE POINT field must first be defined in the Customizing of SAP Project System. To do this, create an alphanumeric key with a maximum of 20 digits, and for every key, specify a descriptive text for information that can later be called via the F4 help when maintaining the reference points in the BOM or the network. *Reference point*

In the activities, you can also enter a reference point that represents several reference points of BOM items. You can do this by defining a key that ends with an asterisk (*). The reference point 130* shown in Figure 2.41, for example, represents the reference points 1301 and 1302.

Finally, you need to specify that the values of the REFERENCE POINT field of BOM items and activities will be compared during a bill of material transfer. To do that, in Customizing Transaction CN38, enter the technical name of the REFERENCE POINT field for the objects BOM items and network activities (see Figure 2.42).

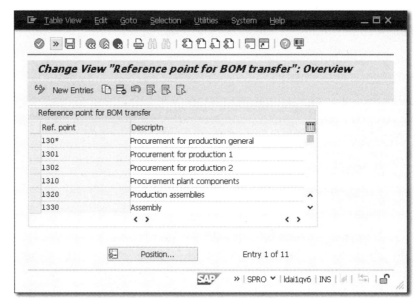

Figure 2.41 Example of the Definition of Reference Points

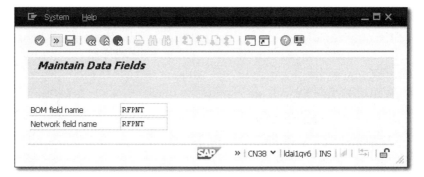

Figure 2.42 Specification of the Reference Point Field as Relevant to the Bill of Material Transfer

After you have defined the reference points in Customizing, you must enter these in the detail data of the relevant BOM items and activities. If you are already using standard networks as templates, you can enter reference points that are already in the activities of the standard networks.

[+]

Using Alternative Fields to Control the BOM Transfer

If you want, you can also specify other fields from activities and BOM items as transfer criteria, provided they have the same data structure. Prior to the introduction of the REFERENCE POINT field, for example, the SORT STRING field of the BOM items and a user field of the activities were often used.

If you call Transaction CN33 (Bill of Material Transfer), first select the projects to which material components are to be assigned and the bill of material items that are to be used for the assignment (see Figure 2.43).

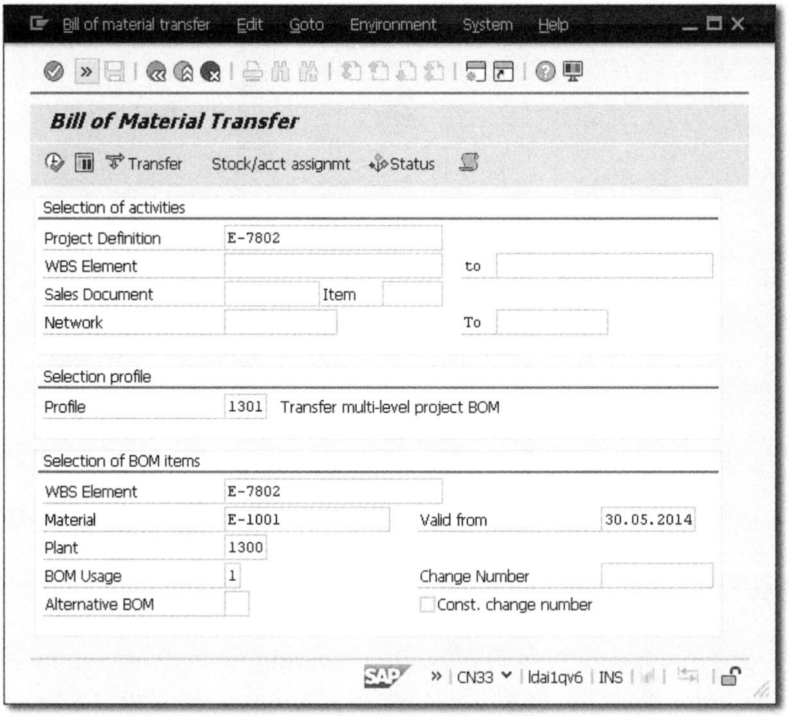

Process of the bill of material transfer

Figure 2.43 Initial Screen of the Bill of Material Transfer

For the bill of material transfer, you can use material or WBS BOMs. If necessary, you can also assign sales order BOMs which are identified, in addition to a material number, according to a sales order item. By specifying parameters for the bill of material transfer, you can control, for example, whether the BOM is to be exploded on multiple levels, or in which stocks the material components are to be managed; or, you can define additional filter criteria for selecting the BOM items (see Figure 2.44). If you want to avoid a manual parameter entry, you can define *bill of material transfer profiles* in the Customizing of SAP Project System that contains all controlling parameters (except for the stock management information; this could also be determined via the Procurement indicator). The profile can then be selected in the initial screen of the bill of material transfer.

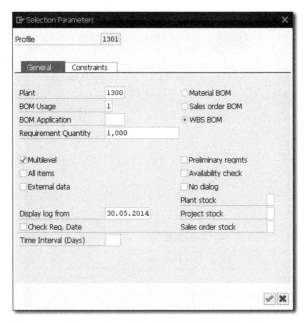

Figure 2.44 Parameters of the Bill of Material Transfer

If you then perform the bill of material transfer, the system automatically assigns all BOM items to activities that have the same reference point (see Figure 2.45). If you set the ALL ITEMS indicator in the bill of material selection parameter, you additionally get an overview of the items that cannot be also assigned due to missing reference points. In this case, you can still manually assign these positions to network activities before saving. If a unique automatic assignment is not possible because several of the selected activities have the same reference point, for example, the system issues an error message.

A significant advantage of the bill of material transfer is that you can adapt the material planning of your projects very efficiently to later BOM changes. If you have assigned BOM items to network activities using the bill of material transfer and the BOM is changed at a later stage (items are deleted, new items are added, or item data is changed), you can repeat the bill of material transfer for the changed BOM and the relevant networks. The system does not make a duplicate assignment, but only determines the BOM changes and suggests appropriate adjustments to the material components.

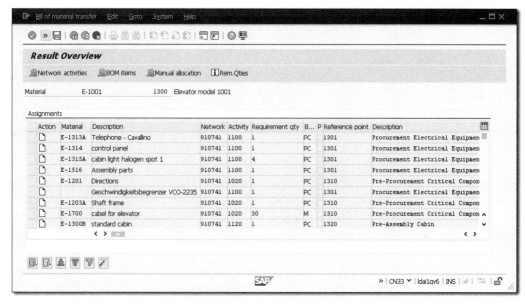

Figure 2.45 Example of the Result of a Bill of Material Transfer

iPPE Project System Integration

As of ECC Release 6.0, you can also assign material components to network activities via the *iPPE*. Using the iPPE, you can enter and further process master data of multivariant products in a model for engineering and production. This enables you to, for example, create complex product structures in the iPPE by at first using abstract elements like nodes, variants, alternatives, or relationships, and then using them later for mapping BOM data. The iPPE objects are edited in iPPE Workbench Professional (Product Designer; see Figure 2.46).

Integrated Product and Process Engineering

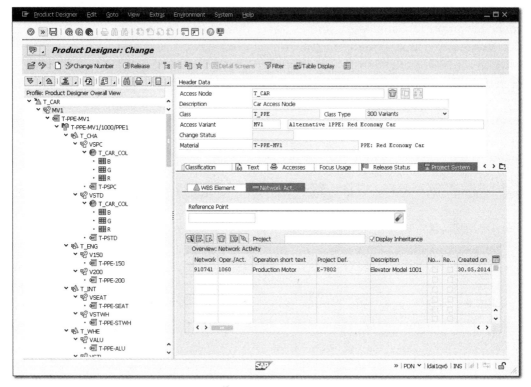

Figure 2.46 Example of Linking an iPPE Object to a Network Activity in iPPE Workbench Professional

Particularly when developing new products, parallel to the product structure creation, projects can be helpful to, for example, map the creation of prototypes or test parts. For this reason, you can link iPPE nodes and variants to WBS elements or network activities and then switch between the objects of the iPPE and SAP Project System. You can make these assignments in both the Product Designer, in the detail area of nodes or variants on the PROJECT SYSTEM tab, and in the Project Builder, in the detail screen of WBS elements or activities on the IPPE-PS tab. However, this tab is only available for projects if you set the IPPE PROJ. REL. indicator in the project or network profile in the Customizing of SAP Project System (see Chapter 1, Section 1.2.2 and Section 1.3.2).

The assignment can also be automated using *reference points*. Define the reference points for the iPPE PS integration in the Customizing of SAP Project System and store them both in the Project System and in the iPPE objects. Note that the reference points of the iPPE PS integration are not identical to the reference points of the bill of material transfer.

After assigning the iPPE objects to network activities, material can also be transferred from the iPPE product structure to SAP Project System. This takes place in the filter screen of iPPE Workbench Professional by selecting an appropriate initial object and then calling the TRANSFER TO PROJECT SYSTEM function.

2.3.2 Project Stock

The project stock is a form of individual stock management where material stocks with a reference to WBS elements can be managed as individual stock segments. Using the options NON-VALUATED STOCK, VALUATED STOCK, or NO PROJECT STOCK in the basic data of the project definition, you specify for a project whether a non-valuated or a valuated project stock management of material will be possible, or whether individual project stocks cannot be used (see Chapter 1, Section 1.2.1).

When the non-valuated project stock is used, every WBS element of the project represents a separate stock segment from the logistics point of view. Material movements with a reference to non-valuated project stock take place without being valuated. For example, when a material managed in a project stock is consumed by a network activity (goods issue for reservation), this does not cause actual costs for the activity, and no postings are made in financial accounting. The calculation of MRP networks determines that no planned costs for material components will be managed in the non-valuated project stock. The stockholding WBS element is debited with the actual costs for the external procurement only when the goods or invoice receipt for purchased parts is posted to the project stock. The cost flows in material procurements (in-house production and external procurement) with a reference to the non-valuated project stock are discussed in detail in Chapter 4, Section 4.5.1.

Non-valuated project stock

Project Controlling with Non-valuated Project Stock

When using a non-valuated project stock, the planned and actual costs for the material consumption are not completely disclosed for the network activities or the assigned production orders.

If you implement the non-valuated project stock, a meaningful cost object controlling is only possible on the level of the stockholding WBS elements or the entire project after the period-end closing.

By implementing planning networks (see Chapter 1, Section 1.3.2), you can also determine planned costs for material components managed in the non-valuated stock. Because these planned costs do not raise the assigned values of the higher level WBS elements, this prevents duplicate assigned values due to the planned material costs for the activity and the actual costs for the WBS element or production order.

Valuated project stock

Due to these disadvantages of the non-valuated project stock, the valuated project stock was provided as of SAP R/3 4.0. When using the valuated project stock, an accounting document reflecting the corresponding value flow is created with every material movement referencing the project stock. The network costing can determine planned costs for material components to be managed in the valuated project stock. The later consumption of the material by the activity results in actual costs for the activity and in the corresponding postings in financial controlling. Purchasing documents and production orders created in the course of material procurement for the project stock cause commitment, stock, and actual costs for the stockholding WBS element. The value flows for material procurements referencing valuated project stocks are discussed in detail in Chapter 4, Section 4.5.1.

Non-valuated project stocks are used primarily by companies that already implemented project stocks before SAP R/3 4.0 and want to stick to them for upward compatibility. You also need to work with non-valuated stocks if you want to use a sales order stock of the item category D for the stock management of material components in the project. Normally, however, it is recommended that you implement the valuated project stock if this is permitted by your business processes. Decision support for working with valuated and non-valuated project stocks can be found in the SAP Library.

Basically, a project stock is an individual stock per WBS element. Therefore, if necessary, you can manage a separate material stock for every subtree and separately valuate the procurement and stock costs for the stockholding WBS elements. While this is certainly positive from a controlling point of view, a stock management per WBS element has disadvantages from a logistics point of view. Because the individual stock segments are managed separately from an MRP point of view, a material requirements planning process (see Chapter 4, Section 4.5.1) creates separate purchase requisitions or planned orders for every stock segment, regardless of whether there is enough material available in another stock segment. If the same material is also required for other stock segments, however, it may make more sense to create a single purchase requisition or a single planned order covering the entire required quantity instead of triggering separate procurement processes for every stock segment. This enables you to negotiate better conditions with the vendor, for example, or to optimize the material production. To avoid the logistic disadvantages of individual stock management, you can use *requirements grouping* in SAP Project System.

Requirement grouping

In the simplest case, you use requirements grouping by setting the AUTOMATIC REQUIREMENTS GROUPING indicator in the project definition before saving it for the first time, or by storing the indicator in the project profile as a default value already. The top WBS element is then automatically identified in the BASIC DATA as a *grouping WBS element*. If the requirements grouping is not to take place for the top WBS element, you can also identify any other WBS element as a grouping WBS element before saving. Instead of managing a separate stock for every WBS element, automatic grouping causes all requirements and stocks of the project referencing the project stock to be managed exclusively on the level of this grouping WBS element. This means, in material requirements planning, only one WBS element is used as an individual stock segment, and all purchase requisitions, orders, or production orders referencing the project stock are assigned to this WBS element.

Automatic grouping

If you want to use several WBS elements of a project for a requirements grouping or make a cross-project requirements grouping, you need to use a manual requirements grouping. For a manual requirements grouping, on the BASIC DATA tab you identify those WBS elements for which

Manual requirements grouping

you want to group requirements as grouping WBS elements. Then, you assign the WBS elements the stocks that are to be grouped to the various grouping WBS elements. This assignment can be performed individually (Transaction GRM4) or, using appropriate selection conditions, for several WBS elements (Transaction GRM3).

Grouping WBS elements of type 2

If you want, you can also make the manual requirements grouping depend on the MRP group of the material (see the MRP 1 view in the material master). First, select option 2 (GROUPING WBS ELEMENT FOR SELECTED MRP GROUPS) in the GROUPING WBS ELEMENT field of the WBS elements used to group the requirements and stocks. Then these grouping WBS elements of type 2 are assigned the MRP groups, the materials of which are to be grouped (Transaction GRM5). Finally, you assign the relevant WBS elements to the grouping WBS elements using Transactions GRM3 or GRM4.

Prerequisites for requirements grouping

For the requirements and stocks of a material to be grouped automatically or manually, various prerequisites have to be met:

- The material must be manageable in an individual stock.
- You need to identify the MRP group of the material as relevant for a requirements grouping in the Customizing of SAP Project System.
- The project must permit a valuated project stock.
- To finally enable requirements that are not needed on exactly the same day to be grouped in a material planning process, the material should permit a period lot-sizing process (MRP LOT SIZE field of the view MRP 1 in the material master).

Material planning example

Figure 2.47 again illustrates the difference between material plannings with and without requirements grouping. No requirements grouping is used for sample project E-2606. Requirements for material E-1314 from different project parts are managed in separate stocks (E-2606-2-2 and E-2606-2-3). Although the material is even required on the same requirements date in both project parts, requirements planning has created separate purchase requisitions as planning-related procurement elements. In project E-2608, a requirements grouping is set on the level of the WBS element E-2608-2. The requirements for material E-1314 from different project parts are now managed in a common stock. The material provides a period lot-sizing process. Therefore, requirements planning has created only one procurement element for the total quantity of both requirements—although their requirements dates are different.

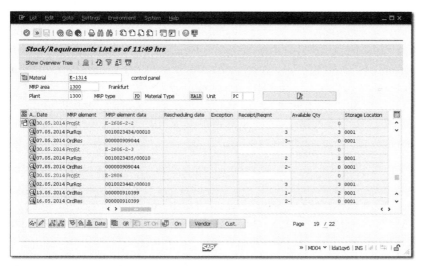

Figure 2.47 Example of a Material Planning with and without Requirements Grouping

> ### Grouping, Pegging, Distribution [+]
>
> The Grouping, Pegging, Distribution (GPD) component developed for the aerospace sector is an enhancement of the standard functions for project-based production procedures. GPD enables you to combine the advantages of optimized material procurement processes on the basis of cross-project requirements grouping with the advantages of detailed procurement cost controlling for individual WBS elements.
>
> The GPD pegging function first determines the proportional assignments of replenishment elements for a grouping WBS element to the objects that caused the requirements. The GPD cost distribution function then allocates the individually incurred costs of the grouping WBS elements to the individual WBS elements containing the original requirements. The SAP library provides further information on the usage of the GPD component.

2.3.3 Availability Check

The requirement dates of material components can either be specified manually or derived from the activity dates. Using the availability check, you can check during your material planning if the material components of the item category L are presumably available on the planned requirements dates, or if there will be a lack of material in the project due to missing stocks and long replenishment lead times, for example.

You can manually trigger an availability check for individual material components or for the entire network from every processing transaction for networks. In the Project Information System: Structures (see Chapter 6, Section 6.1), you can run an availability check for several networks simultaneously. Depending on the settings of the *check control*, you can also run an availability check automatically on every save after creation, release, or every relevant change.

Missing parts

If the availability check detects that a material probably cannot be provided on the planned requirements date, the relevant material components are identified as *missing parts*. Furthermore, the system sets the FMAT (MISSING MATERIAL AVAILABILITY) status on the network header level.

Scope of check

The availability check for material components is controlled by a *scope of check* that you can define using Transaction OPJJ in the Customizing of SAP Project System (see Figure 2.48). The scope of check defines, for example, if the check is to be run on plant or storage location level and which special stocks (quality inspection stock, safety stocks, etc.) are to be considered. The CHECK WITHOUT RLT indicator in the scope of check controls whether the replenishment lead time that you can store in the material master record of a material is to be considered in the availability check. If the indicator is not set, the availability check can suggest dates for missing parts on which the material can be provided.

Planned goods receipts and issues

In the scope of check, you can also define the planned goods receipts and issues to be considered in the availability check. Planned goods receipts can be, for example, purchase requisitions, orders, or planned or production orders that presumably cause a goods receipt before the requirements date of the material component. Planned goods issues represent reservations or planned independent requirements, for example, before the requirements date of the component.

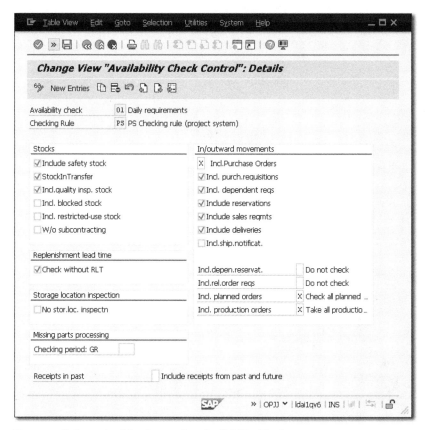

Figure 2.48 Example of the Scope of an Availability Check

In an availability check, the scope of check is determined for every material component using a combination of the value of the AVAILABILITY CHECK field in the material master record (View MRP 3) and a *checking rule*. The checking rule is stored in the *check control* (see Figure 2.49). Using the CROSS-PROJECT field (View MRP 3) in the material master record for components carried in an individual stock, you can also control whether the availability check is run only in the respective individual stock segment, or whether all individual stock segments plus the plant stock are included in the check.

Check control

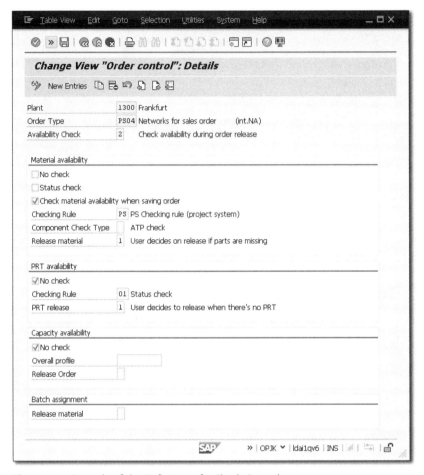

Figure 2.49 Example of the Definition of a Check Control

Checking rules and the check control are created in the Customizing of SAP Project System. The check control (Transaction OPJK) is defined based on the plant, the network type, and the statuses CREATED and RELEASED. In addition to the checking rule, the check control contains settings for automatically running the availability check and controls, for example, whether a release of activities is possible despite lacking material availability, and whether it requires user intervention or is even forbidden.

Material Assignment to Standard Networks

If you use standard networks as templates for operative networks (see Chapter 1, Section 1.3.3) and if operative networks constantly require the same material, you can assign the required material components to the corresponding activities of the existing standard networks. However, the assignment of material components to the standard networks is different from the assignment to activities of operative networks described previously.

Material components

In a first step, one or more material BOMs are assigned to the header of a standard network In a second step, from the assigned material BOMs, you then select those items that are later needed in the operative network and assign them to the relevant activities of the standard network (see Figure 2.50). Material that you have not assigned to any activity of the standard network is not copied to an operative network.

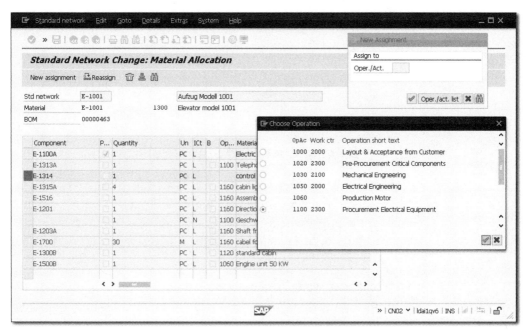

Figure 2.50 Example of the Assignment of Material Components to Activities of a Standard Network

[+]

BOM Explosion in Standard Networks

If a material BOM contains dummy assemblies, these are exploded so that their items can be assigned to standard network activities. Otherwise, the material BOM explosion takes place on only one level in the standard network.

Standard BOM

If you want to assign materials to standard network activities that are not used in any material BOM, you can first create a separate bill of material for the standard network header. You then add the required materials as items to this *standard BOM* and then assign them to the standard network activities. A standard BOM can only be used in the standard network in which it was created.

[◉]

Material Planning

The material for projects is planned by assigning it in the form of material components to network activities. During this assignment, you specify how the material is procured later and—in the case of stock items—in which stocks it is managed. The project stock allows you to manage individual stocks for material with a reference to WBS elements as individual stock segments. There are different options for assigning material components; for example, you can assign material components to activities in standard networks.

2.4 Planning Costs and Statistical Key Figures

Based on the resource and material planning using networks, as described earlier, the system can automatically calculate the planned costs for the procurement and the consumption of resources and material. This form of cost planning is referred to as *network costing*, which is discussed in detail in Section 2.4.6.

If you only use work breakdown structures for mapping projects, you manually plan costs on the WBS element level for the later performance of the individual project parts.

A manual cost planning using WBS elements can also make sense, although you are using networks if these networks are exclusively used for time scheduling, or if you use cost planning on the WBS element level only for a preliminary planning, for example, and want to detail it later via network costing. You can use several options for cost planning with WBS elements, which are discussed in Section 2.4.1 through Section 2.4.4. A significant difference between these options is the level of detail in the planning. Two important criteria for a cost planning's level of detail are the characteristics BY COST ELEMENT and BY PERIOD.

If a cost planning references one or more cost element, this type of cost planning is referred to as a planning *by cost element*. Cost elements are defined in the Cost Element Accounting of Controlling and correspond to the cost-relevant chart of accounts items. Using cost elements, you can structure and classify the consumption of production factors that is valuated with regard to the business purpose. Using cost element reports (see Chapter 6, Section 6.2.2) or hierarchy reports (see Chapter 6, Section 6.2.1) of Reporting, you can analyze costs planned by cost elements with regard to their business purpose-related usage.

Cost planning by cost element

Cost Planning Options by Cost Element   [+]

For a cost planning by cost elements for WBS elements, you can use unit costing (see Section 2.4.2), detailed planning (see Section 2.4.3), and Easy Cost Planning (see Section 2.4.4) in SAP Project System. Calculations using networks (see Section 2.4.6) are always performed by cost element as well.

If a cost planning references the period of the projected cost to be incurred, this type of cost planning is referred to as being period based. Cost planning by date allow you to analyze planned costs for a specific period (for example, monthly) in Reporting and to compare them to the actual costs incurred during a period.

Cost planning by period

Cost Planning Options by Period   [+]

Options of cost planning by period in SAP Project System include the detailed planning (see Section 2.4.3) and network costing (see Section 2.4.6). Easy Cost Planning is only conditionally date-specific (see Section 2.4.4); the other cost planning forms in SAP Project System are period-independent or only reference fiscal years, but not individual periods of a fiscal year.

When you plan costs for WBS elements, you always reference a CO versions. CO versions can be defined in Customizing and contain a number

CO versions

of control parameters for their usages in CO and in SAP Project System (see Figure 2.51).

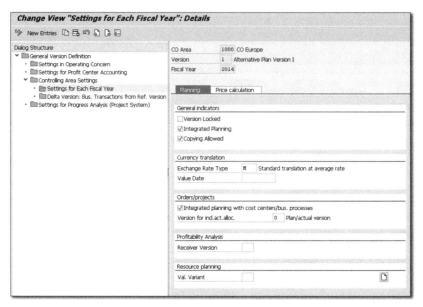

Figure 2.51 CO Version Settings Dependent on Fiscal Year and Controlling Area

Depending on the form of cost planning used, the CO version is either preset in Customizing, or you select it manually when entering the cost planning.

CO versions enable you to plan several different costs for a single WBS element. In an early planning phase of your project, for example, you can select a rough form of cost planning and save the corresponding planned costs in CO version 1. Later, during detailed planning, you can use a more detailed cost planning form to store the planned values in CO version 0. In Reporting, you can then compare your rough planning values to those of the detailed planning. The most detailed planned values of a project should be saved to CO version 0 because the actual costs are also stored in this version. The planned costs of network costing are saved to version 0 by default.

Using the copy functions (Transactions CJ9BS, CJ9B, CJ9FS, and CJ9F), you can copy the planned values of a CO version to another CO version and further process them there, independent of the original CO version. Using Transactions CJ9CS and CJ9C, you can also transfer the actual costs of WBS elements from version 0 as planned costs to a CO version.

The manual cost planning for WBS elements requires the definition of a *planning profile* in the Customizing of SAP Project System (see Figure 2.52). A planning profile contains control parameters for the different cost planning options for WBS elements. The planning profile specifies, for example, if a manual cost planning is to be permitted only for WBS elements with the operative indicator PLANNING ELEMENT set (see Chapter 1, Section 1.2.1) or for all WBS elements. The planning profile to be used is entered in the project definition of a project. In the project profile, you can store a default value for the planning profile of projects.

Planning profile

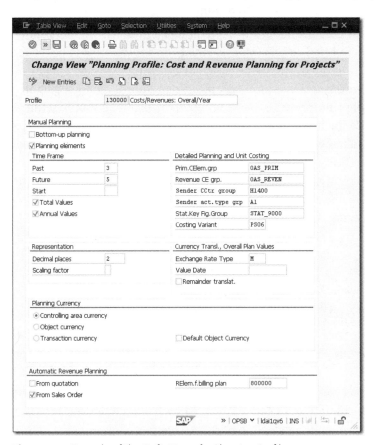

Figure 2.52 Example of the Definition of a Planning Profile

Depending on the form of cost planning used, more settings are necessary in Customizing. These settings and the relevant control parameters of the planning profiles are discussed in the following sections about the different cost planning forms.

If, in addition to the costs, you also want to plan other elements with quantity or time units, for example, you can use the statistical key figure planning function in SAP Project System.

As of EHP 6, new user interfaces as well as a new user role, PROJECT PLANNER AND COST ESTIMATOR, are available, especially for cost planning.

2.4.1 Hierarchical Cost Planning

Overall/structure planning

Hierarchical cost planning on the WBS element level, which is sometimes also referred to as *overall planning* or *structure planning*, is the roughest form of cost planning. It is not based on cost elements or on dates. However, a hierarchical cost planning requires the least planning effort of all planning forms. Depending on the planning profile settings, you can use the hierarchical cost planning to plan *total value total values* (planned values without a reference to fiscal years) or planned values for individual fiscal years. The planning profile then also controls the time horizon to be available for the fiscal year planning. If you want, you can also use the hierarchical cost planning to plan both total values and values referencing fiscal years.

[+] **Restrictions of Hierarchical Cost Planning**

A distribution of planned costs to the periods of a fiscal year is not possible using the hierarchical cost planning. In a hierarchical cost planning, you manually determine the fiscal years for which you want to plan the costs. They are not derived from the planned dates of the projects. In addition, the values of the hierarchical cost planning don't reference cost elements; this form of cost planning is therefore not performed by cost elements.

You perform cost planning by entering total or fiscal year values in the COST PLAN column of the table displayed by Transaction CJ40 for those WBS elements that permit cost planning (see Figure 2.53). More columns (views) inform you about the hierarchical distribution of planned values, planned costs that were planned via other cost planning forms, or the planned values of the previous fiscal year or the sum of all fiscal year values, respectively.

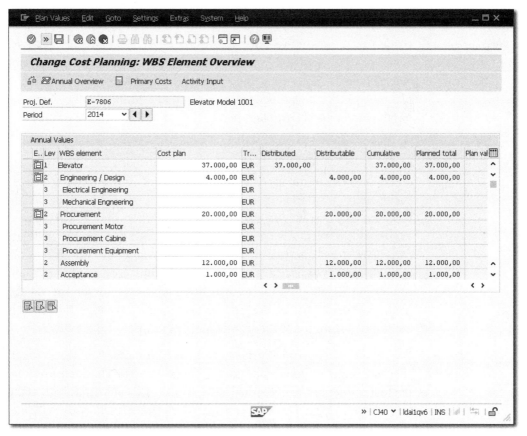

Figure 2.53 Example of a Hierarchical Cost Planning

The PLANNED TOTAL view shows the total of all planned costs for a WBS element in the respective CO version and the corresponding fiscal year, regardless of the cost planning form via which they were entered. In particular, the planned total also includes the planned costs of additive orders (see Section 2.4.7) and networks or network activities (see Section 2.4.6) that are assigned to the WBS element.

Planned total

Copy view and
reassess functions

If you want, you can transfer view values as hierarchical planned values for selected WBS elements using the COPY VIEW function. You can determine the percentage of these values to be copied and whether they are to be added to the original values or transferred as new values. The REVALUATE function enables you to increase or reduce planned values of selected WBS elements by a specific percentage or amount.

Total up function

Using the TOTAL-UP function, you can derive the hierarchical planned values of WBS elements from the total of planned values of the inferior WBS elements. By setting the BOTTOM-UP PLANNING indicator in the planning profile, this function can also be run automatically when saving the hierarchical cost planning.

Currencies during
hierarchical cost
planning

Depending on the planning profile settings, you can use the hierarchical cost planning to plan values in the project controlling area currency, the object currency of the individual WBS elements, or in a freely selectable currency (transaction currency). In the last case, you can store a default value for this currency in the initial screen. When saving, the planned values are automatically converted to the CO area and respective object currencies as well, and saved to the database in all three currencies if the ALL CURRENCIES indicator is set in the controlling area. For total values, conversion details like the exchange rate type are controlled via the planning board profile. For annual values, the exchange rate type is determined from the fiscal year-dependent settings of the CO version.

Planned values
check

You can save the planned values of a hierarchical cost planning without checking them, or you can perform a check first. The check ensures that the total values of the individual WBS elements are at least as high as the total of their annual values, and that the planned values of WBS elements are higher than or equal to the planned values of the hierarchically inferior WBS elements.

Plan line item

If you want, you can define a user status (see Chapter 1, Section 1.6) that permits the business process WRITE PLAN LINE ITEMS. In this case, after setting this status in the project, every change to the hierarchical cost planning is stored in a separate document (plan line item) together with information about the date and the changing user and can therefore be easily traced later.

As of EHP 6, you can also use a Web Dynpro or Excel interface instead of SAP GUI for hierarchical cost planning. This allows for advanced function and configuration options (see Section 2.4.5).

2.4.2 Unit Costing

In Transaction CJ40, you can also create unit costings for planning costs for WBS elements. With unit costing, you can use prices for material, external and internal services from materials management, or purchasing, respectively, for the cost planning of your projects, or refer to CO rates for planning costs for internal activities. Unit costing for WBS elements is cost element-specific but not date-specific.

As with the hierarchical cost planning, the planned values of unit costing can be entered based on the planning profile settings either with a reference to individual fiscal years or independent of fiscal years as total values.

> **Restrictions of Unit Costing** **[+]**
>
> When using unit costing for planning costs for WBS elements, a distribution of values to interim periods is also not feasible. For fiscal year-dependent unit costing, the fiscal years are not derived from the planned dates of the projects, but instead must be selected manually.

When you create a unit costing for a WBS element in Transaction CJ40, you first get an empty list in which you can enter Costing Items item line by line (see Figure 2.54). When creating a costing item, you first specify an *item category*. This item category now determines which data you need to enter for cost planning and which data is automatically determined by the system. In the following text, some of the most important item categories are described.

The item category E (INTERNAL ACTIVITY) is for planning costs for services that are to be provided by cost centers for a WBS element. In a costing item for the item category E, you enter a cost center, the corresponding activity type, and the quantity of the planned activity input.

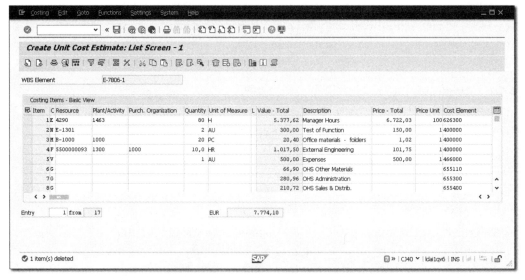

Figure 2.54 Example of the Unit Costing of a WBS Element

Price calculation From the Cost Center Accounting of CO, the system then automatically determines the *price* of the combination of activity type and cost center and thus valuates the planned quantity. From the master record of the activity type, the system uses the cost element for which the planned values are reported, and the text and the unit of measure for the activity.

Using costing items of the item categories F (EXTERNAL ACTIVITY) or L (SUBCONTRACTING), you can plan costs for external activities or subcontracting. For this purpose, you specify a purchasing info record, a plant, a purchasing organization, the planned quantity, and the cost element. From this data, the system automatically determines a price, the unit of measure, and the text, and calculates the appropriate item value.

Service costs are planned using the item category N (SERVICE). Using the quantity and service you specify, the system determines the price, the unit of measure, and the text, and calculates the item value. The cost element is transferred from the master record of the service.

Material costs can be planned in unit costing using the item category M (MATERIAL). Specify the material number, the plant, and the planned quantity, and the system uses this data to determine the price, the unit of measure and the text for the material. The cost element for the item value is derived via the automatic account determination.

If data, such as activity type and prices, purchasing info records, or material master records, are not available, you can freely plan costs in unit costing via the item category V (VARIABLE ITEM). You manually enter a planned quantity, a price, the cost element, and a descriptive text, if you like. The system then only determines the item value by multiplying the price and the quantity.

If you keep implementing similar combinations of costing items for your project cost planning, you can use Transaction KKE1 (Create Base Planning Object) to define *templates* for unit costing. Using the item category B (BASE PLANNING OBJECT), you can then reference these base planning objects in unit costing and use their planned values or even explode their individual costing items and copy them into the unit costing.

Base planning object

Because the individual costing items always reference a cost element, the system can also calculate overhead rates for unit costing. The overhead calculation is controlled by the costing sheet of the respective WBS elements (see Chapter 5, Section 5.3) and takes place automatically when saving the unit costing. If you want, however, you can trigger the overhead calculation when creating a unit costing. In unit costings, overhead rates are reported as items of the item category G (OVERHEAD RATE).

Overhead costs

If you also implement Activity-Based Costing or template allocation (see Chapter 5, Section 5.4) for clearing overhead costs, you can use the item categories X (MANUAL PROCESS COSTS) and P (PROCESS COSTS DETERMINED) in unit costing.

When you save the unit costing for a WBS element, the total of the unit costing is displayed in Transaction CJ40 in the UNIT COSTING view and is included in the value of the view PLANNED TOTAL for the corresponding WBS element. Plan line items cannot be saved for unit costing.

Unit costing for WBS elements is controlled by the *costing variant* you define in the planning profile. Costing variants for unit costing for WBS elements can be defined via Transaction OKKT in the Customizing of

Costing variant

SAP Project System. A costing variant references a *costing type* and a *valuation variant*. The costing type determines the technical properties of costing and usually doesn't require any additional settings in SAP Project System.

Valuation variant The valuation variant of a costing variant uses strategies to control the rates and prices to be applied for determining the planned costs of internal activities, external activities, and material in unit costing. Figure 2.55 shows an example of a possible strategy for determining prices for internal activities. Using the CO VERSION PLAN/ACTUAL field, you can control the CO version from which the prices are to be retrieved.

For calculating the overhead rates for WBS elements, the system always uses the costing sheet in the master data of the respective WBS elements. The costing sheet you can specify in a valuation variant is therefore not applicable in unit costing for WBS elements.

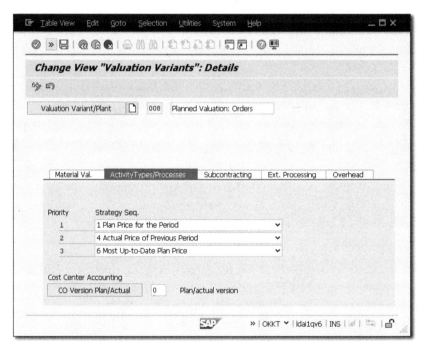

Figure 2.55 Example of Defining a Strategy for Determining Prices in a Valuation Variant

2.4.3 Detailed Planning

Detailed planning for WBS elements is a form of cost planning that considers both cost elements and dates. In a detailed planning for costs on the WBS element level, we distinguish between *cost element planning* and *activity input planning*. You can call detailed planning (cost element and activity input planning) via Transaction CJ40 or directly via Transaction CJR2. Like cost element and activity input planning, you can use detailed planning for planning statistical key figures, or CO resources, or for payment scheduling as well.

In the cost element planning, you select those cost elements from a list (typically primary cost elements) for which you want to plan costs, and enter a planned amount for a fiscal year or a specific consolidation period (see Figure 2.56). This amount can be distributed to individual periods in the period screen of the cost element planning. If a cost element permits the management of quantity information, you can enter a planned quantity in addition to the planned amount in the cost element planning; this planned amount can later be used, for example, for a quantity-dependent application of overhead.

Cost element planning

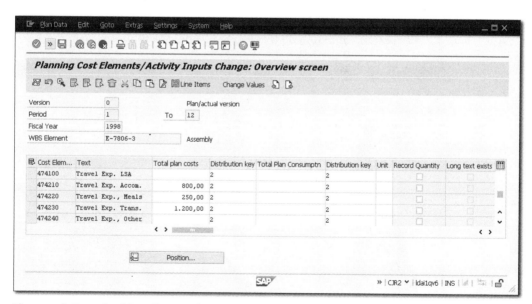

Figure 2.56 Example of Cost Element Planning in the Overview Screen

Distribution key   Using distribution keys, the system can perform the distribution to separate periods automatically. The standard distribution key 1, for exam-
ple, equally distributes to all periods, while key 7 results in a distribution based on the calendar days of the respective periods. The standard
version provides a number of distribution keys. Via the ⌐F1⌐ help for the
DISTRIBUTION KEY field, you can display examples of the various distribution keys. If you want, you can also define your own distribution keys in
the Customizing Transaction KP80 by storing a factor for every period
that determines the division of the values.

Activity input   In the activity input planning, you can plan activities that you want to
planning   use from cost centers in the course of the project. Enter the cost centers,
the respective activity types, and the planned quantities (see Figure
2.57). From the Cost Center Accounting of CO, the system then automatically determines the prices of the individual combinations of cost
centers and activity types during the respective periods and thereby calculates the planned costs. The system uses the prices from the CO version that you entered in the fiscal year/dependent data of the CO version
of your cost planning. The relevant cost elements are transferred automatically from the master record of the activity types. Just like in the
cost element planning, you can manually distribute the values to different periods or automate this process using distribution keys.

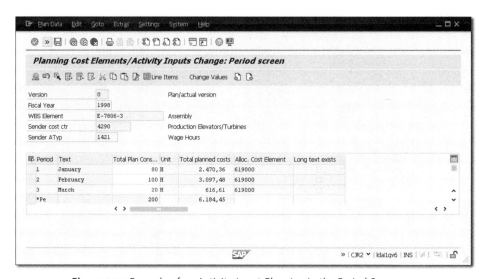

Figure 2.57 Example of an Activity Input Planning in the Period Screen

Restrictions in Detailed Planning **[+]**

In the detailed planning, you need to determine the cost planning periods; so the cost element and activity input periods are not derived from the planned dates of the WBS elements. Therefore, date shifts of projects or project parts don't automatically affect the cost distribution of a detailed planning.

A special function that you can implement when using the activity input planning is the *integrated planning*. In an integrated planning of activity input, not only are the planned costs determined for the WBS elements, but your Planned Activity Input is immediately reported in Cost Center Accounting as scheduled activities for the affected cost centers and can be factored in your company's cost center planning. You also have the option of a planned settlement for cost centers or business processes if you use an integrated planning. To use an integrated cost planning, you need to set the INTEGRATED PLANNING indicator in the relevant WBS elements (this can be predefined via the project profile), and the CO version must explicitly permit integrated planning in the detail screen of the fiscal year-dependent data.

Integrated planning

Because the detailed planning—both as cost element and as activity input planning—always references cost elements, you can also plan overhead rates using the planned data. In contrast to unit costing for WBS elements, this is not handled automatically when saving the cost planning, but must be manually triggered via Transactions CJ46 or CJ47. The calculation of the overhead rates is controlled via the costing sheets of the individual WBS elements.

Overhead rates

Just as in the hierarchical cost planning, plan line items are also written in the detailed planning if this is explicitly permitted by the status of the respective WBS elements. Using these plan line items, you can later analyze every change of the detailed planning separately. In an integrated planning, plan line items are automatically written, whether a status permits this business process or not.

Plan line item

Planning layouts specify the individual entry screens of the detailed planning. SAP provides various planning layouts. If you want, however, you can define your own planning layouts in Customizing. You can use the Report Painter tool to create planning layouts (see Chapter 6, Section 6.2).

Planning layouts

The planning layouts for the different masks of the cost element and activity input planning are grouped in a *planner profile* (see Figure 2.58). You can use predefined planner profiles or create your own profiles in Customizing. The planner profile also controls whether integration with Microsoft Excel is possible.

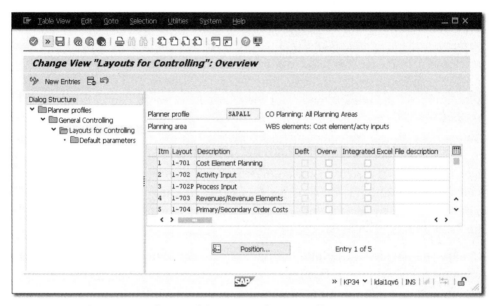

Figure 2.58 Definition of the SAPALL Planner Profile

Planner profile   If you start the detailed planning from Transaction CJ40, the SAP101 planner profile and the planning layouts it contains are automatically used for the cost element and activity input planning. The cost elements, cost centers, and activity types available in the detailed planning via Transaction CJ40 can be controlled via the planning profile of the project definition. In the planning profile, store the corresponding cost element, cost center, and activity type groups, which you can define in advance using Transactions KAH1, KSH1, and KLH1.

If you use Transaction CJR2 for the detailed planning, you can manually select the planner profile via the settings. Using the PPP parameter, you can also store the planner profile to be used in Transaction CJR2 in the SAP user data. In the initial screen of Transaction CJR2, you can select the planning layout you want to use for the planning. If you have not set default parameters in the planner profile, you will have to manually specify information about the CO version, the periods, the cost elements, or the cost centers and activity types of the cost planning later. In addition, you must specify the WBS elements for which you want to plan costs. Instead of specifying single WBS elements or intervals of WBS elements, you can also enter a WBS element group if it has been previously defined in Transaction CJSG.

2.4.4 Easy Cost Planning

The term *Easy Cost Planning* refers to another function that enables you to plan costs for WBS elements. As of EHP 3, you can also use Easy Cost Planning for cost planning at network activity level. Similar to unit costing, the Easy Cost Planning uses existing CO, Purchasing, or MM data in the form of costing items. However, if you want to repeatedly calculate similar costs, the Easy Cost Planning allows you to previously define *costing models* (planning templates) and thereby considerably simplifies entering the required costing data. Cost planning using Easy Cost Planning takes into account cost elements.

Cost planning for WBS elements and networks

> **Easy Cost Planning and Planning Periods**   [+]
>
> Easy Cost Planning determines the period of the planned costs of a project element from the order start date of the element. If the planned duration of an element spans several periods, the planned costs are not distributed automatically. The planned costs are reported in the period containing the order start date of the element. If the order start date of the element shifts, you simply need to call Easy Cost Planning again to automatically adapt the period of the planned costs to the period of the new order start date. If you want to distribute the costs across several periods, you must manually store a latest end date for the items in Easy Cost Planning and adapt that date in the case of retroactive scheduling changes.

Easy Cost Planning for a project can be started from the Project Builder or by using Transaction CJ9ECP. In the left hand area of the Easy Cost Planning, you will find the costing structure, that is, the hierarchical structure of the work breakdown structure. Depending on the structure tree setting in the Project Builder, the Easy Cost Planning displays the identifications or the names of the project elements. If you select an element in the costing structure that permits a cost planning, you can calculate costs for this element in the right hand area.

Item view
There are two different ways of calculation. One option is to display an *item view* and to create a list of costing items as in unit costing for WBS elements (see Section 2.4.2). Depending on the respective item category, you need to manually specify information about cost centers, activity types, material numbers, purchasing info records, cost elements, etc. When this data is transferred, the system automatically uses the costing sheets in the respective project elements to calculate overhead rates and then display the planned costs in the costing structure.

Usage of planning templates
If the same data continues to be relevant for the costing items, you can previously store it in the planning templates. Instead of manually creating costing items and specifying cost centers, activity types, and so on, you can simply reference these planning templates in Easy Cost Planning and automatically derive all necessary costing data. The derivation of the costing data is not static but dynamic, using formulas and activation conditions that you can define in the planning template. Therefore, if you have assigned a planning template to a WBS element in Easy Cost Planning, you first need to specify all parameters that are used in the formulas and conditions of the planning template to derive the relevant costing items and the quantities contained therein. This parameter specification is referred to as *characteristic valuation*. If you want, you can also enter a descriptive text for the assignment of a value to the characteristics.

Figure 2.59 presents an example of using a planning template in Easy Cost Planning. In this example, due to the planning template settings, the valuation of the INTERNAL LABOR HOURS characteristic with a value of 80 HOURS causes activities of cost center 4290 to be automatically planned for two different activity types with the quantities 56 or 24 hours, respectively. The value specified for the ADDITIONAL COSTS characteristic is transferred as the price for a variable item. The planning template stored all other necessary data of the variable item, such as the cost element, for example.

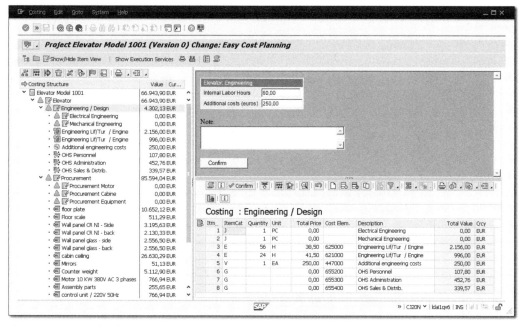

Figure 2.59 Example of a Cost Planning Using Easy Cost Planning

Using the SUBDIVIDE COST ESTIMATE function, you can assign several planning templates to a project element. If you want, you can also manually supplement the costing items derived from the planning templates in the item view with new items. In an Easy Cost Planning worklist, you can store frequently used planning templates as a default quantity and further simplify cost planning.

Assigning several planning templates

Planning templates or costing models are defined in three steps using Transaction CKCM (see Figure 2.60):

Definition of planning templates

1. In the first step, you define the characteristics and their possible values that you want to use in the characteristic valuation and in the definition of formula and conditions.

2. Using these characteristics, the system automatically creates an input screen that can later be used for a characteristic valuation in Easy Cost Planning. In the second step, you can adjust this HTML-based input screen to your specific requirements, if necessary.

235

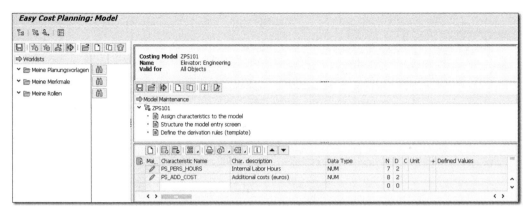

Figure 2.60 Definition of Planning Templates for Easy Cost Planning

3. In the third step, you define the *derivation rules* that specify how to automatically determine costing items from the characteristic values (see Figure 2.61). In this step, you first create all costing items that can show up in the calculation, and then for every item, you determine the conditions that should cause the item to actually be included in a calculation via the ACTIVATION field.

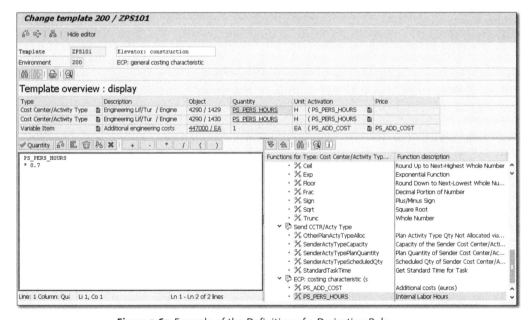

Figure 2.61 Example of the Definition of a Derivation Rule

There is a dedicated editor for defining the conditions; in particular, you can use the planning template characteristics for defining the conditions.

[+]

Using Characteristics in Planning Templates
If you have already defined appropriate characteristics in the central logistic functions, (for example, for classification purposes), you can use these when defining planning templates. If characteristics should only be used for planning templates, you can store class 051 as a constraint in these characteristics.

You also specify the item category for the individual costing items and—depending on the item category—the required costing data such as cost center, activity type, material number, etc. For the QUANTITY and PRICE fields, you can enter fixed values or defined formulas. Formulas are defined via a formula editor where you can use the characteristics of the planning template again.

Just like the unit costing for WBS elements, the costing using Easy Cost Planning is controlled via the costing variant you stored in the planning profile. The valuation variant within the costing variant employs strategies for controlling the rates and prices to be used for internal and external activities or material, for example, when calculating the individual item values (see Section 2.4.2). In Customizing, depending on the CO area, you also specify the CO version in which to save the planned values of the Easy Cost Planning. If necessary, you can also allow for revenue planning using Easy Cost Planning in the Customizing. You can then enter variable items for revenue elements in Easy Cost Planning for billing elements. If you want to use Easy Cost Planning for network activities, you must explicitly activate this function via the respective Customizing activity in Customizing of SAP Project System.

Customizing of Easy Cost Planning

You can also use Easy Cost Planning for cost planning in several CO versions. To do this, not only must you store the standard CO version for Easy Cost Planning in Customizing, but also the CO versions in which you want to allow an additional cost planning via Easy Cost Planning (see Figure 2.62).

Easy Cost Planning in several CO versions

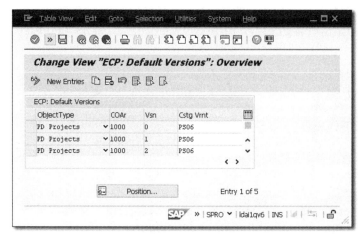

Figure 2.62 Example for Defining Alternative CO Versions for Easy Cost Planning

After you have specified the alternative CO versions for Easy Cost Planning, enable the Easy Cost Planning in several CO versions using Transaction RCNPRECP. If you now start Easy Cost Planning for a project, a dialog is displayed where you can select the CO version in which you want to plan the costs. If you want, you can also copy planned data of the Easy Cost Planning from one CO version to another.

Additional functions More functions of the Easy Cost Planning that are not available in the other forms of cost planning for WBS elements are:

▸ **Usage in simulation versions**
Easy Cost Planning can be implemented for the cost planning in simulation versions.

▸ **Copying**
When creating a project using a template of another operative project, the planned data of the Easy Cost Planning can be copied as well if you want.

▸ **Execution Service**
During the implementation phase of projects, you can use *Execution Services* to post activity allocations, purchase requisitions, or goods issues, for example, for WBS elements directly in Easy Cost Planning. The system suggests the planned data of the Easy Cost Planning for creating the respective documents (see Chapter 4, Section 4.2.3).

As of EHP 6, the COST ESTIMATION ON PROJECTS (FCOM_ECP_OVP) application also provides a Web Dynpro interface for cost planning with Easy Cost Planning. Transaction FCOM_ECP_GEN enables you to automatically configure existing planning templates for the new Web Dynpro interface and use them for cost estimates.

2.4.5 Project Planner and Cost Estimator

With EHP 6, SAP introduced a new role, PROJECT PLANNER AND COST ESTIMATOR (SAP_CO_PROJECT_PLANNER). This role includes several of the described cost planning functions as well as enhanced functions and reports in new Web Dynpro-based editing interfaces. Transaction PFCG enables you to view details of the role and of the linked Web Dynpro applications and to implement modifications, for example, add new applications to the role's menu. After you have assigned the role to a user, the system automatically provides the corresponding role menu when this user calls SAP NetWeaver Business Client (NWBC) (see Figure 2.63).

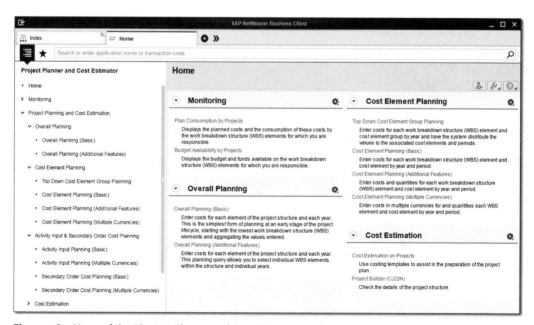

Figure 2.63 Menu of the "Project Planner and Cost Estimator" Role in NWBC

Web Dynpro applications The applications for cost planning with a Web Dynpro-based interface are available as of EHP 6 by default. You can call these applications with the new role in NBWC or start them as Web Dynpro applications, independent of the role and NWBC:

- OVERALL PLANNING
- COST ELEMENT AND ACTIVITY INPUT PLANNING
- TOP-DOWN COST ELEMENT GROUP PLANNING
- ACTIVITY INPUT PLANNING
- SECONDARY ORDER COST PLANNING
- COST ESTIMATION ON PROJECTS

Configuration options Floorplan Manager enables you to configure the interfaces of these applications to adapt them to your requirements. Except for the cost estimation, the technology of all applications mentioned above is based on the BW Integrated Planning infrastructure. One of the advantages of BW Integrated Planning is that you can flexibly integrate report data into the planning applications (see Figure 2.64).

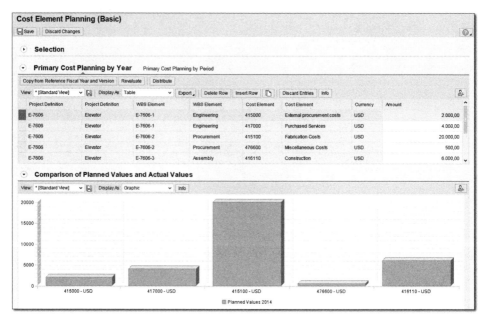

Figure 2.64 Example of Cost Element Planning with the New Web Dynpro-Based Editing Interface

Furthermore, you can use specific functions, for example, for cost distribution or aggregation, and enhanced configuration options. The PROJECT PLANNER AND COST ESTIMATOR view contains several examples of the usage of these additional functions, for example, top-down cost element group planning in detailed planning or planning with multiple currencies. Transaction RSPLAN enables you to define additional customer-specific planning functions if required.

The BW infrastructure also allows for planning via a Microsoft Excel interface. This function is available independent of the PROJECT PLANNER AND COST ESTIMATOR role and NWBC if you use SAP BusinessObjects Analysis or SAP Business Explorer Analyzer (BEx Analyzer). Figure 2.65 shows an example of overall planning in Microsoft Excel using SAP BusinessObjects Analysis.

Microsoft Excel planning

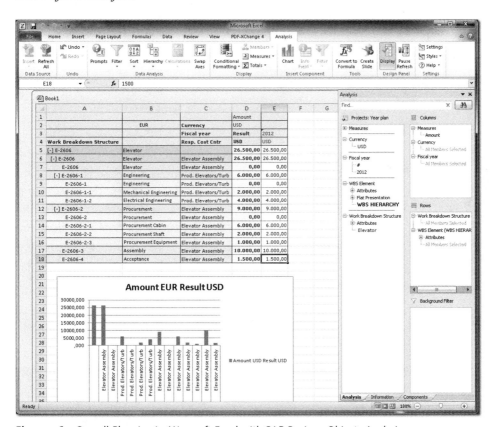

Figure 2.65 Overall Planning in Microsoft Excel with SAP BusinessObjects Analysis

To be able to use applications that are based on BW Integrated Planning, you must implement some settings first. On the one hand, you have to configure SAP Business Warehouse (SAP BW) locally in a client of your SAP ERP system and specify this client for further modeling (Customizing Transactions RSRTS_ACTIVATE_R3IS and RODPS_ODP_IMG). On the other hand, you have to activate necessary SAP Business Warehouse Content (BI Content). You can do this either by using the Data Warehousing Workbench (Transaction RSOR) or by directly activating the BI Content bundle /ERP/FCOM_PLANNING in Customizing Transaction BSANLY_BI_ACTIVATION.

[+] | **Planning Rounds**

In many enterprises, cost planning is carried out regularly, for example, yearly, and for the entire enterprise on the basis of cost centers, internal orders, and projects. In this context, the planning processes must usually be performed by various departments in a certain order and pass the relevant approvals. As of EHP 6, this procedure is supported with *planning rounds* into which the new Overall Planning and Cost Element Planning on Projects applications can also be integrated.

2.4.6 Network Costing

If you use networks for structuring your projects, the network costing function is available for automatically determining planned costs using the activity, activity element, and material component data. Similar to the unit costing for WBS elements or Easy Cost Planning, network costing also uses existing data from CO, Purchasing, or MM for calculating the planned costs. The planned costs always reference cost elements and dates, which means that network costing is a cost element- and date-specific type of planning.

[+] | **Network Costing and Planning Periods**

During network costing, the periods of the planned costs can be derived automatically from the basic dates of the activities, activity elements, and requirement dates of material components. If activities or activity elements span several periods, the system can also distribute the planned costs across these periods. If the dates of network objects are shifted, the distributions of the respective planned costs can be automatically adapted as well.

You can trigger network costing manually from various processing transactions for networks. Depending on the network header settings, network costing can be executed automatically on every save after the network creation or the network release if there was a relevant change to the network. The network costing can then be fully run for all network objects; otherwise, it only recalculates the changed objects (*update*).

To calculate several networks simultaneously, SAP Project System provides Transaction CJ9K. In the initial screen of this transaction, you can select multiple networks and then trigger the calculation of planned costs either directly or via a background job. If the same networks are to be calculated repeatedly, you can save your selection as variants. The usage of asynchronous network costing is particularly necessary if you want to use networks for planning not only costs but also payments.

Asynchronous network costing

The calculation of planned costs will now be described for the different network objects. It's valid for all activities and activity elements that the system only calculates planned costs for these objects if the control key explicitly permits it (that is, if the CALCULATE indicator is set in the respective control key of the activities and activity elements). A similar indicator can also be found in the detail screen of material components. The system will only determine planned costs for the corresponding component during the network costing if this indicator has been set.

Relevancy to costing

For planning costs for internal activities, you need to store a work center, an activity type, and planned work in an internally processed activity (or an internal element). For the combination of the activity type in the activity and the cost center specified in the costing data of the work center (see Section 2.2.1), the system determines a price for every relevant period, and a cost element from the master record of the activity type. As of EHP 3, you can use a customer enhancement to apply deviating prices for calculating the planned costs. The formula in the work center costing data controls the quantity with which to multiply the price for calculating the planned costs. Usually, work centers use the standard formula SAP008 that uses the planned work in the activity for this calculation. The chronological distribution of the costs is determined via the distribution key in the activity or in the work center (see

Internally processed activities

Section 2.2.1). If you haven't stored a distribution key in the activity or in the work center, the system distributes the planned costs equally across the earliest dates of the activity.

Material forecasting values

In internally processed activities, on the ASSIGNMENT tab, you'll find the MATERIAL PLANNING field. During an early project planning phase, you can enter an estimated or empirical value for the later consumption of material in this field. The cost element of this material planning value must have been entered in the network profile of the network. In a later planning phase, the system automatically reduces the material forecast value in Reporting by the value of the material components you assign to the activity.

Externally processed activities

If you use purchasing info records in an externally processed activity (or external element) for specifying the activity to be procured, the system automatically determines a price per unit for this activity and also suggests a planned quantity. The network costing calculates the planned costs for procuring the external activity by multiplying the price and the planned quantity. If you haven't specified any purchasing info record, you need to manually enter a price for calculating the planned costs in the activity. The corresponding cost element can be stored as a default value in the network profile or changed in the activity. The period of the planned costs is calculated by the network costing using the latest end date of the activity.

Invoicing plans

A more detailed form of cost planning for externally processed activities is the use of *invoicing plans*. If you create an invoicing plan for an externally processed activity, you can distribute the planned costs for procuring the external activity to different dates and thus to different periods (see Figure 2.66). In particular, you can also plan outgoing payments, for example, down payments, in invoicing plans using the provided *invoicing rules*. Although payment data is not relevant to costs using an asynchronous network costing, the outgoing payments planned in the invoicing plan are passed on to the PS Cash Management detailed to a daily level for an accurate payment planning (see Chapter 6, Section 6.2.4). The individual dates in an invoicing plan, the distribution of costs or payments to the various dates, and the invoicing rules to be used can be specified manually, derived via milestones, or transferred from an invoicing plan template.

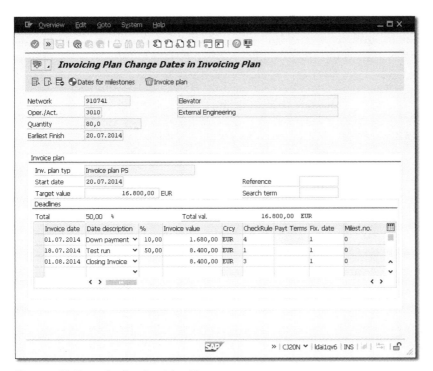

Figure 2.66 Example of an Invoicing Plan

For deriving the invoice plan data from milestones, the milestones must have the SALES DOCUMENT DATE indicator set. During the transfer, the system copies the planned milestone date and the percentage you entered in the milestone to the invoicing plan. With every change to the milestone dates, the invoicing plan dates are automatically adapted. If you specified a usage in the milestone, the system can also determine an invoicing rule. A prerequisite to the automatic determination of the invoicing rule from the milestone usage is that the invoicing plan type and an appropriate date category are stored in the usage definition. In the Customizing of invoicing plans, you can then specify which invoicing rule is to be used for the combination of invoicing plan type and date category.

You can also create invoicing plans using a template. For a template, you can use invoicing plans of other activities or material components, or default invoicing plans defined in the Customizing that the system could

Using templates

245

derive via the invoicing plan type for the network profile. Starting from the earliest end date of the activity, the system calculates the individual dates of the invoicing plan using the start date and the date intervals of the template. If the end date of the activity is shifted, the invoicing plan dates are shifted as well.

[+] **Fixed Dates in the Invoicing Plan**

If the dates of an invoicing plan are to be fixed (that is, independent of project date shifts), you cannot work with templates or derive the dates from the milestones but must enter the dates manually in the invoicing plan. During network costing, the data in the invoicing plans overrides the data of the activity itself.

Service activities   The planned costs for service activities (or service activity elements) are typically composed of the planned costs of the planned services and the expected value of the unplanned activities in the service specifications of the activities. The value of planned activities is calculated from the service conditions of the specified activities and the planned quantity in the service specifications. The cost element for the planned services is specified in the activities or stored as a default value in the network profile. The system determines the periods of the planned costs from the latest end dates of the service activities. As with externally processed activities, you can implement invoicing plans for a detailed cost or payment planning.

Costs activities   Using general costs activities (or cost activity elements), you can plan additional costs that aren't calculated from the data of other activity categories or assigned material components, like travel costs or primary costs for activities that are not procured via purchasing. In the easiest case, you enter an amount and a cost element as a planned value in a general costs activity. The cost element can also be stored as a default value in the network profile.

Unit costing   If you want to plan costs for different cost elements using a general costs activity, you can create a unit costing for the activity. As with unit costings for WBS elements (see Section 2.4.2), in a unit costing for the activity, you can create a table of different costing items for a general costs activity. In particular, you can use the item category V (Variable Item) to manually enter cost elements and corresponding planned costs (prices and quantities). The planned costs of unit costing override the costs planned manually in the detail screen of a general costs activity.

The system automatically determines the periods of the costs planned manually or via unit costing from the basic dates of the general costs activity. If you stored a distribution key in the activity, this key determines the chronological position and the distribution of the planned costs across the duration of the activity. If you haven't entered a distribution key, the system distributes the planned costs equally across the earliest dates of the activity. For a detailed time scheduling of the cost or payment flows, you can also implement invoicing plans for general costs activities as well. Note, however, that you cannot use an invoicing plan and unit costing simultaneously for a general costs activity.

If you assigned material components to activities, the system can use the component data during network costing to automatically calculate planned costs for the later material consumption. The calculation of material costs depends on the item category and the type of stock management for the material components (see Section 2.3).

Material components

For non-stock items without a reference to a material master record or a purchasing info record, you can manually specify a price per unit. The system then calculates the planned costs by multiplying the price with the planned quantity. If you entered a material number for the non-stock item, the system can retrieve the price from the material master record. If you specified a purchasing info record in the component, the price is determined using this purchasing info record. If you want, you can also create an invoicing plan for a non-stock item for a more detailed planning. The data from the invoicing plans overrides the other data of the material components.

Non-stock item

For stock items, the network costing calculates the planned costs from the planned quantity and a price per unit, which is determined from the material master record. For material components managed in the non-valuated project stock, the system only reports planned costs if you use a planning network. For the stock items of a valuated project stock, you can also create a unit costing for a component and therefore calculate

Stock items

the production costs for internally produced material, for example, if no appropriate price for this material is available in the system.

The system determines the period of the planned costs for material components from the requirements date of the components, or from the invoicing plans you assigned to the material components. The cost elements are typically detected automatically via the account determination, or transferred from the unit costings of the material components.

[+] **Network Costing and CO Versions**

By default, the planned costs of network costing are saved to CO version 0. If you want, however, you can copy the planned data to another CO version using Transactions CJ9F or CJ9FS. As of EHP 3, you can use BAdI BADI_NW_CO_VERS_ CK to save the network costing data directly to a CO version other than 0.

Costing variants

In network costing, the overhead rates are automatically calculated in the plan as well. The calculation is controlled by the costing sheets in the activities (see Chapter 5, Section 5.3). Similar to unit costing or Easy Cost Planning, the network costing is controlled via a costing variant. The valuation variant contained in the costing variant uses strategies to define how the prices for internal activities, external activities, and materials that are required for the calculation are to be determined. The costing variants used for calculating a planned and an actual network are specified in the network header, or stored as default values in NETWORK TYPE PARAMETERS.

Header and activity account assignment

Using the ACTIVITY ACCOUNT ASSIGNMENT indicator in NETWORK TYPE PARAMETERS, you decide whether the planned costs—and the later actual costs—are separately managed on every single activity or activity element, or whether the planned costs of a network are only reported as a total on the network header level. Normally, it makes sense to use activity-assigned networks because they are conducive to a more detailed analysis of the planned and the actual costs. In addition, you can assign the activities of activity assigned networks to different WBS elements and assess the aggregated costs of the assigned activities on the WBS element level. Header-assigned networks are typically used in sales and distribution projects where the CO takes place on the sales order item level.

The cost integration with the networks is achieved via an account assignment to network headers. We don't recommend an activity assignment of a header-assigned network to different WBS elements.

No plan line items can be created for planned data from network costings. Therefore, a direct integrated planning or planned settlement is not possible for networks. However, it is possible to achieve an indirect integrated planning and planned settlement for networks that are assigned to plan-integrated WBS elements (see Section 2.4.3). You can achieve this indirect integrated planning using Transaction CJ9Q or CJ9QS to roll up the planned costs of networks or network activities to the WBS elements to which they are assigned. If the WBS elements are plan-integrated, the system writes plan line items for the WBS elements during the rollup, and automatically forwards the planned data for the internal activities as scheduled activities to the corresponding cost centers. You can also use the plan line items for a planned settlement on the WBS elements level.

Integrated planning of networks

However, note the following restrictions for the integrated planning of networks:

▸ The rollup of planned network data cannot be performed in CO version 0 because the planned costs would then be reported doubly on the WBS elements level (see Section 2.4.7).

▸ Overhead rates are not rolled up to the WBS elements. However, you can manually apply the overhead for the WBS elements in the used CO version using Transactions CJ46 and CJ47.

▸ If the planned values of the networks change, you need to reuse Transaction CJ9Q or CJ9QS if you want to adapt the planned data on the WBS elements level.

Compared to the manual cost planning forms for WBS elements, using network costing has many advantages:

Advantages of network costing

▸ Because network costing is always cost element-specific, the system can automatically calculate overhead rates during network costing.

▸ And because network costing is also date-specific—where the periods of the planned costs are directly derived from the dates of the network objects—date shifts directly affect the periods of cost planning.

▸ Invoicing plans and unit costings provide different possibilities for detailing your cost planning. Invoicing plans even enable a payment planning to the day. If you copy activities or networks, all data required for calculating the planned costs is copied as well. You only need to perform network costing for the new objects to determine the planned costs. In this respect, network costing is a copyable form of cost planning.

▸ You can also implement network costing for simulation versions.

2.4.7 Planned Costs of Assigned Orders

Order assignment

WBS elements you identified as account assignment elements cannot only be assigned activities or entire networks, but also other order categories of the SAP system, such as internal orders, service and maintenance orders, or production orders. The assignment can be stored manually in the respective orders or created automatically. Internal orders, for example, can be created during Claim Management and assigned to a WBS element (see Chapter 4, Section 4.8). Maintenance orders can derive the assignment to WBS elements from functional locations, provided you have already stored WBS elements there. Alternatively, you can also use the order assignment to project function, for example, to assign maintenance orders to WBS elements. Production orders referencing project stocks are automatically assigned to the stockholding WBS elements.

Cost planning for orders

Depending on the order category, you have different options for order cost planning. For internal orders, for example, you could use similar forms of cost planning as for WBS elements. The planned costs of service, maintenance, and production orders, however, are calculated in a similar way as the planned costs of networks. In contrast to networks, however, planned costs for production orders are always managed on the level of the respective order headers. An assessment on the level of the individual activities within these orders is therefore impossible. As of EHP 5, as for networks, you can also use activity assigned orders for service and maintenance orders. In Customizing, depending on the respective plant and order type, you define whether header account assignment or activity account assignment is used for an order. In case of activity-assigned orders, you can specify the assignment to WBS elements separately on the level of the individual operations of the service and maintenance orders.

In the Customizing of SAP Project System, you can use Transaction OPSV to control how the planned costs of assigned orders are to be handled on the WBS element level (see Figure 2.67). Using the ADDITIVE indicator in this table, you specify whether or not the planned costs for orders are to be added to the planned costs of the WBS elements.

Order value updating for projects

If the ADDITIVE indicator is set for a specific combination of order category, order type, and CO area, these are called *appended orders*. The planned costs of these orders are rolled up additively to the assigned WBS elements and thus increase the planned total of these WBS elements. This setting is particularly relevant if you want to budget the WBS elements, and the planned total is instructive—you have to know how much to budget for—when assigning budgets (see Chapter 3, Section 3.1).

Additive orders

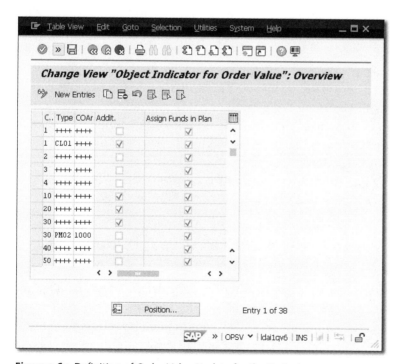

Figure 2.67 Definition of Order Value Update for the Project

Non-appended orders Orders for which the ADDITIVE indicator is not set are referred to as *non-appended orders*. Your planned values are not rolled up to the assigned WBS elements and thus do not increase their planned total. If you work with budgeting in SAP Project System, you might have to consider the planned costs of non-additive orders manually when assigning budgets. For production orders, for example, using non-appended orders makes sense if the planned costs for production are already reported for assigned activities on the WBS element level due to material components.

The ASSIGN FUNDS IN PLAN indicator in the order value updating table for the project controls when the values of assigned orders should represent allotments against the budget of WBS elements. This indicator is discussed in detail in Chapter 3, Section 3.1.5.

2.4.8 Planning Statistical Key Figures

Creating statistical key figures — Statistical key figures enable you to plan and monitor specific units within projects, such as the mileage spent, number of project team members, and so on. You can use Transactions KK01, KK02 (Individual Processing), and KAK2 (List Maintenance) to create and edit statistical key figures. The master data of a statistical key figure merely contains an ID and a name, the unit in which the key figure is maintained, its assignment to a CO area, and the key figure type. The key figure type determines whether the key figure values should be the same for the month of entry and all subsequent months of the current fiscal year (fixed value), as would be the case for the number of project team members, or whether the values apply only to the month of entry (totals value), as, for example, in a monthly planning of miles to be driven.

Planning statistical key figures — You can use Transaction CJS2 to plan statistical key figures at the level of WBS elements, while Transaction CJK2 allows you to plan statistical key figures at the level of networks, activities, and activity elements.

The actual planning process is similar to the detailed cost planning (see Section 2.4.3). In the initial screen, you must define the CO version and the planning period, the project elements to be planned, and the statistical key figures. After that, an overview screen allows you to store a current planned value and, if necessary, a maximum planned value for the entire period. Both the distribution key and key figure type then determine how to distribute the planned values across the planning period. However, you can also call a period screen to change the distribution of planned values across individual periods. Similar to detailed planning, the planner profile and the planning layouts determine the appearance and functional scope of the different entry screens for planning statistical key figures.

As of EHP 3, you can also plan the statistical key figures directly in a separate tab within the Project Builder (see Figure 2.68). However, in contrast to the planning transactions described previously, the Project Builder does not allow you to call a period screen, for example.

Planning in the Project Builder

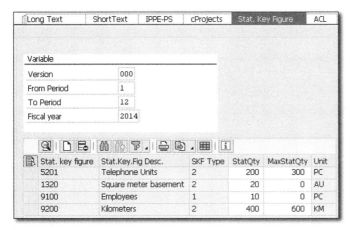

Figure 2.68 Planning Statistical Key Figures in the Project Builder

With regard to activities and activity elements, you can use the planning function for statistical key figures in the Project Builder to determine the planned work for the activity. The prerequisites for this are that the WORK field in the INTERNAL tab is left blank, that you have defined a statistical key figure record for the conversion, and that you have set the WORK CALCULATION indicator. The conversion then occurs based on the following formula:

Value of the "Work" Field in Hours =
Planned Quantity × Statistical Key Figure Rate

The duration of work is always calculated in terms of hours, but is then converted into the respective time unit of the activity or activity element.

Predefining key figures

You can use Transaction CNSKFDEF to predefine the key figures to be planned or the statistical key figure record for statistical key figure planning in the Project Builder. Then you can make these default settings dependent on, for example, the controlling area, project profile, order type, or individual projects.

To use the statistical key figure planning function in the Project Builder, you must explicitly activate this function in the Customizing section of SAP Project System. If required, you can separately activate the function for the following object types: WBS elements, network headers, activities, and activity elements.

Using statistical key figures

In addition to planning statistical key figures, you can also enter actual data of statistical key figures for released project elements and compare this data with the planned values in Reporting. Transaction KB31N enables you to do so.

If required, you can even use statistical key figures for calculations in the context of period-end closings. For example, statistical key figures may be useful to determine periodic transfers or template allocations (see Chapter 5, Section 5.4).

[◉] **Project Cost Planning**

Depending on your requirements, you can use different cost planning options for projects in SAP Project System. If you work with networks, the system can automatically calculate the planned costs using the data of activities, activity elements, and material components, and report them separately per activity or activity element, respectively.

If you only work with WBS elements, hierarchical cost planning, unit costing, detailed planning, and Easy Cost Planning or cost estimation represent various manual forms of cost planning. The planning of statistical key figures not only enables you to plan the costs, but also other key figures for projects.

2.5   Revenue Planning

For some project types, particularly for sales and distribution projects, a revenue planning, in addition to the cost planning, is important to make assumptions about the later profits or profitability of a project during the planning phase. For projects, you can plan revenues on the WBS elements level or, if you use the integration into SD, using sales documents linked to projects. WBS elements for which you want to plan revenues must be identified as billing elements (see Chapter 1, Section 1.2.1). A revenue planning on the network level is not possible.

Similar to cost planning using WBS elements, there are different possibilities with different levels of detail for revenue planning as well. If you want, you can also perform several revenue plannings for one billing element and save them in different CO versions.

2.5.1   Hierarchical Planning

Using Transaction CJ42, you can perform a hierarchical revenue planning for billing elements of a project. For this reason, there are similar functions as in the hierarchical cost planning (see Section 2.4.1). This form of revenue planning does not reference any revenue element and is therefore not revenue element-specific. Depending on the planning profile settings of the project, you can plan the revenues as total values or with a reference to individual fiscal years, or both. A distribution of the revenues to individual periods of a fiscal year is not possible in the hierarchical revenue planning.

Revenue planning functions

2.5.2   Detailed Planning

The detailed planning of revenues enables you to plan values for different revenue elements and to distribute these values to individual periods of a fiscal year either manually or automatically using distribution keys. This form of revenue planning is both revenue element- and date-specific. The periods of planned revenues, however, cannot be derived from the planned dates of the billing elements but must be specified manually.

For the detailed planning of revenues, there are the same functions as for cost element planning (see Section 2.4.3). In particular, this form of revenue planning is again controlled by planning layouts and planner profiles. You can perform the detailed planning of revenues via Transaction CJ42 or by calling Transaction CJR2. In the planning profile, you determine the revenue element group that is to be available during the detailed planning via Transaction CJ42. To plan revenues using Transaction CJR2, your user must be assigned to a planner profile with an appropriate planning layout for revenue planning.

2.5.3 Billing Plan

Using a billing plan, you can make a very detailed planning—similar to the invoicing plans. A billing plan always references a revenue element that you must store in the planning profile of the project. If you want, you can also use billing plans for planning incoming payments to the day. The update of planned data always references CO version 0. In contrast to hierarchical planning or detailed planning, you can use billing plans for revenue planning in simulation versions.

Creating items of a billing plan

In a billing plan, you distribute a target value (that is, the entire total revenue) to different dates. To do this, you create the different items within a billing plan, each including information about the planned date, amount, or percentage, respectively, of the target value, and the *billing rule* to be used. Using the billing rule, you can control whether an item is revenue-relevant, that is, updated in the revenue plan, or just relevant to down payments. Items that are relevant to down payments are updated to the day, along with the other items in the financial plan of a project in PS Cash Management (see Chapter 6, Section 6.2.4).

You can manually create the items of a billing plan. The dates of the manually created items are handled as fixed dates; that is, changes to dates regarding the project do not affect the dates of the billing plan in this case. However, you can also create the items automatically by transferring milestone data or referencing a template.

When transferring milestone dates, the system copies the milestone dates and the billing percentage stored in the milestone to the billing plan and might also suggest a billing rule. The billing rule is then determined from the combination of billing plan type and date category stored in the usage of the milestone. If the milestone dates change, the dates of the billing plan are also adapted automatically when saving the project. A prerequisite for transferring milestone dates is that the SALES DOCUMENT DATE indicator is set in the relevant milestones (see Chapter 1, Section 1.4).

Transferring milestone dates

If you create a billing plan referencing a template, the system determines the dates and the percentage distribution of the amounts for the billing plan from the item data of the template. The system adjusts the dates to the start date and the percentage distribution of the amounts to the target value. When dates of the billing element are changed, the dates of the billing plan are automatically adjusted after a scheduling, if you worked with a template. You can use other billing plans as templates or define default billing plans in the Customizing of SAP Project System.

Using templates

In nearly every processing transaction of work breakdown structures, for example, in Project Builder, you can assign billing plans to billing elements of a project. If you want, you can also implement billing plans in simulation versions for a revenue planning. A special possibility of creating billing plans for WBS elements is to use sales pricing, which is discussed in Section 2.5.4. The billing plans that you assign to WBS elements are exclusively for planning revenues and possibly payments; they cannot be used for automatic invoice creation.

Billing plans for WBS elements

However, you can also create billing plans in SD for customer quotation or sales order, provided the respective item category permits this (see Figure 2.69). If the sales document item is assigned to a billing element, the planned data of the billing plan is automatically updated to the revenue planning or financial budgeting of the billing element and can therefore be analyzed on the WBS element level. A prerequisite is that you must have enabled the update of data from quotations or orders in the planning profile of the project.

Billing plans in sales documents

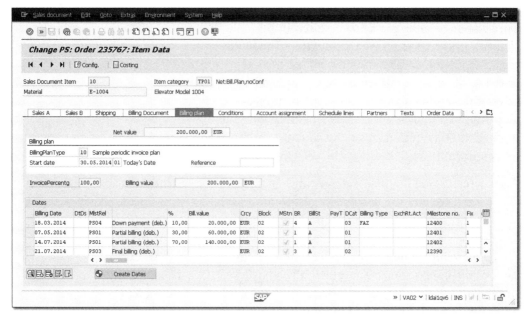

Figure 2.69 Example of a Billing Plan of a Sales Document Item

Milestone billing In contrast to the billing plans for WBS elements, the items of a billing plan for a sales document item can also be used for billing during the project implementation. The actual revenues are then automatically transferred to the billing element. If you created items of a billing plan using milestone data, you can use the milestone billing function (see Chapter 4, Section 4.6.1).

[!]

> **Prioritization of Billing Plans**
>
> Note that the values from billing plans for WBS elements override the values from sales documents. If you want to use billing plans for WBS elements only for a forecast or as a template for billing plans in sales documents, you should delete them after creating the appropriate sales documents.

Even if you didn't create billing plans in a sales document item, you can update planned revenues from the sales document items to the revenue planning of the billing elements to which the items are assigned. The system then determines the value and the revenue element via the conditions of the items, and the billing dates from the respective delivery scheduling data.

2.5.4 Sales Pricing

Using sales pricing for SD projects, you can derive and save prices for the services or material produced for the project from the planned data of these projects. Typically, the data of sales pricing is used particularly for the creation of quotations and the revenue planning of SD projects for which sales prices cannot be determined based on standard prices. If you can use existing standard prices and fixed conditions for SD projects, sales pricing is usually not required. In this case, the quotation is not created via sales pricing, but directly in SD.

SAP Project System provides two options for creating sales pricings: You can use Transaction DP81 to create sales pricings for projects that were created due to a customer inquiry and are linked to this inquiry; or, you can use the Project Builder or Transaction DP82 to create sales pricings for projects that don't reference a customer inquiry. These two options will be explained in the following text.

During a presales phase, special documents can be created in SD in which customer inquiries about the price or availability of services or material can be saved. These documents are referred to as *customer inquiries* and are essentially requests for submitting a quotation to the customer. If you created a project for the creation of quotations in SAP Project System, you can assign sales document items to WBS elements of this project and thus establish a link between the sales document items and the project. If you now create a sales pricing for the project or a sales document item via Transaction DP81, the system can use both the SD data in the sales document and the planned data of the project.

Project-assigned customer inquiries

During sales pricing, a two-step aggregation of the planned data of the project takes place (planned costs, statistic indicators, planned material and activities, and so on). Which planned data is considered during sales pricing, and how and according to which criteria the data is aggregated, is controlled via a dynamic item processor profile (*DIP profile*) that must be stored in the detailed data of the sales document items.

Sales price basis The result of the first aggregation step is presented in the *sales price basis view*. Figure 2.70 shows an example for such a sales price basis view. In this example, the planned costs of a project were aggregated according to their cost elements. In addition to the aggregation itself, the DIP profile controls how the aggregated values (dynamic items) are presented in the upper area of this view. The lower area of the sales price basis view has more details about the aggregated items. In particular, the lower area allows for a manual change to items by an amount, quantity, or percentage. If you change items, the amount transferred to the sales pricing deviates from the original amount.

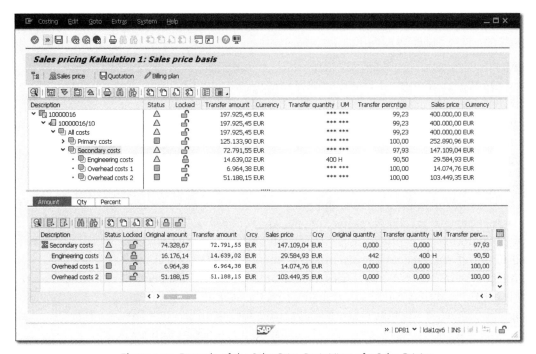

Figure 2.70 Example of the Sales Price Basis View of a Sales Pricing

Sales price view During the second aggregation step, the aggregated and possibly manually changed items of the sales price basis are automatically linked to material numbers. Depending on the DIP profile settings, these can be, for example, material numbers from material components of the project, or fixed material numbers stored in the DIP profile for project activities or for the material to be produced using the project. The material numbers are sorted and grouped into sales document items. Using the *pricing* function of SD, the system can now determine a sales price for the individual items using the material numbers and the SD data of the inquiry (customer number, sales organization, and so on). The sales document items and the corresponding sales prices are shown in the *sales price view*. The sales price view corresponds to a customer view of the sales pricing. Figure 2.71 shows an example of a sales price view. The upper area shows the hierarchy of all sales document items.

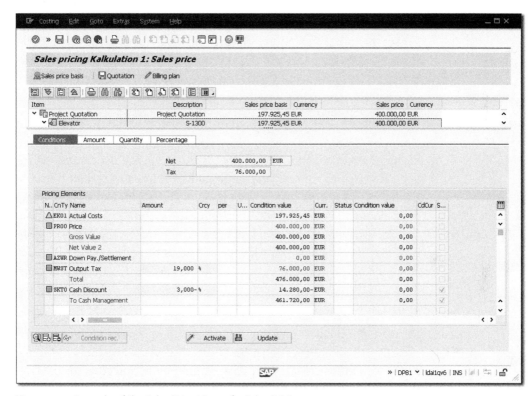

Figure 2.71 Example of the Sales Price View of a Sales Pricing

The lower area lists details about the sales prices of the items, that is, the conditions determined by the system during pricing. If you want, you can adjust the sales price of an item by adding more conditions. In a sales pricing, you can toggle between the sales price view and the sales price basis view at any time to implement changes.

Billing plan and
quotation creation
The sales pricing data can be used for different purposes:

- You can save the data to a document and add a descriptive document text. Thus, you can create and compare several different sales pricings for a project.

- You can create a billing plan, which is automatically assigned to the billing element of the billing structure used in the sales pricing. As a target value of this billing plan, the system suggests the total value of sales prices.

- You can create a customer quotation. The system then automatically uses the link to the inquiry, the account assignment to the project, and particularly the items and sales prices determined using the sales pricing. The quotation can be further processed in SD, and can later serve as a basis for creating a customer quotation.

Projects without
customer inquiry
You can also perform sales pricings for projects without an inquiry, if necessary. The SD data required for a sales pricing must then be stored in the project definition. The sales organization, the distribution channel, the division, and the DIP profile can be entered as default values in the project profile or manually in the control parameters of the project definition, if necessary. For specifying the customer, an appropriate partner determination procedure must be entered on the project definition level that enables you to enter a customer number on the PARTNER tab of the project definition (see Chapter 1, Section 1.2.1). Sales pricings for projects that do not reference any inquiries can be created using the Project Builder or directly via Transaction DP82.

Simulation
versions
During the quotation phase of SD projects, you can use simulation versions (see Chapter 1, Section 1.9.2) to create several structures for a project; to plan different dates, capacity requirements, and costs for the later implementation; and to compare this planning. In particular, you can also use the data of the simulation versions for sales pricings and the creation of quotations. A prerequisite for this is that the project definition and the billing element already exist as operative objects.

Definition of
DIP Profiles
Sales pricings are basically controlled by the DIP profile of the sales document items or the project definition. You create DIP profiles in the Customizing of SAP Project System using Transaction ODP1. In addition to using DIP profiles for creating sales calculations, they can be used for a

resource-related billing (see Chapter 4, Section 4.6.2) or a results analysis (see Chapter 5, Section 5.6). Therefore, the settings of the DIP profile are specified with a reference to one of these usages (see Figure 2.72).

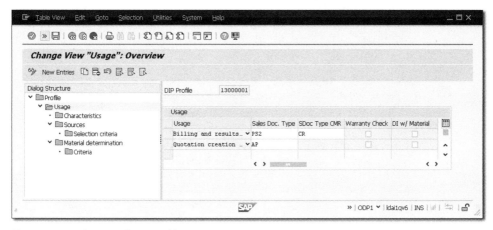

Figure 2.72 Definition of DIP Profiles

If you use it for controlling the sales pricing, first store the document type using those quotations that can be created from the sales pricing. Then, decide which characteristics are relevant for determining the dynamic items, dynamic and the material numbers. Also, specify how the first aggregation step is to be performed and presented in the sales price view using these characteristics. Possible characteristics are cost element, object number, cost center, activity type, and so on. If you want, however, you can use a customer enhancement to consider additional characteristics as well.

Controlling the sales pricing

Then you specify the sources from which the sales pricing can retrieve values. For every source, you can define additional selection criteria or determine standard percentages. Possible sources are, for example, Easy Cost Planning, planned costs, totals records, and statistical key figures. Using a customer enhancement, you can also define additional sources.

> **Further Information on DIP Profiles**   **[+]**
>
> A very detailed documentation of the definition of DIP profiles, their various application areas, and the available customer enhancements can be found as an attachment to SAP Note 301117.

Via the material determination of a DIP profile, you control the aggregation of the dynamic items to material numbers. You can manually enter the material numbers in the table for material determination; however, you can also transfer material numbers from material components of the projects. The material numbers to actually be determined during sales pricing are controlled using selection criteria that you define for the individual material numbers.

[◉] **Revenue Planning of Projects**

Similar to cost planning, SAP Project System also provides several possibilities for planning revenues for WBS elements. By linking sales document items to WBS elements, you can plan revenues in SD as well, which can then be updated as planned revenues to projects. Using sales pricing, you can create customer quotations directly in SAP Project System using the planned data of projects.

2.6 Summary

This chapter dealt with the different project planning functions of SAP Project System. For WBS elements, there are functions for time scheduling cost planning, and revenue planning. Networks provide functions for scheduling, resource and material planning, and network costing. If you use both WBS elements and networks for structuring projects, planned data can be exchanged between the WBS elements and the assigned networks or network activities.

Within the approval phase, funds for project execution are made available through budgeting. The budget management functionality of SAP Project System enables you to monitor assigned funds and prevent budget overruns.

3   Budget

Companies often use the term "budget" very differently. It therefore makes sense to first explain what we mean by budget in the context in which it is used in SAP Project System and to differentiate it from the terms "planned costs" and "actual costs."

In the planning phase of a project, you can estimate or calculate the costs for the subsequent execution and save these costs as *planned costs* for the different project objects. Depending on which form of cost planning you use for this, the planned costs in this case are stored as total values, with reference to fiscal years or individual periods, by cost element, or without any reference to a cost element. If required, you can also enter several different planned costs for the same object and store them in different Controlling (CO) versions.

You can compare the planned costs against the *actual costs* in the execution phase of a project. The actual costs correspond to the funds that are actually required to execute individual parts of the project based on services used by the cost centers of your own company or by suppliers, materials consumed, overhead costs allocated, and so on. Actual costs are updated in SAP Project System by the account assignment of corresponding documents on project objects and always refer to cost elements.

You document an approved cost structure for executing the different parts of the project by distributing the budget to WBS elements of a project. A project is typically budgeted in its approval phase—that is, before the project execution is even started. In SAP Project System, budget does not refer to individual cost elements and therefore represents the approved framework for all costs of the project, including both the primary and secondary costs (an exception in this case is *exempt cost elements*). Although you can still change the budget values of a project retroactively, unlike CO versions for planning costs, there is only one relevant budget value for an object at any time.

In Reporting, you can evaluate the budget values and planned and actual costs together. After you budget a project, you generally use the *availability control* function to automatically calculate assigned *funds* for the budget of a WBS element and to prevent budget overruns. In this sense, budget is not only an approved cost structure but also represents a binding budget for a project.

Integration with Investment Management | You can only perform budgeting and budget monitoring via the functions of SAP Project System; however, you can also use an integration of SAP Project System with Investment Management to manage budgets across projects. These two options are discussed in Section 3.1 and Section 3.2. Another option for cross-project budgeting is to integrate with SAP Portfolio and Project Management (SAP PPM). Chapter 7 discusses SAP PPM as well as the integration scenarios with SAP Project System.

[+] **Budget and Networks**

Note that budgets can only be assigned to WBS elements in SAP Project System; networks cannot be budgeted.

However, the costs of networks or network activities, to which WBS elements are assigned, are included in the assigned funds for the budget of the WBS elements and are taken into account for the availability control.

3.1 Budgeting Functions in SAP Project System

Budget profile | Depending on your requirements, you can use different functions in SAP Project System to manage your project budgets. In this case, the management of budgets for individual projects is controlled by the budget profile in the project definition of the projects. Figure 3.1 shows an example of defining a budget profile. You can define budget profiles in

Customizing of SAP Project System using Transaction OPS9 and store them as default values in project profiles. The individual settings options for a budget profile, along with the different functions of budget management, are explained in the following sections.

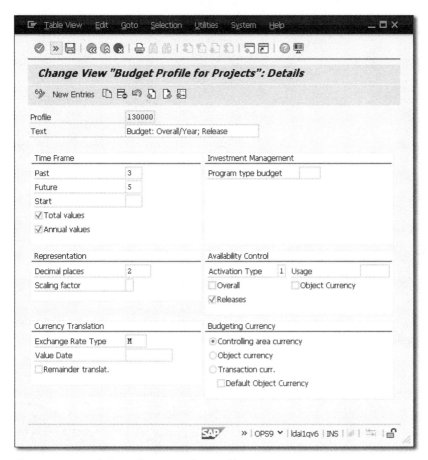

Figure 3.1 Example for Defining a Budget Profile

3.1.1 Original Budget

The first step in managing a budget for a project is to allocate an *original* budget in Transaction CJ30 (see Figure 3.2). All WBS elements of a project are displayed in tables in this transaction.

Transaction CJ30

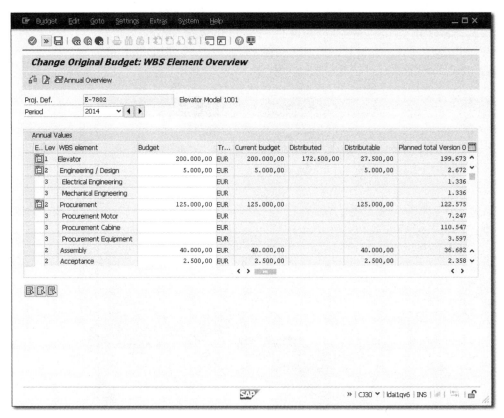

Figure 3.2 Example for Distributing the Original Budget

In the (view) BUDGET column, you can enter the values for the original budget of the individual WBS elements; however, the budgeting for a project is usually preceded by cost planning, which acts as an indicator for allocating budgets. The planned costs of the WBS elements are therefore displayed in the PLANNED TOTAL view in Transaction CJ30, and you can copy these planned costs as the original budget using the COPY VIEW function, which you can call from the transaction menu. You can use the percentage rate in this case to specify whether you want the planned costs to be copied completely, partially, or at more than 100%. In the transaction settings, you define which CO version should be used to display the planned total. In addition, you can use the REVALUATE function to increase or decrease budget values of selected WBS elements by a certain percentage or amount.

Planned Total of a WBS Element	**[+]**

The planned total of a WBS element is calculated from the total values from the hierarchical cost planning, detailed planning, unit costing, Easy Cost Planning, and from the values of all assigned additive orders and networks or activities.

The budgeting of a project must be hierarchically consistent by the time the availability controlis activated. This means that the system checks within a project structure to verify whether the budget values of WBS elements of a lower-level exceed the budget value of the WBS element for the next highest level.

Hierarchical consistency

You can analyze the hierarchical distribution of the budget values manually within the project structure using the DISTRIBUTED and DISTRIBUTABLE views or activate an automatic check in Transaction CJ30. A project is typically budgeted top-down. This means that the person responsible for the budget successively distributes the original budget of the highest WBS element to the WBS elements of lower levels. In contrast to this method, however, you can also use the TOTAL UP function to derive the original budget of WBS elements from the budget values already distributed on WBS elements of lower levels and therefore ensure hierarchical consistency.

Top-Down Distribution of Budget	**[+]**

You *don't* have to split the budget of a WBS element completely onto lower-level WBS elements, but you can also distribute parts of the budget further, or you can abandon the distribution of the budget altogether. This means that you don't have to perform budgeting to the lowest level of a project.

Depending on which settings you've selected in the budget profile of a project, you can enter the original budget of the project as overall values or as fiscal-year-dependent values. Alternatively, you can enter both overall and original budgets with reference to fiscal years for WBS elements. With fiscal-year-dependent budgeting, the budget profile also controls the interval that should be possible for budgeting. With the COPY VIEW function, you can use budget values from a previous year

(Previous Year view) as a template for the budget values of a fiscal year if required.

Overall budget and fiscal-year budget

If you allow both overall values and fiscal-year-dependent values for the distribution of original budgets, then the overall budget of a WBS element must be greater than or equal to the total of its individual fiscal-year budgets by the time the availability control is activated. You can manually check this using the Cumulative view (total fiscal year values) and Remainder view (difference from overall value and total fiscal year values) for each WBS element. Alternatively, you can activate an automatic check.

Figure 3.3 shows the results of a check in which the distribution of an original budget is inconsistent. The first error message indicates a hierarchically inconsistent distribution: a higher budget was distributed than available in a fiscal year. The other error messages refer to the fact that in total more fiscal-year budgets were distributed than overall budgets.

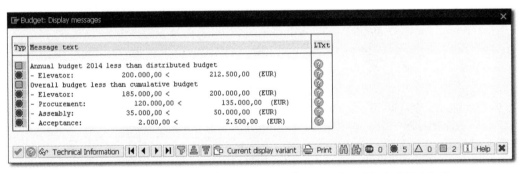

Figure 3.3 Example of Error Messages for Inconsistent Budget Distribution

Budgeting currencies

Using the budget profile, you also control the currencies in which the WBS elements can be budgeted. You can allow the uniform CO area currency and the object currency of the individual WBS elements in the project or a transaction currency of your own choice for budgeting. However, the budget values entered are always converted into object and controlling area currencies of the WBS elements. The annual values in this case are converted using the rate type that was defined in the fiscal-year-dependent values of CO version 0. The total values are converted based on the budget profile settings.

Depending on the budget profile settings, you can run the hierarchical consistency check and the cumulative annual values check against the overall budget of a WBS element either in the CO area currency or in the object currency of the WBS elements, but you should note that consistency checks in the object currency can only be run for projects in which the object currency within the project structure is uniform.

When you save the distribution of the original budget, the system creates a unique document (*budget line item*) with additional information about the document date and the name of the person who created the document. Before you save the distribution, you can enter more detailed document texts for the entire budget distribution or for individual WBS elements, which you can then evaluate later in Reporting or in Transaction CJ30 along with the other data for the budget line items.

Budget line item

Provided you don't use the special SAVE WITHOUT CHECKING function for saving the budget values, the system also automatically performs the checks for hierarchical consistency and for consistency of the overall value and cumulative values when you save and thereby prevents inconsistent budget values from being saved. After you save the distribution of the original budget, all budgeted WBS elements are automatically assigned the BUDG (budgeted) status. This status prevents the budgeted WBS elements from being deleted directly and from hierarchical changes to these WBS elements and all lower-level objects.

BUDG status

3.1.2 Budget Updates

In the course of a project, you may need to change the project budget of individual WBS elements. You can use Transaction CJ30 for this and adjust the original budget accordingly. When you save the budget, a new budget line item that allows the subsequent change to be analyzed is then created. However, instead of changing the original budget, it generally makes more sense to use *budget updates*. In this context, a distinction is made between *budget supplements*, *budget returns*, and *budget transfers*. Based on the budget updates and the original budget of WBS elements, the system then calculates a current budget for each WBS element.

When you work with budget updates instead of changing the original budget, the initial, original budget remains unchanged. You can therefore compare the original budget with the current budget at any time in Reporting. In suitable budget reports, you can analyze how the current budget was achieved based on supplements, returns, or transfers. Because the line item documents of budget updates always contain information on the senders and recipients of budget values, you can also retroactively trace the flow of budget values. To prevent changes to the original budget values, thereby forcing the use of budget updates, you can define a user status that does not allow the BUDGETING business transaction, but does allow business transactions for updating a budget (see Chapter 1, Section 1.6).

Transactions CJ36 (to project) and CJ37 (in project) are available in SAP Project System to enter budget supplements. You can enter the amounts for WBS elements, by which the current budget of these WBS elements is to be increased, in both transactions. You can post supplements for individual fiscal years or overall values. When you save the supplements, the system performs corresponding consistency checks exactly as it does when you distribute an original budget. You can also enter document texts that are then saved in a budget line item with the other data of the budget supplement.

The difference between Transactions CJ36 and CJ37 is that with a supplement in the project (Transaction CJ37; see Figure 3.4), the increase in the current budget of a WBS element results in the distributable budget of the higher-level WBS element being reduced accordingly. If there is no more distributable budget available on the higher-level WBS element, then you cannot post a supplement on the lower-level WBS element within the project due to the hierarchical consistency check. With supplements in a project, you can only supplement as much budget as is still available for distribution at the higher-level.

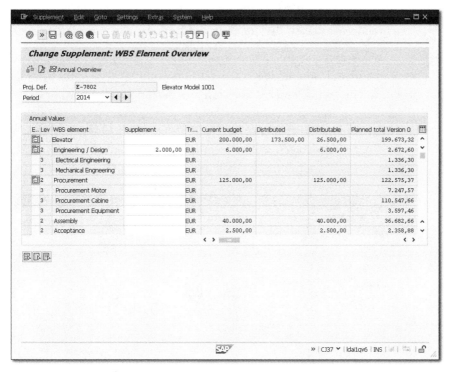

Figure 3.4 Example of a Supplement in the Project

In contrast, with a supplement to the project (Transaction CJ36), the increase in the current budget of a WBS element automatically results in the current budget of the hierarchically higher-level WBS element being increased by the same amount. This occurs regardless of whether a distributable budget existed on this WBS element. The distributable budget of the higher-level WBS elements therefore remains constant. A supplement to the project therefore results in an additional budget being made available for a project "externally."

Supplement to project

Like budget supplements, you can also enter budget returns using Transactions CJ35 (from project) and CJ38 (in project). You use budget returns to reduce the current budget of WBS elements by a certain amount; however, a budget return must not impair the consistency of the budget values. When you post a return in project for a WBS element, this automatically increases the distributable budget of the higher-level WBS element. When you enter a return from project for a WBS element,

Budget returns

the current budgets of the higher-level WBS elements are also automatically reduced—that is, they're extracted from the entire project budget.

Budget transfers You can use budget transfers for different purposes—for example, to move a budget from one WBS element to another WBS element (see Figure 3.5). The WBS elements here can even belong to different projects. If the WBS elements belong to a project, then they must nevertheless not be within the same hierarchy branch. The system also automatically makes transfers between WBS elements of lower hierarchy levels to the WBS element of higher hierarchy levels.

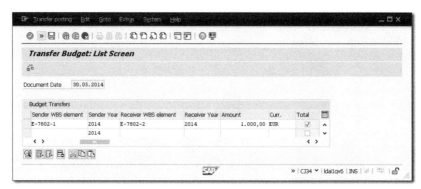

Figure 3.5 Example of a Budget Transfer

You can perform transfers for overall values or individual fiscal years. You can also transfer a budget of a WBS element for a fiscal year to another WBS element and another fiscal year if required. Finally, you can also transfer budget values of a fiscal year to another fiscal year for a WBS element (*advance* or *carryforward*). For each transfer, you can enter a document text that is saved in a budget line item with the relevant data of the transfer.

3.1.3 Budget Release

In some cases, it is useful to separate the distribution of budget values from the actual release of budgets for executing projects or individual parts of a project. This is also frequently necessary if budgeting with reference to fiscal years is not detailed enough and the budgets are to be made available successively within a fiscal year. However, bear in mind that you need to carry out an additional step to release budgets when managing project budgets.

In SAP Project System, you can use Transaction CJ32 to enter released budget values for WBS elements of a project. Similar to the distribution of original budgets, you can release overall or fiscal year values depending on the settings of the budget profile. You can enter amounts manually in the RELEASE column or use the COPY VIEW function to copy values from other views, such as the values of the CURRENT BUDGET or PLANNED TOTAL views (see Figure 3.6).

Released budget values

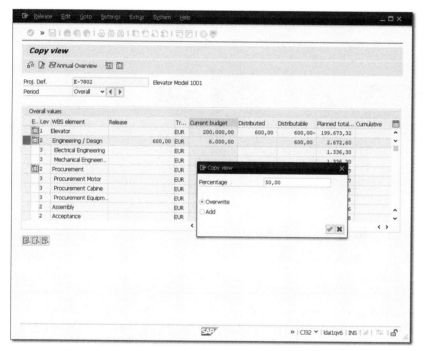

Figure 3.6 Example of the Budget Release Using the Copy View Function

In this case, you can select at what percent you want the values to be copied and whether the values are to be added to existing releases or whether they should overwrite existing values.

You can also activate a check manually or automatically for releases when you save them. The check ensures that the releases of WBS elements don't overrun the releases of the higher-level WBS elements

Consistency checks

(hierarchical consistency). Each WBS element is also checked to ensure that the released budget does not exceed the current budget. If you're working with both overall values and fiscal year values, then the release of the overall values must ultimately be greater than or equal to the total of the annual releases. Each budget release is documented by a budget line item, to which you can add a descriptive document text before you save the release.

Mass release of budgets

You can also enter releases simultaneously for several projects in Transaction IMCBR3. You can copy the budget or planned values in full or with a release percentage weighted as a released budget. If required, you can perform this mass release for the total values and all fiscal year values simultaneously or restrict the mass release to an individual fiscal year.

[◉] **Budget Values in Project System**

A distinction is made in SAP Project System among an original budget, the current budget, and, if necessary, budget releases. In addition to the currency in which they were entered, all budget values are also saved to the database in the object currency of the individual WBS elements and in the CO area currency of the project.

3.1.4 Budget Carryforward

In Transaction CJCO, you can transfer a budget that was not consumed for a project within one fiscal year into the following fiscal year. The system uses the difference of the fiscal year budget and the distributed values and actual costs to calculate the budget amount that is carried forward from one fiscal year into the next fiscal year for each WBS element. These actual costs include the costs of the WBS element with budget carried forward, the actual costs of all assigned orders and networks, and the actual costs of lower-level WBS elements without a separate budget. Note that the planned costs of apportioned orders and networks are not deducted from the fiscal year budget when the carryforward is calculated. Budgets are typically carried forward as part of a company's year-end closing. Because commitments are ignored when the budget values to be carried forward are calculated, you should use a commitment carryforward in Transaction CJCF before you carry forward budgets.

You can also carry forward the budget for a project several times. If in the old fiscal year actual costs were posted to the project at a later stage, then a new budget carryforward results in the budget, which was already carried forward into the next year, being posted back to the previous year. However, in this case only the maximum amount of budget that was previously carried forward in total into the next year can be posted back to the previous year. If necessary, you can also carry budget forward in the form of a test run and use detailed lists to first analyze the planned carryforwards before you start an actual update run.

Carryforward several times

Other tools available for managing project budgets in SAP Project System include the following:

Additional budgeting tools

- Plan/Budget Consistency Check for Projects (Transaction IMCOC3)
- Transfer Plan to Project Budget (Transaction IMCCP3)
- Adjust Plan/Budget to Agree with Assigned Values for Projects (Transaction IMPBA3)
- Currency Recalculation of Plan/Budget for Projects (Transaction IMCRC3)

Restrictions of Transaction IMPBA3   **[+]**

Note that the ADJUST PLAN/BUDGET TO AGREE WITH ASSIGNED VALUES FOR PROJECTS function ignores statuses that don't allow changes to planning or budgeting. The transaction for adjusting plans/budgets to assigned values for projects is therefore not available in the SAP menu; you can only start it by calling Transaction IMPBA3 directly.

For more information about the functions of the transactions listed previously and each consistency check executed, see the program documentation, which you can call from the transactions.

3.1.5   Availability Control

A main task of managing budgets for projects is to contrast the budget with the individual project parts—that is, their approved cost structures, the planned commitment, and actual costs based on purchase orders and activity inputs or material withdrawals, for example. For this reason, different standard reports are available in the reporting area of SAP Project System.

However, availability control also enables the system to determine relevant funds automatically in the background and to compare these assigned funds with the corresponding budget values. By doing so, the availability control can warn you of imminent budget overruns before they occur or even notify you of the allotment of excess funds on WBS elements when they are created.

Availability control process

As soon as the availability control for a project is active, the system performs different steps for postings on a WBS element of the project or for postings to assigned apportioned orders or networks or network activities. The system first determines the relevant WBS elements of the project carrying budget. If a posting is made on a WBS element that does not have its own budget, then the system searches successively for a WBS element carrying budget at the higher level.

Assigned values

The system then determines the associated funds for the WBS elements carrying budget. The assigned value of a WBS element carrying budget consists of the following:

- Actual costs or statistical costs on the WBS element carrying budget
- Actual costs and static actual costs of lower-level
  WBS elements without their own budget
- Commitments on the WBS element carrying budget and on lower-level WBS elements without their own budget
- The maximum from the planned and actual costs and the commitments of assigned apportioned networks and orders

The individual contributions to the assigned values of a WBS element carrying budget warrants further explanation. Actual costs resulting from goods withdrawals and documents from FI or CO, for example, belong to the actual costs that are included in the calculation of assigned funds. In particular, debits due to settlements are also included in the calculation of the assigned value. Credits caused by settlements are only considered if the settlement took place on a budget-controlled object. Commitments are created due to purchase requisitions, purchase orders, or funds reservations.

Values of assigned orders or networks are either already included in the calculation of assigned values with the CREATED status or included once the orders have been released. You can use the ASSIGNED FUNDS IN PLAN indicator in the DEFINE ORDER VALUE UPDATING FOR ORDERS FOR PROJECTS table (Transaction OPSV) in Customizing of SAP Project System to determine which of the two statuses for which you want the values to be included in the assigned funds calculation. In this case, you can implement the setting based on the order category, order type, and CO area of the orders.

Apportioned orders

Assigned Values of Networks and Orders

[+]

With the exception of planning networks, the values of assigned orders or networks are included in the calculation of assigned values by the time the RELEASED status is assigned. In particular, the planned values of assigned apportioned orders represent funds against the budget of WBS elements. The planned values of material components for valuated stock are not included in the total of assigned values, however.

If you want to exclude certain costs (for instance, overhead costs) as assigned values, then you can enter the corresponding cost elements as *exempt cost elements* based on the CO area in Transaction OPTK in Customizing of SAP Project System. These exempt cost elements are therefore not checked as assigned values against the budget of WBS elements. Revenues are generally ignored when assigned values are determined.

Exempt cost elements

After the system has determined the relevant WBS elements carrying budget and calculated the corresponding assigned values due to a posting on a project, a check takes place in the last step of the availability control. This check compares the available budget of WBS elements carrying budget with their assigned funds.

If the availability control determines that certain tolerance limits you defined are exceeded by assigned values, then the system performs one of the following three actions:

Availability control actions

▶ **Warning**
When the user who made the posting on the project saves the data, he receives a warning message that refers to the exceeded tolerance limit. The user can now either save the corresponding document or

postpone the document for the time being if necessary to consult with the project manager first.

▶ **Warning and email to project manager**
The user who makes the posting receives a warning message and decides whether or not to save the posting document. When the document is saved, the system generates an email to the person responsible for the WBS element carrying the budget for which the limit was exceeded and to the person responsible specified in the project definition. The email contains information about the WBS element in question, the level by which the tolerance limit has been exceeded, the business transaction that triggered the action, and its document number.

▶ **Error message**
With this action, documents that would lead to the specified tolerance limits being exceeded are not saved. The user receives a corresponding error message.

First, consider what effects the use of the ERROR MESSAGE action could have internally (for instance, when you enter invoices in FI). In general, the ERROR MESSAGE action is only used for select business processes.

Business transaction groups

You define the tolerance limits and the relevant action that the system should take when the tolerance limits are exceeded in the DEFINE TOLERANCE LIMITS Customizing transaction based on the budget profile and the *transaction groups* (see Figure 3.7). Business transaction groups in this case represent the groupings of business transactions.

The business transaction group for FINANCIAL ACCOUNTING DOCUMENT therefore covers postings in FI, the business transaction group for BUDGETING covers subsequent budget changes, and so on. The business transaction group for ORDERS FOR PROJECT covers planning cost changes of assigned, apportioned orders and also the assignment of orders with assigned values. Postings on assigned orders (for instance, the account assignment of a purchase order), however, are checked in the business transaction group (PURCHASE ORDER) provided for the posting.

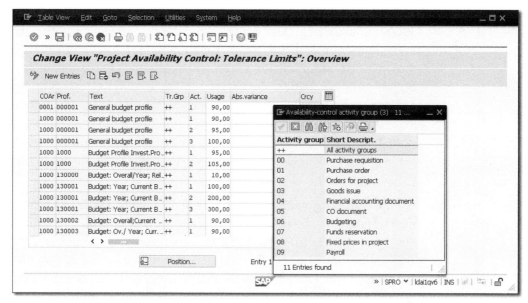

Figure 3.7 Defining the Tolerance Limits of Availability Control Based on Business Transaction Groups

The business transaction group for ALL BUSINESS TRANSACTION GROUPS is used to define actions for a tolerance limit for all business transaction groups for which you do not want to specifically implement other settings. However, if you implement settings for a business transaction group of a tolerance group, then these have priority over the settings of the business transaction group for ALL BUSINESS TRANSACTION GROUPS. Only the business transactions for which you defined tolerance limits and actions in the DEFINE TOLERANCE LIMITS table are taken into account during the availability control check.

Assigned Values of Goods Receipts	[+]

Although the business transaction of the goods receipt generates assigned values, you should note that it is ignored during the availability control check. Therefore, use the PURCHASE ORDER business transaction group for the check and, if necessary, don't allow account assignments to be changed for the goods receipt posting.

The tolerance limit settings for projects with the budget profile 130001 illustrated in the example in Figure 3.7 result in a warning message (Action 1) being issued each time a purchase requisition is posted (business transaction group 00), which leads to more than 90% of the available budget being consumed. If purchase requisitions exceed the available budget, the system reacts by issuing an error message and therefore prevents the purchase requisitions from being posted (Action 3). All other business transactions only result in a warning message being issued and an email being sent to the corresponding person responsible in the project (Action 2) if the budget is exceeded.

For the availability control, you specify in the budget profile of a project which budget is to be used as the basis for the check, in which currency you want the availability control to be implemented, and when the availability control should be activated. Depending on the budget profile settings, you can perform the availability control check against the current, still distributable total or annual budget or (if you are working with budget releases) against the released, overall, or annual budget that can still be distributed.

Just as with the consistency checks for budgeting, you can also carry out the availability control either in the CO area currency of the project or in the object currency of the WBS elements. However, the latter only works if the object currency within the project is uniform; in other words, it is identical for all WBS elements of a project. Using the object currency for the availability control is particularly relevant if you have also carried out the budgeting in the object currency. The postings on the project will mainly be entered later in the object currencies or in foreign currencies, and you will have to anticipate widely fluctuating exchange rates between the object and foreign and CO area currencies.

You can use two options to activate the availability control for a project. If you select setting 1 (AUTOMATIC ACTIVATION DURING BUDGET ALLOCATION) in the ACTIVATION TYPE field of the budget profile (see also Figure 3.1), then the availability control for a project is automatically activated when you enter a relevant budget. If you want the availability control to check funds against the current budget, then the activation already takes place when the original budget is distributed. If you want the check to reference the released budget, then the availability control is only activated automatically once you have released the budget.

> **Automatic Activation during Budget Allocation for WBS Elements without Budget** **[+]**
>
> Suppose you want to use activation type 1 but also plan on activating the availability control, even though you don't yet want to distribute or release any budget. In this case, perform budgeting or release a budget (the availability control is activated) and then immediately return the budget again (the availability control remains active).

If you select activation type 2 (BACKGROUND ACTIVATION) in the budget profile, then either you can manually activate the availability control in the background or this can be done automatically by the system. You can manually activate the availability control of a project in Transaction CJBV. To activate the availability control automatically, define a job in Transaction CJBV for all relevant projects that regularly checks in the background whether the funds of the projects exceed the usage level specified in the budget profile. If this is the case, then the availability control is activated automatically for the corresponding projects.

If you don't want to use the availability control function for managing budgets for projects, then you can select activation type 0 (CANNOT BE ACTIVATED) in the budget profile. Selecting this setting means that you cannot activate an availability control manually or automatically. However, you may also need to deactivate an availability control that is already active. To do this, you can use Transaction CJBW in the SAP Project System menu. If you only want to exclude individual WBS elements of a project from the availability control, then you can define a user status that does not allow the AVAILABILITY CONTROL business process (see Chapter 1, Section 1.6) and set it in the corresponding WBS elements.

Deactivating the availability control

In Transaction CJ30 or CJ31, you can call information about the availability control and conduct a detailed analysis of the budget values already available and still distributable and all relevant Customizing settings (see Figure 3.8). If, in the case of an active availability control, you make changes later to the relevant Customizing settings of the budget

Availability control analysis

profile, tolerance limits, exempt cost elements, or the order value update for the project, then you should reconstruct the availability control for all affected projects in Transaction CJBN. You will find more useful information about availability control in SAP Notes 178837, 165085, and 33091.

Figure 3.8 Analysis of Availability Control in Transaction CJ30

> **Budgeting Functions in SAP Project System**
>
> In SAP Project System, you can distribute budget values hierarchically to WBS elements of your projects. Depending on requirements, you can distribute budgets as overall budgets, fiscal year budgets, or releases of less than one year. You can use budget updates to make subsequent changes to your budgeting. The availability control ensures that the system automatically issues warning or error messages or sends email to the relevant project managers when specific tolerance limits of the budget values are exceeded.

3.2   Integration with Investment Management

If several projects split budgets or if you want other plans that are not mapped using projects to be taken into account when budgets are allocated, then an isolated consideration of individual project budgets is not sufficient. However, you cannot manage a budget across projects simply by using the aforementioned SAP Project System tools. Nevertheless, by using the integration of SAP Project System with Investment Management in the SAP system, not only can you plan, distribute, and monitor the budgets of projects, but you can also do this simultaneously for the budget values for internal or maintenance orders at a higher level.

Investment programs in Investment Management form the basis for the comprehensive planning and budgeting of costs for a company's plans or investments. When you create investment programs, you make an assignment to a *program type* in each case through which the system automatically derives default values and control parameters. Investment programs consist of an *investment program definition* with general specifications and default values for the entire program and hierarchically arranged *investment program positions*.

Investment programs

You can structure investment programs based on any criteria, such as geographical factors, the size of the plan, or the organizational setup of your company. After you create the structure of an investment program, you can use this structure to plan costs hierarchically and to allocate budgets. Figure 3.9 shows an example of the structure of an investment program and budget values that were distributed at different levels for the programs involved.

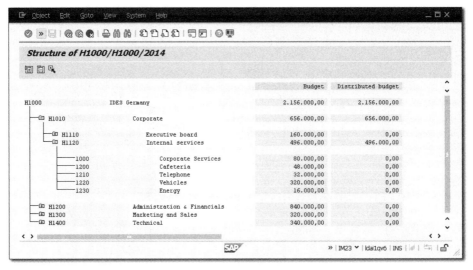

Figure 3.9 Example of an Investment Program

Investment measures
Maintenance orders, internal orders, and projects that you assign to investment program positions are called *investment measures*. Investment measures are used for the detailed planning of plans or investments but are also used in particular for their operational execution.

In Reporting in Investment Management, different CO data of investment measures can be analyzed in aggregated format at the level of investment program positions. Investment measures are created and edited in the corresponding applications. For example, you create and edit maintenance orders in Plant Maintenance, internal orders in CO, and projects in SAP Project System.

Appropriation requests
Even before you create investment measures in the relevant applications, you can create *appropriation requests* in Investment Management to map project proposals, investment requirements, development ideas, or other plans in the stages before their possible implementation in the system. You can define numerous pieces of investment-relevant information and documents in an appropriation request. In particular, you can create several variants within an appropriation request to map different implementation options and plan their costs, for example. As for investment measures, you can also assign investment program positions to appropriation requests.

Using statuses and workflows, you can map multilevel approval processes for appropriation requests in Investment Management. After you approve an appropriation request, you can transfer this to the investment measure. For projects, you can therefore use appropriation requests to enter project proposals, plan their costs, initiate approval processes, and, finally, create operative projects from the appropriation requests.

Creating Projects from Appropriation Requests	[+]
When you create projects from appropriation requests, you can use operative and standard work breakdown structures as a template. However, networks assigned to templates are not copied in this case. When you transfer an appropriation request into a project, the project receives various sets of master data, the assignment to investment program positions, and the planned costs of the appropriation request.	

After you have assigned appropriation requests and investment measures to investment program positions, you can roll up their planned costs to the relevant investment program positions in Transaction IM34 in Investment Management. Therefore, you don't have to plan costs twice (that is, at the level of appropriation requests on the one hand and at the level of investment program positions on the other). However, you can also plan costs directly on the program positions or change uploaded planned costs (Transaction IM35) if required.

Rollup of planned values

The cost planning of investment programs is generally used as the basis for a budgeting process in Investment Management. A first step in this case involves allocating budget values at the level of the different positions of an investment program. A second step entails distributing the budget values of a program position in Investment Management to the assigned investment measures.

Budgeting process

You perform the budgeting of program positions in Transaction IM32 in Investment Management similarly to the budgeting of projects in SAP Project System. In Investment Management, contrary to SAP Project System, you can differentiate between budgets according to different budget types (for instance, costs that can be capitalized or additional costs that cannot be capitalized). However, by separately using budget types when managing budgets, you prevent budget values from being distributed from program positions to assigned investment measures. We therefore will not discuss the use of budget values any further in the following sections.

Depending on the settings of the investment program, you can distribute the overall values or budget values with reference to the fiscal years manually or by copying planned values. This allows the system to ensure the hierarchical consistency of the budget distribution. You can make necessary budget changes of an investment program in the form of budget supplements (Transaction IM30) or returns (Transaction IM38; see Section 3.1.2).

Following the budgeting of the program positions, you can now distribute the budget values of the positions further to each assigned investment measure; you can do this in Transaction IM52 in Investment Management. You can distribute the budget values manually or use the planned values of the individual investment measures as a template. If required, you can also use Transaction IM52 to post budget supplements or returns between investment program positions and the assigned investment measures. In SAP Project System, the budget distributed to a project this way can now be used to distribute it further to lower-level WBS elements within the project structure (see Section 3.1.1).

Controlling the budget distribution The linking of budget values of an investment program position with the budget values of assigned investment measures is controlled by the BUDGET DISTRIBUTION OF OVERALL VALUES and BUDGET DISTRIBUTION OF ANNUAL VALUES indicators in the master data of the investment program position. Both indicators have the following significance:

▶ If the BUDGET DISTRIBUTION OF OVERALL VALUES and BUDGET DISTRIBUTION OF ANNUAL VALUES indicators are set in an investment program position, then the assigned investment measures can only receive your overall budget and your fiscal year budget through the distribution of budget values of the program position. For the projects, the budget values can then be distributed further within the hierarchical project structure.

- If only the BUDGET DISTRIBUTION OF OVERALL VALUES indicator is set, then the assigned investment measures can only receive your overall budget from the higher-level program position. However, you can distribute the annual budgets at investment-measure level (regardless of the fiscal-year-dependent values of the program position). Only the BUDGET DISTRIBUTION OF ANNUAL VALUES indicator—that is, a distribution of annual budgets without a simultaneous distribution of overall budgets—cannot be set.

- If neither of the two indicators is set in an investment program position, then you can budget the assigned investment measures separately. Although you can compare the budget values of the program position and the assigned measures with each other in Reporting in Investment Management, an automatic check does not take place to determine whether the budget values of the measures exceed the budget of the program position.

The operative processing of investments or plans, and therefore also the corresponding postings, are performed at the investment-measure level and can be monitored there using an active availability control. For this reason, an active availability control is not possible for investment program positions. However, by setting the BUDGET DISTRIBUTION OF OVERALL VALUES indicator in the master data of a program position you can ensure that the budget values of the assigned measures in total cannot exceed the budget of the program position. In principal, this corresponds to a type of availability control for investment programs in terms of assigned investment measures.

To ensure that the data can be exchanged between maintenance, internal orders, and projects on the one hand and investment programs on the other (rollup of planned costs, budget distribution, aggregated evaluations in Investment Management, and so on), you must create corresponding assignments. Investment program positions are assigned for projects at the WBS elements level. You can create the assignments between the WBS elements and program positions both in Investment Management and SAP Project System in the maintenance transactions for work breakdown structures (see Figure 3.10).

Assigning projects

Figure 3.10 Example of Assigning a WBS Element to an Investment Program Position

To create assignments, you must meet several prerequisites. Program positions must allow an assignment. In the master data of a program position, you can decide whether assignments can be made to appropriation requests, orders, or projects. However, investment measures can only be assigned to *end-node positions*. These are program positions for which no other program positions are assigned at a lower-level.

A project is typically only assigned to one investment program position. In this case, you make the assignment at the top WBS element level of the project. As part of budget distribution in Investment Management, this WBS element then receives a budget from the higher-level program position. The project manager can then distribute this budget further to the lower-level WBS elements of the project (see Section 3.1.1).

Several investment program positions However, you may want a project to receive a budget from different "buckets," which means that it is assigned to several investment program positions. In this case, you can choose between two options for the assignment:

▶ **Multiple assignments**
In the maintenance transactions of SAP Project System, you can assign a WBS element (for example, the top WBS element) to several different program positions and consequently compare each assignment by specifying a percentage.

However, you only use these types of multiple assignments to ensure that the planned, actual, and budget values of the project (taking into account the weighting percentage rates) can be evaluated on the different program positions along with the values of other assigned investment measures. Nevertheless, if you use a multiple assignment, then you cannot distribute the budget from the assigned investment program positions at a later stage.

▶ **Assigning several WBS elements of a project**

If you also want to distribute budget values of different program positions on the project, then your second option is to assign different WBS elements of a project to each program position. These WBS elements do not necessarily have to be WBS elements of the highest level of the project. Furthermore, they don't have to be on the same level within the project structure. However, you can only assign a WBS element to an investment program position if a higher-level or lower-level WBS element is not yet assigned to a program position.

If you distribute a budget of different investment program positions to each assigned WBS element, then the system automatically rolls up the budget values to the higher-level WBS elements. This ensures that the hierarchical consistency of the budget values is maintained within the project structure. The project manager can then distribute the budget further to lower-level WBS elements if required.

If the BUDGET DISTRIBUTION OF OVERALL VALUES indicator or the BUDGET DISTRIBUTION OF ANNUAL VALUES indicator is set in an investment program position, then the assigned WBS elements can only receive a budget through the budget distribution of the program position. After you assign the WBS elements, you can no longer assign budgets separately in SAP Project System. As long as the WBS elements have not yet received any budget from the program position, the lower-level WBS elements cannot yet receive any budget in a hierarchically consistent format either. To prevent a WBS element from receiving a budget in the SAP Project System before it has already been assigned to an investment program position, you can make a mandatory assignment to an investment program position for WBS elements before the first budgeting.

Mandatory
assignments

You can do this in two different ways:

▶ You can control the relevant fields for an assignment as required fields by using the field selection for WBS elements (see Chapter 1, Section 1.8.2). Because you don't want all WBS elements to be assigned to program positions, you must specify suitable influencing fields and values when you define the field selection.

The assignment is generally made at the top WBS element level of a project. Therefore, to do this you specify the INVESTMENT PROGRAM field as the mandatory field in the field selection based on the influencing LEVEL field and the value 1.

▸ You can enter a program type in the budget profile of a project to make a mandatory assignment to an investment program position for WBS elements (see Figure 3.1). This entry ensures that the project is only budgeted after a WBS element of the project has been assigned to an investment program for this program type.

[+] **Displaying the Assignment Fields**

The fields for assigning investment program positions are not displayed by default in the detail screen of the WBS elements. However, when you define your own tabs (see Chapter 1, Section 1.8.2) you can also include these fields in the detail screen of WBS elements.

Investment projects

The integration of SAP Project System with Investment Management can be used not only for pure exchange of data between projects and investment programs but also for the project settlement. Here, the goal is to allocate the costs collected on a project to *assets under construction* (AuC) and also to allocate *completed assets* from Asset Accounting. You can define *investment profiles* in Investment Management Customizing for this purpose and enter these profiles in the master data of WBS elements. WBS elements or projects in which investment profiles are defined are also called *investment projects*. Chapter 5, Section 5.9 explains in detail how investment profiles are defined and used and discusses in depth the processes for settling projects specifically available for investment projects.

[◉] **Budget Management across Projects in Investment Management**

You can use Investment Management functions to manage budgets across projects at the level of the investment program. By assigning projects to investment programs, the planned costs of the projects can be rolled up into Investment Management, and budgets from Investment Management can be distributed to the projects.

3.3   Summary

By distributing budgets to projects, in addition to the planned costs, you can manage an approved cost structure for your projects and monitor funds against this cost structure by using availability control. In addition to using SAP Project System functions to manage budgets, you can also use the integration with Investment Management to manage budgets across projects.

In the execution phase, you can compare the previously planned dates, resource and material requirements, and costs and revenues with the corresponding actual data and thereby monitor the execution and progress of your projects.

4   Project Execution Processes

In the execution phase of projects (depending on the type of project), capacity activities of your company are used; external resources are involved in the execution; material is purchased, produced in-house, consumed, and delivered; invoices from suppliers are entered; invoices are sent to customers; various internal cost allocations are made; and so on. Although many of these processes are triggered in projects, they are processed across different departments.

Implementation phase

Due to the integration of SAP Project System into other applications of the SAP system, you can update almost all project-related data automatically on the relevant projects or evaluate this data in the Reporting of the projects regardless of whether the corresponding documents are created in Purchasing, Production, Sales, or external and internal accounting. Therefore, this data doesn't need to be entered several times. In particular, you can compare the actual data of the project execution with the relevant planning data at the level of the projects. In Reporting, you can use progress analysis or special tools to identify variances in the project planning when needed, such as ProMan or progress tracking.

We discuss the different aspects and processes for implementing a project in this chapter. Note that the individual sections are not in any chronological order; instead, they are sorted by topic, because different processes are typically executed in parallel in the execution phase of projects. When constructing an elevator, for example, the engineers can start with the final assembly of the elevator, use materials, and confirm their time data while missing material is procured in Purchasing and invoices are created in Financial Accounting (FI) for materials already delivered.

4.1 Actual Dates

You can use actual dates to document the period required to implement a work package in projects. Different functions are available for entering actual dates depending on whether you use work breakdown structures (WBS) or networks to structure your projects. We discuss these in the following sections.

4.1.1 Actual Dates of WBS Elements

You can enter actual dates for WBS elements in WBS. A distinction is made in this case between the actual start and actual finish date of a WBS element. The actual start date documents the time that the execution of the WBS element begins and the actual finish date records the time it ends. The setting of an actual start date for a WBS element is automatically documented by the PCNF (PARTIALLY CONFIRMED) system status at the WBS element level. If you also set an actual finish date, the WBS element is automatically assigned the status CONF (CONFIRMED). If the CONF status is active in a WBS element, then a warning is issued each time you make a subsequent change to the actual dates of this WBS element. Provisional actual dates for WBS elements only result from actual dates of assigned activities, and therefore cannot be entered manually for WBS elements.

Prerequisites for actual dates of WBS elements

You must fulfill several prerequisites to enter actual dates for WBS elements. To define an actual start date in a WBS element, the WBS element must have the PREL (PARTIALLY RELEASED) or REL (RELEASED) status and no other status can prevent the setting of the actual date. Setting an actual finish date for a WBS element requires the status to be REL and all lower-level WBS elements and, if necessary, the assigned activities must have the CONF status.

Entering actual dates

You can use three options to enter actual dates at the WBS elements level:

▸ **Manual entry**
Manually enter actual dates for WBS elements. Similar to the manual planning of dates, you enter the actual dates in a table or, if required, in a graphic in the detail screen of the WBS elements, depending on the relevant editing transaction.

▸ **Extrapolation**
Use the EXTRAPOLATE DATES function to calculate actual dates from the actual dates of the lower-level WBS elements.

▸ **Determination of actual dates**
Use the DETERMINE ACTUAL DATES function to derive the actual dates of WBS elements from the actual dates of the assigned activities.

Actual dates of WBS elements cannot be derived automatically from FI, Controlling (CO), or Purchasing documents, for example. Instead, the relevant project manager has the responsibility of entering actual dates for WBS elements.

4.1.2   Actual Dates of Activities

Actual dates of activities (or activity elements) are typically entered using confirmations (see Section 4.3). In this case, you differentiate between the actual dates from partial confirmations, which are practically interpreted as provisional actual start dates and actual finish dates, and the actual dates from final confirmations, which represent the actual execution period. The actual dates of confirmations for an activity are automatically updated in the activity, provided you have not explicitly prohibited this in the confirmation. The actual start date of an activity is determined from the earliest actual start date of all confirmations of the activity. Similarly, the actual finish date is determined from the latest actual finish date of all confirmations. If required, you can also change the actual dates manually at activity level. Actual dates of activities cannot be derived automatically from material documents or vendor invoices, for example. The REL (RELEASED) status is required for creating confirmations for an activity and entering actual dates.

Confirmations

Note that the actual dates of network activities can affect the subsequent schedulings of the network. If an activity has the CONF system status due to a final confirmation, then the system automatically sets the planned dates of the earliest and latest date of the activity on the actual dates of the activity. If the activity has relationships to other activities, then the planned dates of these activities would also be adapted accordingly to the scheduling logic if rescheduling were performed (see Chapter 2, Section 2.1.2).

Shift order indicator

If an activity has the PCNF status due to partial confirmations, then the SHIFT ORDER indicator determines in the scheduling parameters how the actual dates of the activity are to be handled for a subsequent scheduling. If the SHIFT ORDER indicator is set, then the system calculates the earliest and latest date according to the normal scheduling logic. However, in this case the system uses the planned duration as the relevant duration for the scheduling minus the duration already confirmed. This setting can be useful if, for example, you have already done some work before the originally planned period but want to prevent all subsequent activities from also being scheduled much too early.

Scheduling example 1

Figure 4.1 shows a corresponding example. A partially confirmed activity called ELECTRICAL ENGINEERING is assigned to the WBS element of the same name. It was documented in the partial confirmation that three days were already worked (see actual date bar of the activity in Figure 4.1—the lowest date bar) but this work was started a week earlier than originally planned (to compare, see the forecast date bar of the activity, that is, the highest date bar in the lower part of the screen in Figure 4.1). Subsequent scheduling that resulted in the SHIFT ORDER indicator being set has calculated the new start date of the activity (see the basic date bar of the activity, that is, the middle date bar in the lower part of the screen) according to the normal scheduling logic.

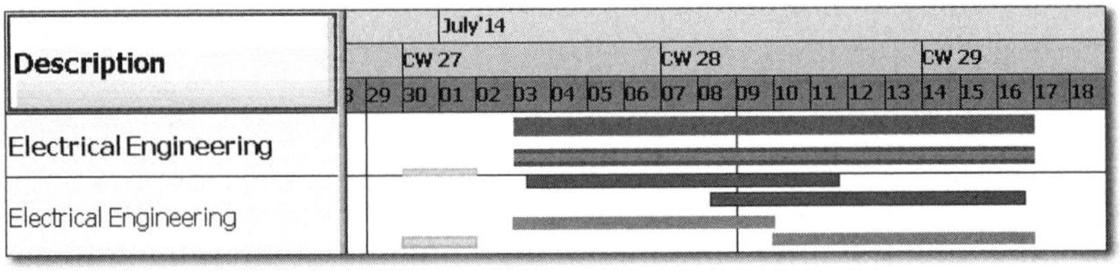

Figure 4.1 Example of Scheduling a Partially Confirmed Activity in Which the Shift Order Indicator Is Set

However, the original duration minus the duration already worked was used as the duration for the scheduling. At the WBS element level, the actual date of the activity is shown as a provisional actual date (thinner, bright date bar in the upper part of the screen).

If the SHIFT ORDER indicator is not set for a rescheduling, then the system automatically sets the earliest start of a partially confirmed activity on the actual start date of the activity. As the duration, the system uses the planned duration for scheduling the earliest finish date and uses the planned duration minus the duration already confirmed for scheduling the latest date. Figure 4.2 shows an example of the partially confirmed ELECTRONIC ENGINEERING activity. The basic dates displayed in Figure 4.2 (middle date bar in the lower part of the screen) now result from a scheduling for which the SHIFT ORDER indicator was not set. Compare the basic dates with the scheduling dates displayed in Figure 4.1.

Scheduling example 2

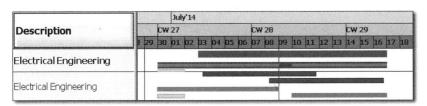

Figure 4.2 Example of Scheduling a Partially Confirmed Activity in Which the Shift Order Indicator Is Not Set

In addition to entering actual data, you can also specify forecast data in a partial confirmation. Therefore, in addition to the actual start and finish dates you can also specify a forecast remaining duration or a forecast finish for performing the activity. This forecast data is automatically taken into account for subsequent schedulings. If you have specified a forecast remaining duration, then this duration is used for rescheduling. If you entered a forecast finish date when partially confirming an activity, then the system automatically sets the finish dates of the activity to this date for a rescheduling.

Forecast dates in confirmations

If you don't want actual dates from confirmations to affect the subsequent schedulings, then you can prevent the actual dates of the confirmations from being updated on the activities by setting the NO DATE UPDATE indicator in the confirmations or confirmation parameters. You can also use a corresponding field selection to prevent a forecast remaining duration or a forecast finish date from being entered in the confirmations.

4.1.3 Actual Dates of Milestones

Percentage of completion

To document that milestones of a project have been reached, you can enter an actual date for these milestones. You must do this manually for milestones that are assigned to WBS elements. You can enter actual dates for milestones on activities manually or derive them from confirmations of activities. To copy the actual finish date of a confirmation as the actual date of a milestone, the confirmation parameters must allow this (SET MILESTONE DATES AUTOMATICALLY indicator; see Section 4.3), and the degree of processing of the confirmation must be greater than or equal to the percentage of completion that the milestone represents (PERC OF COMPL. field in the milestone). You can use actual dates of activity milestones to unlock billing items within milestone billing and therefore control the creation of invoices (see Section 4.6.1).

SAP Fiori — confirming project milestones

The SAP Fiori app CONFIRM PROJECT MILESTONE is another option for manually entering a milestone actual date (see Figure 4.3). By means of this app, you can confirm actual dates for milestones via a tablet or smartphone when you're in the field. You can call the app directly from the SAP Fiori Launchpad, from an analytical app, or from the fact sheet for milestones (see Chapter 1, Section 1.7.6). In contrast to manual entry of actual dates of milestones in SAP ERP transactions, in this app you don't need to access the milestone confirmation via the project structure; you can directly search for a milestone to open its confirmation.

[+]   **Relationship between Planned and Actual Dates**

Note that the planned dates of milestones are automatically set on the actual dates of the milestones. If you want to perform a planned/actual comparison of milestone dates, then you must use project versions or forecast dates (see Chapter 2, Section 2.1).

Figure 4.3 SAP Fiori App for Entering Actual Dates of Milestones

4.2 Account Assignment of Documents

Costs, revenues, or perhaps even payments on projects are updated on WBS elements and network activities or on activity elements by using the account assignment of corresponding documents (that is, activity allocations, invoices, goods receipts and issues, billing documents, down payments, and so on). If you've assigned orders such as plant maintenance, production, and internal orders to projects, then documents can also be assigned to these orders. In Reporting, you can analyze the corresponding costs of the assigned orders in an aggregated format at the level of the project, but the project is not updated automatically. However, you can settle the costs of the assigned orders on the project as part of period-end closing (see Chapter 5, Section 5.9) if required.

Prerequisites To perform the account assignment of documents on WBS elements or network activities, the status of the objects must allow a corresponding account assignment. Although you can assign purchase requisitions or purchase orders by default to projects in the CRTD (CREATED) system status, you cannot post goods or invoice receipts. For the account assignment of documents that results in actual costs, the status in the relevant account assignment objects of SAP Project System must be REL (RELEASED). Furthermore, the master data of WBS elements must also allow an account assignment of documents. If required, you can use the ACCOUNT ASSIGNMENT ELEMENT operative indicator to determine whether you want an account assignment to be possible for each WBS element (see Chapter 1, Section 1.2.1).

4.2.1 Commitments Management

When you update data on projects due to the account assignment of documents, you differentiate between actual costs and commitments. Although actual costs indicate the actual consumption of goods and services in figures, commitments simply correspond to obligations based on purchase requisitions, purchase orders, or funds commitments. By using commitments, you can proactively analyze liabilities that may result in actual costs at a later stage; however, commitments are not yet entered for accounting purposes. If you activated the availability control (see Chapter 3, Section 3.1.5), then commitments are taken into account as funds of the budget of WBS elements. In other words, commitments bind funds in advance for the subsequent actual costs.

Activating the commitments management
To enable the system to update commitments on SAP Project System projects, you must activate the commitments management for projects. You can do this for the relevant controlling areas in Customizing by using Transaction OKKP (see Figure 4.4). In Reporting, depending on the settings of the reports you can analyze commitments separately or according to purchase requisition commitments, purchase order commitments, or commitments for funds commitments (see Chapter 6, Section 6.2).

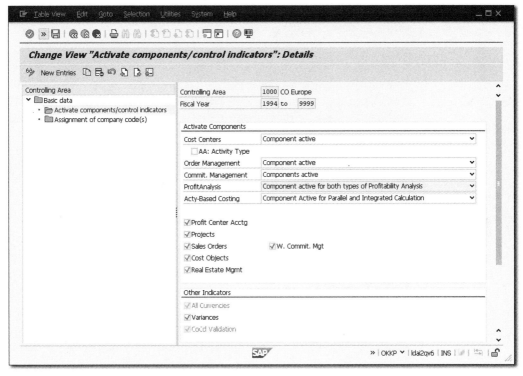

Figure 4.4 Activating the Commitments Management

As soon as commitments management is active, the system uses the (remaining) quantity and the price for each unit of measure to calculate a purchase requisition commitment for the planned delivery date for each purchase requisition that you assign to a project. The system also updates this purchase requisition commitment on the project. In this case, the purchase requisitions can be created manually in Purchasing and assigned to a WBS element, or they can be created automatically based on externally processed and service activities or externally procured material components of a network. The purchase requisition commitment is (according to the relevant account assignment) shown separately on the WBS elements, network headers, or activities. Purchase requisitions that are automatically created within Materials Requirement Planning (MRP) runs are an exception in this case—that is, they don't lead to corresponding purchase requisition commitments. Only

Purchase requisition commitments

the purchased orders for these purchase requisitions result in the commitments being displayed.

[+] **Displaying Commitments**

For header-assigned networks, the commitments are displayed on the network header; for activity-assigned networks, they are displayed at the level of individual activities. Commitments for material components are updated on the corresponding network headers or activities for non-stock items. Commitments for stock items can only be displayed in SAP Project System if they are managed in the individual requirements stock. The commitments are then updated on the relevant segments of the individual requirements stock.

Purchase order commitments

If you create a purchase order for a purchase requisition that is assigned to a project, then the purchase requisition commitment is reduced in accordance with the quantity transferred in the purchase order. If the entire quantity of the purchase requisition is copied into the purchase order, then the purchase requisition commitment is also reduced completely. Using the value of the purchase order, the system simultaneously determines a purchase order commitment and updates it on the corresponding account assignment objects, from which it can be evaluated in the delivery date period of the purchase order.

Based on the Goods Issue indicator for the purchase order, the purchase order commitment is reduced and the corresponding actual costs are updated by posting either a goods receipt or the invoice receipt that refers to the purchase order. If only a portion of the quantity or values of the purchase order is posted in this case, a portion of the purchase order commitment will be converted into actual values. The purchase order commitment is reduced entirely if you post a complete goods receipt or invoice receipt or you manually set a Delivery Completed indicator to document that no more deliveries are expected even though the quantity or value of the purchase order has not yet been reached. As long as you have not yet posted a goods or invoice receipt for the purchase order item, you can lock the item or, in certain circumstances, delete it. In both cases, the purchase order commitment of the item is reduced completely.

Funds commitments

You can use Transaction FMZ1 in SAP Project System to create *funds commitments* if you want to reserve funds for later costs but are still unsure of which business transactions will result in these costs. The amount of a funds commitment is shown as a corresponding commitment on the WBS element, network, or activity to which you have assigned the funds commitment. In addition, the funds commitment amount is taken into account when the assigned values are being calculated and is therefore included in the availability control of projects. You can either reduce the commitments for funds commitments manually by entering the corresponding reduction amounts in Transaction FMZ6, or this can occur automatically when vendor invoices are entered in FI if the corresponding funds commitment is specified in the account assignment block of the invoice.

4.2.2 Manual Account Assignment

In contrast to externally processed activities and service activities or material components in networks, purchasing documents or documents for settling costs cannot be created automatically for work breakdown structures. Instead, you have to create these documents manually in SAP Project System, Purchasing, CO, or FI and assign them to WBS elements. For statistical WBS elements (see Chapter 1, Section 1.2.1), you must also always specify another account assignment object in these documents in addition to the WBS element, because updating statistical WBS elements is not cost-effective and only occurs for information purposes.

The following list contains examples of some transactions from different applications of the SAP system that may be relevant within the execution phase of projects and that you can use to enter documents and then assign them to WBS elements:

Examples of document entries

- ▸ Transaction ME51N (Create Purchase Requisition)
- ▸ Transaction ME21N (Create Purchase Order)
- ▸ Transaction KB21N (Activity Allocation)
- ▸ Transaction MIGO (Goods Movements)
- ▸ Transaction FB60 (Vendor Invoices)

Additional functions are available in FI to manage documents relating to a project in the form of *debit and credit own payment chains*. These functions are usually used for long-term construction projects for which various down payment invoices, final invoices, and deductions are supposed to be entered and monitored. Employees can also enter times for WBS elements in the Cross-Application Time Sheet (CATS; see Section 4.3.3). The transfer of this time data into CO then generates an activity allocation between the cost center of the employees and the corresponding WBS elements.

4.2.3 Execution Services

If you used Easy Cost Planning to plan your costs at the WBS elements level (see Chapter 2, Section 2.4.4), then you can post different documents, such as internal activity allocations, purchase requisitions, or goods issues, directly from Easy Cost Planning after you release the WBS elements. The main advantages of this option are that you do not have to know how to use several different transactions to create these documents and you can use the planning data of the various costing items as a template. Consequently, you can reduce the overall time and effort required to create these documents and prevent errors from occurring when you enter the required data. Posting a document from Easy Cost Planning is called *Execution Service*.

Depending on which Execution Service you select from the list of available Execution Services in Easy Cost Planning, the system only proposes the data from relevant costing items in each case. If you select the GOODS ISSUE Execution Service, for example, only data of the items for item category M (MATERIAL) is offered, and so on. From the proposed items, you can now only select the specific items for which you want to perform the Execution Service. If necessary, you can still change the proposed data or supplement missing data before you make a posting.

When you make a posting, a corresponding document is created and automatically assigned to the selected WBS element. If warnings are issued or errors occur when you post a document, then you can analyze the corresponding messages in a log. You can use a document overview to display a list of the documents already posted using the Execution Service and, if required, go directly to the display of the documents or perform cancellations. Figure 4.5 shows an example of the INTERNAL ACTIVITY ALLOCATION Execution Service being used on the ENGINEERING/

DESIGN WBS element of the elevator project. Two activity allocations that have already been posted are displayed in the document overview.

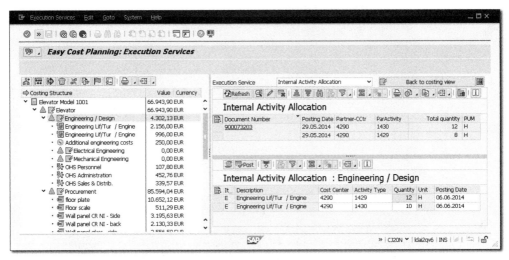

Figure 4.5 Example of the Execution Service for an Internal Activity Allocation

To use Execution Services, you must first define an Execution Service profile in the Customizing activity of SAP Project System and assign the relevant project profiles (see Figure 4.6). In the Execution Service profile, you first define which Execution Services should be available when using the profile. The following Execution Services are available for selection:

Execution Service profile

► INTERNAL ACTIVITY ALLOCATION

► PURCHASE REQUISITION

► PURCHASE ORDER

► RESERVATION

► GOODS ISSUE

You then implement additional detailed settings on the selected Execution Services (see Figure 4.7). For example, for the PURCHASE REQUISITION Execution Service, you define the document type you want to be used for creating purchase requisitions for WBS elements. For the GOODS ISSUE Execution Service, you specify the movement type to be used, and so on.

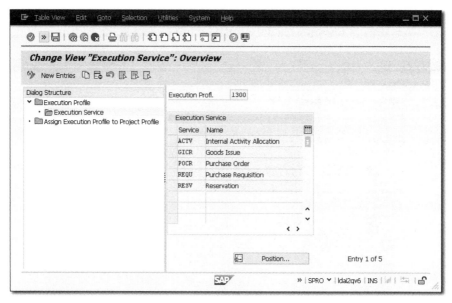

Figure 4.6 Defining an Execution Service Profile

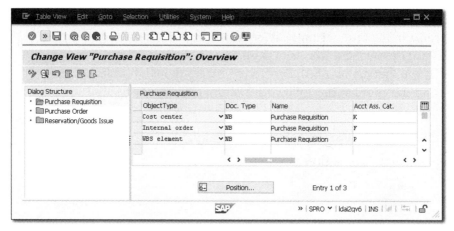

Figure 4.7 Defining the Settings for Execution Services

4.3   Confirmations

You can use confirmations to document the processing status of activities or activity elements and, if required, also specify forecast data for their continued progress. Because confirmations can affect actual dates (and possibly planned dates) of projects and capacity requirements, actual costs, status and milestone information, and possibly even goods movements or billing documents, they play an important role in the execution phase of projects with networks. To enter confirmations for an activity (or an activity element), the activity must be released and the control key of the activity must allow a confirmation (see Chapter 1, Section 1.3.2). In Customizing of SAP Project System, you must also have defined *confirmation parameters*, which control the properties of the confirmations.

Confirmations and Locks   **[+]**

Confirmations have an immediate effect on network data. Therefore, note that when you enter a confirmation for an activity or activity element the entire network is always automatically locked.

Where confirmations are concerned, we generally differentiate between *partial confirmations* and *final confirmations*. If you want to document that a portion of the planned services of an activity was already performed but you still expect additional confirmations for this activity later on, then you enter a partial confirmation for this activity. A partial confirmation is a confirmation for which the FINALCONF indicator is not set (see Figure 4.8). Partial confirmations set the PCNF (PARTIALLY CONFIRMED) status in the confirmed activity.

Partial confirmations

The *degree of processing* of a partial confirmation indicates to what percent the activity has already been processed and can be used within a progress analysis to determine the percentage of completion (see Section 4.7.2). The system automatically calculates the degree of processing from the proportion of the actual total amount of work that has already been confirmed for an activity to its planned or forecast total work. However, you can also define an alternative degree of processing manually in the confirmation if required. In the example shown in Figure 4.8, the degree of processing for the ELECTRICAL ENGINEERING activity results from the ratio of the actual work (10 HR + 15 HR) and the forecast total work (10 HR + 15 HR + 30 HR).

Degree of processing

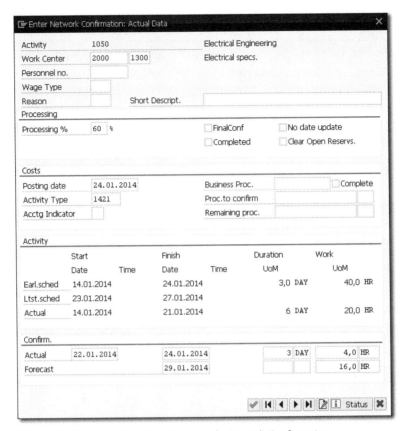

Figure 4.8 Example of the Detail Screen of a (Partial) Confirmation

Remaining work   You can use the WORK CENTER, ACTUAL WORK, and FORECAST WORK
(REMAINING WORK) fields in a partial confirmation to document which
work center has performed which degree of work and to forecast how
much work you still expect has to be performed. Based on the total
amount of work already confirmed and the planned or forecast total
amount of work, the system can propose the remaining work that is still
to be completed. If you activated the calculation of capacity requirements, then the remaining work is taken into account as a (remaining)
capacity requirement in the capacity planning. By setting the COMPLETED
indicator in a partial confirmation, you can indicate that no more
remaining work is required.

| Dependency of Fields in Confirmations | **[+]** |

The fields for the degree of processing, actual work, and remaining work and the work planned and forecast in total are connected. Depending on which field or fields you specify for a confirmation, the system automatically calculates the value of the other fields. You can also enter values for all three editable fields manually. If the degree of processing differs from the value calculated by the system, the system then issues a warning message.

You specify the execution period of the relevant partial activities in the ACTUAL START and FINISH fields of a partial confirmation. If you want to document that activities were not only performed on workdays, then you can also specify an ACTUAL DURATION. If the NO DATE UPDATE indicator is not set in a confirmation, then the actual dates are forwarded to the activity. If the activity is assigned to a WBS element, then the actual dates are incorporated into the provisional actual dates of the WBS element (see Section 4.1.1). If milestones are assigned to the activity, then the milestones can use the actual finish date of the confirmation as the actual date (see Section 4.1.3) so that billing items in sales orders are unlocked (see Section 4.6.1).

Actual and forecast dates

The actual dates of the activity are derived from the earliest actual start date and the latest finish date of all confirmations for this activity. Depending on the settings in the scheduling parameters, the actual dates of partially confirmed activities can then have different effects on the subsequent schedulings (see Section 4.1.2). In a partial confirmation, you can also forecast a finish date for performing the activity or a residual remaining duration if required. The forecast data is then taken into account the next time the network is scheduled.

By setting the FINALCONF indicator in a confirmation, you document that an activity has been processed completely (for which the degree of processing is 100%) and you don't expect any more confirmations. However, if another confirmation is entered for an activity that has been finally confirmed, then the system issues a warning message. This is controlled by the CONF (CONFIRMED) status that the system automatically sets in the activity when a final confirmation is made.

Final confirmation

As with a partial confirmation, you can also enter actual work and actual dates in a final confirmation. But because a final confirmation represents the complete processing of an activity you cannot (in contrast to partial confirmations) enter forecast data for the continued progress of the activity or for residual remaining work. The final confirmation of an activity results in the scheduled dates of the activity being automatically adjusted on the actual dates (see Section 4.1.2). If a WBS element or milestones are assigned to the activity, then the actual dates of the final confirmation can also be transferred to these objects. In addition, the system automatically sets the remaining capacity requirement of an activity that has been finally confirmed to zero, even if the work originally planned or forecast may not have been fully confirmed.

Reasons for variances
You can use short and long texts in partial and final confirmations to enter more detailed descriptions for the confirmed activities. If a variance from the planned performance occurred when the activity was performed, then in addition to a corresponding description you can specify the reason for the variance—for example, machine breakdown, operating errors, and so on. The reason for a variance in a confirmation can be used for evaluation purposes; furthermore, by specifying the reason for a variance the user status of the activity is changed automatically so that milestone functions of assigned milestones can be triggered. To use variance reasons, you must have already defined this in Customizing of SAP Project System using Transaction OPK5. If you want a reason for the variance to initiate a status change in the activity, then you must specify which system or user status is to be set when defining the variance reason. You can also change the status of an activity in a confirmation manually, without referring to a variance reason, by branching from the confirmation into the status management of the activity and setting the required status.

Calculating actual costs based on confirmations
Based on the confirmations of an activity, not only are actual or forecast dates forwarded to the activity, the status of which may be changed and the remaining capacity requirement adjusted, but actual costs of performed work are also automatically updated on the activity. To ensure that the system can calculate the actual costs for confirmed work, you must specify a work center, activity type, and the corresponding actual work in the confirmation, provided this data is not already proposed based on the planning data. When you save the confirmation, the system uses the combination of the activity type you specified and the cost

center of the work center to automatically calculate an activity price that can be used to estimate the confirmed work. The actual costing variant of the network controls which strategy is to be used to calculate the price (see Chapter 2, Section 2.4.6). After you save the confirmation, the system writes an accounting document that is assigned to an activity. This document results in the actual costs of the confirmed work being added to the activity (price multiplied by the actual work) and the same amount being simultaneously reduced in the cost center of the work center.

If material components are assigned to an activity, then you can branch from a confirmation for this activity into a list of assigned material components (stock items) and make goods issue postings to document the consumption of components. When you save a confirmation, the system writes a corresponding activity-assigned material document that results in actual costs on the activity. The goods issue for the non-valuated project stock is an exception (see Section 4.5.1). The actual costs are calculated from the withdrawn quantities and the price of the relevant material. The actual costing variant of the network controls which strategy is used to calculate the price (see Chapter 2, Section 2.4.6). For material components that were identified for a *backflush*, the system automatically posts goods issues amounting to the planned quantities for a final confirmation. If you enter a final confirmation and all assigned material components have not yet been withdrawn, then the system can automatically clear the reservations that are still open when you set the CLEAR OPEN RESERVS. indicator in the confirmation.

Goods movements for confirmations

The accounting documents for posting the actual costs based on confirmed work and the material documents based on material withdrawals are posted with the relevant confirmation document. If errors occur, then you can eliminate the reason for the errors or cancel the confirmation. For performance reasons, you can also separate the actual cost calculation and the posting of backflushes from the posting of the confirmation document and perform these later in the background. If problems occur, then you must postprocess the incorrect data records. You control the separation of backflushing processes by using process controls that you can define in Customizing of SAP Project System and then enter in the confirmation parameters.

Process control

You can also specify a personnel number and, if necessary, a wage type, for a confirmation. Your confirmation data can then be transferred to Time Management and subsequently used there for evaluation purposes or for calculating incentive wages. By setting the No HR Update indicator, you can also prevent confirmation data from being forwarded to Time Management.

Split confirmations If, in addition to having planned activity work at the work center level of the activity within the capacity planning, you have performed a distribution to capacity splits, for example, to individual personnel resources (see Chapter 2, Section 2.2.2), then you can also confirm the individual capacity splits separately. SAP Note 543362 elaborates on the effects of split confirmations and any additional activity confirmations on the activity data.

Cancelling If necessary, you can also cancel an entered confirmation by using
confirmations Transaction CN29. If you entered several confirmations, then you receive a list of the confirmations, from which you can select the confirmation that you want to cancel. When you cancel a confirmation, you can enter a long text with details about the reason for the cancellation. With the exception of the set user status, cancelling a confirmation results in all confirmed data being undone at the level of the activity; however, for performance reasons you can also perform a *vague cancellation* of confirmations. Although the posting of actual costs, actual work, capacity requirements, and material movements is undone consistently, forecast data or statuses are not adjusted. For more information about vague cancellations, see SAP Note 304989.

Confirmation Before you can enter confirmations for activities, activity elements, or
parameter capacity splits, you must define *confirmation parameters* in Customizing of SAP Project System (Transaction OPST) for the combination of the network type and the plant of the relevant networks (see Figure 4.9).

You can use confirmation parameters to control which data and CO indicators you want the system to propose when you create a confirmation, whether confirmation processes are executed online or in the background, and how errors that occur when actual costs and goods movements are posted should be handled. In addition, you use confirmation parameters to control different checks for confirmation data.

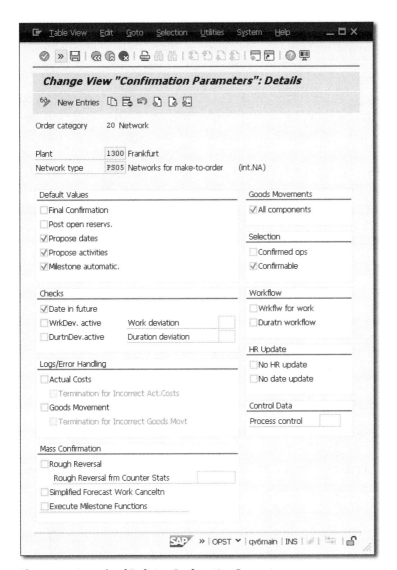

Figure 4.9 Example of Defining Confirmation Parameters

You can use the DATE IN FUTURE indicator in the confirmation parameters to specify whether future dates can also be confirmed or only dates up to the current date in each case. If you set the WRKDEV. ACTIVE (consider permissible deviations of the work) indicator in the confirmation parameters, then the system issues a warning message each time you

Deviations in confirmed work/ duration

315

want to save a confirmation for which the total from the actual and remaining work exceeds the planned work. If you want to have a limited overrun of the planned work without a warning message being issued, you can enter a percentage amount in the WORK DEVIATION field of the confirmation parameters. This is the percentage by which the planned work can be exceeded without a warning message being issued. If a confirmation is saved despite the defined tolerance limits being exceeded and despite a warning message, then the system can (due to the WRKFLW FOR WORK indicator in the confirmation parameters) automatically trigger a workflow, which informs the person responsible for the network of this deviation. Warning messages and workflows can also be created in the same way if there are deviations in the entered actual and remaining durations of the original planned duration for an activity.

Field selection | You can also define a *field selection* for confirmations in Customizing of confirmations in SAP Project System. You can use the field selection to do the following:

▶ Control which fields you want completely hidden for a confirmation

▶ Control which fields are only supposed to be displayed but cannot be changed by users

▶ Control which fields are ready for input

▶ If necessary, control which fields must always be filled before you save the confirmation

If required, you can make the field selection settings dependent on the relevant network type, network profile, work center, or control key of the activity.

Because confirmations are integral for executing a project with networks, there are many different ways in which you can enter confirmations. The most important options are explained in the following sections.

4.3.1 Individual Confirmations

You can use individual confirmations to create partial or final confirmations for individual activities, activity elements, or capacity splits of a network. You enter these individual confirmations in a detail screen (see Figure 4.8). You can create individual confirmations using Transaction CN25. If you only want to specify a network number in the initial screen of this transaction, then you receive a selection list of activities or activity elements for the network first. In the confirmation parameters, you can specify whether confirmed activities and confirmable activities should be included in this list. *Confirmable activities* are activities whose control keys allow, though do not necessarily provide for, confirmations (see Chapter 1, Section 1.3.2).

As the person responsible for the network, you can also create individual confirmations in various maintenance transactions for networks—for example, in the Project Builder or Project Planning Board. You can also create individual confirmations using the information system for structures in SAP Project System (see Chapter 6, Section 6.1) or in capacity reports (see Chapter 6, Section 6.3.3).

You can use the CNW1 Internet service to enter individual confirmations through the Internet or intranet. This enables members of the project team and authorized partners to confirm data online directly from the location of the project execution by using only an Internet browser. You can process the confirmation data directly in the SAP system in exactly the same way as an individual confirmation; however, unlike the confirmations that you create directly in the SAP system, you can't enter any long texts for confirmations with the Internet service and you can't change any statuses manually or post goods movements manually.

Internet confirmation

4.3.2 Collective and Summary Confirmations

If you want confirmations for several activities or different networks to be entered simultaneously (for example, by a central administrator), collective confirmations are available for this in SAP Project System. When you use collective confirmations, you enter the confirmation data in tables (see Figure 4.10). You can also branch to the detail screen of a confirmation if necessary. In the default area of a collective confirmation, you can enter values for the individual columns of the collective confirmation, which the system transfers to the data entry section as default values for all activities.

Collective confirmation

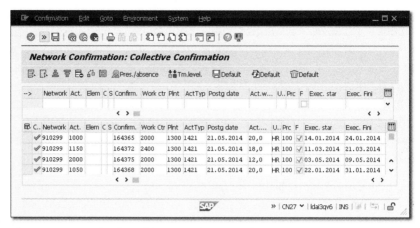

Figure 4.10 Example of a Collective Confirmation of Activities

Pool of confirmations

If you have entered activities or activity elements in a table of a collective confirmation, then you can save the list for these objects as a *pool of confirmations*. With subsequent collective confirmations, you can constantly refer to this pool of confirmations and avoid having to enter the activities or activity elements manually each time. You can enter collective confirmations by using Transaction CN27, through the Internet via the CNW1 Internet service, or in the information system for structures (see Chapter 6, Section 6.1).

Confirmation workflow

You can also send *confirmation workflows* in the information system for structures. To do this, you select the activities or activity elements that are to be confirmed from a report and you send this list as a pool of confirmations to the project member responsible. The project member then receives a work item for entering the actual data, which he can use to branch directly into the collective confirmation of the pool of confirmations.

Summary confirmation

You can use a *summary confirmation* to simultaneously confirm all activity elements of an activity that have not yet been confirmed manually. To do this, select the corresponding activity in Transaction CN25, go to the summary confirmation, by pressing [F7], and enter a degree of processing. The degree of processing is forwarded to the assigned activity elements and used to calculate the confirmation data; however, the activity is not confirmed by a summary confirmation per se.

4.3.3 Cross-Application Time Sheet (CATS)

Many companies use the CATS as a key transaction for entering the time data of their employees. Each employee, or only particular employees (such as cost and work center supervisors or administrators assigned to enter employee time data), can use CATS to enter working times for a group of employees. The time data entered using CATS can then be transferred into other applications, such as CO or SAP Project System, and consequently generate internal activity allocations, or confirmations automatically. To document when and for what purpose work was performed, the working times in CATS must be assigned *working time attributes* (in particular, account assignment objects) that establish how the data is processed further in the SAP system.

If you have performed work for a network activity, then in CATS you will enter how many working hours you performed on the relevant days and the activity ID (see Figure 4.11). If required, you can add descriptive texts or forecasts for still outstanding work to your details, or you can document that the activity is to be confirmed. Depending on the settings of CATS, the system can automatically add additional information, such as activity or attendance types, to your details.

Confirming activities using CATS

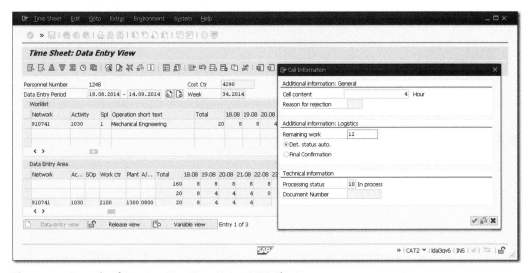

Figure 4.11 Example of Entering Time Data Using CATS Classic

The time data entered for the network activity is first saved in a separate CATS database table and cannot be displayed yet in the project. Once the data has been transferred into SAP Project System, the data from CATS is used to generate the individual confirmations that refer to the network activity. The individual confirmations result in the creation of a corresponding accounting document and the activity debited with the actual costs of the work.

Transferring data into other target applications
You can also enter working times for maintenance orders or service orders in the same way in CATS. The transfer of data into the corresponding target applications results in confirmations for these orders. You can also transfer time data into Human Resources (HR) to enter attendances and absences, travel activities, or to create remuneration documents. In addition, you can enter time data or statistical key figures relating to costs centers, costs objects, business processes, internal or sales orders, and particularly WBS elements in CATS. In these cases, the working time data is transferred into CO, which leads to the corresponding activity allocations being created. You can also use CATS to enter suppliers' services. This data is then transferred into the services area of Materials Management (MM) and service entry sheets are created (see Section 4.4.2).

The data is transferred into the relevant target components via transfer reports. The following transfer reports are available, among others:

▶ The RCATSTPS report (Transaction CAT5) to transfer data into SAP Project System

▶ The RCATSTCO report (Transaction CAT7) to transfer data into CO

▶ The cross-component RCATSTAL report (Transaction CATA), which you can use, in particular, to transfer common data into HR, CO, plant maintenance, or customer service, and into SAP Project System (however, you can only transfer data separately into MM using Transaction CATM)

The transfer reports are usually scheduled as background jobs, which means that the working time data is transferred automatically to the target components at regular intervals.

Depending on the settings of CATS, there may be two additional steps to perform between entering the time data and transferring it: the time data is explicitly released by the person who entered it and the project manager approves it. The approval procedure can be supported by an approval workflow from CATS.

Releasing and approving working time data

There are different application interfaces you can use to enter time data with CATS:

CATS—application interfaces

▶ For example, you can use CATS classic (Transaction CAT2) or CATS for Service Providers (Transactions CATSXT and CATSXT_ADMIN) directly in the SAP system.

▶ You can use CATS regular (CATW service) to enter time data through the Internet.

▶ You can also use CATS notebook locally (for example, installed on a laptop) to enter time data offline. If you later connect CATS notebook with an SAP system, the data from CATS notebook and CATS is synchronized in the SAP system.

You can use customer enhancements to make various changes to the different application interfaces. To enter time data via mobile end devices—for example, a smartphone—you can download a mobile application from the SAP Store if required.

You can make it easier for employees to enter time data in CATS by using *worklists*. A worklist is a default area in CATS in which time data and working time attributes are automatically imported and can be copied into the data entry section of CATS using a copy function. The worklist can be filled by account assignment objects or working time attributes that were entered earlier by the employee, by pools of confirmations that you created in SAP Project System, or by capacity requirements on the work center to which the employee is assigned. In particular, data for workforce planning on personnel resources (see Chapter 2, Section 2.2.2) can also be copied automatically into the

Worklist

worklist of CATS of the corresponding people. You can also use a customer enhancement or a BAdI to combine worklists.

Prerequisites
for CATS Time data is always entered using CATS with reference to a personnel number. Therefore, to use CATS corresponding personnel numbers for internal and external employees who want to enter working times through CATS must be available in the SAP system. External employees who want to enter activities using CATS are normally grouped under one or a few personnel numbers. You can create the personnel numbers manually in the SAP system as *HR mini master records*. You need at least Infotypes 0001 (ORGANIZATIONAL ASSIGNMENT) and 0002 (PERSONAL DATA) to do this; we also recommend that you use Infotype 0315 (TIME SHEET DEFAULTS). If you're using SAP HR Management, then you can also copy the required data directly from HR. As a result, additional data such as Infotype 0007 (Planned Working Time) of the employees can also be used in CATS for information purposes or for performing checks.

Data entry profile Before you can use CATS, you must have defined data entry profiles in Customizing of the cross-application components. Data entry profiles control the interface and functions of CATS (see Figure 4.12). You can manually define the data entry profile together with the personnel number when you access CATS. However, the initial screen is usually skipped, and a personal number and data entry profile are firmly assigned directly to the SAP users using the PER and CVR user parameters.

Depending on the data entry profile, you can also define a field selection in Customizing for the data entry section or the worklist of CATS. You can use the field selection to control which working time attributes the employees can or must enter. You can use various customer enhancements and BAdIs to adapt the interface and functions of CATS to meet your own requirements. Customizing of CATS contains a detailed description of the possible enhancements.

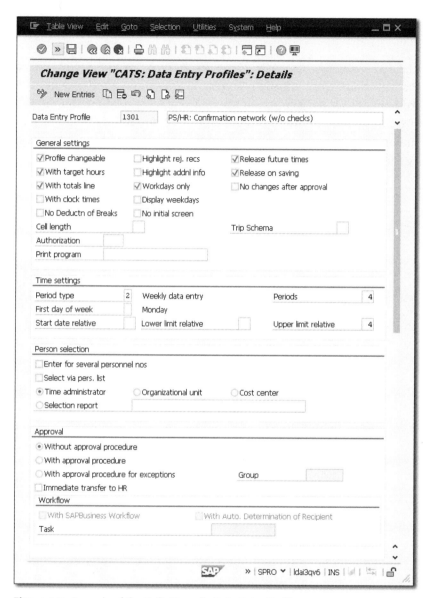

Figure 4.12 Example of the Definition of a Data Entry Profile

4.3.4 Additional Confirmation Options

In addition to individual, collective, and summary confirmations or using CATS, other options are also available for confirming activities or activity elements. These options are outlined briefly in the following text.

SAP Fiori—Confirm Network Activity

The SAP Fiori app Confirm Network Activity provides you with a mobile option for confirming activities. You can call the app directly from the SAP Fiori Launchpad, from an analytical app, or from the fact sheet for network activities (see Chapter 1, Section 1.7.6). Figure 4.13 shows an example of an activity confirmation using this app. Note that not all fields and functions of confirmation are available here.

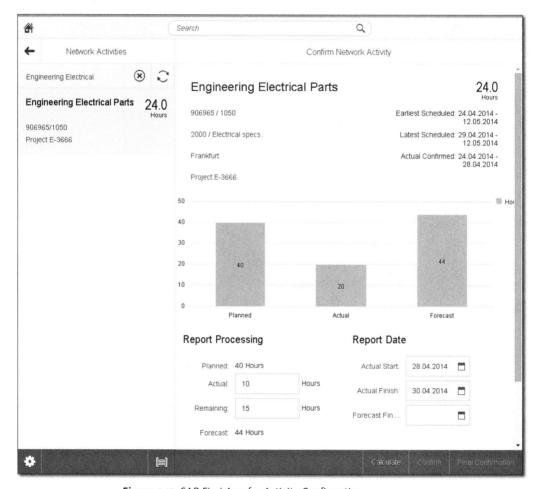

Figure 4.13 SAP Fiori App for Activity Confirmation

You can use the standard KK4 interface to connect external *plant data collection* (PDC) systems to SAP Project System and, by doing so, copy data from external systems into the SAP system for confirmation purposes. This interface can also make activity data available in the PDC system for plausibility checks.

Plant data collection (PDC)

To import confirmation data into SAP Project System, you can use the `AddConfirmation` BAPI. This BAPI can help you to develop your own interfaces for the exchange of data with any other systems or Internet applications, for example.

BAPI

Lastly, you can also use the Progress Analysis Workbench to enter confirmations for activities and activity elements (see Section 4.7.2).

4.4 External Procurement of Services

This section describes purchasing processes that were automatically triggered due to purchase requisitions of externally processed activities and service activities or elements. Similar processes can be run for WBS elements in Purchasing when you manually assign purchasing documents to WBS elements (see Section 4.2).

4.4.1 Externally Processed Activities

A purchase requisition or a new item within a purchase requisition can be created automatically for an externally processed activity (and also for an externally processed element) depending on the setting of the RES./PURC. REQ. indicator. In the process, the system checks whether all of the data (that is, the material group, purchasing group, unit of measure, etc.) required for creating the purchase requisition or purchase requisition item can be copied from the activity data. If the data cannot be copied, then the system issues an error message, and you must add the missing data to the activity.

You can use a customer enhancement to make further adjustments automatically to different data of the purchase requisition when you save the purchase requisition. Subsequent changes to the activity also directly affect the purchase requisition. Due to the purchase requisition, commitments are shown on the activity (or on the network header in the case of a header-assigned network).

Determining the source of supply

You can directly process the purchase requisition further in Purchasing. If you have not already made reference to a purchasing info record or an outline agreement in the activity and you know the supplier, then you must first select the supplier. You can do this using an automatic source determination, for example, in which the system searches for suitable source list entries, quota arrangements, info records, or outline agreements for the external service and proposes one or several suppliers. You can also carry out bid invitations if required. In Purchasing, requests for quotations (RFQs) are sent to different suppliers, their bids are entered and compared with one another, and a supplier is ultimately selected. If necessary, you can also assign a fixed supplier to the purchase requisition manually.

Purchase order handling

The purchase requisition data can then be used by Purchasing to create a purchase order. The purchase order is assigned to an activity and, consequently, the purchase requisition commitment is reduced on the activity, and a corresponding purchase order commitment is simultaneously increased (see Section 4.2.1). The PURCHASE ORDER EXISTS indicator is also automatically set in the activity. Unlike the purchase requisition, which only represents an internal document that cannot be used outside the company, the purchase order is the request directed to an external supplier to deliver an external service by the specified delivery date; consequently, a purchase order also has an external effect. In Purchasing, you can link the added processing of the purchase requisition and the creation of the purchase order to *release procedures*, which are automated approval processes.

Workflow for purchase order-related changes

If a purchase order exists for an externally processed activity and if you subsequently make a purchase order–related change to the activity—for example, you change the delivery date, the activity quantity, or the activity type—then the purchase order is not adjusted automatically. However, you can activate a workflow in the PARAMETERS FOR NETWORK TYPE (see Chapter 1, Section 1.3.2), which you can use each time you make a purchase order-related change to inform the purchaser responsible of this change and to allow the purchaser to change the purchase order directly (see Figure 4.14).

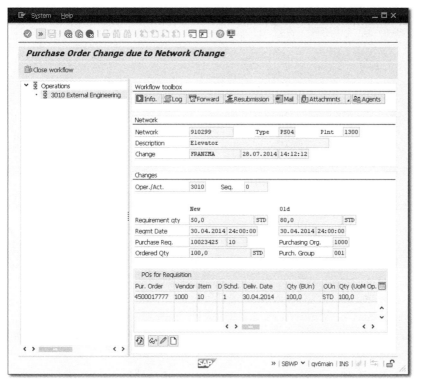

Figure 4.14 Example of a Workflow after a Purchase Order-Related Change to an Externally Processed Element

Special functions are available in Purchasing to monitor purchase order handling further. In particular, you can also use progress tracking to monitor purchase order-related events (see Section 4.3).

Monitoring purchase order handling

Depending on which account assignment category you defined in Customizing of SAP Project System for procuring activities externally for networks, the activity performed by the supplier can be documented using a goods receipt or an invoice receipt. If the account assignment category allows for a valuated goods receipt, then posting a goods receipt for the purchase order results in actual costs on the activity based on the net price of the purchase order. Otherwise, actual costs are only updated on the activity once the invoice is received. The purchase order commitment of the activity is reduced accordingly in each case (see Section 4.2.1). If there are price differences in the purchase order net price when the invoice is received or checked, then the resulting costs can be shown on the activity.

Advantages and Restrictions of Valuated Goods Receipts

The advantage of using a valuated goods receipt is that you can already see the actual costs when the activity is performed regardless of when the supplier sends you an invoice. You should note, however, that the costs are not checked against the budget of WBS elements due to a goods receipt posting (see Chapter 3, Section 3.1.5).

4.4.2 Services

A purchase requisition that was automatically created as a result of a service activity (or service element; see Chapter 2, Section 2.2.5) triggers similar purchasing processes as the purchase requisitions of an externally processed activity. You can assign suppliers to the purchase requisition manually, the system can determine a supplier automatically by using the source determination, or you can perform bidding procedures. You can use the purchase requisition data to create a purchase order and consequently commission the services of suppliers. The purchase requisition and purchase order are each assigned to the activity and result in the commitments being increased and decreased accordingly. Subsequent changes to the activity have a direct effect on the purchase requisition but not on the purchase order. However, if the activity date, amount, or type changes, then the purchaser responsible can be automatically informed of these purchase order-related changes. Note that subsequent changes to the services specifications of a service activity are not sufficient to trigger the standard workflow when purchase order-related changes are implemented.

Service entry Unlike purchasing processes for an externally processed activity, a *service entry* and *service acceptance* always take place for service activities. In a service entry, an employee or the supplier documents which planned or unplanned services were performed in relation to the purchase order. If the value of the unplanned services exceeds the limit you allowed for in the activity (see Chapter 2, Section 2.2.5), then the system issues an error message for the service entry. Service entries are executed by using service entry sheets (see Figure 4.15). These entry sheets can be created directly in Transaction ML81N or via CATS and then transferred to MM (see Section 4.3.3).

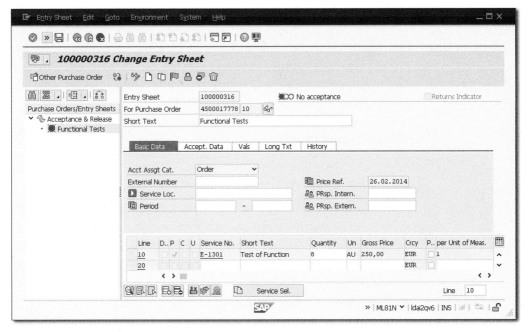

Figure 4.15 Example of a Service Entry Sheet

After services have been documented in the service entry sheet, they must be checked and accepted by one or more of the people responsible depending on the system setting. Once this service has been accepted, the system creates a material document (similar to the goods receipt posting for externally processed activities), which results in actual costs and a reduction in the purchase order commitment on the activity. An invoice verification can then be performed on the activity for adjustment postings if necessary.

Service acceptance

4.5 Material Procurement and Delivery

Chapter 2, Section 2.3.1 described how material components could be assigned to network activities to plan the procurement and subsequent consumption of materials in the project. The item category and procurement type for the assignment specified how a material is to be procured and in which stock the stock items are to be managed. The following section explains how the different procurement types are executed and, in particular, the associated value flows for the project.

Delivery notes If material has to be delivered to the customer or construction site during project execution, then delivery notes can be created for the required shipping tasks in SAP Project System. This option, known as a *delivery from project*, is discussed in Section 4.5.2, and Section 4.5.3 introduces ProMan, a tool that you can use to monitor logistical data of all project-related procurement measures.

4.5.1 Material Procurement Processes

Assigning the required material to activities in the form of material components is the starting point for procuring material for network activities. Depending on the setting of the RES./PURC. REQ. indicator for a material component, the procurement of the material can be triggered automatically if the status is CREATED, triggered for a release, or triggered manually at a later stage.

Non-stock Items

Vendor selection Similar to external processing, purchasing processing is triggered for non-stock items (see Section 4.4.1). Based on the purchase requisition for the material component, this means that a supplier selection takes place in Purchasing. A purchase order is created, and a goods receipt or invoice receipt is entered. Non-stock items and externally processed activities use, in particular, the same account assignment category to ensure that the value flow is also processed in the same way. Purchase requisitions and purchase orders are therefore assigned to the activity to which the non-stock item is assigned and produce corresponding commitments on the activity (or on the network header for header-assigned networks). The goods or invoice receipts are also assigned to the activity and result in actual costs and a simultaneous reduction of the commitment. Non-stock items are procured directly through Purchasing (direct procurement) and not through MRP.

Non-stock items are not managed in a stock (either plant stock or individual requirements stock). Therefore, no inventory costs are incurred. The goods and invoice receipt of a non-stock item corresponds directly to the material consumed being posted by the activity.

Stock Items

Many different procurement types are available for stock items depending on the material master data, the project settings, and so on (see Chapter 2, Section 2.3.1). In the simplest scenario, only one reservation is created for a stock item in SAP Project System; this reservation represents a request to MRP to procure the material in the required quantity by the planned requirements date. Depending on whether you selected the RESERVATION FOR NETWORK, RESERVATION WBS ELEMENT, or RESERVATION SALES DOCUMENT procurement type, the reservation refers to the plant stock stand, a stock-managing WBS element, or a sales order item as an individual requirements stock segment. The task of MRP is to ensure the availability of the material.

Reservation

The MRP controller can use a *material requirements planning run* to calculate material shortages and for the system to generate procurement proposals automatically if requirements aren't covered by the available stock and the fixed purchasing or the previously planned production receipts. Depending on the material and planning run settings, procurement proposals can be purchase requisitions or planned orders (planned procurement elements). Based on the lot-sizing procedure selected, you can calculate the quantities and dates of the procurement elements in such a way that you can combine requirements for different dates to optimize the in-house production costs or, because of greater order quantities, improve purchasing conditions. This procurement quantity calculation must be performed separately for each stock segment (see Chapter 2, Section 2.3.2).

Requirements planning

If you selected the PURCH. REQUISITION + RESERVATION procurement type for a material component, then in addition to creating the reservation the system generates a purchase requisition for the material (regardless of whether sufficient stock is available). Therefore, an MRP run is generally unnecessary for this procurement type.

Dependent
requirements If a valid BOM (assembly) exists for a material, then this is exploded
within a multilevel planning run, and procurement proposals are also
created for the BOM items (dependent requirements); this action triggers the related procurement. If the assembly is managed in the project
stock, then the dependent requirements are also managed in this stock
(if this is allowed by the settings in the material master and the BOM
items). If there is a valid work breakdown structure BOM for the assembly, then this is used instead of the material BOM to explode the BOMs.

You can perform planning runs for all stock segments simultaneously
but also separately for individual requirements stock segments, such as
individual stock-managing WBS elements (Transaction MD51; see Figure 4.16). If a planning run identifies critical situations (for example, if
the start date of a planned order was scheduled in the past), then the system creates exception messages that inform the MRP controller of this
situation. The MRP controller can then postprocess the data manually.
However, adjustments to project data, such as changing the requirements date of a material component, don't take place in the planning
run or as part of further processing.

Figure 4.16 Initial Screen of Material Requirements Planning for Project Stocks

You can then convert the planned procurement elements created by a planning run into exact procurement elements. You convert purchase requisitions into purchase orders in Purchasing and planned orders into production orders in Production. If the planned order refers to a WBS element as a stock segment and there is a separate project routing for the material and the WBS element, then this project-specific routing is used to create the production order. The exact procurement elements refer to the same stock segments as the planned procurement elements. In Purchasing or Production, you can now process the procured materials further. If the required material is finally delivered or goods were produced in-house, then the material is posted into the stock provided and is now available for consumption. In the last step of this process, the material can be withdrawn by the activity, and this withdrawal can be documented using a goods issue that refers to the reservation number of the material component.

Exact procurement elements

The value flow of the procurement process just described will now be explained in an example of procuring a material produced in-house using valuated project stock. Based on the assignment of a stock item to an activity that refers to the valuated project stock, the system shows planned costs for the subsequent consumption of the material. The planned costs are calculated within the network costing on the basis of the planned quantity and requirements date of the component (see Chapter 2, Section 2.4.6). The costing variant in the network header is used for this calculation. The creation of the reservation for the material component and also the subsequent planning run do not result in any changes to the project's costs.

Value flow for in-house production

If a material is to be produced in-house, then the planning run creates a planned order that can be converted into a production order. The production order is assigned to the stock-managing WBS element and can therefore be evaluated with the project in Reporting of SAP Project System. The production order contains planned costs for producing the material and a planned increase of the same amount to ensure that a change to the total planned costs does occur on the stock-managing WBS element. Confirmations of work performed on the production order result in actual costs on the order that you can also analyze at aggregated levels on the stock-managing WBS element.

Inventory costs If the material production was completed and a goods receipt posting of the material performed in the project stock, then the stock-managing WBS element is credited with the costs for the material stock in the form of statistical actual costs (value type 11), and the production order is debited by the same amount. The following strategy is used to evaluate the material in the stock and therefore calculate the inventory costs:

1. If you already posted a goods receipt for the material in the project stock, then this standard price of the individual requirements stock segment is used. If required, you can manually change the standard price of the material for the individual requirements stock segment in Transaction MR21.

2. The evaluation that you make available in customer enhancement COPCP002 is used.

3. The system transfers the evaluation from a marked costing of a sales order item assigned to the WBS element, an activated SEIBAN costing, or a unit costing that you have created for the material component in the network.

4. The production order costing is used to calculate the evaluation.

5. The price in the material master determines evaluation.

Period-end closing If there are still variances on the order after the material has been delivered to the project stock and the production order has been reduced accordingly, then you can settle these variances on the stock-managing WBS element or directly on the profitability analysis during period-end closing.

The consumption of the material by the network activity—the goods issue for the reservation—ultimately results in the activity being credited with actual costs in accordance with the evaluation of the material and the inventory costs being simultaneously reduced at the level of the WBS element.

[+] **Prerequisites for Displaying Inventory Costs**

To enable the inventory costs to be shown on the stock-managing WBS element as statistical actual costs, you must create the relevant material stock account of FI and the cost element for type 90. The General Ledger (G/L) account determination can be controlled separately from the collective stock by using separate valuation classes for the project stock in the material master data.

When you externally procure a stock item for the valuated project stock, the purchase requisition, purchase order, and goods receipt of the material are assigned to the stock-managing WBS element, which results in commitments and inventory costs on the WBS element. Depending on the price control, the inventory costs are calculated based on the standard price or moving average price. If differences occur with the order value, then these can be shown as price differences on the stock-managing WBS element with a corresponding account control. The final consumption of the delivered material by the activity results in actual costs on the activity and reduces the inventory stock at the level of the WBS element accordingly. If you created the purchase requisition using a planning run, then a purchase requisition commitment is not created for performance reasons. In this case, only the purchase order results in a commitment being created on the stock-managing WBS element.

Value flow for external procurement

If you require dependent requirements for the in-house production of a material that is managed in the valuated project stock, then these requirements (provided they allow individual requirements management) are also managed in the project stock. The planned costs for the consumption of dependent requirements are shown as planned costs at the level of the production order. Within the framework of procuring individual requirements and dependent requirements, resulting purchase requisitions, purchase orders, production orders, and goods receipts automatically refer to the stock-managing WBS element and result in commitments and, in particular, inventory costs on the WBS element, as explained earlier. The consumption of dependent requirements by the production order results in actual costs on the order. The inventory costs for the dependent requirements are simultaneously reduced at the level of the stock-managing WBS element.

Valuated product stock—dependent requirements

Value Flow for Valuated Project Stock [◉]

When you use the valuated project stock, material movements for the individual requirements stock are managed based on quantities and values.

> Planned and actual costs for the consumption of the material are shown on the consuming object (network activity or production order). The inventory costs of the material and, if necessary, commitments for its external procurement are posted on the stock element (WBS element).

Non-valuated project stock—value flows

The logistical process of procuring material for non-valuated project stock (external procurement and in-house production) is utterly the same as using valuated project stock. However, you cannot group the requirements of several WBS elements when you use non-valuated project stock (see Chapter 2, Section 2.3.2). Unlike valuated project stock, material movements are entered based on quantities, not values. This means that no planned or actual costs are shown for the consumption of individual requirements materials at the level of the consumer (activity or production order). Planned costs for material that is managed in non-valuated project stock can only be shown on planning networks, because planning networks don't affect planning and therefore prevent assigned values from being displayed twice.

If necessary, commitments are posted at the level of the stock element (the WBS element) due to purchase orders. However, the goods receipt of an externally procured material or of a dependent requirement in the non-valuated project stock does not result in inventory costs; instead— as for direct procurement of material for the WBS element—the goods receipt results in actual costs on the stock-managing WBS element. The goods receipt of an in-house-produced material in the non-valuated project stock does not result in a value flow; therefore, no changes are made to the costs, either on the stock-managing WBS element or the supplying production order. As part of period-end closing, the actual costs of the production order are finally settled on the WBS element, based on internal activities and material withdrawals from the general plant stock.

Collective stock—value flows

As is the case when you use valuated project stock, both a quantity and value flow take place for stock items that are managed in collective stock (RESERVATION FOR NETWORK procurement type) each time goods are moved. Therefore, you can determine planned and actual costs for the consumption of material managed in collective stock at the level of the consumer (network activity or production order). However, because materials managed in collective stock are procured for a general stock—that is, without reference to a WBS element as the individual requirements stock segment—the costs that are incurred as part of the procurement, and in particular the inventory costs, cannot be assigned directly to any project and therefore cannot be shown at the project level.

Advance Procurement

If you have material produced in-house with a very long in-house production time or purchased parts for which bidding procedures must be performed within purchasing processes, then you may need to trigger the procurement of the material for projects even though the actual consumers—that is, the corresponding network activities or production orders—have not yet been created in the SAP system. These consumers are only created later as part of the project detail using subnetworks or based on planning runs in MRP, but if the activities or orders for which material is required to implement them do not yet exist, then you cannot assign material components to these either, and therefore you cannot plan the consumption of the required material yet. Nevertheless, you can use advance procurement to trigger the procurement of material without having to plan the consumption of the material beforehand.

Using advance procurement

To perform the advance procurement of a material, you have to assign the material as a stock item to an existing activity of the project structure and select the PRELIM. PREQ procurement type for purchased parts and the PLNDINDEPREQ procurement type for material produced in-house. Because it is not yet clear at this stage where the material will actually be consumed, no planned costs are shown for these components.

Advance procurement types

A preliminary purchase requisition triggers a purchasing process. From the point of view of planning, the preliminary purchase requisition is fixed and is not deleted by material planning runs. The planned independent requirements for the advance procurement of material produced in-house results in the production of the material being triggered for the next MRP run. You can then post the material delivered and produced in-house in a stock.

As soon as you have created the activities or orders for your project that will consume the material you procured in advance, you can assign the material to these objects once again. However, this time you must use a simple reservation as the procurement type, one that relates to the same stock segment in which the material procured in advance is also managed. You can use this reservation to finally withdraw the material procured in advance from the stock. When you use the collective stock or valuated individual requirements stock, the planned and actual costs for consumption can be shown on the consuming object—that is, the network activity or production order.

4.5.2 Delivery from Project

If parts of the project are carried out by a different company in a different location (for example, onsite at the customer location) and material is required for this purpose, then you must plan and implement corresponding deliveries. The SAP system supports you with various shipping functions for picking, packaging, and transporting the material, but to enable corresponding tasks to be performed in shipping delivery notes that contain a list of the material to be delivered must be created. The creation of these types of delivery notes in SAP Project System for material in projects or assigned production orders is called *delivery from project*.

Delivery information

To create a delivery, the system requires information about the shipping point, ship-to party, planned goods issue date, and sales area. You must specify this *general data* manually if the system cannot derive it from assigned sales order items or *delivery information*. Delivery information (see Figure 4.17) can be assigned to WBS elements, activities, or network headers (for header-assigned networks), and material components can be created directly in maintenance transactions for projects or centrally using Transaction CNL1.

When you create a delivery from a project (Transaction CNS0), you first select the material components to be delivered by specifying a project, WBS element, network, or an assigned sales order and suitable filter criteria. With the exception of assemblies (see Chapter 2, Section 2.3.1), you can select all stock items that are assigned to a network activity of the project or to a production order for the project. The components can be produced in-house or procured externally and managed in a collective, sales order, or project stock.

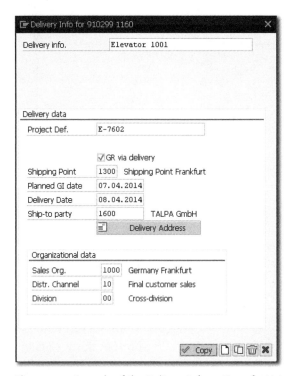

Figure 4.17 Example of the Delivery Information of a Network Activity

The system uses the planned goods issue date in the general data of the delivery to calculate the availability of the selected material components and proposes a delivery quantity for each component (see Figure 4.18).

Calculating the delivery quantity

The proposed delivery quantity is each available quantity of a component that is still open; the open quantity results from the difference in the requirement quantity and the already withdrawn quantity or the quantity in the delivery. You can check the different pieces of quantity information in the detail screen of a material component for the delivery. As soon as you have saved a delivery for a project, you can use the document directly in shipping for all other follow-up actions. In SAP Project System, you can analyze deliveries from projects using Transaction CNS0 or ProMan.

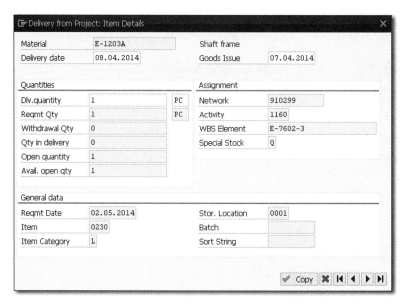

Figure 4.18 Example of Calculating the Delivery Quantity of a Material Component

4.5.3 ProMan

Project-oriented procurement

When you use the aforementioned procurement processes just for material or services (including external services) for a project, this results in a whole range of logistical data in SAP Project System, Purchasing, Production, Shipping, and so on. You can use ProMan (Transaction CNMM) to evaluate this data centrally in a transaction. Traffic lights in ProMan indicate exceptional situations—for example, overdue purchase orders or missing material stocks. You can also execute different procurement tasks directly in ProMan if required.

When you call ProMan, you first specify the project for which you want to analyze procurement measures. You can restrict the data selection further by specifying additional filter criteria in the initial screen of ProMan. In the main screen of ProMan, you see the project structure on the left and the different tabs (views) on the right, and data for the objects selected in the project structure is displayed in tables (see Figure 4.19). In the project structure, you can either select one object or several similar objects simultaneously, such as all material components of a network.

To enable data from documents and orders to be analyzed in ProMan, Views in ProMan you must link these objects to the selected project. You can do this by assigning them automatically or manually to the project or by assigning them to a stock-managing WBS element. Consequently, data for dependent requirements in production orders can be analyzed in ProMan if these are managed in the project stock. However, if the dependent requirements are managed in collective stock, then there is no longer a link to the project and the data for the dependent requirements is therefore not displayed in the ProMan views.

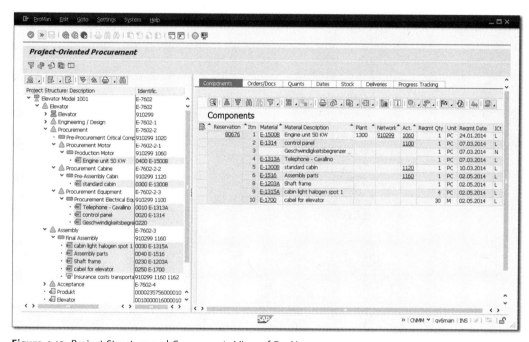

Figure 4.19 Project Structure and Components View of ProMan

The following list contains the different views in ProMan with some selected data in each of these views:

▶ COMPONENTS
Reservation number, material number, network activity, requirement quantity, and date

▶ ACTIVITIES /ELEMENTS
Network activity or activity element, activity quantity, information record, supplier, PURCHASE REQUISITION EXISTS indicator

▶ ORDERS/DOCUMENTS
Purchase requisition, purchase order, planned and production orders, material documents, COMPLETED, CANCELLED, and DELIVERY COMPLETED indicators, and so on

▶ QUANTITIES
Quantities in purchase requisition, purchase order, planned or production order, and in material documents

▶ DATES
Requirement date, delivery date in purchase requisition and purchase order, posting date of material documents, scheduled dates of planned and production order

▶ STOCK
Unrestricted use stock, quality inspection stock, and blocked stock of material

▶ DELIVERIES
Reservation number, delivery from project, delivery quantity, material provision date

The display of views in tables allow you to perform different functions and adjustments, such as calculate totals or subtotals, print out data, use filter and sort criteria, and so on. You can then store any changes to the interface in your own layouts.

As of EHP 3, you can use the BAdI `BADI_CNMM_CUST_ENH_SCR` to define custom fields and display those fields in a separate tab in ProMan.

You can also display progress tracking data (see Section 4.7.3) for a selected material component in a separate tab as of EHP 3.

Hotspots Underlined data in the different views is called a *hotspot* that enables you to go to the details of the data when you click on it. Examples of hotspots in ProMan are reservations, purchase requisitions, purchase orders, material documents, deliveries, planned and production orders, material masters, and project structure data. For more detailed analysis, you can also branch from ProMan to the requirements/stock list of the material or to order reports.

In addition to analyzing data, you can also use ProMan to execute different procurement tasks. You can execute the following functions in ProMan (the possible functions here depend on which object you have selected in the project structure and which view you are in at the time):

Executable functions

▸ Generate purchase requisitions or reservations

▸ Perform planning runs

▸ Group purchase requisitions

▸ Create purchase orders

▸ Post goods receipts and issues

▸ Make transfers between stock types

▸ Generate deliveries

After you have executed a function in ProMan, you can refresh the views and then check the result of the function directly in ProMan. In addition to this, as of EHP 3 you can change the assignment of material components via drag-and-drop in the structure tree; this is similar to the process in the Project Builder.

You can use ProMan fully without having to perform any prior Customizing activities; however, if necessary, you can define ProMan profiles and exception profiles in Customizing. You can use a ProMan profile, which you can select in the initial screen of ProMan, to control which documents and orders are read by the database and which views you want to be displayed in ProMan (see Figure 4.20).

ProMan Customizing

In addition, the ProMan profile refers to an exception profile. Exception profiles define when you want the relevant traffic lights in ProMan to indicate exceptional situations. You can even define the conditions for displaying traffic lights by using the same functions as those used for defining substitutions or validations (see Chapter 1, Section 1.8.4 and Section 1.8.5).

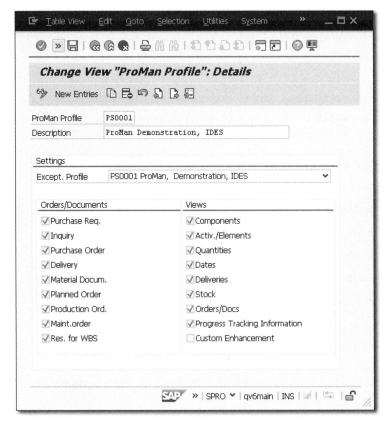

Figure 4.20 Example of Defining a ProMan Profile

4.6 Billing

You bill a project using corresponding functions from Sales based on sales order items that are assigned to WBS elements of the project. Due to this assignment, the resulting payment flows and actual revenues of billing documents are updated on the billing elements of the project and can therefore be compared to the planned revenues (see Chapter 2, Section 2.5). Two functions for controlling billing processes in Sales using project data are explained in the following sections: the *milestone billing* and *resource-related billing* of projects.

4.6.1 Milestone Billing

When you create a billing plan for a sales order item, you can derive the billing date, billing percentage, and the billing rules from the milestones of a project (see Chapter 2, Section 2.5.3). As long as the milestones of the project have not yet been reached, the corresponding items of the billing plan are used exclusively for revenue and payment planning. In other words, they are locked for a billing. However, a lock can be automatically released if the milestone of the corresponding invoice date receives an actual date. You can either set this actual date manually in the milestone or (if it is an activity milestone) it can be set automatically due to an activity confirmation (see Section 4.1.3). A billing run in Sales then automatically generates down payment requests or invoices based on the unlocked items in the billing plan. If the sales order item is assigned to a WBS element, then the resulting actual revenues or down payment requests are updated in the project. This process is called *milestone billing* and is illustrated next using the example of the elevator project.

Let us suppose that the customer agreed to a down payment of 10% of the target value of 200,000 EUR (268,400 USD) at the start of the project, a partial invoice of 30% when an agreed-upon project goal is reached, and a final invoice when the project is completed. Corresponding milestones called Down Payment, Partial Payment, and Final Invoice were defined in the project and copied to the billing plan of the sales order. In SAP Project System, planned revenues of 60,000 EUR (80,534 USD) for the planned date of the Partial Invoice milestone and additional planned revenues of 140,000 EUR (188,000 USD) for the planned date of the Final Invoice milestone are shown in revenue reports. In payment reports of PS Cash Management (see Chapter 6, Section 6.2.4), you can also analyze the planned down payment (billing rule 4) of 20,000 EUR (27,000 USD), taking into account the payment conditions for the planned date of the Down Payment milestone.

An activity confirmation creates an actual date in the Down Payment milestone and documents the fact that the milestone has been reached. The actual date is automatically forwarded to the billing plan of the sales

Down payments

order and unlocks the down payment item. The billing of the sales order in Sales results in a down payment request (FAZ document type) of the agreed-upon amount being automatically created for the unlocked item (see Figure 4.21).

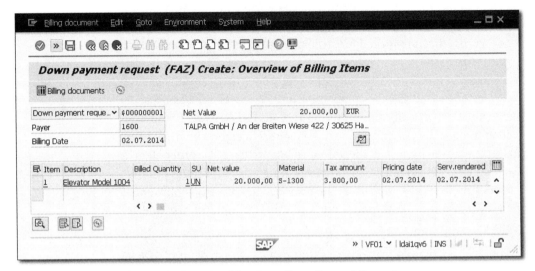

Figure 4.21 Example of Creating a Down Payment Request

The amount is shown as a down payment request in the payment reports in SAP Project System. If the customer's down payment is entered in FI for the down payment request, then you can also analyze this using the payment reports of SAP Project System. The amount of the down payment request is reduced accordingly.

Partial invoices

If the PARTIAL INVOICE milestone is also reached during the course of the project, then the second item of the billing plan is automatically unlocked due to the actual date of the milestone. The billing of the sales order now creates a partial invoice (controlled by billing rule 1 of the item). The down payment made by the customer can be settled proportionately or completely (see Figure 4.22). Actual revenues in the amount of the partial invoice are now shown on the billing element of the project in the revenue reports of SAP Project System. You can use payment reports in SAP Project System to track the invoice-related payment made by the customer that has been entered in FI.

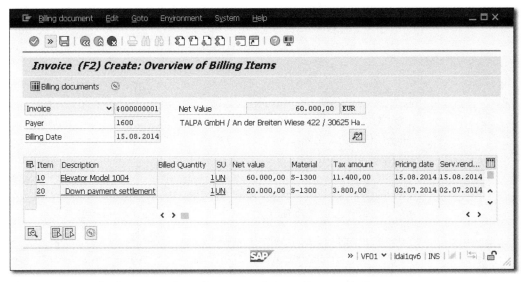

Figure 4.22 Example of Creating a (Partial) Invoice with Down Payment Settlement

If the last FINAL INVOICE milestone is reached in the project and the corresponding item is unlocked in the billing plan, then the billing of the sales order creates an invoice in which all of the down payments of the customer, which have not yet been settled, are deducted from the receivables. Based on this final invoice, the remaining actual revenues are posted on the project and can be analyzed in Reporting. The actual receipt of payment is also shown later in the payment reports of SAP Project System.

Final invoice

4.6.2 Resource-Related Billing

If the required services and materials for implementing the project have not yet been established before the start of the project, then you cannot agree on any fixed prices for the project processes with the customer. In these cases, you cannot bill fixed amounts in the way you could in the preceding example. Instead, you can create a billing using the actual costs of the project. For the billing, you use billing requests in which you can verify for the customer the services performed, material consumed, and additional costs incurred. This form of billing is called *resource-related billing*.

Like sales pricing (see Chapter 2, Section 2.5.4), resource-related billing is also controlled by a DIP profile that is stored in the sales order item assigned to the project. The DIP profile controls how the actual data of the project or the relevant billing structure for individual items of a billing request are to be summarized. For more information about defining DIP profiles, see Chapter 2, Section 2.5.4 and SAP Note 301117. If you use SAP HANA as the database, then individual item values can be aggregated directly in the database. This considerably accelerates resource-related billing that is based on individual items. When you start the resource-related billing for the sales order item (Transaction DP91), you can analyze and, if necessary, still change the two-tier summarization of the actual data in the EXPENSES view and SALES PRICE view.

Expenses view   The EXPENSES view contains hierarchically structured actual data, such as actual costs or statistical key figures entered in the project execution, summarized as dynamic items in accordance with the DIP profile settings. In the EXPENSES view, you can now decide which of the dynamic items are to be billed or temporarily postponed or which should not be included in the billing request (see Figure 4.23).

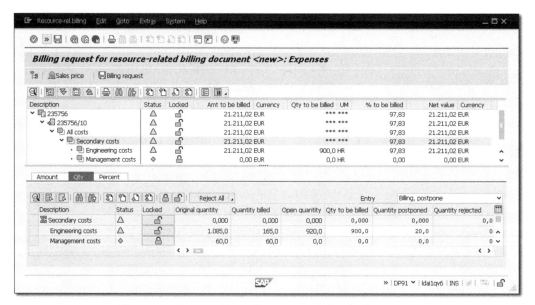

Figure 4.23 Expenses View of a Resource-Related Billing

In a second summarization stage, the DIP profile converts the dynamic items for material numbers. These can be material numbers of the consumed material components of the project or material numbers of defined material master records specifically used for the purpose of confirming an activity. Pricing occurs automatically based on these material numbers and, if necessary, on sales order data, such as the customer number, sales organization, and so on. The SALES PRICE view displays the hierarchically structured material numbers that are combined for individual sales document items. In the SALES PRICE view, you can also analyze the conditions of the different sales document items determined via the pricing and change or add additional conditions (see Figure 4.24). You can now create a billing request that includes the summarized items and any items you adapted. The billing of the request in Sales finally posts the corresponding actual revenues on the project.

Sales price view

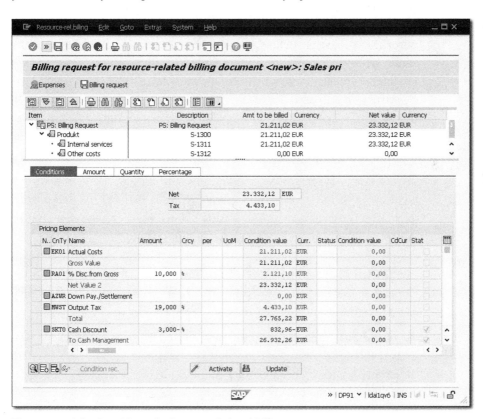

Figure 4.24 Sales Price View of a Resource-Related Billing

Resource-related
billing

You can combine the milestone billing (based on a billing plan in the sales order) and the resource-related billing of the sales order. Consequently, by using milestones in the project, you can control when resource-related billings are possible and whether resource-related down payment requests (billing rule 4) or billing requests (billing rule 1) are created in the process. This includes all combinations of fixed down payments, fixed billing documents, resource-related down payments, and resource-related billing documents.

Billing between
company codes

In international companies, employees from different company codes are frequently involved in the project execution. The costs between the company codes are normally settled on a resource-related basis. Let's look at an example of a cross-company code process for the elevator project.

The elevator is to be built and sold in Germany, but parts of the construction are to be carried out by employees in the United States. Therefore, the project structure contains branches for both the company codes of Germany and the United States. In the company code for Germany (the requesting company code), a purchase order is created for the construction and assigned to the corresponding part of the project. In the company code for the United States (the delivering company code), a sales order is created because of the purchase order and assigned to the branch of the project for the US company code.

In the course of the project execution, the employees in the United States post their activities on the branch of the project provided for this purpose. The actual costs that result from these postings can now be billed on a resource-related basis with reference to the sales order. The billing leads to actual revenues on the branch for the company code for the United States. In contrast, the corresponding invoice receipt in the company code for Germany results in actual costs on the object to which the purchase order was also assigned.

DIP profile

As of the Enterprise Release, the new source INTERCOMPANY-LINE ITEMS is available for defining DIP profiles (see Chapter 2, Section 2.5.4). With this source, you can use an alternative option to the one explained previously to map the resource-related billing of project activities between company codes. In this case, rather than a sales order being created for each individual project it is only created once (or once for each fiscal year) in the delivering company code, with the requesting company code as the customer. Only structures for the requesting company code are required within the projects themselves in this scenario. Employees of the delivering company code can also use these structures to directly post the activities they have performed. These cross-company code activities are automatically collected in the new source. A resource-related billing in Transaction DP93 based on the cross-company code activities finally performs all of the required adjustment postings in accounting and posts revenues for the delivering company code.

Redesign of Resource-Related Billing between Company Codes	**[+]**
Note that resource-related billing between company codes was redesigned in 2011 in order to eliminate various restrictions of the previous solution, such as "redundant" postings in FI if the reconciliation ledger was used or in case of real-time integration. This redesign also included the provision of new functions, such as collective processing.	
You can find more information on this redesign and the necessary settings in Customizing in SAP Note 1461090 and in the attachment to this note in particular.	

4.7   Project Progress

With very complex projects in particular, it is important to provide the project and subproject managers with tools that they can use to monitor the progress of the project efficiently and to identify variances in the project planning as soon as possible. In addition to the different reports from Reporting (see Chapter 6), SAP Project System has its own functions for this purpose: milestone trend analysis, progress analysis, and progress tracking. These functions are explained in the following sections.

4.7.1   Milestone Trend Analysis

Milestone trend analysis is used to display the date situation of important project events simply and clearly, which enables you to immediately identify any variances in your planning and trends of such variances. To

Presentation of the project status

do this, the planned and actual dates of the milestones relevant to project progress are compared graphically or in tables at different times in the milestone trend analysis.

Figure 4.25 shows an example of the graphic display of a milestone trend analysis. On the vertical time line, you can see the dates of the different milestones; on the horizontal time line, you can see the period when the milestones had these dates. A horizontal curve for a milestone therefore means that its dates have not changed over the course of time—that is, progress is being made on schedule. Conversely, an ascending curve indicates that a deadline has been delayed, whereas a descending curve shows that a milestone has been reached early compared to the original planning. You can perform milestone trend analyses using Transaction CNMT or in the Project Planning Board (Transaction CJ2B).

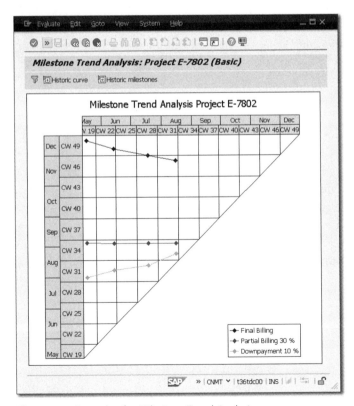

Figure 4.25 Example of a Milestone Trend Analysis

To perform a milestone trend analysis, the projects that you want to analyze must contain milestones for which the TREND ANALYSIS indicator is set or was set earlier on the project (see Chapter 1, Section 1.4). The HISTORICAL CURVE view of the milestone trend analysis shows the dates over time of the milestones for which the TREND ANALYSIS indicator is currently set. The HISTORICAL MILESTONES view also displays milestone dates, but it displays those for which the indicator is not currently set, although it was set at an earlier time.

The second prerequisite for the milestone trend analysis is that you must create project versions (see Chapter 1, Section 1.9.1) to retain the dates of the milestones for the different times in the system. Note in this case that you must set the MTA RELEVANT indicator for the project versions to ensure that they can be used for a milestone trend analysis.

Prerequisites of milestone trend analyses

4.7.2 Progress Analysis

You can use *progress analysis* to compare the actual status of a project with the planned project progress to enable you to determine any schedule or cost variances early on and take any necessary measures (that is, stop the project, allocate more budget, change scheduling, etc.) to control the situation. You can analyze the progress for individual parts of the project or on an aggregated basis for the entire project, whereby the different parts of the project can be weighted very differently.

The progress analysis determines the following key figures for this in both aggregated and nonaggregated form and makes them available in a special progress version:

Percentage of completion, costs of work performed

▸ Planned percentage of completion—POC (planned)

▸ Actual percentage of completion—POC (actual)

▸ Budgeted costs of work scheduled—BCWS

▸ Budgeted costs of work performed—BCWP

The earned values are an expression of the value of the relevant percentage of completion in each case and are calculated from the product of a percentage of completion and a reference factor (overall costs) that reflects the total value of the work to be performed. This reference factor can be displayed by the planned costs or the budget. The following therefore applies:

$$BCWS = POC \text{ (planned)} \times overall\ costs$$
$$BCWP = POC \text{ (actual)} \times overall\ costs$$

BCWS, BCWP, ACWP In business literature, planned and actual earned values are generally known as the *Budgeted Costs of Work Scheduled* (BCWS) and *Budgeted Costs of Work Performed* (BCWP) values.

To make statements on the cost variances, another key figure is used, namely the actual costs incurred. These are frequently called *Actual Cost of Work Performed* (ACWP) values in the literature within the progress analysis.

SV, CV You can now calculate *Schedule Variances* (SV) and *Cost Variances* (CV) from these key figures as follows:

$$SV = BCWP - BCWS$$
$$CV = BCWP - ACWP$$

The SV value is a measurement for schedule variances in your project. If SV is positive, this means that the value of the current progress exceeds the planned value; therefore, your project is progressing "faster" than planned. However, if SV is negative, there is a scheduling delay in your project; you have not yet reached the level of progress originally planned by this date.

The CV value reflects the costs variances. If the CV value is positive, this means that the value of the current project progress is greater than the resulting actual costs that were used for it. However, if CV is negative, more actual costs have been incurred in your project than should be the case due to the actual project progress.

CPI, ECV The cost variance can also be expressed by the *Cost Performance Index* (CPI), in which

$$CPI = BCWP \div ACWP$$

The CPI indicates how the value of your actual project progress behaves in relation to the actual costs. If you adopt a continuous development of a project corresponding to the CPI value, then forecasts for the anticipated expected Costs Value (ECV) total costs are also made using the following formula:

$ECV = total\ planned\ costs \div CPI$

If required, you can also analyze cost and schedule variances separately for different cost elements. This can be useful if you want to look at the development of internal or external services or the use of material separately.

The planned and actual degrees of completion are the starting points for calculating cost and schedule variances. You can determine these degrees of completion using *measurement methods*. The following measurement methods are available by default:

Measurement methods

▶ **Start-finish 0–100**
The percentage of completion is 0% until such time as the finish date of the object has been reached. The value then changes from 0% to 100%. The planned finish date is used for the planned percentage of completion, and the actual finish date is used for the actual percentage of completion. This method is only useful for objects for which the duration is shorter than the period between two progress analyses and for which a more specific method cannot be used.

▶ **Start-finish 20–80**
When the planned or actual start date is reached, the planned or actual percentage of completion is set to 20%. When the finish date is reached, the percentage of completion increases to 100%. An average value is achieved by using 20% as the initial value (considered across several evaluation periods). However, you should only use this method if the duration of the object is not too long and a more specific method cannot be used.

▶ **Time proportionality**
With this method, the percentage of completion increases in proportion to the duration of the object, taking into account the relevant factory calendar. The system uses the planned start and finish dates for the planned percentage of completion, the actual start and finish dates for the actual percentage of completion, or, in the case of a PARTIALLY CONFIRMED status, the actual start date and the planned duration of

the object. This method is useful if you can assume a linear increase in the progress of the project.

▶ MILESTONES
The percentage of completion for WBS elements and activities is copied from the corresponding field of assigned milestones that are identified as being relevant for the progress analysis (see Chapter 1, Section 1.4). The system takes into account the planned date of the milestone for the planned percentage of completion and the actual date for the actual percentage of completion. The milestone technique can be useful if you can define objective criteria for achieving milestones.

Other standard methods
The progress version for each of the preceding methods decides whether the forecast or basic dates are used to determine the planned degrees of completion. Other standard methods include the following:

▶ **Cost proportional**
You use this method to calculate the planned percentage of completion of an object from the ratio of cumulative planned costs up to the period of the progress analysis and the overall planned costs of the object; the actual percentage of completion results from the ratio of the actual costs to the overall planned costs. In terms of which CO version of the planned costs is to be used, you specify this in the progress version. You can only use this method in planned data if you have performed a cost planning by date. This method is useful for objects for which progress can be derived from cost development; these can typically be general cost activities, externally processed activities, or assigned production orders.

▶ **Quantity proportional**
You determine the degrees of completion with this method as you do with the cost-proportional method. However, instead of cost information you use a statistical key figure here to calculate the degrees of completion. To use this method, you must have defined a suitable statistical key figure of the TOTALS VALUES type and assigned it to the method. In addition, you must perform planning by date for the key figure and post actual values for this key figure within the execution phase. This method is useful if you can derive the progress of an

object by preferably using quantities such as the amount of work performed or the number of products completed.

▶ **Secondary proportionality (apportioned effort)**
This method copies the percentage of completion of one object from the percentage of completion of another reference object. Therefore, a prerequisite for using this method is that a fixed relationship can be assumed between the progress of the object and the reference object stored in the object (for example, quality inspection and production).

▶ **Degree of processing from confirmation**
This method copies the actual percentage of completion from the degree of processing of confirmed activities or activity elements (see Section 4.3). You can only use this method when you use networks or to determine actual degrees of completion. Because the degree of processing is usually derived from the confirmed activity, this method is useful if you can measure the progress of the object on the internal activity performed, because this is often the case for internally processed activities.

▶ **Estimates**
You manually specify the percentage of completion for individual periods of the object using this method. To prevent an early overestimate of the actual progress when determining estimates, you can store a maximum percentage of completion in this measurement method (generally 80%) that can only be exceeded once an actual finish date has been entered. This method is often used for WBS elements whose percentage of completion does not increase in a linear direction and cannot be derived from assigned activities or milestones.

▶ **Actual = planned**
This method, which you can only use for the actual percentage of completion, copies the planned percentage of completion as the actual percentage of completion.

You can use different methods to determine the planned and actual degrees of completion. However, it generally makes sense to use the same method in the planned and actual data to compare the progress data better (the DEGREE OF PROCESSING method is an exception here).

We recommend that you determine the degrees of completion for WBS elements with assigned activities at the level of the activities and aggregate these degrees of completion on the WBS elements using suitable weighting factors, such as the planned costs of the activities, for example.

Measurement method determination

When you perform a progress analysis, the system determines the measurement methods to be used for the individual objects according to the following strategy:

1. You determine the method using a BAdI.[1]

2. You explicitly store one measurement method and one progress version in the object.

3. The progress version involves the planned method being copied as the actual method and vice versa (this is not possible for the ESTIMATES and SECONDARY PROPORTIONALITY methods).

4. You enter a measurement method in Customizing as the default value for the object type.

5. The system uses the 0–100 method.

You cannot assign measurement methods to assigned orders manually. Instead, you can only store a default value in Customizing.

Settings in Customizing of the Progress Analysis

Defining measurement methods

Corresponding measurement methods for determining degrees of completion using the methods described previously are already defined in Customizing of SAP Project System in the standard system. You can define additional measurement methods if required. Figure 4.26 shows an example of defining your own measurement method. The start-finish rule is used as the measurement technique in this example. However, unlike the 20–80 method, a start percentage of completion of 50% is used here.

You can use the MAX POC (maximum percentage of completion) field to define a percentage of completion that must not be exceeded as long as

---

1 You can find more detailed information on this BAdI and a sample implementation in SAP Note 549097.

a finish date has not been set. A maximum percentage of completion is relevant for the DEGREE OF PROCESSING, TIME, COST, QUANTITY, and SECONDARY PROPORTIONALITY methods and, in particular, the ESTIMATES method.

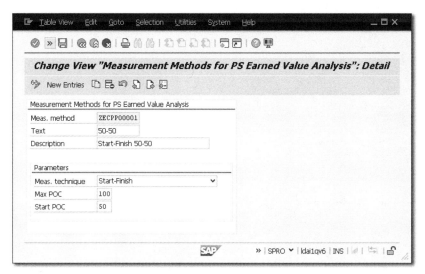

Figure 4.26 Example of Defining a Measurement Method

The measurement techniques are defined as fixed techniques in the SAP system. However, you can also determine customer-specific percentages of completion using the INDIVIDUAL (USER EXIT) measurement technique and customer enhancement CNEX0031.

Depending on the CO area, progress version, and object type or order type, you can store default values for the measurement methods in Customizing of SAP Project System, which are used to determine planned and actual percentages of completion (see Figure 4.27).

Default values for measurement methods

When you perform a progress analysis, the percentages of completion are updated in a progress version in the form of statistical key figures. Progress key figures are already delivered by default for aggregated and nonaggregated percentages of completion and for percentages of completion relevant to the results analysis. You can also define your own progress key figures if required. In Customizing of SAP Project System,

Statistical progress key figures

you must assign the progress key figures to CO areas and to the relevant usages.

Figure 4.27 Defining the Default Values for the Measurement Methods of Different Object Types

Progress version

A progress version is a CO version with the exclusive use of PROGRESS ANALYSIS. Figure 4.28 shows the definition of a progress version in Customizing of SAP Project System. When you perform a progress analysis, you specify the progress version in which you want the progress data to be saved. If you do not derive the measurement methods of objects using a BAdI, then you must also store a progress version in the objects, either to be able to enter a measurement method manually or to derive the measurement method using default values from Customizing.

You also specify the following control parameters in the progress version:

▶ EV BASIS
Reference factor for calculating the earned values from the percentages of completion (planned costs or budget values)

▶ POC WEIGHTING
Value for weighting the percentages of completion when aggregating data at the next highest level (for example, planned costs)

▶ PLANNING TYPE and
EARLY/LATESet of dates to be used for methods that depend on planned dates

▶ REFERENCE
Controls whether the planned method should be copied to the actual method and vice versa if each of the other methods were not explicitly entered

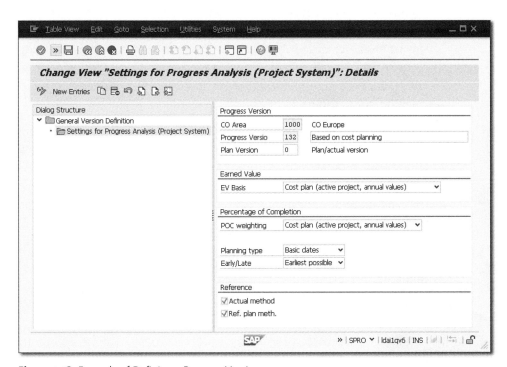

Figure 4.28 Example of Defining a Progress Version

Performing and Evaluating the Progress Analysis

You can use Transactions CNE1 (INDIVIDUAL PROCESSING) and CNE2 (COLLECTIVE PROCESSING) to perform the progress analysis. As of SAP ECC Release 6.0, you can also use the Progress Analysis Workbench for the progress analysis (Transaction CNPAWB). When you start the progress analysis in individual or collective processing, in addition to selecting the objects, flow control, and progress version in the initial screen you also specify the periods up to which the actual values are to be taken into account. When you use the TIME PROPORTIONALITY method, you can also enter a specific date instead of the period to calculate the percentages of completion based on precise dates. When you perform the progress analysis, the system determines measurement methods for the selected objects, calculates the percentages of completion in nonaggregated and aggregated format for the cost element groups provided, and updates these percentages of completion in the progress version as statistical key figures. The system then calculates the earned values based on the percentages of completion and writes these values into the progress version. As of EHP 6, you can also enter multiple progress versions in the initial screens of Transactions CNE1 and CNE2. Because the project structure is read only once during execution, the calculation of progress values for multiple progress versions and thus different measurement methods can be accelerated.

As part of progress value determination, you can also make adjustment postings for past periods (for example, if planned costs are changed) that, along with the original earned values, will lead to *adjusted progress values* in the progress version. You can analyze the original progress values and the adjusted values separately. Because the percentages of completion can also be used as part of the results analysis (see Chapter 5, Section 5.6) in addition to the aggregated and nonaggregated percentages of completion, a percentage of completion is also updated as a separate statistical key figure for the results analysis. SAP Note 189230 contains some information that you may find useful when troubleshooting within your progress analysis.

Progress Analysis Workbench

After you perform the progress analysis, you can analyze the data in the Project Planning Board using special progress reports or also in the Progress Analysis Workbench (see Figure 4.29). However, in addition to using the Progress Analysis Workbench for the common analysis of progress data, statuses, dates, costs, and different master data of projects you can also use it to change data. Consequently, the many functions you can perform in the Progress Analysis Workbench include confirming activity elements, setting different system and user statuses, entering planned and actual dates of WBS elements, changing user fields and customer-specific fields, and, in particular, maintaining percentages of completion in tables. You can also export data from the Progress Analysis Workbench to Microsoft Excel, enter percentages of completion or dates for WBS elements, activities, and milestones there, and then import the data back into the SAP system.

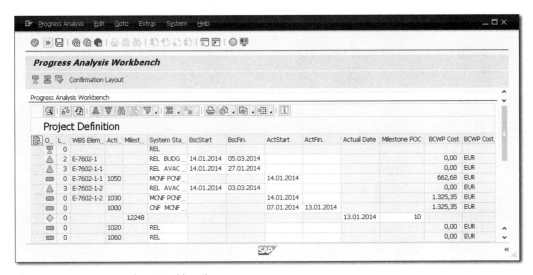

Figure 4.29 Progress Analysis Workbench

As of EHP 3, in the Progress Analysis Workbench you can now choose between the flat, tabular display shown in Figure 4.29 and a structure tree display to navigate to and edit individual objects. In addition, you can also easily toggle between a STANDARD LAYOUT and a CONFIRMATION LAYOUT. The confirmation layout contains fewer fields than the standard layout and is therefore less complex when it comes to entering data.

Display versions

4.7.3 Progress Tracking

The use of progress tracking in SAP Project System is relevant for projects for which the punctual procurement and delivery of material components play a key role for the execution of the project. You can use progress tracking to track any events for the material components in the projects and, if required, enhance these events with status information and additional deadline information. The events may have equivalent events in the SAP system documents, such as a purchase order or goods issue and receipt, but they can also be defined completely independent of the SAP system.

In Purchasing, you can use the progress tracking function to track the scheduled dates of purchase orders. Therefore, you must distinguish between the two progress tracking objects: *material component* and *purchase order*. As of EHP 3, two more progress tracking objects are available in SAP Project system: *WBS elements* and *network activities*. It makes sense to use progress tracking for WBS elements and network activities, for example, if you want to keep your project structures as small as possible and at the same time require the detailed tracking of dates for scheduled events. For each progress tracking object, separate transactions and Customizing activities are available. The following sections describe the progress tracking process for material components as an example.

Progress tracking process

When you perform progress tracking for material components (Transaction COMPXPD), you first select the material components for which you want to process or analyze events in the progress tracking. This is a two-step selection process. If you're performing the progress tracking for a component for the first time, then you must assign the events for which you want to analyze dates to the material component first. To do this, you can create new events for the components directly in the progress tracking or use *standard events* and *event scenarios* that you already defined in Customizing of SAP Project System. If required, you can also automate the assignment of events using a BAdI.

You can now enter up to four dates for each event of a material component: an original, planned, forecast, and actual date. You can enter these dates in progress tracking manually or by using a mass change, copy them from other components using copy functions, or calculate them using scheduling in progress tracking. In particular, you can also determine the dates automatically from SAP system documents using a BAdI.

You can then analyze the event dates of the different material components in progress tracking. In this case, traffic lights can indicate if there are any variances (between the planned and forecast dates of an event, for example) or if planned dates have been overrun even though a corresponding actual date for the event of a component was not entered (see Figure 4.30).

If you want to analyze the dates of material components in greater detail, then you can assign subitems to the components and enter event dates for each subitem. You can also store status information with descriptive texts for each material component.

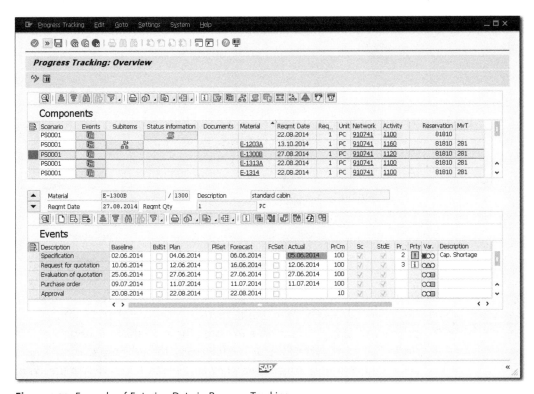

Figure 4.30 Example of Entering Data in Progress Tracking

Customizing of progress tracking

To use progress tracking, you must define a progress-tracking profile in Customizing of SAP Project System (see Figure 4.31). You can use this profile, which you must enter in the initial screen of progress tracking, to control which date types (original, planned, forecast, or actual) are to be displayed for events, which variances should be highlighted by traffic lights, and the details for scheduling event dates.

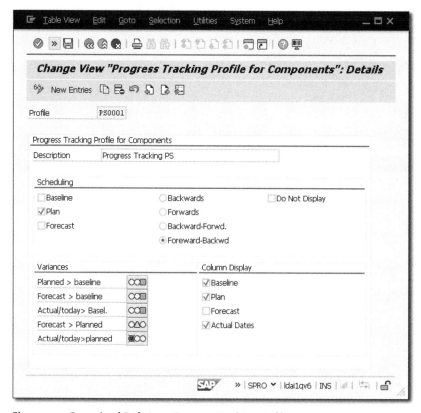

Figure 4.31 Example of Defining a Progress Tracking Profile

Standard events and scenarios

You generally also have to define standard events and event scenarios in progress tracking Customizing to assign these events to material components in progress tracking at a later stage. In the simplest scenario, a standard event only consists of a key and a text. If you derive the event dates using a BAdI execution, then you can also specify whether a derived date in the application should be modifiable for a standard event. After you define a standard scenario, you can define a sequence of standard events for the scenario (see Figure 4.32). You can use time intervals between two events, which you can then use in progress tracking to schedule event dates. If you also want to store status information in progress tracking for material components, then you must also define status Infotypes in Customizing, which are used to structure the statuses. You can also use these infotypes to conduct an authorization check of the status information.

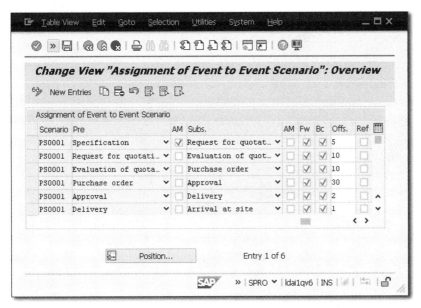

Figure 4.32 Assigning Standard Events to a Scenario

You can use the EXP_UPDATE BAdI to adapt the functions of progress tracking to meet your own requirements. This BAdI consists of methods that you can use to assign event scenarios or events to components automatically or to influence the time intervals for scheduling. In particular, you can use a method of this BAdI to derive event dates automatically for material components from purchase requisitions, purchase orders, goods movements, and so on. As of EHP 5, you can also use the EXP_ENHANCE BAdI to add customer-specific functions and adapt the user interface.

EXP_UPDATE

4.8   Claim Management

You can use Claim Management to document unforeseen project events or variances in project planning as claims for a project. You can also initiate required activities and tasks in a claim and track the related processes or calculate the costs that result from a variance and integrate them into the cost planning of the project in question. In Reporting, you can use specific reports to evaluate claims. The INTERNAL CLAIM and EXTERNAL CLAIM notification types are delivered by default for Claim Management. You can also create your own notification types for Claim Management in Customizing.

Examples of internal and external claims

Examples of why you might want to create internal claims include internal, unforeseen capacity and material bottlenecks, necessary adjustments to specifications and project planning data, unexpected deadline delays, and problems with partners or suppliers during project processing. You can use external claims to document subsequent requests or complaints made by customers or other companies involved in implementing the project. These are just some examples for using claims; theoretically, the functions of Claim Management are not defined using special scenarios.

Creating claims

You can create, edit, and display claims in the SAP system using Transactions CLM1, CLM2, and CLM3. You can also create claims through the Internet or intranet using the SR10 service. SAP already provides a predefined form for this in which you can enter the data for the claim; however, you can also define your own forms. You can use standard workflows of Claim Management to inform the corresponding people responsible that a claim has been created and to optimize processes for further processing or approval of claims.

When you create a claim in the SAP system, you must first specify the notification type of the claim and the partner type of the notification that determines the additional partner data (for example, customer or supplier numbers) that can be specified in the claim. You then enter a description for the claim in the detail screen of the claim. You can enter more detailed explanations for the claim in different long texts that can vary in terms of the long text type.

You can use a filter function for long text types to enable you to select specific information at a later time. Examples of long text types are Reasons Long Text or Consequences Long Text. However, you can define the description of a maximum of four long text types in Customizing. By linking Claim Management to document management and the Business Document Services of the SAP system, you can also link any other documents to the claim.

You can also enter additional information in a claim, which includes details about the partners involved (customers, suppliers, users responsible, etc.), relevant documents from Purchasing or Sales, system and user statuses, and activities and tasks. Contrary to activities, you can enter a partner and status for each task. For example, you can enter a WBS element in a claim and, as a result, create the reference to a project (see Figure 4.33).

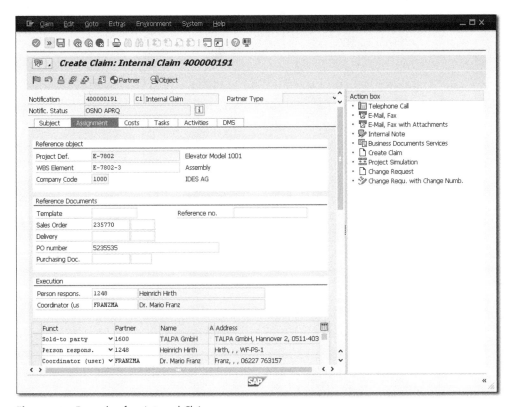

Figure 4.33 Example of an Internal Claim

When processing the claim, you can use an *action box* to execute various function modules depending on the status of the claim and the settings in the claim Customizing. For example, some of these function modules could include starting and documenting calls, sending faxes and email, or creating other claims or simulation versions (see Chapter 1, Section 1.9.2). The system can automatically log activities that you executed from the action box as an activity or task in the claim. In Customizing, you can adjust the action box to reflect your own needs and add other activities.

You can also store information about the expected costs to be incurred due to a variance. In the simplest case, you only enter an estimated amount in the claim. Alternatively, you can also create a detailed costing in the claim and copy the calculated total amount as the estimated costs. If you created a costing in the claim, then you can also integrate this costing into the cost planning of the project in question. This cost integration is technically implemented using a cost collector—that is, an internal order.

When you save the claim, the system automatically creates an internal order called NOTIFICATION followed by the name of the claim and copies the estimated costs of the claim into the internal order as planned costs. At the same time, the assignment of the claim is also copied to the WBS element in the cost collector and the organizational data of the internal order using this assignment is derived. Assigning the internal order to the WBS element means that you can now also analyze the planned costs in Reporting of the project. On the cost collector, you can also post actual costs incurred due to variances; however, in this case you normally have to settle the internal order. Alternatively, you can also post the actual costs directly to the project. Nevertheless, a planned/actual comparison is then no longer possible at the level of the cost collector; instead, it is only possible at the level of the project.

The MKOS (cost collector created) system status automatically documents the creation of the cost collector in the claim. If the estimated costs subsequently change in the claim, then the planned costs of the internal order are also automatically adjusted. If you want to prevent the planned costs of the internal order from being changed manually (that is, regardless of the claim), then you must define a user status for the internal order that will not allow the UNIT COSTING PLANNING and PRIMARY COSTS PLANNING business processes. This status does not affect a change to the planned costs caused by changes to the estimated costs of the claim, because for costing the claim the business process PRIMARY COSTS UNIT COSTING is used. Setting or undoing the DLFL (deletion flag) status in the claim automatically results in the status also being set or undone in the internal order.

To ensure that the system creates a cost collector when you save a claim, various prerequisites must be met in the claim and the relevant WBS element. For example, you must enter a WBS in the claim, the estimated costs of the claim must be calculated using a costing, and (if the claim requires approval) the claim must be approved. Furthermore, the WBS element must be an account assignment element and have the PREL (PARTIALLY RELEASED) or REL (RELEASED) status. If Profit Center Accounting is active and you want to create business area balance sheets in the company code of the WBS element, then you must also enter a profit center and business area in the WBS element.

Prerequisites of cost integration

Another prerequisite for creating a cost collector automatically is that you create an implementation of the `NOTIF_COST_ CUS_CHECK` BAdI and set the E_CREATE_COST_COLLECTOR indicator to X in the CHECK method. If required, you can program additional conditions in the method to create a cost collector. The CO properties of the internal order are defined by a *CO scenario*, which you must assign to the relevant notification types in claim-specific Customizing. For this reason, a CO scenario is delivered with the standard system. The cost collector is always created as an internal order for the CL01 order type. With the exception of the status profile, you should not make any changes to this order type. In the DEFINE ORDER VALUE UPDATING FOR ORDERS FOR PROJECTS Customizing table, you can use this order type as a reference to decide whether the planned costs of the cost collector should be added to the planned total of the WBS element (see Figure 2.62 in Chapter 2, Section 2.4.7).

Customizing of claims entails general notification Customizing and claim-specific Customizing. In general notification Customizing, you can

Customizing of claims

create new notification types or make adjustments to both of the standard INTERNAL and EXTERNAL CLAIM notification types. In terms of a message type, you can define in general notification Customizing which partners, reasons, activities, or tasks can be entered in a claim or which function modules can be executed from the action box. In addition to the cost collector settings described previously, claim-specific Customizing involves defining the long text types that can be used to structure information in the claim.

4.9 Summary

In the execution phase of projects, various documents are produced in the SAP system due to project-related business transactions. These documents are assigned to the corresponding projects, which consequently results in commitments, costs, and revenues as well as payments being updated on the projects. To monitor projects or parts of projects over time, you must enter actual dates for WBS elements and activities and compare these actual dates to the planned dates. Tools for analyzing the progress of projects support you in identifying cost and schedule variances in your planning.

To determine all relevant data for a period and make it available for Enterprise Controlling (CO), you need to perform various periodic activities during project planning and execution.

5   Period-End Closing

Chapter 2 and Chapter 4 explained how project costs and revenues could be planned and posted. However, the planning data based on detailed planning and even the actual costs based on the direct assignment of activity allocations, internal, material documents, or invoices are usually incomplete. In most cases, you have to take into account portions of overhead costs from cost centers that are not directly related to the services rendered (for example, administrative cost centers). Adjustment postings may have to be made for allocated activities due to changed prices. Interest profits and losses may have to be considered as well, particularly for cost-intensive projects lasting several years. To make your project data available for the relevant Enterprise CO analyses, you may also want to add key figures (such as forecast data and so on) to your data. Finally, projects often serve to collect costs and revenues only on a temporary basis and forward the costs and revenues collected in a period to other receivers.

SAP Project System provides various functions for handling all of these tasks. These functions are normally executed periodically. In this chapter, we will discuss several general aspects pertaining to the execution of the relevant functions before we delve into the various period-end closing activities that must be executed for projects.

Periodic activities

> **Planned and Actual Periodic Activities**   **[+]**
>
> Planned periodic activities are often referred to as *allocations*, whereas actual periodic activities fall under the general term of *period-end closing*. SAP Note 701077 has a range of useful information about periodic activities in SAP Project System.

5.1 Processing Types

Individual processing The various period-end closing activities can be executed for each project or each part of a project individually in *individual processing* or for several projects at the same time in *collective processing*. Figure 5.1 shows a typical initial screen for individual processing. By specifying the project definition, you can select all WBS elements for this project simultaneously. If you enter a WBS element instead of the project definition, then the WITH HIERARCHY indicator determines whether the WBS element is to be selected on its own or whether all lower-level WBS elements in the hierarchy are to be selected. The WITH ORDERS indicator determines whether the assigned networks and orders should also be included in the selection.

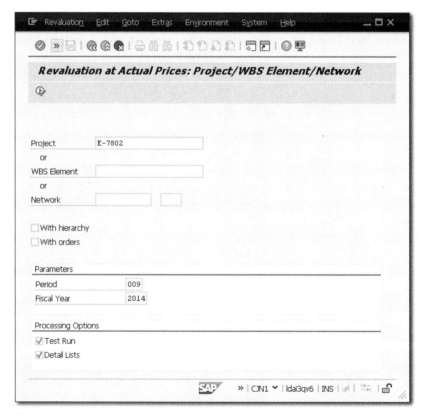

Figure 5.1 Initial Screen for Revaluation at Actual Prices in Individual Processing

Depending on the transaction, the initial screen may also include other fields—for example, fields that allow you to control which periods and parameters are to be used for process control. The settings for process control allow you to define whether a test run or a detailed list is to be created at the end of execution, for example. With a test run, you can analyze the result of the execution without the data being updated.

To use collective processing, you must first use Transaction CJ8V to define *selection variants*—that is, lists of all projects or parts of projects that should be taken into account. You can also use dynamic selections and status selection profiles as filter criteria for object selection (see Chapter 6, Section 6.1). In the variant attributes, you must specify at least one meaning for the selection variants before you save.

Collective processing

Defining Selection Variants [+]

Selection variants are a generic function in SAP systems, which can be used for many purposes (collective processing, calling reports, etc.). You can use the variant attributes to make settings for the display and ready-for-input status of fields, for example. Specifically, you can select certain fields as selection variables. The value of the field is then automatically filled at runtime with variable date calculation (for example, with the current date), user-specific fixed values, or fixed values that you maintain centrally in Table TVARVC.

As a rule, the period-end closing of projects cannot be viewed in isolation from other periodic activities in your company. Instead, it depends on other business transactions, such as price calculation in Cost Center Accounting. You must adhere to certain sequences. For example, the actual costs must be calculated in Cost Center Accounting before the actual costs of your projects can be revaluated, which, in turn, must happen before you can calculate the overhead costs based on your actual costs.

To plan and monitor the process of period-end closing, which may be a cross-departmental process, you can use the *Schedule Manager* rather than individual transactions for individual periodic activities. In the Schedule Manager (Transaction SCMA), you can use a TASK LIST (see Figure 5.2) and a MONTHLY and DAILY OVERVIEW to structure the various

Schedule Manager

periodic activities, add explanatory documents if necessary, and schedule and monitor various tasks. You can use a monitor to analyze in detail the execution of tasks, restart tasks if necessary (if errors occur during execution), or navigate to project maintenance—for example, to enter missing master data.

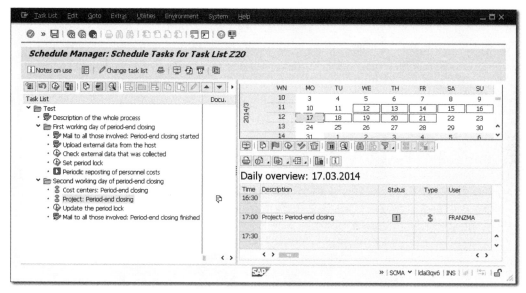

Figure 5.2 Example of a Task List in the Schedule Manager

Flow definitions

The actual planning and execution of the various period-end closing activities in the Schedule Manager are based on *flow definitions*, which can be included as tasks in a task list and scheduled (see Figure 5.3). You can use the Workflow Builder to define the sequence of period activities in a process flow in the form of individual steps and, if necessary, integrate the sending of information to users or user decisions. By creating a flow definition for the multilevel worklist of the Schedule Manager, you ensure that if one step in the flow definition is executed incorrectly only the incorrect objects are processed again when the flow definition is executed a second time.

The following section describes the various functions available in SAP Project System for a period-end closing. The screenshots for the individual functions are all taken from the transactions for individual processing.

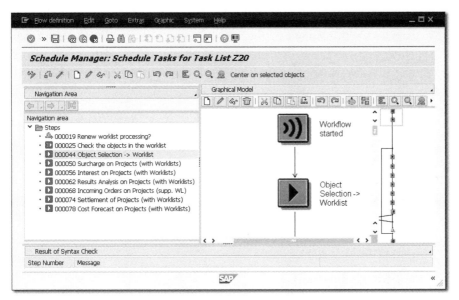

Figure 5.3 Example of a Flow Definition

5.2 Revaluation at Actual Prices

If your projects incorporate activities of cost centers or business processes during the project execution phase (for example, via confirmations or the assignment of activity allocations internal to WBS elements), then relevant prices based on the activity type are used for the revaluation of the activities and the calculation of the corresponding cost flows.

Some companies use *actual price calculation* to calculate the price of the individual activity types iteratively for the valuation of actual activities as part of the period-end closing. Actual prices are calculated based on the relationship between the actual costs and the actual service rendered by the cost center or business process. Depending on the procedure used, the costs and activities of the individual periods are analyzed separately (periodically differentiated price), as total values (average price), or as values cumulated up to the analysis period (cumulated price).

Actual price calculation

However, because the actual price calculation is not executed until the period-end closing, the iteratively calculated actual price is not available when the actual activity is posted. Therefore, the activities are normally valuated with planned prices initially. After the actual prices are calculated, you can make the relevant adjustment postings (in other words, execute a revaluation at actual prices for your projects).

5.2.1 Prerequisites for Revaluation at Actual Prices

To use the REVALUATION AT ACTUAL PRICES function, various prerequisites must be fulfilled. Internal activity allocations must have been executed or process costs posted for a project. In Customizing, you must have defined whether and how the revaluation is to be executed using the REVALUATION indicator in the fiscal year-dependent parameters of the CO version (or the relevant actual version). The indicator can be set in one of three ways:

▶ **0 (no revaluation)**
No revaluation takes place. This usually means that all actual activities are valuated with the planned price.

▶ **1 (revaluation with separate procedure)**
Revaluations are possible and are executed as differences based on the original allocation with a separate procedure (ACTUAL PRICE CALCULATION). The original allocations remain unchanged. As a result, you can trace the deviation between the valuations at the actual price and the planned price.

▶ **2 (revaluation in the original procedure)**
Revaluations are possible and result in a change to the original allocations. The differences between the valuations at the actual price and the planned price cannot be traced with this setting. Changing the existing allocation records is particularly useful if no planned price exists and, therefore, no valuation has taken place with the original posting.

As a final prerequisite for revaluation at actual prices, an actual cost calculation must be executed in Cost Center Accounting or activity-based costing (Transaction KSII or CPII). The actual price calculation is largely controlled by the METHODS indicator in the fiscal year-dependent parameters of the CO version and the PRICE indicator of the actual allocation price, which is copied as a default value from the master data of the relevant activity type.

5.2.2 Executing the Revaluation at Actual Prices

You can use Transactions CJN1 (individual processing) and CJN2 (collective processing) to revaluate work breakdown structures and networks in SAP Project System.

Revaluation—work breakdown structures/networks

Figure 5.1 showed the initial screen of individual processing. In addition to selecting the objects, you specify the PERIOD and the FISCAL YEAR for revaluation here and the relevant indicators for process control. If you repeat the revaluation for a period, then only the differences that arise due to subsequent price changes are posted. If necessary, you can also cancel the revaluations executed in the update run. The original activity allocations remain unchanged.

If no activities were included in the period, if no actual price exists, or if the project was already valuated with the current actual price, then no posting occurs. If the status of the project or the cost center to be credited prevents posting, then the system issues an error message to that effect.

5.2.3 Dependencies of the Revaluation of Actual Prices

It's generally useful to set period locks for the actual project costs for the ACTUAL ACTIVITY ALLOCATIONS (RKL) and INDIRECT ACTUAL ACTIVITY ALLOCATIONS (RKIL) activities (Transaction OKP1) before you execute the revaluation at actual prices. After you execute the revaluation at actual prices, you can also set a period lock for the REVALUATION activity (RKLN) if necessary.

Setting period locks

> **Overhead Restrictions When Using Revaluation at Actual Prices** [!]
>
> Note that when you use the revaluation at actual prices as part of the application of overhead (see Section 5.3) no percentage overhead rates can be calculated on the basis of costs for cost element category 43 (INTERNAL ACTIVITY ALLOCATIONS). Because the revaluation would lead to changed costs of these

cost elements, you would need to execute a new application of overhead, which would lead to changed costs for the credited cost center. This would result in a recursion.

Note also the sequence in which you execute the overhead application, settlement (see Section 5.9), actual price calculation, and revaluation. You may have to execute settlements again before and after the revaluation at actual prices (or after a reversal of revaluation) to ensure that the settlement receiver receives consistent revaluation data. In the SAP Library, you'll find an example of revaluation at actual prices with a repeated settlement. Here, the connection between settlements to cost centers, price calculation, and revaluation is discussed in detail.

5.3 Overhead Rates

Not all cost centers in a company can allocate their costs to specific projects or other CO objects via activity allocations, distributions, or assessments. Administrative cost centers, for example, do not generally have a direct relationship with a project; this means that an activity-related allocation of costs is not possible for these cost centers. Instead, these costs centers are credited and the project is simultaneously debited, usually via applications of overhead. The calculation of overhead rates is based on the costs or quantities that were posted to the project with reference to the relevant cost elements, such as labor or material costs.

5.3.1 Prerequisites for the Allocation of Overhead Rates

Costing sheet

The calculation of overhead rates is controlled by a *costing sheet*, which must be entered in the relevant WBS elements or network activities or (in the case of header-assigned networks) in the network headers. For WBS elements, you can define a default value for the costing sheet in the project profile. In the network header, the costing sheet is derived from the valuation variant of the costing variant of the network, but it can also be changed manually. If you assign activities to a WBS element, then these activities use the same costing sheet as the WBS element.

Otherwise, they use the costing sheet of the network header as a default value.

You define costing sheets in the Customizing settings of SAP Project System. A costing sheet consists of a key and a description to which rows are assigned respectively (see Figure 5.4). A row in a costing sheet may contain either a *base* (base row) or an *overhead*, together with a *credit* and an indication of which rows are to be used to calculate the overhead rate and the credit. You can also use totals rows in a costing sheet to give subtotals and sum totals. The rows are processed from top to bottom for the overhead calculation.

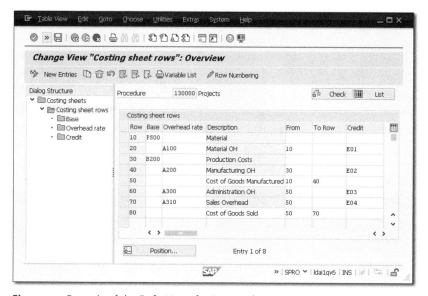

Figure 5.4 Example of the Definition of a Costing Sheet

You use the base rows within a costing sheet to determine which cost elements are to be used as a basis for calculating the overhead costs. Bases are also defined in Customizing. Depending on the controlling area, you can assign individual cost elements or cost element intervals to a base. If necessary, you can also assign individual origins or origin intervals to distinguish between the costs of different materials. To do this, an origin must be defined in the costing view of the material masters.

Calculation base

Overhead rate

The overhead rate in a row of a costing sheet determines the rate at which the overhead is applied. An overhead rate may be defined as a percentage (calculated on the basis of the costs of the cost elements to which the overhead is to be applied), or it may be quantity based if the cost elements of the base rows allow you to enter absolute quantities. Percentage or quantity-based overhead rates can be defined on the basis of validity periods, the overhead type (planned, actual, or commitment), or, for example, organizational units and master data belonging to the objects to which the overhead is to be applied (see Figure 5.5). The *dependency* you assign to the overhead rate determines which columns are available when defining various percentages or amounts for each unit of measure. You can define your own dependencies in Customizing if necessary.

Credit

The credit that you enter in an overhead row of the costing sheet determines which objects (cost centers, internal orders, or business processes) are to be credited by the calculated overhead value and which overhead cost element (cost element category 41) is to be used to allocate the overhead (see Figure 5.6). You can also define validity periods in the credit definition and, if necessary, determine which percentages of the credit are to be posted as fixed or variable proportions.

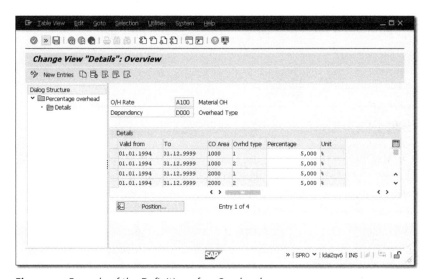

Figure 5.5 Example of the Definition of an Overhead

Figure 5.6 Example of the Definition of a Credit

5.3.2   Executing the Application of Overhead

You can execute an application of overhead for planned costs (Transactions CJ46 and CJ47), as well as for actual costs of a project (Transactions CJ44 and CJ45), and, if necessary, based on commitments (Transactions CJO8 and CJO9). However, a credit is only executed for the calculation of actual overhead rates. The calculation of planned overhead rates is automatically executed in the planned costs of a project as part of network costing, as part of unit costing for WBS elements, or when you use Easy Cost Planning to plan costs. In the actual costs for a project, however, the calculation must be explicitly triggered as part of the period-end closing or scheduled as a regular background job.

In addition to selecting the objects and defining the process control, you must also specify the period for which the application of overhead is to be executed on the initial screen of the overhead calculation. For actual costs, the overhead rates are calculated for the specified period only. For planned costs, you can also specify a range of periods for processing; however, all periods in the range must be within the same fiscal year.

Settings

You can repeat the overhead rate calculation for a project any number of times. In this case, the system only determines the differences between the current and previous runs and posts these differences to the object. The difference amount may be a positive or a negative value. If necessary, you can also execute a reversal of the application of overhead.

Error log If errors occur during execution (for example, due to the status of the objects, invalid costing sheets, or missing percentages), then you can analyze these sources of errors in an error log. Provided that you have enabled the output of detailed lists in process control, you can also display a list with details of the amounts for each sender and receiver and the overhead cost element used (see Figure 5.7).

Depending on the number of objects to be processed and complexity of the calculation, overhead calculations may require high performance levels. For this reason, in SAP HANA the application of overhead that is based on line items was optimized. You can use this optimization if you deploy the SAP HANA version of SAP ERP or utilize SAP HANA in a *sidecar approach*. In this approach, the line items are replicated to an SAP HANA database. This can be done virtually in real time. As a result, the data from application of overhead can be loaded from this in-memory database (instead of the SAP ERP database) to considerably increase performance. SAP Note 1658547 provides further information on this option.

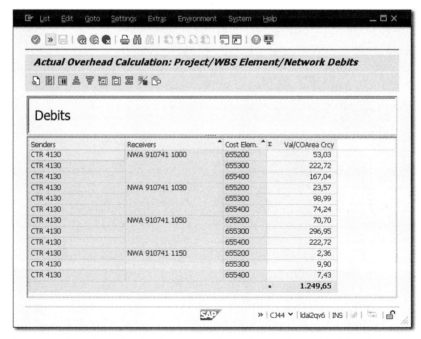

Figure 5.7 Actual Overhead Calculation of Network Activities and Activity Elements

5.4   Template Allocations

With the application of overhead described in the previous section, all overhead costs are allocated using quantity-based or percentage overhead rates based on the quantities or costs of selected cost elements. Template allocation, on the other hand, enables a much more differentiated calculation and allocation of overhead costs. With template allocation, you first use suitable *functions* to calculate quantities that were used by the senders (that is, the cost centers or business processes) in the project. The costs to be allocated are then calculated by valuating these quantities with the prices that have been defined.

> **Advantages of Template Allocation**   [+]
>
> Because you can access almost any function module and table field in the SAP system when defining functions for the template allocation, overhead costs can be allocated according to cause when you use template allocation.

5.4.1   Prerequisites for Template Allocation

To execute a template allocation for projects, you must first define appropriate *templates* in Customizing with Transaction CPT2. A template contains a list of the senders whose costs are to be allocated and the relevant functions and formulas that determine how the quantities are to be calculated, which are valuated with prices later to allocate costs. If necessary, you can use *methods* (that is, logical conditions) to dynamically control the determination of the senders and the activation of the individual rows of a template. Special editors are provided in template maintenance to help you define formulas and methods. By specifying an allocation time in a template, you can determine whether the costs should be allocated periodically or whether an allocation can only be executed once for the start or end period of the object, for example. Figure 5.8 shows an example of a template for the allocation of overhead costs among networks. In this example, the quantity is determined by the number of network activities, and the sender is a business process.

Template

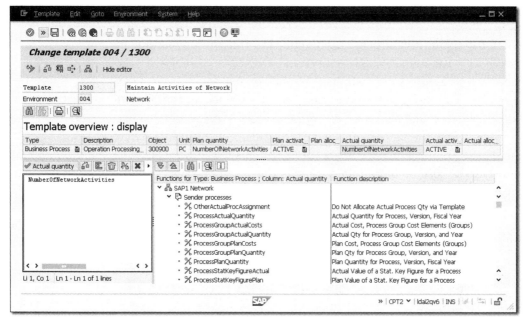

Figure 5.8 Sample Definition of a Template

Environment

You always create a template with reference to an *environment*. This environment contains the functions that you can use to define the template. The two environments 004 (NETWORK) and 005 (WBS ELEMENT) are provided for the definition of projects. These comprise diverse functions as standard. However, you can also add new functions if necessary (Transaction CTU6). These may be standard functions defined by SAP. Alternatively, you can define your own functions that access table fields of the SAP system, standard function modules, or user-defined ABAP function modules.

Determination rules and overhead keys

After you have defined a template, you must assign it to one or more combinations of *costing sheet* and *overhead key* (determination rule) in Customizing Transaction KTPF. You also need to define the combination of costing sheet and overhead key in the master data of the relevant WBS elements, activities, or network headers. When you execute a template allocation for a project, the system can then use this combination to automatically determine the relevant template. The overhead key in the master data of the objects and in the determination rule is used exclusively for the assignment of objects with the same costing sheet to various templates. You can define any overhead key in SAP Project System Customizing settings.

To ensure that the template allocation can also calculate the costs to be allocated using the quantities that were calculated via the functions and formulas of the template, you must also define the prices in accounting with which the quantities are to be valuated. For the allocation of costs from cost centers, you can define the prices based on activity types—for example, with Transaction KP26 for the planned data of a project or Transaction KBK6 for the actual data of a project. For the allocation of costs from business processes, you can define the prices with Transaction CP26 for the planned project data and KBC6 in the actual data of a project, for example.

5.4.2 Executing Template Allocation

You can execute a template allocation for planned costs (Transactions CPUK and CPUL) and actual costs (Transactions CPTK and CPTL) of projects. The calculation of planned template allocation is automatically executed in projects as part of network costing, unit costing for WBS elements, or when you use Easy Cost Planning to plan costs. For actual costs of projects, however, the calculation must be explicitly triggered as part of the period-end closing.

On the initial screen of the template allocation, you select the objects and specify the periods of a fiscal year for which the allocation is to be executed. You can execute the template allocation for several periods simultaneously for both planned and actual costs.

In the results display of the template allocation, you can analyze the amounts of the allocated costs and the relevant sender and receiver objects in each case (see Figure 5.9). If you have executed template allocation for several periods, then you can navigate to a period screen and display the distribution of the allocations among the various periods. If problems occur during template allocation, then you can navigate to a log showing the relevant messages—that is, warning or error messages. If necessary, you can also display the sender and receiver master data or access the *template evaluation*.

Results display

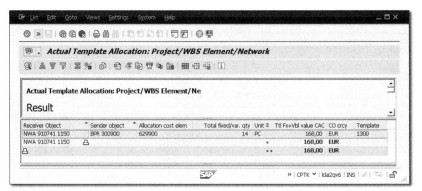

Figure 5.9 Result of a Template Allocation for Actual Costs of a Project

Template evaluation

From the template evaluation, you can branch to all relevant details of the template used. For example, you can find out which functions and formulas were used to execute the quantity calculation or which method activated an allocation row. If you executed a template allocation for several periods, then you can use the template evaluation to analyze each period separately.

5.5 Interest Calculation

In SAP Project System, you can calculate interest based on your costs and revenue data or payment flows and post costs to your projects for interest losses or revenue for interest profits. The interest calculation function is available for both the planned and actual data of a project.

Both planned and actual interest calculation take the form of a *balance interest calculation*. With this type of calculation, the balance of costs, revenues, or payment data is first calculated, and then the interest is calculated in the balancing objects (for example, certain WBS elements of your project). The interest is cumulated over the interest period and posted to the balancing object. Where possible, the balances calculated by the system are accurate up to the day. The relevant date is the posting date of the document or, in the case of payments, the payment date. Because interest is taken into account in balancing, compound interest can also be calculated.

The *interest profile* used determines which objects are to be considered as balancing objects. The system uses the *interest indicator* to determine which interest rate is relevant and which accounts are to be used for posting the interest. The combination of interest profile and interest indicator determines which value categories (that is, which cost elements and commitment items) are to be included in the balancing and interest calculation. You can control and evaluate the interest calculation of different value categories (for example, costs, revenues, and payments) separately.

Interest profile and interest indicator

> **Interest Calculation of Investment Projects**
>
> For investment projects, special interest calculation is used. For WBS elements with an investment profile, all costs, revenues, or payments that are already activated in the asset under construction are taken into account independent from the individual value categories.

[+]

The transaction currency of the interest calculation is identical to the controlling area currency, which means that the interest is posted to your projects in the CO area currency.

5.5.1 Prerequisites for Interest Calculation for Projects

Before you can use the interest rate calculation for projects, you must make some settings in Customizing. If you have additional requirements for planned or actual interest calculation, you can also define customer enhancements—for example, to influence the values and line items for which interest is to be calculated and the interest that has actually been calculated.

Interest Indicators and Interest Rates

Figure 5.10 shows the definition of interest indicators (Transaction OPIE) in the Customizing settings. Interest indicators for projects can only have interest calculation type S (BALANCE INTEREST CALCULATION). Interest calculation type P (ITEM INTEREST CALCULATION), whereby interest is calculated for each payment item, is not available for projects.

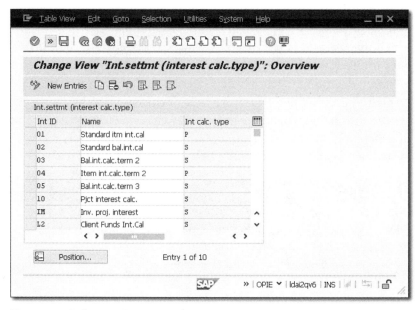

Figure 5.10 Definition of Interest Indicators

General and time-dependent terms

With the interest indicators, you define general and time-dependent terms and the interest rate that is to be used for the interest calculation. In the general conditions (Transaction OPIH), you define the calendar type (for example, a banking calendar or the Gregorian calendar) on which the interest calculation is based. The calendar type determines the number of interest days per month and year that are used, for example, to calculate a daily interest rate based on an annual interest rate. A banking calendar always consists of 30 days per month, whereas the Gregorian calendar always uses the exact number of days per month. In addition, you can define a minimum amount for the interest (and other control data) in the general conditions. An interest calculation will then only be executed as of this minimum amount. In the time-dependent terms, you define which interest rate is to be used based on the interest indicator, currency, transaction type (debit or credit interest), and the EFFECTIVE FROM and AMOUNT FROM fields. The interest rate can be derived from reference interest rates (a discount rate, for example) or defined manually.

Interest Profile

Interest profiles are defined in Customizing and can be defined as a default value in the project profile. When you execute the interest calculation, a logical inheritance of the interest profiles occurs. In other words, an object that does not have its own interest profile uses the interest profile of the higher-level object, and so on. However, if an object has its own interest profile, then this interest profile is also used.

The interest profile determines which objects are to be included as balancing objects in the interest calculation. Figure 5.11 shows the definition of an interest profile. The settings for (hierarchy) processing in the interest profile have the following effects:

Balancing objects

▶ If you select DERIVE AUTOM. as the processing type in the interest profile, then the processing logic depends on the project type.

▶ In the case of WBS elements with an investment profile (investment projects), only the costs that are already activated in an asset under construction are taken into account in the interest calculation. If you want to also take into account the costs of assigned networks and orders, then you must first settle their costs to the WBS element. Planned interest calculation is not possible for investment projects.

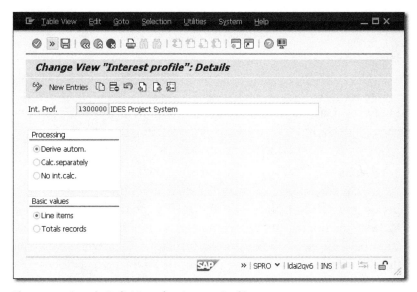

Figure 5.11 Sample Definition of an Interest Profile

▸ For projects with billing elements (customer projects), the system takes into account the billing element and all lower-level objects in the billing hierarchy in the interest calculation. Balancing and posting of the calculated interest then takes place in the billing element. But if the billing element or a lower-level WBS element has an investment profile, then the logic of the investment projects applies to these objects.

▸ For objects that don't have an investment profile and are not subordinate to a billing element (cost projects), balancing and posting of the interest occurs separately in the individual account assignment objects (in WBS elements, network headers or activities, or assigned orders).

▸ When interest is calculated for objects that have an interest profile with the CALC. SEPARATELY indicator, lower-level objects are ignored. Logical inheritance does not occur with this interest profile. You can also use this indicator to override the automatic derivation of hierarchy processing. The NO INT. CALC. indicator allows you to do the same thing; interest is not calculated for objects that have an interest profile in which this indicator is set.

Basic interest calculation values

You also make the settings for the BASIC VALUES for the interest calculation in the interest profile. The two possible values have the following effects:

▸ **Line items**
The interest calculation is exact to the day with reference to the posting or payment date of the line items. Postings in periods for which interest has already been calculated (value dates in the past) and changes to the interest rate within a period (interest rate changes) can be taken into account with this option.

▸ **Total values**
As a basis for interest calculation, total values are created for each period and dated to the middle of the period to calculate the interest. With this setting, the interest calculation is not exact to the day. However, performance is better in this instance than it would be if line items were used as the base values for the interest calculation.

Special Characteristics of Line Items and Total Values

Line items are always used for the first actual interest calculation; however, in subsequent interest calculation runs only the line items of the last four periods before the last run are selected. Independent of the settings in the interest profile, totals records are used for any periods prior to the last four periods. With the planned interest calculation, line items can only be used for planned payments. But in order for any line items to be written for planned payments you must first configure a number range for exact-to-the-day payment planning (Activity FIPA) in Customizing (Transaction KANK). The system always uses totals records for the interest calculation for planned costs and revenues.

With reference to the interest profile, you must make detailed settings in Customizing. Figure 5.12 shows the relevant transaction, Transaction OPIB. In the detailed settings, you create a reference between the interest profile and the interest indicator you want to use.

Detailed settings for the interest profile

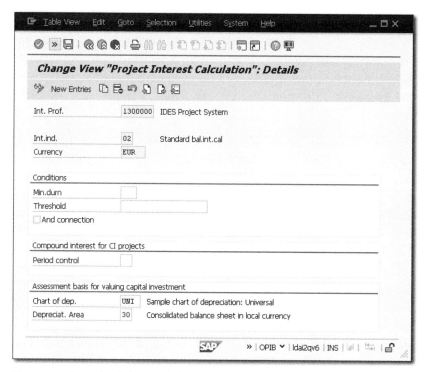

Figure 5.12 Example of the Detailed Settings of an Interest Profile

You can also define conditions (minimum durations or threshold values) to determine exactly when an interest calculation is to be executed. For investment projects, you also need to define which valuation area should be used as an assessment basis for the interest calculation, and, if applicable, you use the PERIOD CONTROL field to determine when compound interest is to be calculated (for example, once a quarter rather than at each interest calculation run).

Interest relevance Finally, you need to define (in Customizing) which values are to be used as a basis for calculating the interest. To do this, you require value categories, which include all relevant cost and revenue elements and commitment items. For each value category, you can then define the interest relevance depending on the interest profile and interest indicator in Customizing Transaction OPIC.

Update Control

You use update control to determine the cost elements in CO in which the interest is to be updated. For technical reasons, an update to the profit and loss account in FI takes place first, which is controlled by *posting specifications*. The definition of cost elements for the relevant General Ledger (G/L) accounts ensures that the update to CO will occur directly.

Posting specifications Figure 5.13 shows the definition of posting specifications. Depending on the two business transactions of *interest earned* and *interest paid posting*, and, if necessary, depending on the interest indicator, company code, and business area, you define (using account symbols for encryption) which profit and loss accounts in the relevant chart of accounts in FI are to be used in each case for debit and credit. If you don't require a differentiation based on business areas, for example, then you can define the wildcard character "+" in the relevant field. By defining cost elements for the G/L accounts that are used for the debit posting for interest paid and the credit posting for interest earned, you ensure that the interest is posted to these cost elements in CO. If you use PS Cash Management, then you must ensure that no commitment items for financial Transaction 30 are assigned to the G/L accounts in your posting specifications to prevent an update to PS Cash Management.

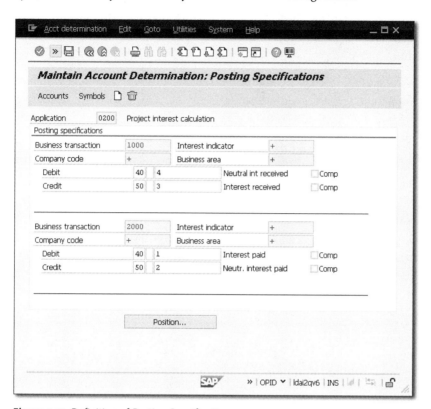

Figure 5.13 Definition of Posting Specifications

Balances in FI and CO   **[!]**

Note that you must enter a credit and debit account in the posting specifications for both interest earned and interest paid. This gives a balance of zero in FI. However, to prevent a balance of zero in CO you must not define any cost elements for the G/L accounts for the debit postings for interest earned or the credit postings for interest paid.

Finally, you must assign the relevant activities KZRI (ACTUAL INTEREST CALCULATION) and KZRP (PLANNED INTEREST CALCULATION) to a number range in Customizing.

5.5.2 Executing the Interest Calculation for Projects

For the interest calculation of projects, you can use Transactions CJZ3 and CJZ5 for planned data and Transactions CJZ2 and CJZ1 for actual data. The initial screens for the actual and planned interest calculation are identical.

With actual interest calculation, you select the relevant objects, specify the parameters for process control, and specify the period up to which the interest calculation is to be executed. You can also select a limit for a specific day from the menu.

With planned interest calculation, you can either specify the period for the interest calculation (which has advantages in terms of performance) or—if you don't select a restriction—execute an interest run for the entire period. The start of the period is determined on the base date of the first costs incurred, and the end of the period is determined on the basis of the scheduling data of the objects. You also must specify the CO version that will serve as a basis for the interest calculation on the initial screen.

When you execute the interest calculation, the system proceeds as follows:

1. The system uses hierarchy processing to determine the relevant balancing objects based on the project type and the interest profile used. The interest profile may be logically inherited in this case.

2. Balancing occurs for the relevant periods at the level of the balancing objects for the value categories selected as relevant in Customizing. If necessary, subtotals may be created for a specific day or period.

3. The system uses the interest indicator to calculate the interest rate and uses update control to determine the costs elements for updating the interest.

4. The system calculates the interest and posts it to the balancing object. A source document is written, which can be evaluated in the information system.

After the interest calculation is executed, you can display logs for error messages and for the update. After an update run, you can analyze the list of objects and interest-relevant line items that were included in the balancing and can view the interim balances with information about the interest rate, number of interest days, and calculated interest (see Figure 5.14).

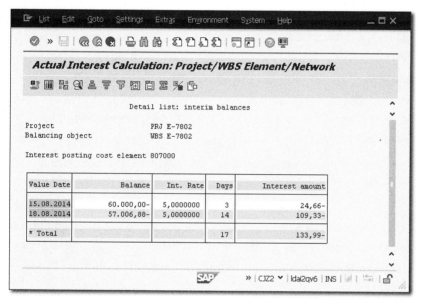

Error logs and cancellation

Figure 5.14 Displaying the Interim Balances of an Actual Interest Calculation

You can also cancel the interest runs by using the transactions specified earlier. Although all previous interest postings for the specified period are canceled in the planned interest calculation, only the most recent interest run is canceled in the actual interest calculation.

Determination of Accounting Data Related to a Specific Period   [◉]

By using functions for revaluation of actual prices, overhead allocation, template allocation, and interest calculation, you can correct the accounting data of your projects or determine overhead rates or interest profit and losses. In this way, you can ensure that all relevant costs and revenues for your projects are available for further allocations or period-end closing activities at the end of the period.

5.6   Results Analysis

The results analysis revaluates the costs and revenues for your projects. Depending on the method used, inventory values and reserves and the cost of sales and the calculated revenue affecting income can be calculated as part of the results analysis. With the settlement of this results analysis data (see Section 5.9), adjustment postings can be made in FI and in the Profitability Analysis (PA) and CO-PA, or the values in FI and CO-PA can be reconciled.

Results analysis data   The calculation of the results analysis data depends, on the one hand, on the results analysis method (that is, the formula for calculating the results analysis data) and the status of the object in which the results analysis is executed (control of the creation and cancellation of inventories and reserves).

The objective of results analysis and the specified dependencies is illustrated by the following example.

A sales and distribution project (for example, the construction and sale of an elevator) is spread over four periods. The planned costs $C(p)$ are $80,000 against a planned revenue $R(p)$ of $120,000. The customer has agreed to milestone billing of 50% of the target revenue for the second period, an additional 25% for the third period, and a final invoice for the remainder in the fourth period.

At the end of each period, you execute the results analysis with two different methods for different purposes. First, you need to calculate the reserves for unrealized costs or any impending losses. In addition, you should ensure that interim profits are calculated for the planned milestone billings of your project if the revenue exceeds the calculated cost of sales. You therefore select REVENUE-BASED METHOD WITH PROFIT REALIZATION and settle the results analysis values to CO-PA.

As a second results analysis method, select COST-BASED POC METHOD, which allows you to calculate the revenue affecting net income—which is based on the actual costs and, where relevant, the revenue in excess of billings—and to identify unrealized profits.

Following the revenue-based method with profit realization, the calculated cost of sales $C(c)$ and the calculated revenue affecting income $R(c)$ are determined as follows:

$C(c) = C(p) \times R(a) \div R(p)$
where R(a) = actual revenue
$R(c) = R(a)$

Capitalized costs $C(z)$ are calculated as follows if the actual costs $C(a)$ are greater than the calculated costs:

$C(z) = C(a) - C(c)$ *if* $C(a) > C(c)$

Conversely, if the cost of sales is greater than the actual costs, then reserves are calculated as follows for unrealized costs $C(u)$:

$C(u) = C(c) - C(a)$ *if* $C(c) > C(a)$

With the cost-based POC method, the planned costs and revenues are weighted with the ratio of actual to planned costs to calculate the costs and revenues affecting income. The following formulas are used:

$C(c) = C(a)$
$R(c) = R(p) \times C(a) \div C(p)$

If the actual revenue is less than the calculated revenue, then a revenue in excess of billings $R(z)$ is calculated as follows:

$R(z) = R(c) - R(a)$ *if* $R(c) > R(a)$

However, if the actual revenue is greater than the calculated revenue, then the system calculates a revenue surplus $R(r)$ as follows:

$R(r) = R(a) - R(c)$ *if* $R(a) > R(c)$

The use of the formulas and rules of these two results analysis methods are now illustrated using the aforementioned sales and distribution project as an example.

In Period 1, the project is released and actual costs of $20,000 are incurred, but no actual revenue is earned. The revenue-based method with profit realization thus gives a calculated revenue equal to the actual revenue and a calculated cost of sales of zero. The settlement to CO-PA in results analysis version 0 produces the following values in the PA:

Actual revenue: 0
Calculated cost of sales: 0
Result: 0

The RELEASED status also causes capitalized costs to the order of $C(b)$ = $20,000 to be created and posted to FI as part of settlement to CO-PA. This produces the following display in the profit and loss statement:

Expense: $20,000 (actual costs)
Revenue: $20,000 (increased inventory)

With the cost-based POC method, the calculated cost of sales is equal to the actual costs. For the revenue affecting income:

$R(c)$ = $120,000 × $20,000 ÷ $80,000 = $30,000

This gives a revenue in excess of billings $R(z)$ of $30,000. If you were to settle the results analysis data to CO-PA (which is a purely hypothetical analysis, because only the data of results analysis version 0 is settled to CO-PA), then the following picture would emerge in the PA and in the profit and loss statement:

Calculated revenue: $30,000
Cost of sales: $20,000
Result: $10,000
Expense: $20,000 (actual costs) + $10,000 (profit)
Revenue: $0 (actual revenue) + $30,000 (revenue in excess of billings)

Period 2 In Period 2, an additional $30,000 is posted to the project as actual costs, which means that the actual costs have increased to $C(a)$ = $50,000 in total. In addition, the agreed-upon milestone billing is executed in the amount of $60,000. The revenue-based method with profit realization gives the following figures:

$C(c)$ = $80,000 × $60,000 ÷ $120,000 = $40,000
$R(c)$ = $60,000
$C(z)$ = $50,000 − $40,000 = $10,000

The settlement to CO-PA transfers the difference values compared with the previous period and gives the following new values in the PA and in the profit and loss statement:

Actual revenue: $60,000
Calculated cost of sales: $40,000
Result: $20,000
Expense: $50,000 (actual costs) + $20,000 (profit)
Revenue: $60,000 (actual revenue) + $10,000 (increased inventory)

If you use the cost-based POC method, then the following results analysis values are calculated:

$C(c) = \$50,000$
$E(c) = \$120,000 \times \$50,000 \div \$80,000 = \$75,000$
$R(z) = \$75,000 - \$60,000 = \$15,000$

A hypothetical settlement would give the following values in CO-PA and FI:

Calculated revenue: $75,000
Calculated cost of sales: $50,000
Result: $25,000
Expense: $50,000 (actual costs) + $25,000 (profit)
Revenue: $60,000 (actual revenue) + $15,000 (revenue in excess of billings)

In Period 3, additional actual costs of just $5,000 arise. The second milestone billing of $30,000 results in a total actual revenue of $90,000 in this period.   Period 3

The revenue-based method then calculates the following values affecting net income:

$C(c) = \$80,000 \times \$90,000 \div \$120,000 = \$60,000$
$R(c) = \$90,000$

Due to the relatively small increase in costs and the second milestone billing, the calculated cost of sales is now higher than the actual costs.

Therefore, the capitalized costs are canceled and reserves for unrealized costs are calculated instead:

$C(u) = \$60,000 - \$55,000 = \$5,000$

The following values are shown in CO-PA and FI after settlement:

Actual revenue: $90,000
Calculated cost of sales: $60,000
Result: $30,000
Expense: $55,000 (actual costs) + $5,000 (reserves) + $30,000 (profit)
Revenue: $90,000 (actual revenue)

The results analysis according to the cost-based POC method produces the following values:

$C(c) = \$55,000$
$R(c) = \$120,000 \times \$55,000 \div \$80,000 = \$82,500$

In contrast to Period 2, the actual revenue is now greater than the calculated revenue, which means that a revenue surplus in the form of reserves is created as follows:

$C(u) = \$90,000 - \$82,500 = \$7,500$

A CO-PA settlement would give the following results:

Calculated revenue: $82,500
Calculated cost of sales: $55,000
Result: $27,500
Expense: $55,000 (actual costs) + $7,500 (revenue surplus) + $27,500 (profit)
Revenue: $90,000 (actual revenue)

Period 4
In Period 4, additional actual costs of $30,000 are posted to the project, with the result that the planned costs are exceeded by $5,000. The final settlement results in the agreed target revenue of $120,000. You complete the project. Due to the status change, any inventories and reserves are canceled in the results analysis.

Because the actual costs exceed the planned costs, the actual costs are taken as the cost of sales in the revenue-based method. Due to the status, the existing reserves are canceled. After settlement to CO-PA, the following values are shown in the PA in FI:

> *Actual revenue: $120,000*
> *Calculated cost of sales: $85,000*
> *Result: $35,000*
> *Expense: $85,000 (actual costs) + $35,000 (profit)*
> *Revenue: $120,000 (actual revenue)*

In the cost-based POC method, the calculated revenue is now set as equal to the actual revenue. A settlement to CO-PA would produce the same results in CO-PA and FI as the cost-based method.

In addition to the results analysis methods outlined previously, a range of other methods is provided in the standard system, which you can also use for results analysis. The selection of a results analysis method depends on various business-related factors, such as the required results analysis data (Are inventory costs and reserves required?) and how is it to be used (that is, for internal information purposes or in the financial statements) and the relevant legal requirements.

Other results analysis methods

The results analysis methods provided in the standard system are listed here (you'll find a detailed description of these methods with explicit examples in the SAP Library):

- ▶ (01) Revenue-based method with profit realization
- ▶ (02) Revenue-based method without profit realization
- ▶ (03) Cost-based POC method
- ▶ (04) Quantity-based method
- ▶ (05) Quantity-based POC method
- ▶ (06) POC method on basis of revenue planned by period
- ▶ (07) POC method on basis of project progress value determination
- ▶ (08) Derivation of cost of sales from "old" resource-related billing of CO line items
- ▶ (09) Completed contract method
- ▶ (10) Inventory determination, without planned costs, without milestone billing

- ▶ (11) Inventory determination, without planned costs, with milestone billing

- ▶ (12) Inventory determination, reserves for follow-up costs, without milestone billing

- ▶ (13) Inventory determination "WIP at actual costs" for objects not carrying revenue

- ▶ (14) Derivation of cost of sales from resource-related billing of dynamic items

- ▶ (15) Derivation of revenue from resource-related billing and simulation of dynamic items

5.6.1 Prerequisites for the Results Analysis

The results analysis method, the status dependencies of the inventories and reserves, and other settings to control the results analysis are all found in *valuation methods* in Customizing. The valuation method is determined by the *results analysis keys* of the relevant objects and the *results analysis version* that you specify when you execute the results analysis. Updating of the results analysis data into SAP Project System, CO-PA, and FI is controlled by results analysis cost elements, *line IDs*, rules for updating the results analysis cost elements, and posting rules. We will now briefly discuss the relevant Customizing activities.

Results analysis key
A valuation can only be determined and a results analysis can only be executed for WBS elements that have a results analysis key. However, the costs of lower-level objects can also be automatically factored in the results analysis in projects. You can use various predefined results analysis keys provided in the standard system. You can also enter results analysis keys manually in WBS elements, define them as a default value in the project profile, or use strategies to derive them along with the settlement rule (see Section 5.9.1).

Results analysis cost elements
The values from the results analysis are updated to the analyzed WBS elements using results analysis cost elements—that is, cost elements of cost element type 31. The results analysis data is evaluated in the cost reports of SAP Project System using the relevant results analysis cost elements.

When you execute the results analysis, you specify a results analysis version, into which the data from the results analysis is updated. Because the determination of the valuation method also depends on the results analysis version, you can perform several results analyses with various methods for the same object and save the data from the results analysis to a separate CO version. However, only the values of results analysis version 0 can be settled to the PA.

Results analysis version

Figure 5.15 shows an example of the definition of a results analysis version in Transaction OKG2 in Customizing.

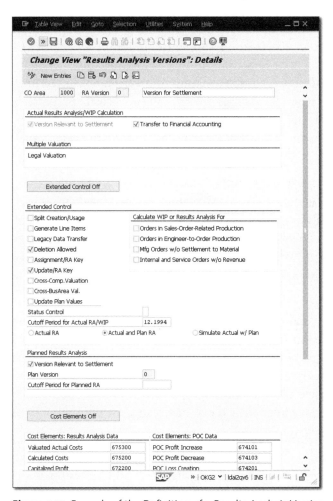

Figure 5.15 Example of the Definition of a Results Analysis Version

You can use the VERSION RELEVANT TO SETTLEMENT and TRANSFER TO FINANCIAL ACCOUNTING indicators in the results analysis version to control the relevance of the results analysis data for settlement and the simultaneous automatic transfer to FI. If profit center accounting is active, then a posting for the profit center defined in the master data of the settlement object is executed simultaneously, provided that the TRANSFER TO FINANCIAL ACCOUNTING indicator is set in the results analysis version. In the EXTENDED CONTROL settings of the results analysis version, you can determine whether the version is also to be used for a planned results analysis.

Additional indicators are provided in extended control—for example, for defining whether the creation and consumption of inventories or reserves by various cost elements is to be updated, whether line items are to be created during the results analysis, or (if the nonvaluated project stock is used) whether work in process can be calculated separately for assigned orders depending on their results analysis keys. For performance reasons, line items are not often written during the results analysis.

The results analysis version, together with the results analysis key, indicates a valuation method. The results analysis method that is to be used for the results analysis is defined in the valuation method. A results analysis method is defined in the various valuation methods that are provided in the standard system. When defining valuation methods, no distinction is made between maintenance with and maintenance without expert mode.

Figure 5.16 shows the maintenance of a valuation method without use of the expert mode in Transaction OKG3 in Customizing. In addition to the results analysis method, you can define the status here for which inventories and reserves are to be canceled. Inventories and reserves are always created once the status changes to RELEASED. By specifying a profit basis, you can control which planned costs are to serve as a basis for the results analysis.

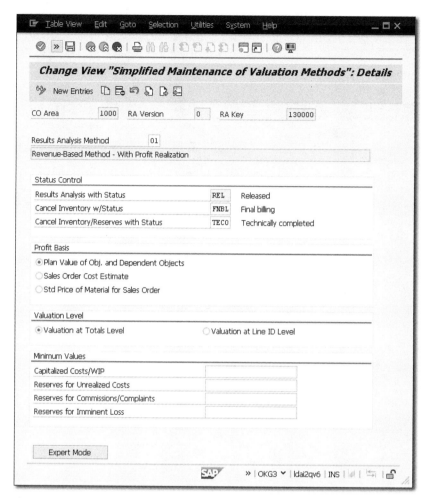

Figure 5.16 Example of the Definition of a Valuation Method

You can also define the valuation level (summary allocation of the results analysis data in accordance with the default settings in expert mode or allocation by line ID) and the minimum values required for the update of inventories and reserves.

Figure 5.17 shows the expert mode for defining valuation methods. Depending on the status, you can define additional detailed settings here for valuation and for the cancellation of reserves and inventories or for calculating planned values as a basis for the results analysis. By using

Expert mode

the indicators for the extended control of the results analysis, you can define which periods should be taken into account in the results analysis or which procedure should be used to handle manually entered results analysis data, for example.

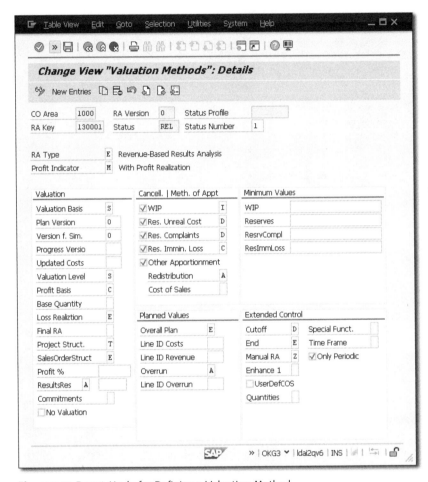

Figure 5.17 Expert Mode for Defining a Valuation Method

Project structure indicator

Note, in particular, the PROJECT STRUCT. indicator provided in expert mode for the valuation method. The most important values of this indicator are explained in the following list:

▶ **Project structure indicator A**

Project structure indicator A is used by default—in other words, if you use the simple maintenance option for defining a valuation method. When you use this indicator, a results analysis is only possible for billing elements of a project. During the results analysis, the values of all lower-level WBS elements and all assigned networks and orders are automatically summarized at the level of billing elements for the purpose of results analysis. One advantage of this scenario is that you only have to settle the billing elements, because the results analysis data of these WBS elements incorporates the values of all lower-level objects.

Using Project Structure Indicator A **[!]**

The following must be ensured if you use project structure indicator A:

▶ A results analysis key must only be defined in the billing elements for which you want to determine results analysis data and not in planning or account assignment elements.

▶ A settlement must only be executed for the highest billing element in which data was used for the results analysis. Therefore, you can use an appropriate strategy to derive the settlement rules (see Section 5.9.1).

▶ The project structure should not contain other billing elements above or below the billing elements for which you want to execute a results analysis.

▶ **Project structure indicator B**

If the project structure also contains billing elements at levels below the highest level and if you are interested in both the overall result of the project and the result of the individual levels, then you can use project structure indicator B. In this scenario, results analysis data is updated for each billing element for which a results analysis key is defined. To determine the results analysis data, all planned data and actual data of this element and the lower-level objects are taken into account. Thus, as with indicator A, you have a complete result for the highest billing element in the structure. However, only the difference between the results analysis data of this element and the results analysis data of the lower-level elements is updated in the highest billing element.

► **Project structure indicator T**

For projects with a cross-company code structure, we recommend that you establish separate results analysis data for the billing structures of each company code. To do this, you can use project structure indicator T in expert mode. When you use this indicator, data is similarly summarized in the relevant billing elements. However, in contrast to indicator B, the values of the lower-level billing elements and their assigned WBS elements and orders are ignored in the summarization.

► **Project structure indicator E**

If you want to determine separate results analysis data for each individual WBS element of a project in isolation, use project structure indicator E. In this case, only the values in the WBS element to be analyzed and the values of the assigned orders are summarized for the results analysis. WBS elements located at lower-levels in the hierarchy, and their assigned orders are ignored.

► **Other project structure indicators**

Other possible project structure indicators are C, Q, and U. For information about using these indicators, refer, for example, to the [F1] help of the PROJECT STRUCTURE field in a valuation method in expert mode.

Line IDs
Line IDs allow you to classify results analysis data in accordance with FI requirements. Various line IDs are provided in the SAP standard system. If necessary, you can also create your own line IDs based on the CO area in Customizing (see Figure 5.18). In Transaction OKG5 in Customizing, you must assign to the line IDs all cost elements under which debits and credits are posted and that were already taken into account in the results analysis.

Figure 5.19 shows the relationship between cost elements and line IDs. You can make each assignment dependent on the results analysis version, fixed and variable portions, the debit and credit indicator, or a validity period, for example. For subsequent posting in FI, you must determine for each assignment whether the cost elements must be capitalized, do not have to be capitalized, or can be capitalized. In addition, you can determine what percentage of each assignment cannot be capitalized and, if necessary, which portion can be capitalized.

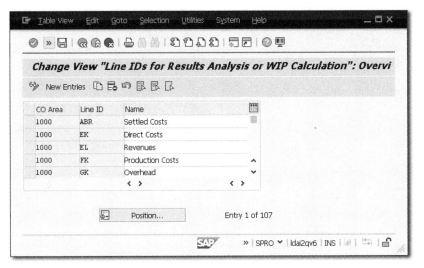

Figure 5.18 Defining Line IDs

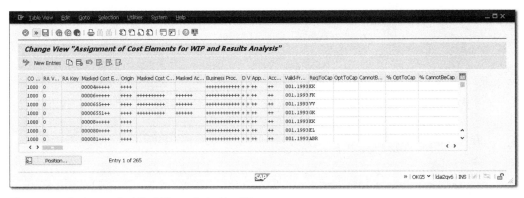

Figure 5.19 Assignment of Cost Elements to Line IDs

The next Customizing activity requires you to define the results analysis cost elements under which the results analysis data is to be updated in Transaction OKG4 (see Figure 5.20). First, assign each line ID to a category, which determines how the results analysis data can be grouped, for example, according to inventory, reserve, direct costs, revenue, and so on. Depending on the category, you can then assign various cost element types for each grouping to the line IDs.

Update rules

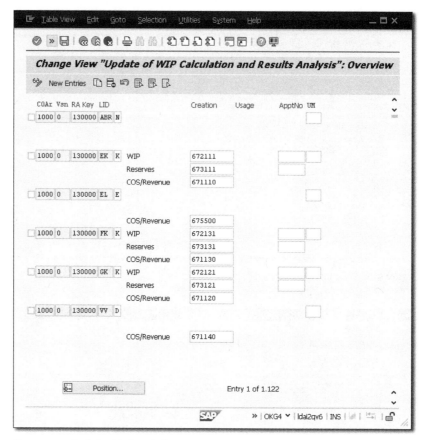

Figure 5.20 Defining Update Rules

Finally, use Transaction OKG8 in Customizing to define posting rules to control the transfer of the results analysis data to FI (see Figure 5.21). A posting rule consists of the assignment of individual results analysis cost elements or entire results analysis categories to a profit and loss account and a balance sheet account. Results analysis categories correspond to the assignments of cost elements to line IDs that you have already made in Transaction OKG5; for example, WIP (WORK IN PROGRESS, REQUIRES CAPITALIZATION).

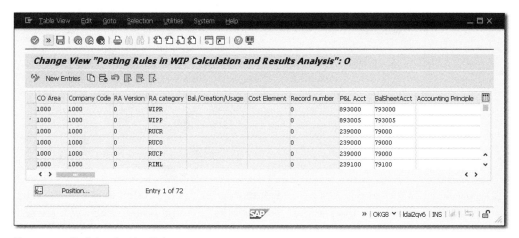

Figure 5.21 Defining Posting Rules

5.6.2 Executing the Results Analysis

Before you perform an actual results analysis for a project, you should set a lock period to ensure that all results analysis data determined up to and including the lock period is not changed by the results analysis. This is of particular relevance if you can no longer make any postings to FI for these periods. The standard system is preconfigured in such a way that the lock period for all valuation methods is always the prior period to the results analysis period. However, you can change this setting, if necessary, in expert mode and define a different lock period in the results analysis version.

Lock period

You can perform a planned results analysis with Transactions KKA2P and KKAJP. For the actual results analysis, use Transactions KKA2 and KKAJ. In Transaction KKG2, you can also manually enter the cost of sales for a project depending on the settings. On the results analysis initial screen, select the relevant WBS elements, the results analysis period, and the relevant results analysis version. When you execute the results analysis, the system uses the results analysis version and the results analysis key of the objects to determine which valuation method is to be used to analyze the data. The results analysis data is then calculated on the basis of the status of the WBS elements that are to be analyzed. Depending on the settings of the valuation method, you may also be able to enter additional results analysis data manually.

> ### Time-Dependent System Statuses
>
> Because the time of the results analysis may differ from the time for which a status that is relevant for the results analysis has been set, the assignment of the results analysis data to the relevant periods may be incorrect in the results analysis. To avoid this potential problem, activate time dependency for the system status in Customizing. The system then stores the date for which the status was set (for example, for the status RELEASED, TECHNICALLY COMPLETED, or FINAL BILLING) and takes this into account in the results analysis. For the planned results analysis, you can also plan the time of a status change.

Flexible error management

With flexible error management, which you can define in Customizing, you can influence the messages that may be issued when you execute the results analysis. You can, for example, convert the WARNING MESSAGE type into an error message for certain results or vice versa or suppress messages completely. Figure 5.22 shows the result of a results analysis.

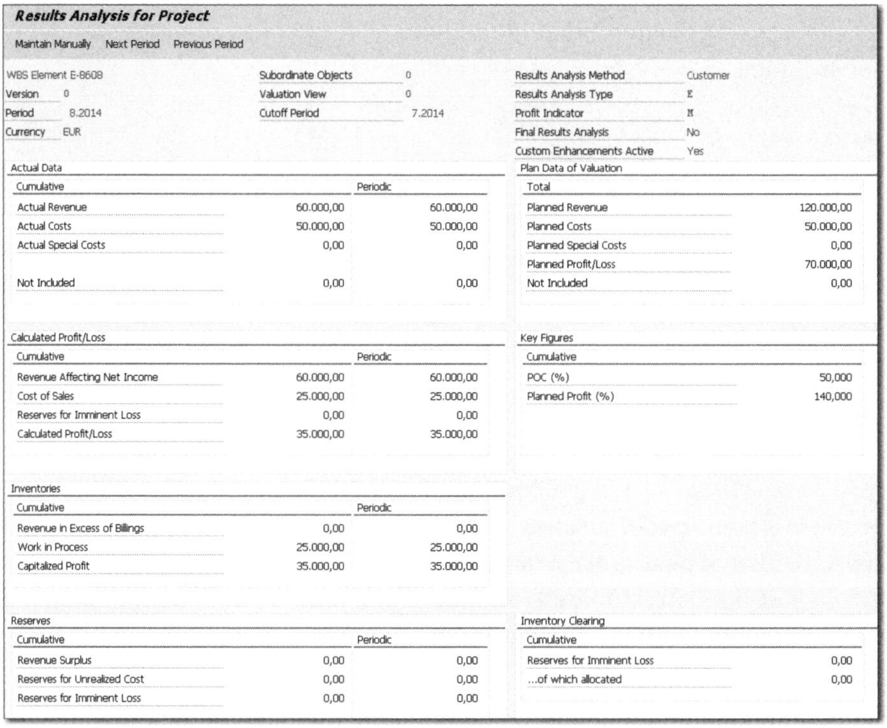

Figure 5.22 Example of the Result of a Results Analysis

Make sure that you save the result so that the results analysis data is updated. If the CO area currency differs from the company code currency, then the results analysis is executed in both currencies. In this case, you need to save the results twice so that the data is updated. The results analysis data is not posted to the PA or FI until project settlement (see Section 5.9).

Updating of results analysis data

5.7 Project-Related Incoming Orders

For sales and distribution projects, you can use project-related incoming order determination to calculate additional CO key figures for *incoming orders*, for the *order history*, for *open order values*, and for *open order value reduction* and to evaluate these in SAP Project system reporting or settle them to the results analysis, thereby making them available for analysis in company-wide profitability and sales accounting.

Based on the key figures from incoming order determination, you can forecast the results for your sales and distribution projects in terms of costs, revenues, and, in some cases, quantities. Evaluation of the order history allows you to trace how the results of your projects change due to newly received sales orders, changes to orders, or rejections.

We will now use the simple example of our elevator project to explain how project-related incoming order determination works and how it is used. Costs were planned by cost element for the project, amounting to $80,000.

Example of project-related incoming order determination

The assignment of a sales order item to the project results in an update of the planned revenue to the amount of $120,000. Accordingly, the project-related incoming order determination shows corresponding costs and revenue for the open order values of $80,000 and $120,000, respectively, for special cost elements of the incoming orders in the category INCOMING ORDERS: NEW ORDER (IONO).

Over the course of the project, actual costs of $40,000 are posted to the project and billing amounts to $60,000. In the results analysis, $40,000 is posted as the cost of sales and $60,000 as revenue affecting income if you use a revenue-based method, for example (see the example in Section 5.6).

A new project-related sales order determination then shows the analyzed values in the Order Balance: Reduction by Billing Documents (OBRB) category. The new open order values for the costs and revenue of the project are based on the original open order values minus the reduction amounts — in this case, minus the results analysis data:

open order value (revenue) = $120,000 – $60,000 = $60,000
open order value (costs) = $80,000 – $40,000 = $40,000

Other changes occur as the project progresses. First, additional actual costs of $5,000 and actual revenue of $30,000 are posted to the project. In addition, a new sales order item is assigned to the project, which results in additional planned revenue of $30,000. The planned costs of the project are then also increased to $15,000. The results analysis for the project then calculates the cost of sales as $57,000 and revenue affecting income of $90,000. The subsequent project-related incoming order determination then shows revenue of $30,000 and costs of $15,000 as the difference, because of the previous execution under the Incoming Orders: Changed Order (IOCO) category. The changes to the results analysis values — that is, $30,000 for the revenue affecting income and $17,000 for the cost of sales — are, in turn, used as reduction amounts under the OBRB category. The new open order values for the project are therefore as follows:

open order value (revenues) = $120,000 – $90,000 + $30,000
= $60,000
open order value (costs) = $80,000 – $57,000 + $15,000
= $38,000

Figure 5.23 shows the Incoming Orders/Balance hierarchy report (see also Chapter 6, Section 6.2.1), with the values from the preceding example.

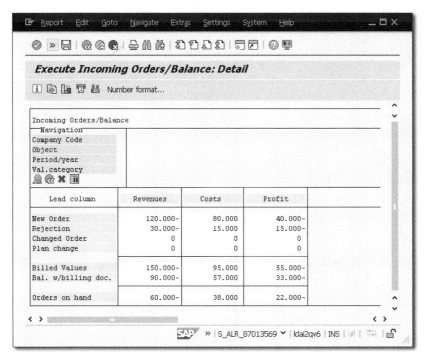

Figure 5.23 Evaluation of Project-Related Incoming Orders

When the incoming order data is determined, a distinction is made between WBS elements that are fully invoiced and those that are not. As long as a billing element does not have the system status FNBL (FINAL BILLING), the open order values are calculated as follows:

Status dependency

open order value (revenue) =
incoming orders (revenue) – revenue affecting income
open order value (costs) =
incoming orders (costs) – cost of sales

Incoming orders are determined on the basis of the revenues planned by revenue element in the billing element and the costs planned by cost element in the objects of the billing structure of the WBS element. As illustrated previously, the reduction amounts for the orders on hand are calculated on the basis of the analyzed actual data of results analysis version 0. If you have not yet executed a results analysis, then the reduction amount is zero, and the open order values are therefore equal to the incoming orders.

If a billing element has the FINAL BILLING status, then both the incoming orders and the reduction amounts are calculated from the analyzed actual data of results analysis version 0. In other words, the reduction amounts are equal to the incoming order data in this case, and the open order values are thus equal to zero.

If the actual revenue exceeds the planned revenue, then the incoming order revenue is equal to the actual revenue regardless of the status of the billing element. Similarly, if the actual costs exceed the planned costs, then the incoming order costs are equal to the actual costs.

5.7.1 Prerequisites for Project-Related Incoming Order Determination

Incoming order cost elements

As an initial prerequisite for using project-related incoming order determination, you must create secondary cost elements under which costs, revenues, and, if necessary, quantities for incoming orders are to be updated. Use the following cost element categories:

▸ 50 INCOMING ORDERS: SALES REVENUES

▸ 51 INCOMING ORDERS: OTHER REVENUES

▸ 52 INCOMING ORDERS: COSTS

If the project-related incoming orders are to be settled in the CO-PA at a later stage, it is often useful to classify the incoming order cost elements in accordance with the value fields in the results analysis.

Next, you must assign the relevant cost elements of the costs and revenues and the results analysis cost elements to the incoming order cost elements in the Customizing settings. You can make this assignment for cost element intervals or cost element groups based on the CO area and results analysis key (see Section 5.6.1). For the subsequent evaluation, you must assign the incoming order cost elements to corresponding value categories in Transaction OPI2 (see Chapter 6, Section 6.2.1).

If you want to settle the data from project-related incoming order determination in the PA, then you will need a suitable PA transfer structure transfer structure, which determines the mapping of the incoming order cost elements to value categories of the PA when settlement occurs (*see* Section 5.9.1). In addition, the operating concern to which the data is to be settled must include the characteristic SORHIST, and a number range for the I ORDER-REL. PROJECT activity type must be maintained. You can define a number range in Transaction KEN1 in the PA Customizing settings. You assign the SORHIST characteristic to an operating concern in Transaction KEQ3. The indicator has the following four possible categories:

Settings in CO-PA

- ▸ **AENA (New order)**
  This category comprises cost element categories 50, 51, and 52, and is created when sales order items are created for billing elements.

- ▸ **AEGA (Order change)**
  This category only contains cost element category 50, and is created if changes are made to conditions or quantities in relevant sales orders.

- ▸ **AEAB (Cancellation)**
  This category comprises cost element categories 50, 51, and 52, and is created when sales order items are cancelled for billing elements.

- ▸ **AEPA (Plan change)**
  This category comprises the two cost element categories 51 and 52, and is created when relevant changes are made to the cost structure of the project.

For project-related incoming order determination, you must also make settings in SAP Project System Customizing for the relevant results analysis keys (*see* Figure 5.24). For example, you use the indicators in the HIERARCHY LEVEL IN BILLING STRUCTURE SECTION of a results analysis key to determine whether the entire order history is to be determined for the project as a whole or for the individual billing elements. However, the ORDER CHANGE and PLAN CHANGE categories of the order history are always determined at the level of the individual billing elements. You also specify the CO version of which the data is to serve as the basis for the incoming order determination.

Results analysis key

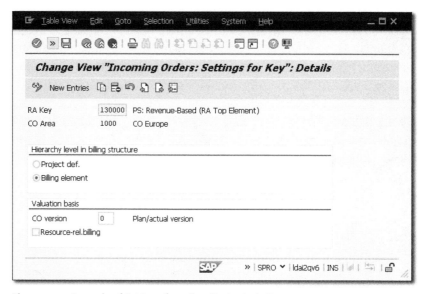

Figure 5.24 Example of Settings for a Results Analysis Key

Billing elements for incoming orders

The billing elements in which you want to calculate the key figures for incoming orders must also meet certain requirements. First, the billing elements must have a results analysis key and must be released so that the AUTOMAT. WIP/RESULTS ANALYSIS business process is permitted. In addition, sales order values must have been updated under value type 29 in the billing elements. This update can occur via a sales order item assigned to the project or, if necessary, with a BAPI from an external system. The planning profile of the project should also allow for an update of the planned revenue of the sales order to the project (see Chapter 2, Section 2.5.3).

5.7.2 Executing the Project-Related Sales Order Determination

Typically, you execute the determination of project-related sales orders immediately after the results analysis for projects. You can use Transactions CJA2 and CJA1 in SAP Project System to do so. On the initial screen, you select the relevant objects by specifying sales orders, projects, or individual WBS elements, and you specify the period for which an order determination is to be executed and the process control.

When you execute the project-related incoming order determination, the results analysis key of the billing elements and their status (final billing or not final billing) determine how the OPEN ORDER VALUE and INCOMING ORDERS key figures are calculated. Figure 5.25 shows the detailed list of a project-related incoming order determination.

Incoming order determination

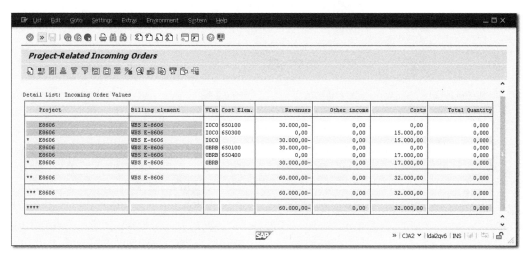

Figure 5.25 Detail List of a Project-Related Incoming Order Determination

You can evaluate the calculated key figures in Reporting, in which the INCOMING ORDERS/BALANCE hierarchy report is available as standard for this purpose (see Figure 5.23). If necessary, you can also settle the calculated key figures to the PA and then evaluate them using the relevant reports at the operating-concern level.

You can also execute an incoming order determination several times for the same period; however, when the key figures are calculated on the basis of the planning data generally only the changes since the previous execution are considered. Note that when the incoming orders are determined all incoming orders between the last execution and the current execution are considered, regardless of the period for which the changes were made.

If necessary, you can also cancel a project-related incoming order determination. This may be necessary if you want to subsequently delete the billing indicator or the results analysis key from a WBS element for which you have already determined incoming orders. It might also be useful to cancel the incoming order determination and execute it a second time if you executed several incoming order determinations within a period but are interested in the overall changes to the key figures when compared with the previous period.

5.8   Cost Forecast

Estimate to completion

In previous chapters, we discussed how you can plan the costs of projects and how commitments and actual costs can be posted to projects as part of the execution phase. However, if deviations in the form of delays, expected overtime, and so on occur during the execution of your projects, then an analysis of the current planned and actual costs and commitments won't suffice if you want to make meaningful forecasts on how the costs of your projects will develop. The objective of the *cost forecast* is to calculate the *cost to complete* (estimate to completion) for each cost element for future periods based on the planned, commitment, actual, and, in particular, forecast data of the networks. The cost to complete is copied with the commitments and actual costs of CO version 0 into one or more special forecast versions, which can be used as default values for a realistic prediction of costs.

The cost to complete is calculated as follows when you execute the cost forecast.

For internal processing activities, the calculation of the cost to complete depends on the status of the activities and when they occur relative to the key date of the cost forecast. If an internal processing activity has not yet been confirmed, which means that it does not yet have an actual date, then the cost forecast assumes that all of the planned work still has to be completed. For an activity that occurs after the key date, the cost to complete is based on the normal costing for the activity. For an activity that is completed before the key date, the system uses the key date period to valuate all of the planned work.

If part of the planned work of an activity occurs before the key date and part occurs after, then the system allocates all of the work to the period between the key date and the planned end date, taking into account the allocation key, and calculates the period-based cost to complete for this period. In all three cases, the *estimated costs at completion* (estimate at completion) correspond to the cost to complete.

For a partially confirmed internal processing activity, the cost to complete is calculated from the forecasted remaining work (see Chapter 4, Section 4.3), distributed across the period between the planned actual date and end date of the activities. The end date is based on the forecasted end date or forecasted remaining duration or on the calculated end date (see Chapter 4, Section 4.1.2). The estimated costs at completion are based on the total actual costs of the confirmed activities and the cost to complete. If an internal processing activity has been confirmed, then the cost to complete for the activity is zero. The estimated costs at completion correspond to the actual costs of the activity.

With externally processed activities and service activities, calculation of the cost to complete depends on whether purchase requisitions and purchase orders have been created. If no purchase requisitions or purchase orders have been entered for an activity, then the time at which the activity takes place, relative to the key date of the cost forecast, becomes significant again. If the planned start date is after the cost forecast key date, then the cost to complete is calculated using the normal costing for the activity. If the start date is before the key date, then the planned costs are revaluated in the key date period. If an invoicing plan is used, then the planned costs for dates before the key date are moved to the key date, whereas costs for dates after the key date are copied unchanged. Because no actual costs or commitments exist yet, the estimated costs at completion correspond to the cost to complete in each case.

Externally processed and service activities

If a purchase requisition or purchase order exists for an activity, then the cost to complete is set to zero (even if an invoicing plan is used). The estimated costs at completion are based on the total actual costs or commitments for the activity.

For general costs activities, the calculation of the cost to complete depends on whether actual costs have been posted. For a general costs activity without actual costs, the calculation of the cost to complete

Costs activities

depends on when the activity occurs relative to the key date of the cost forecast. In this case, the logic used for internal processing activities that have not yet been confirmed is employed. If you used an invoicing plan for cost planning, then the planned costs for dates before the key date are set to the key date, whereas costs for dates after the key date are copied unchanged as the cost to complete. The estimated costs at completion correspond to the cost to complete.

If actual costs have already been posted to a general costs activity, then the cost to complete is based on the difference between the planned and actual costs of the activity. The distribution key is used for distribution across the period between the key date of the cost forecast and the end date of the activity. If the actual costs exceed the planned costs, then the value of the cost to complete is zero. The estimated costs at completion are based on the total of the actual costs plus the cost to complete.

Material components The calculation of the cost to complete for material components depends on the item category of the component (see Chapter 2, Section 2.3.1).

For non-stock items, the planned costs of the component are factored into the calculation of the cost to complete for the activity. If a purchase requisition, purchase order, or goods receipt/invoice receipt exists for the component, then only the commitments or actual costs are used for the calculation.

For stock items, you need to distinguish between components for which a goods issue has been posted and those without a goods issue. If a goods issue has not yet been posted, then the cost of completion for the activity is calculated from the planned costs of the component. The period for the planned costs determination is based either on the requirements date, if this is after the cost forecast key date, or, if not, on the cost forecast key date. The estimated costs at completion for the component correspond to the cost to complete. If a goods issue has been posted for a component, then the cost forecast first calculates the difference between the planned quantity and the quantity issued and then calculates the cost to complete for the open quantity. In this case, the estimated costs at completion are equal to the total of the actual costs and the cost to complete.

5.8.1 Prerequisites for and Restrictions of the Cost Forecast

It is only useful to use the cost forecast if you use networks and work breakdown structures. The networks must be activity assigned and must be both appended and apportioned (that is, planning networks used solely for planning purposes are ignored). Moreover, only the CO version 0 values of costing-relevant activities that are assigned to a WBS element are considered.

The cost to complete for project stock-related material components cannot be calculated as part of the cost forecast. Only plant stock-related stock items are included in the cost forecast calculation, whereas the planning data of WBS elements is ignored in the cost forecast. However, the commitment costs and actual costs of the WBS elements are copied, together with the values of the assigned networks, into the forecast version and can therefore be taken into account when calculating the estimated costs at completion.

To update the cost to complete and copy the commitments and actual costs, you require a forecast version, which you must specify when you execute the cost forecast. Version 110 is available by default. However, you can also create your own CO versions in Customizing for the cost forecast (see Chapter 2, Section 2.4), which must then have the exclusive usage FORECAST COSTS.

Forecast version

To factor in date changes due to confirmations, it usually makes sense to execute rescheduling before the cost forecast. The cost of completion is then calculated on the basis of your current time scheduling. Before you execute the cost forecast, you should also have executed the overhead calculation for the commitment values and actual values so that all commitments and actual costs are copied into the forecast version. However, you don't have to manually execute a planned application of overhead, because planned overheads are automatically calculated as part of the cost forecast.

5.8.2 Executing and Evaluating the Cost Forecast

You can use Transactions CJ9L and CJ9M to execute a cost forecast. In addition to selecting the objects and selecting process control, you also enter the key date for calculating the cost of completion and the forecast version. When you execute the cost forecast, the system calculates the cost of completion for the selected objects based on the key date and copies this cost of completion to the forecast version. The system also copies the commitments and actual costs to the forecast version so that they can be used to calculate the estimated costs at completion.

Example of a cost forecast

Figure 5.26 shows an example of the result of a COST FORECAST (as you can see, only the result of an individual activity of a project is displayed in the detailed list of the cost forecast). In this example, planned costs are shown for an internal processing activity for periods 7 to 9. Due to a partial confirmation in period 8 and the forecasted remaining duration in the confirmation, the cost forecast also calculates a cost to complete for period 10. Also, due to the forecasted remaining work the estimated costs at completion differ significantly from the planned costs.

The FORECAST (12CTC1) hierarchy report is available as standard for analysis of the cost to complete and the commitments and actual costs at the time of the cost forecast. Because the values are calculated by cost element, however, you can also define your own cost element reports to evaluate the cost forecast (see Chapter 6, Section 6.2.2).

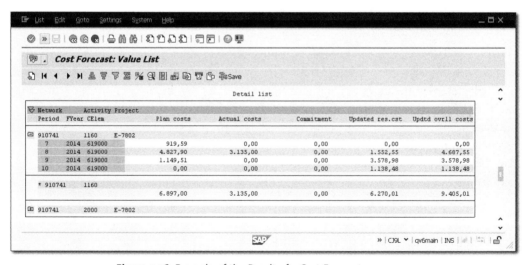

Figure 5.26 Example of the Result of a Cost Forecast

5.8.3   Forecast Workbench

As of EHP 3, an additional cost forecast transaction is available: the Forecast Workbench (Transaction CNFOWB). In contrast to the transactions described previously, the Forecast Workbench allows you to not only execute and evaluate a cost forecast but also to change forecast costs and quantities manually.

The Forecast Workbench consists of an initial screen and the actual evaluation or editing screen. The initial screen (see Figure 5.27) allows you to select the project or a subtree of it and to enter a period and fiscal year.

Initial screen

The Forecast Workbench enables you to view three forecast versions simultaneously:

Forecast versions

▶ Automatic Forecast Version
This CO version enables you to calculate forecast values similar to Transaction CJ9L if you select the Execute New Project Forecast function in the initial screen of the Forecast Workbench.

▶ Past Forecast Version
You can use this CO version to compare different cost forecasts with each other.

▶ Current Forecast Version
The current forecast version is the forecast version you want to make changes to in the Forecast Workbench.

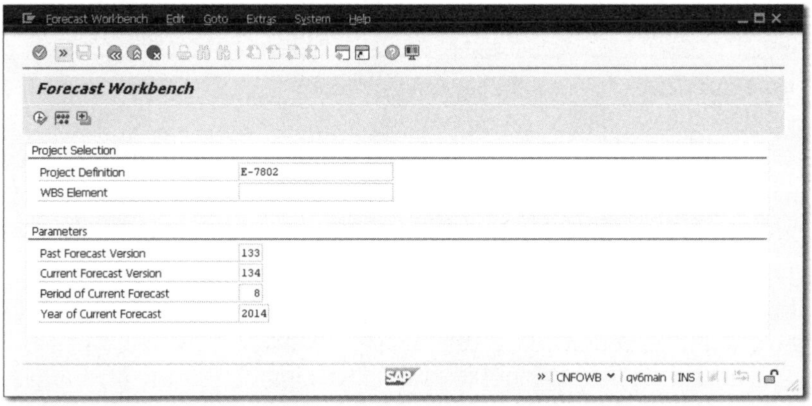

Figure 5.27 Initial Screen of the Forecast Workbench

You can select the current—and (optionally) past—forecast version in the initial screen of the Forecast Workbench. You define the automatic forecast version and a default value for the current forecast version in Customizing depending on the respective CO area. In Customizing, you must also define which planning versions you want to use to display the planned costs and quantities for WBS elements and networks. The ACTUAL COST INFORMATION FOR BASELINE function in the initial screen allows you to start copying the actual data into the current forecast version.

Editing screen The evaluation or editing screen of the Forecast Workbench consists of the following elements: a structure tree for navigation within the project structure and for selecting one or more objects and a table that displays the forecast details for the selected objects (see Figure 5.28). Each combination of objects and cost elements or statistical key figures displays in a separate row in that table.

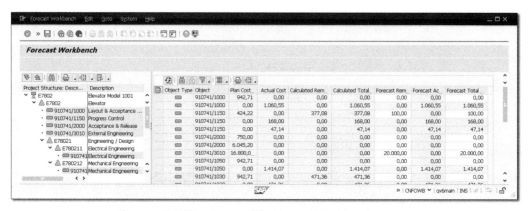

Figure 5.28 Editing Screen of the Forecast Workbench

The separate columns list information about planned, actual, remaining, and total costs and quantities for the different forecast versions and the planning version. In this context, the cost and quantities of the automatic forecast version are referred to as *calculated* costs and quantities, the values of the past forecast version are called *past* values, and those of the current forecast version are called *forecast values*. The fields related to the remaining and total forecast values are ready for input so that you can manually enter or change forecast values in the Forecast

Workbench. In that case, the system distributes the forecast values similarly to the previous distribution as of the period specified in the initial screen.

| Determination of Additional Period-Based Project Key Figures | [◉] |

Based on the results analysis, sales order determination, and cost forecast, you can revaluate the accounting data of your projects at the end of the period and determine additional key figures, such as costs that can be capitalized and reserves, incoming orders, and open order values as well as cost to complete and costs at completion.

5.9   Settlement

In general, project structures serve only as temporary cost objects. In other words, the costs that are posted during the execution phase of a project are typically allocated to one or more other receivers as part of the period-end closing—that is, they are *settled*. The costs are allocated to various receivers in accordance with the purpose of the settlement. The following list describes some examples of project settlement:

Project settlement options

▶ **Settlement to Profitability Analysis (CO-PA)**
You can use the results analysis to calculate inventory costs or reserves for a project, for example (see Section 5.6). The settlement of these analyzed costs to CO-PA means that the information is made available to the PA for detailed Enterprise CO while automatic adjustment postings can be made concurrently in FI.

▶ **Settlement to Asset Accounting**
or investment projects, cost portions—which can or must be capitalized—can be settled to AUC or completed *assets*. In Asset Accounting, you can then use these values for relevant depreciations, for example.

▶ **Settlement to cost centers**
When you settle the costs of projects to cost centers, you can use these values in Cost Center Accounting—for example, for price calculation.

In addition to the preceding settlement receivers, you can also settle project costs to other orders, projects, cost objects, sales order items, or G/L accounts, for example, depending on your Enterprise CO requirements.

You use *settlement rules* to determine which portions of which costs can be settled to which receivers with which amounts. These rules must be defined in the relevant senders—that is, in WBS elements or network activities, for example. Although settlements are generally only executed for actual data of projects, you can also settle planning data to cost centers, business processes, or (if you have previously executed a planned results analysis) to PA for plan-integrated WBS elements. Then you can use the planning data in Cost Center Accounting or Activity-Based Costing for planned price calculation, for example. Planning data belonging to projects that are not plan-integrated can also be transferred to the results analysis without settlement. This occurs via a *planning data transfer* from WBS elements with a results analysis key.

5.9.1 Prerequisites for Project Settlements

Various prerequisites must be fulfilled in SAP Project System Customizing and in the master data of the relevant projects before project settlements can be executed.

Settlement rule   In order for the costs of a WBS element or network header or activity to be settled, a settlement rule must be defined in the relevant object. A settlement rule consists of control parameters—in particular, a *settlement profile*—and between one and 999 *distribution rules*. Figure 5.29 shows an example of the distribution rules of a WBS element.

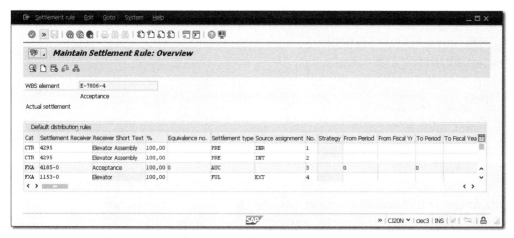

Figure 5.29 Example of the Distribution Rules of a Settlement Rule

In a distribution rule, you have to first define the settlement receiver. You can also execute settlements to various receivers by creating several distribution rules within a settlement rule. The settlement profile determines which settlement receivers can be used in the settlement rule.

Next, you can define which portions of the costs are to be settled to the settlement receiver. Costs can be distributed as a *percentage*, using *equivalence numbers*, or *by amount*. With a settlement by amount, the amount rule category determines whether the specified amount is to be settled periodically or whether the amount simply represents the upper limit for all settlements. In the first case, a negative balance may occur in the object due to the settlement by amount, whereas in the second case only the actual debit is settled periodically as a maximum.

In addition, costs are often supposed to be distributed among various receivers based on the specific cost elements. To do this, you can define a *source assignment* in a distribution rule (depending on the parameters of the settlement rule), which refers to a cost element interval or cost element group. The distribution rule then only applies to debits for these cost elements. This means that debits, which can or must be capitalized, can be settled to Asset Accounting while the other cost portions are settled to cost centers for investment projects, for example. In Asset Accounting, valuation areas can be used to make a further distinction between cost portions that can or cannot be capitalized based on the purpose of the valuation if required. The system posts portions of a valuation area that cannot be capitalized as nonoperating expenses.

The settlement type of a distribution rule controls additional details of the settlement to the receiver. The following settlement types are available:

▸ **PER (periodic settlement)**
During settlement, only the costs of the relevant settlement period are settled in accordance with the settlement rule.

▸ **GES (full settlement)**
With full settlement, both the costs of the settlement period and the unsettled costs from previous periods are settled.

For investment projects, that is, for WBS elements with an investment profile, the following additional settlement types are also available:

- **AUC (capitalization of assets under construction)**
  This settlement type is used to settle the costs of WBS elements to assets under construction. Distribution rules for the AUC settlement type cannot be created manually. Instead, they are automatically created during the first settlement, provided that an asset under construction exists for the WBS element.

- **PRE (preliminary settlement)**
  Distribution rules for the PRE settlement type are used for settlement before the distribution rules for settlement type AUC. With settlement type PRE, you can therefore settle cost portions that are not to be capitalized.

If necessary, you can also enter a validity period for distribution rules, which is taken into account when settlement is executed. After a distribution rule is used in a settlement, only the end date of the validity period can be changed.

Settlement rule parameters

The parameters for the settlement rule essentially consist of the settlement profile, an allocation structure, and, if necessary, a source and PA transfer structure. You must define all of these profiles in advance in the Customizing settings.

Settlement profile

The settlement profile (see Figure 5.30) is the central profile for settlement. In a settlement profile, you define, for example, which receiver types can or must be used in the settlement rule and how costs are to be distributed. By setting the TO BE SETTLED IN FULL indicator, you ensure that an object can only be completed or flagged for deletion if its balance is zero. In addition to other control indicators, you can also define default values for the other profiles of the parameters of a settlement rule in a settlement profile.

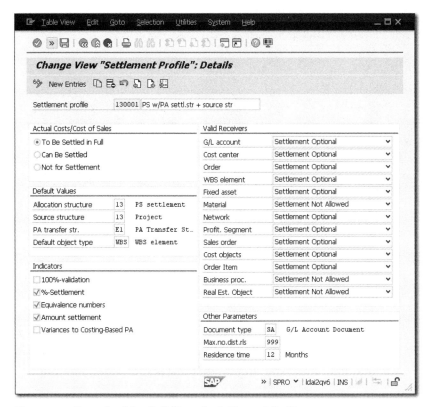

Figure 5.30 Example of the Definition of a Settlement Profile

The allocation structure (also referred to in some cases as *settlement structure* in Customizing) determines which (source) cost elements are to be settled under which (settlement) cost elements to the relevant receiver types. An allocation structure therefore consists of one or more assignments. Each assignment refers to source cost elements (that is, an interval of cost elements or a cost element group under which debits may be posted) and to settlement cost elements (see Figure 5.31) under which the debits can be allocated during settlement. Settlement cost elements are defined on the basis of the individual settlement receivers. If necessary, the source cost elements can be retained during the settlement to the receivers. To do this, set the BY COST ELEMENT indicator for the relevant receiver types in the allocation structure. For performance

Allocation structure

reasons, a settlement using a smaller number of settlement types is often preferred to a settlement by cost elements.

[◉]

Definition of Allocation Structures

When defining an allocation structure, note that the structure includes all source cost elements under which debits may be posted and that each of these source cost elements may appear only once within the allocation structure.

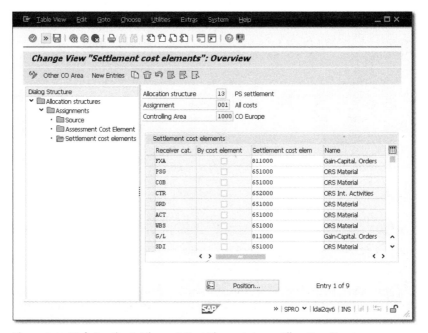

Figure 5.31 Defining the Settlement Cost Elements in an Allocation Structure

Source structure   A source structure consists of one or more source assignments. An assignment includes the debit cost elements that are to be settled in accordance with the same distribution rules during settlement. When you enter a distribution rule, you can restrict its validity to the cost elements in a source assignment by specifying this assignment. In the example shown previously in Figure 5.29, all costs of the INT and INR source assignments are settled to a cost center, whereas all other costs are settled to the AUC or the completed asset.

You only require a PA transfer structure as part of project settlement if you want to settle costs to Profitability Analysis. Because data in the results analysis has a reference to value fields, you use the PA transfer structure to determine which cost elements are to be assigned to which value fields. You have to create one or more assignments in a PA transfer structure for this purpose. Each assignment refers to source cost elements (a cost element interval or cost element group) and to a value field. If necessary, you can also define various value fields within an assignment for fixed and variable portions.

PA

Defining PA Transfer Structures

If you execute a results analysis before project settlement to the results analysis, then you must ensure that the PA transfer structure incorporates all relevant results analysis cost elements.

[!]

There are various options for creating settlement rules for WBS elements and network headers or activities. You can define the settlement profile and thus also all relevant settlement parameters as default values for WBS elements in the project profile for networks in the network type. If the same distribution rules are to be used for all WBS elements and, if necessary, for all networks in a project, then you can define these distribution rules at the project definition level when you create the project (with or without a template). When you save, this settlement rule is accepted by all WBS elements and, depending on the settings in the network parameters, by the assigned networks. When you create new WBS elements or networks for the project, the settlement rule from the project definition is also copied to these elements or networks.

Creating settlement rules

Another efficient method for creating settlement rules for WBS elements and networks is to use strategies to determine settlement rules. Figure 5.32 shows the definition of a strategy to generate a settlement rule for WBS elements. You can use this strategy to determine the settlement profile, the results analysis key (see Section 5.6.1), and the receivers of the settlement rule. The receivers are also defined by specifying the ACCOUNT ASSIGNMENT CATEGORY in the strategy.

Strategies for settlement rules

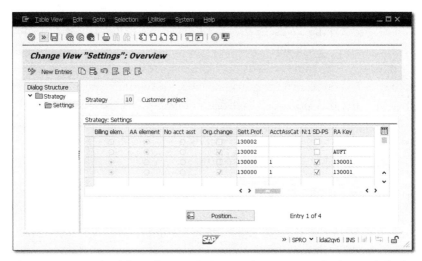

Figure 5.32 Example of the Definition of a Strategy for Generating Settlement Rules for WBS Elements

Account assignment categories

The following account assignment categories can be used when defining a strategy:

- **No receiver**
  No distribution rule is generated.

- **Profitability segment**
  A distribution rule is created for a profitability segment in Profitability Analysis. The characteristic values in this case are derived from the WBS element and the sales document items that are assigned to the WBS element. If several sales document items are assigned to a WBS element, then the indicator N:1 DS-PS in the strategy determines whether a settlement rule is to be generated.

- **Requesting cost center**
  A distribution rule is generated with the COST CENTER receiver type. The system copies the requesting cost center of the WBS element as the receiver cost center.

- **Responsible cost center**
  A distribution rule is generated with the COST CENTER receiver type. The system copies the responsible cost center of the WBS element as the receiver cost center.

▶ **Copy rule from higher-level object**
The WBS element copies the settlement rule of the higher-level WBS element or the project definition.

> **Copy Rule from Higher-Level Object**   **[+]**
>
> If the copy rule from higher-level object option is used, then a settlement rule is only generated by default if the WBS element did not previously have a settlement rule. However, as of EHP 3, you can also use the BAdI WBS_SETTLE-MENT_RULE_NEW to pass on settlement rules to WBS elements with existing settlement rules.

You can define the determination of the account assignment category, the settlement profile, and, if necessary, the results analysis key separately within a strategy for billing elements, account assignment elements, and WBS elements that prohibit billing or account assignment. In addition, the ORG. CHANGE indicator allows you to determine that the settings you make are only valid if the current WBS element and the object that is directly above this in the hierarchy differ in their assignment to a company code, business area, or profit center.

When you have defined a strategy in SAP Project System Customizing settings, you must assign this setting to the relevant project profiles. Finally, you must generate the settlement rules for WBS elements. To do this, access Transaction CJB2 (Individual Processing) or CJB1 (Collective Processing), select the relevant objects, and execute settlement rule generation. The system uses the project profile to determine the relevant strategy and (if possible) generates settlement rules and, if necessary, results analysis keys for the selected WBS elements.

Settlement rules

You can use a BAdI for greater control of the generation of settlement rules in Transaction CJB1 or CJB2. For example, you can adjust the determination of strategies to meet your own requirements or restrict the selection of sales document items for customer projects. You can then display additional information about the generation of the settlement rules in a log and, if necessary, in a detailed list.

[+] | **Avoiding Generated Settlement Rules**

Note that automatic generation of settlement rules with Transaction CJB1 or CJB2 is not possible for investment projects. If you also want to prevent the generation of settlement rules for other WBS elements, then you can define a user status that prevents the AUTOMATICALLY GENERATED SETTLEMENT RULES (SRGN) business process. This has no effect on the manual creation of settlement rules.

Strategies for networks
You can also define strategies to determine settlement rules for networks in the Customizing settings. In a strategy for a network, you define the sequence in which the system should execute various types of strategies to determine settlement rules (see Figure 5.33). You can use the following types of strategies to determine which settlement rules to use:

- ▸ Generate settlement to WBS element
- ▸ Copy settlement rule of the WBS element
- ▸ Copy settlement rule of the project definition
- ▸ No settlement rule
- ▸ Manual maintenance of settlement rule
- ▸ Automatic generation of settlement rule

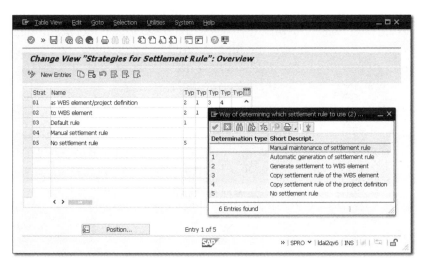

Figure 5.33 Defining Strategies for Generating Settlement Rules for Networks

With the AUTOMATIC GENERATION OF SETTLEMENT RULE type, the system uses a *default rule* as a settlement rule. You define which rule is to be used in PARAMETERS FOR NETWORK TYPE. The default rules provided are preconfigured by SAP and cannot be changed. One possible default rule for networks is NETWORK: TO SALES ORD./WBS ELEMENT, which results in a settlement to an assigned sales order item or a WBS element.

Default rule

You also define the strategy that is to be used to determine settlement rules for networks in PARAMETERS FOR NETWORK TYPE. However, in contrast to WBS elements, you don't have to execute any additional transactions to generate the settlement rules for networks using strategies.

Sometimes, it doesn't make sense to enter default distribution rules in the project definition or to generate settlement rules automatically. You must then manually create distribution rules for the relevant operational objects. To do this, you can navigate from the object master data to distribution rule maintenance (shown in Figure 5.29) and, if necessary, from there to maintenance of the settlement parameters. As soon as a settlement rule exists for an object, it is documented for the object as system status SETC (settlement rule created).

Manual entry of distribution rules

You can use the RKASELRULES_PR report for an overview of the settlement rules of projects. On the initial screen of this report, you use selection variants to determine which projects are to be analyzed. If necessary, you can use details of the settlement parameters and settlement receivers as additional selection criteria. After you execute the report, it returns a table listing the distribution rules of the selected object. You can then navigate to the master data of the sender and receiver or to the settlement rules display.

5.9.2 Executing Project Settlements

For individual and collective processing of project settlements, you can use Transaction CJ9E or CJ9G for planned settlement and Transaction CJ88 or CJ8G for actual settlement in SAP Project System. Figure 5.34 shows the initial screen for individual processing of actual settlement for a project.

Individual and collective processing

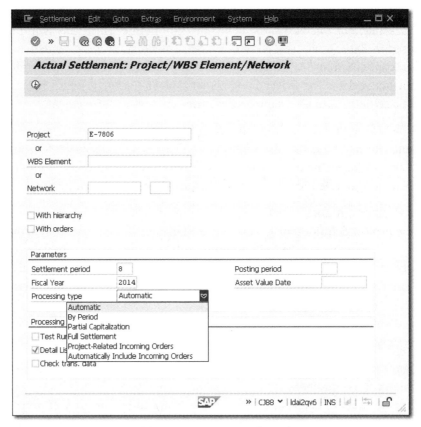

Figure 5.34 Initial Screen of the Actual Settlement of a Project

In addition to selecting the relevant objects and specifying process control, you define the period for which you want the settlement to be executed on the initial screen. Depending on the settlement type of the relevant distribution rules, the settlement either takes account of debits from the specified settlement period only or factors in costs from previous periods. If the settlements are not to be posted to the settlement period—for example, because this period is already locked against posting—then you can specify a later period as the posting period, provided that this is still in the same fiscal year as the settlement period.

On the initial screen of project settlement, you also enter a PROCESSING TYPE, which controls additional details of the settlement process. The following processing types are available:

▶ AUTOMATIC
   With this processing type, distribution rules with settlement type PER are executed before settlement rules with settlement type FUL. For investment projects, settlements to assets with settlement type FUL are only taken into account after the relevant WBS elements are completed.

▶ BY PERIOD
   With this processing type, only distribution rules with settlement types PER, PRE, and AUC are taken into account. Settlement to assets(s) under construction will be carried out last.

▶ PARTIAL CAPITALIZATION
   With this processing type, distribution rules for assets with settlement type FUL are used if the WBS element is not completed.

▶ FULL SETTLEMENT
   This processing type is used for settlement rules with distribution rules of settlement type PER only to check whether a balance still exists in the object after settlement due to debits in previous periods. If so, the system issues an error message, and you must execute settlement for the previous periods first.

Finally, if you also want to settle data from project-related incoming orders to the results analysis as part of settlement, then you can use the two processing types PROJECT-RELATED INCOMING ORDERS and AUTOMATICALLY INCLUDE INCOMING ORDERS.

When you execute project settlement, you can then analyze the result in a basic list and, depending on the process control settings, in a detailed list (see Figure 5.35). You can navigate from the detailed list to the display of the sender and receiver master data or to the display of the settlement rules if necessary. If errors occurred during the execution—for example, because the status of an object prevented settlement or settlement rules were missing—then you can display the relevant messages.

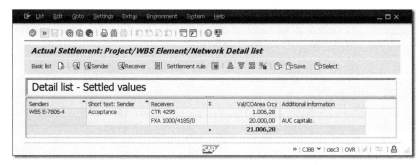

Figure 5.35 Detailed List of an Actual Settlement

You can repeat project settlement for the same period any number of times. In this case, the system only takes into account the postings that have been made since the last settlement. You can also cancel settlements in individual and collective processing; however, a cancellation run only cancels the most recent settlement. If, for example, you executed several settlements for a period and now want to cancel project settlement for the entire settlement period, then you must execute several cancellation runs.

5.9.3 Settlement of Investment Projects

For investment projects, you must take into account several special features regarding project settlement. If you assign an investment profile to a WBS element, the system may (depending on the investment profile settings) automatically generate one or more assets under construction when the WBS element is released. Data belonging to the WBS element, such as the name or the requesting cost center, is copied to the AUC. You define investment profiles in Investment Management Customizing using Transaction OITA (see Figure 5.36).

Distribution rule With the first settlement of the WBS element, the system automatically generates a distribution rule for settlement type AUC for settlement to the assigned asset under construction. If you don't want to settle all costs of the WBS element to this asset under construction, then you must manually enter additional distribution rules for the debits to other receivers that are not to be capitalized. Use settlement type PRE to ensure that these distribution rules are taken into account before settlement to assets under construction as part of project settlement. You can use an appropriate source structure to distinguish between the cost portions that are to be capitalized and those that are not (shown in Figure 5.29).

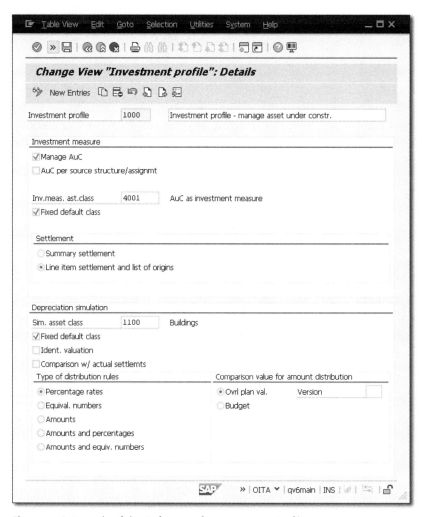

Figure 5.36 Example of the Definition of an Investment Profile

Once the asset under construction phase is completed, create a completed asset. You can do this in the Asset Accounting transactions or directly when maintaining the WBS element. Next, define a distribution rule in the WBS element with settlement type FUL for the cost portions to be capitalized, and enter the completed asset as the settlement receiver. Note, however, that this distribution rule is only taken into account in the project settlement if you have selected PARTIAL CAPITALIZATION or AUTOMATIC as the processing type and completed the relevant WBS elements—in other words, if you have set the system status to TABG.

When the WBS elements have been completed, the debits that have been settled to the assets under construction are automatically reposted to the completed assets at the same time that the full settlement to the asset takes place. However, other debits can still be posted to the WBS elements. The relevant cost portions are then settled to the asset as part of the next project settlement.

Line item settlement

You can also execute line item settlement for investment projects, provided that this is permitted by the investment profile. With line item settlement, you can create a separate, specific distribution rule for each debit posted (that is, for each line item). Therefore, an exact data origin can be determined for each line item, from the completed asset, to the original debit, to the investment project. You can also define a general settlement rule in addition to your line item settlement rules. The system then uses this rule for all line items for which no separate settlement rule has been assigned. You can enter line item distribution rules in Transaction CJIC.

Multilevel settlement

Although *direct settlements* are generally used for sales and distribution projects or overhead cost projects, *multilevel settlement* may be useful for investment projects. With direct settlements, the sender objects settle their debits to the relevant receivers directly. With a multilevel settlement for investment projects, you first settle all costs to the WBS elements with an investment profile and then settle all debits from these WBS elements to assets under construction, assets, and other receivers. The system uses the settlement rules to automatically determine whether a direct settlement or a multilevel settlement should be executed in each case. This means that you only need to execute one settlement run, even in the case of a multilevel settlement. This multilevel settlement of investment projects may be necessary especially if you use assigned networks or orders without an investment profile, because these cannot automatically settle their costs to assets under construction. Multilevel settlement may also be useful if you want to archive and delete assigned orders during the asset under construction phase of projects lasting several years. For reasons of traceability, this is not possible if you settle the orders to AUCs directly.

If you use multilevel settlement, look at the dependencies explained in the next section. You should also note the special features related to the interest calculation for investment projects (see Section 5.5).

5.9.4 Project Settlement Dependencies

To ensure that a project settlement can take into account all debits belonging to a period, you must first execute all relevant period-end closing activities. In particular, you must execute the overhead allocation and template allocation. If you also use revaluation at actual prices, interest calculation, and results analysis, then you should also execute these period-end closing activities before project settlement. A settlement must be executed before and after revaluation in certain cases (see Section 5.2.3). If you determine project-related incoming orders (see Section 5.7), then you must execute a separate settlement of this data based on the processing type you use for settlement.

Consider the particular problems associated with the hierarchically aggregated display of values in the SAP Project System reports after a multilevel project settlement. To ensure that no incorrect data is displayed in a WBS element in the structure overview or in hierarchy reports after a multilevel settlement (see Chapter 6, Section 6.1 and Section 6.2.1), the system executes an *elimination of internal business volume*. An elimination of internal business volume means that the system generates internal allocation records that remove the settlements posted in a WBS element. Consequently, no duplicate actual costs from settlement and from the aggregation of values are displayed for this WBS element.

Elimination of internal business volume

To ensure that values can be displayed correctly in the structure overview and in hierarchy reports with the elimination of internal business volume, note the following points in relation to multilevel settlement:

- ► Always settle the WBS elements to higher-level WBS elements that are directly above them in the hierarchy and not to lower-level WBS elements or to WBS elements that are several levels higher.

- ► Always settle assigned network headers or activities and orders to the assigned WBS element.

- ► Don't subsequently change the hierarchical position of the settled objects.

For more details about the elimination of internal business volume after multilevel settlement, see SAP Note 51971.

5.10 Summary

SAP Project System comprises a range of functions that help you make adjustment postings based on changed actual prices, applications of overhead, and interest calculations as part of period-end closing for your projects. With the results analysis and determination of project-related incoming orders, you can calculate additional key figures and make these available for Enterprise CO. The cost forecast provides information about the expected cost to complete and costs at completion for your projects and also takes into account the forecast data from confirmations. Finally, you can use project settlement to allocate the costs and revenue data for your projects to other receivers in the SAP system.

Flexible and clear reporting of all project-related data is integral to project management. SAP Project System provides accounting and logistics reports of different levels of detail for this very purpose.

6   Reporting

To monitor and control projects, you need reports that enable you to provide information about the current cost, revenue, schedule, and capacity situation of your projects. For this reason, different standard reports are available in Reporting of SAP Project System. If required, you can customize these reports or define your own reports. Reporting in SAP Project System is roughly divided between *Project Information System: Structures* and *Project Information System: Financials*. Other reports are also available for special logistical evaluations and for analyzing project progress. This chapter will describe the different evaluation options you can use in SAP Project System.

Reporting with SAP Business Warehouse   [+]

Companies that use SAP Business Warehouse (BW) for reporting purposes can also use predefined SAP Business Content for SAP Project System. This SAP Business Content consists of different extractors, update rules, characteristics, key figures, InfoCubes, queries, and roles. You can find details on content for SAP Project System in the SAP Library using the following keywords:

▶ PRODUCT LIFECYCLE MANAGEMENT • PROGRAM AND PROJECT MANAGEMENT

▶ FINANCIALS • CONTROLLING • OVERHEAD COST CONTROLLING • OVERHEAD PROJECTS

As of EHP 6, *simplified reporting* offers new objects and queries for evaluating accounting data when using SAP BW. The new reports are similar to existing ERP reports and permit an improved hierarchy presentation of projects and direct access to transaction data. In other words, loading of accounting data no longer requires replication but is done at the runtime of new reports.

Note, however, that the project structures still need to be replicated to be able to evaluate them using the new reports. By default, the new simplified reports are also integrated with the project planner and cost estimator role (see Chapter 2, Section 2.4.5).

6.1   Project Information System: Structures

The focus of Project Information System: Structures is on evaluating master data, schedules, and statuses of project objects; however, it can also show cost and revenue data. In Project Information System: Structures, you differentiate between the structure or project overviews and individual overviews. Although individual reports only allow you to evaluate one document or object type at a time (that is, only from WBS elements or only from activities), you can use the structure/project structure overview to evaluate several object types simultaneously. Before we describe the structure/project structure overview and individual overviews in more detail, we will first deal with the data selection that is common to all reports of Project Information System: Structures (and also Project Information System: Financials).

Data selection   Figure 6.1 shows the initial screen of a report in Project Information System: Structures in SAP Project System. You can determine areas in the selection area of the initial screen for which you want to evaluate data. These areas include individual values or whole intervals of project definitions, work breakdown structure (WBS) elements, networks and orders, and so on. You can use indicators to specify whether the data you want to select from the database for your evaluation is data of operational objects or data of versions, standard structures, or previously archived objects.

Database profile   The *database profile* that you use influences the appearance of an initial screen and the selection options available there, but in particular it influences the selection of data. You can assign a database profile as a parameter value for the PDB parameter ID in the user master data (Transaction SU01) or as a default value in a *PS info profile*. If the database profile allows this, you can make changes to the database profile temporarily when you call a report, or you can select a different database profile.

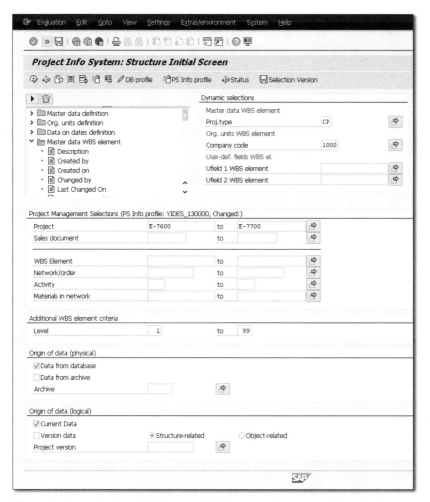

Figure 6.1 Example of an Initial Screen of the Structure Overview with an Active Dynamic Selection

Figure 6.2 illustrates how a database profile is defined in Customizing Transaction OPTX. You can use the database profile to specify which objects and data are to be read from the database and which project view should be used to define how that data is displayed in the report in accordance with the project structure or arranged on the basis of the project cost centers responsible, for example. SAP Note 423830 contains a detailed description of the different indicators for a database profile and their interdependencies.

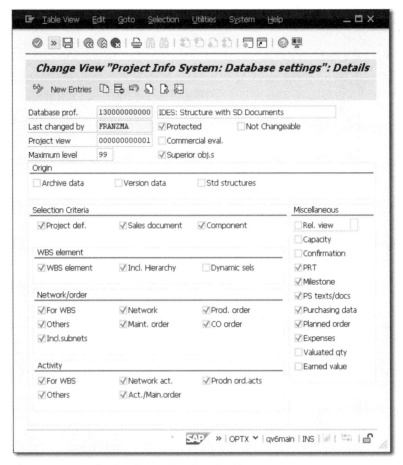

Figure 6.2 Example of Defining a Database Profile

Dynamic selection | You can use *dynamic selection* and *status selection* profiles to further restrict the object selection you made in the initial screen of a report. Figure 6.1 shows a dynamic selection of the object selection according to the project type and company code of WBS elements. The specifications in dynamic selections act as filters for selecting objects from the database. With a suitable dynamic selection, you can reduce the amount of data selected and thereby influence the performance of the evaluation considerably. You can define which fields should be available for the dynamic selection. To do this, you need to create a selection view for the PSJ logical database with the CUS origin in Transaction SE36. Note that the definition of your own selection view for the dynamic selection is cross-client.

In addition to the field values of dynamic selection, you can also use statuses as filter criteria for selecting objects. To do this, you must first define a *status selection profile* in Customizing of SAP Project System using Transaction BS42. You store different rows consisting of system or user statuses in a status selection profile (see Chapter 1, Section 1.6). You can use NOT, AND, or OR conditions for each row to specify how you want the combination of these statuses to be used as a filter. In the initial screen of a report, you can then select the status selection profile for the different object types as an additional restriction for selecting data from the database.

Status selection profile

Dynamic Selection Using Status Combination Codes   **[+]**

As of EHP 3, you can use status combination codes (see Chapter 1, Section 1.6) as an alternative to status selection profiles as filter criteria in the dynamic selection process when selecting objects. Because status combination codes are stored in the master data of project objects instead of a separate database table—as is the case with the actual statuses—using status combination codes as filter criteria instead of status selection profiles leads to a considerable increase in system performance during object selection processes in reporting.

If you made a more complex selection in the initial screen of a report, then you can save this selection as a *selection variant*. When you then call the report again at a later time and you want to make the same selection you don't have to enter all of the selection criteria again manually. Instead, you only need to select the selection variant you saved.

Selection variants

Properties of Data Selection   **[!]**

Note that you generally cannot select any other data from the database within the evaluations. In other words, your data selection determines which data is available for the evaluation. Similarly, you cannot further restrict the amount of data selected within the report; instead, you can only influence the display of this data by using field selections or filter functions. This means that the data selection you make in the initial screen of a report also influences the performance of the evaluation considerably.

Selection versions You can also save the data of reports of Project Information System: Structures as *selection versions*. When you call a report, you can then decide whether you want to select the current data from the database or the data of a selection version for the evaluation. You can create any number of selection versions and, if required, assign them a validity period. If the datasets for evaluation are very large, then you can also schedule the creation of a selection version in the initial screen of a report as a background job. In this case, the system could automatically execute the data selection at night, for example. When creating a selection version, you can specify a number of days after which the system is to delete the version automatically. You can also delete the selection versions manually.

Project views In addition to using the database profile to control the data selected, you can use the PROJECT VIEW field of the database profile to determine the hierarchy that will be used to display data when you call hierarchically arranged reports of Project Information System: Structures and Project Information System: Financials. Some of the following project views are delivered in the standard system:

- ▶ Project structure
- ▶ Profit center
- ▶ Cost centers
- ▶ Investment programs
- ▶ Sales view
- ▶ Characteristics hierarchy from summarization (see Section 6.4)

You can also create your own project views for predefined hierarchy types in Customizing Transaction OPUR. In addition, you can use a customer enhancement to define a hierarchy structure for project views for hierarchy type 99.

[+] **Project View Properties**

You cannot select any more data from the database in the project view. Instead, you can only define how the data in the information system will be displayed. The data in structure reports is hierarchically displayed most effectively when you use the project structure as a project view.

For more information about data selections in the reports of SAP Project System, also refer to SAP Notes 107605 and 700697.

6.1.1 Structure/Project Structure Overview

You can use the *structure overview* and *project structure overview* to simultaneously evaluate the data of all project objects and orders and sales documents assigned to them (customer inquiries, customer quotations, and sales orders).

Structure Overview

PS info profile

Figure 6.3 shows the evaluation of a project in the structure overview (Transaction CN41). The display of data and different functions of this report are determined by a *PS info profile* that you can either assign to users using the PFL parameter ID or manually select when you call the report. The PS info profile is essentially an overall profile in which several subprofiles are combined. Some PS info profiles and all required subprofiles are delivered in the standard system. You can also define your own PS info profiles using Transaction OPSM in Customizing of SAP Project System or branch directly to the editing area of lower-level profiles from a PS info profile.

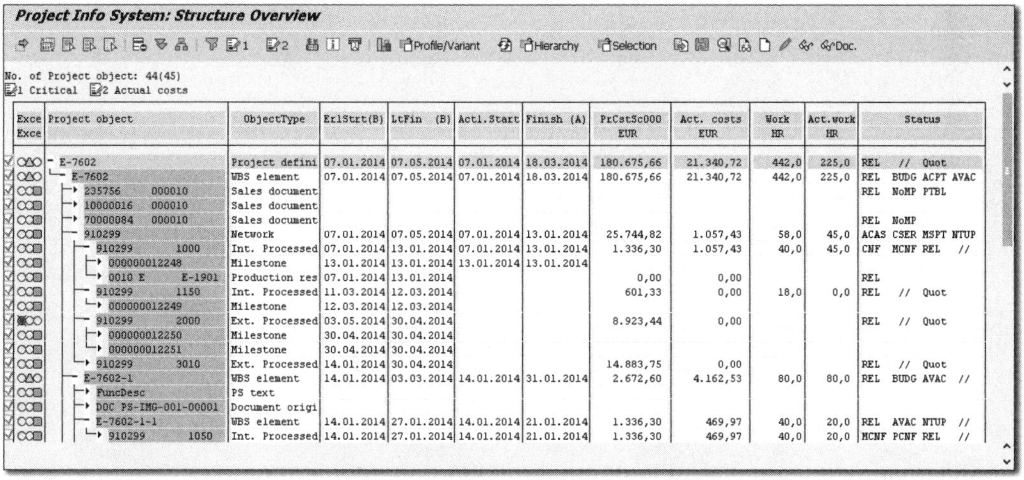
Project Info System: Structure Overview

1 2 Profile/Variant Hierarchy Selection Doc.

No. of Project object: 44(45)

1 Critical 2 Actual costs

Exce Exce	Project object	ObjectType	ErlStrt(B)	LtFin (B)	Actl.Start	Finish (A)	PrCstSc000 EUR	Act. costs EUR	Work HR	Act.work HR	Status
	E-7602	Project defini	07.01.2014	07.05.2014	07.01.2014	18.03.2014	180.675,66	21.340,72	442,0	225,0	REL // Quot
	E-7602	WBS element	07.01.2014	07.05.2014	07.01.2014	18.03.2014	180.675,66	21.340,72	442,0	225,0	REL BUDG ACPT AVAC
	235756 000010	Sales document									REL NoMP PTBL
	10000016 000010	Sales document									
	70000084 000010	Sales document									REL NoMP
	910299	Network	07.01.2014	07.05.2014	07.01.2014	13.01.2014	25.744,82	1.057,43	58,0	45,0	ACAS CSER MSPT NTUP
	910299 1000	Int. Processed	07.01.2014	13.01.2014	07.01.2014	13.01.2014	1.336,30	1.057,43	40,0	45,0	CNF MCNF REL //
	000000012248	Milestone	13.01.2014	13.01.2014	13.01.2014	13.01.2014					
	0010 E E-1901	Production res	07.01.2014	13.01.2014			0,00	0,00			REL
	910299 1150	Int. Processed	11.03.2014	12.03.2014			601,33	0,00	18,0	0,0	REL // Quot
	000000012249	Milestone	12.03.2014	12.03.2014							
	910299 2000	Ext. Processed	03.05.2014	30.04.2014			8.923,44	0,00			REL // Quot
	000000012250	Milestone	30.04.2014	30.04.2014							
	000000012251	Milestone	30.04.2014	30.04.2014							
	910299 3010	Ext. Processed	14.01.2014	30.04.2014			14.883,75	0,00			REL // Quot
	E-7602-1	WBS element	14.01.2014	03.03.2014	14.01.2014	31.01.2014	2.672,60	4.162,53	80,0	80,0	REL BUDG AVAC //
	FuncDesc	PS text									
	DOC PS-IMG-001-00001	Document origi									
	E-7602-1-1	WBS element	14.01.2014	27.01.2014	14.01.2014	21.01.2014	1.336,30	469,97	40,0	20,0	REL AVAC NTUP //
	910299 1050	Int. Processed	14.01.2014	27.01.2014	14.01.2014	21.01.2014	1.336,30	469,97	40,0	20,0	MCNF PCNF REL //

Figure 6.3 Evaluating a Project in the Structure Overview

Defining a PS
info profile Figure 6.4 illustrates how a PS info profile is defined. You can use the
fields in the ACTION SELECTION section of the PS info profile to specify
which action you want the system to execute when you double-click on
an object or data field in the report. Possible actions might include
branching to the display, changing the object, or displaying the long text
or change documents for the object. The STRUCTURE OVERVIEW profile in
the PS info profile controls how the structure overview is displayed.
This profile contains lower-level profiles that define the display, sorting,
grouping, filtering, and highlighting colors of objects (exceptions) and
indicators that determine how the data is aggregated and displayed.

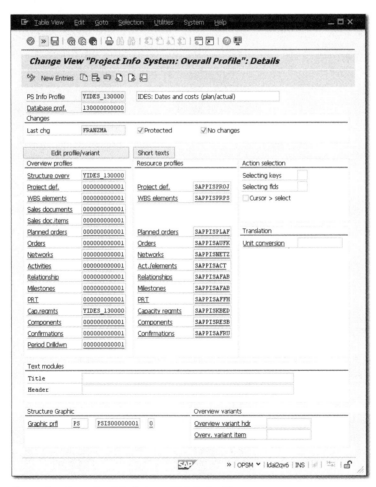

Figure 6.4 Example of Defining a PS Info Profile

You can change many of the settings in the report itself:

▶ You can use a field selection to determine which fields are displayed.

▶ You can change the sequence of field columns and their width with a mouse click.

▶ You can define filters and, if required, sorting, grouping, and summarization criteria or determine whether you want the values to be displayed in aggregated or nonaggregated format. Grouping, sorting, and summarization are only possible in the structure overview if you remove the hierarchical display of objects.

▶ Specifically, you can also define exceptions in the report using traffic lights or colored highlighting—for example, to indicate that planned dates have been overrun or to emphasize objects with special characteristics.

If the PS info profile or the corresponding subprofiles allow this, you can save changes that you made in the report as changes in the Customizing profiles and also generate new profiles in the report.

In addition to the different options you can use for adjusting data in the report and printing report data, you can use the following functions in the structure overview:

▶ Display, change, mass change, and create objects

▶ Confirm activities, create and send pools of confirmations

▶ Perform availability checks for material components

▶ Update data (refresh)

▶ Graphically display data as structure, hierarchy, network, Gantt chart, and portfolio graphics or display total curves and histogram displays

▶ Send report data and export the data into Microsoft Excel format or as HTML or ASCII files

▶ Use periodic displays of costs, commitments, or revenues

▶ Branch to individual overviews, reports of Project Information System: Financials, or logistical reports, such as capacity reports or reports for displaying reservations, purchase requisitions, or purchase orders for a selected object

To better compare data with each other (for example, planned quantities or amounts with the actual values), you can also select difference columns in the structure overview and display the difference as absolute amounts or percentages. When you evaluate project or simulation versions in the structure overview, you can also compare the version data and the operative data row by row.

[+] **Using Structure Overviews**

Due to the wide range of functions of the structure overview, the option to evaluate structure, schedule, and CO data of all project-related objects simultaneously and, in particular, to branch to the editing area of all objects, the structure overview of some companies is used as the main transaction for managing projects.

Project Structure Overview

Just as in the structure overview, in the project structure overview (Transaction CN41N), which is available as of SAP ERP 6.0, you can simultaneously evaluate data for project definitions, WBS elements, assigned networks and orders, and different sales documents. Although the interface of the structure overview is based on a "classic" display, the SAP List Viewer (ALV) interface is used to display objects and data in the project structure overview (see Figure 6.5).

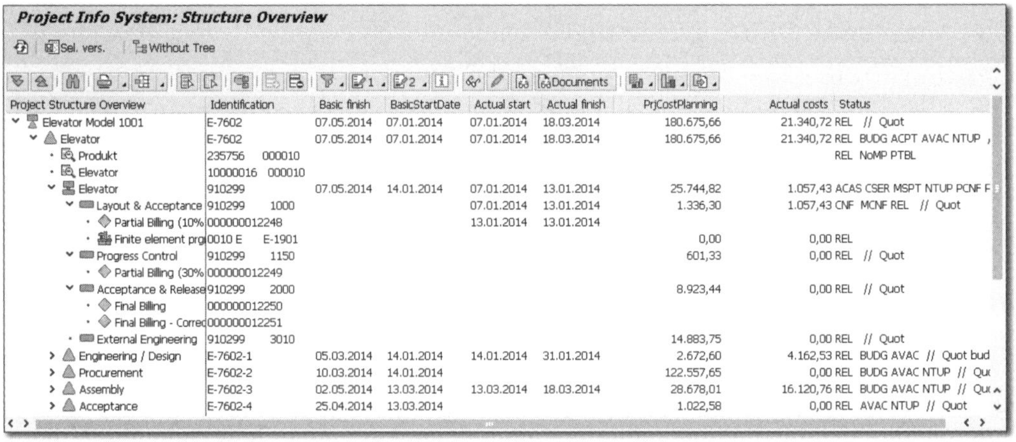

Figure 6.5 Evaluating a Project in the Project Structure Overview

The advantage of the interface of the project structure overview is that you can make changes to the selection of columns and their sequence and width easily and save these changes as *layouts*. You can save as many layouts as you wish and later select which layout you want to use to display the data. When you save a layout and set the USER-SPECIFIC indicator for this layout, only you can select or change this layout; otherwise, all users would be able to use your layout. If you identify a layout as an initial layout, then this layout is used instead of the standard layout the next time you call the report.

Layouts

The project structure overview, nevertheless, has nowhere near the range of functions that the structure overview has to offer. The following list identifies the functions of the project structure overview:

Functions of the project structure overview

▶ Display with or without hierarchy tree

▶ Print preview and print of current view or the complete hierarchy

▶ Filter function

▶ Display and change objects, display long texts

▶ Update data

▶ Graphical display of data as structure, hierarchy, or network graphics

▶ Export data—for example, as a file—to XLS in DOC, RTF, TXT, HTML, or HTM format

Note that you cannot evaluate project versions or customer-specific fields in the project structure overview.

Object Currency in the Structure and Project Structure Overview   **[+]**

By means of a customer extension, you can release the display of accounting data in the object currency in the structure and project structure overview as well as in the project planning table and the evaluation of the progress analysis. As a result, all relevant fields are available not only in the CO area currency but also in the respective object currency and can be added accordingly to the layout of reports or to field selection. The aggregation of data in the object currency only takes place as long as the object currency is uniform within the structure.

6.1.2 Individual Overviews

You can use individual overviews to evaluate data for individual documents or object types. As with the structure and project structure overviews, two different interfaces are also available for you to use with the individual overviews. You can use enhanced individual overviews that are based on a classic display of data or you can also use ALV-based individual overviews for your evaluation purposes.

Individual overviews in Project Information System: Structures The following individual overviews are all available in Project Information System: Structures (the transaction codes shown here refer to the enhanced and ALV-based overviews):

▸ Project Definitions (Transaction CN42/CN42N)

▸ WBS Elements (Transaction CN43/CN43N)

▸ Planned Orders (Transaction CN44/CN44N)

▸ Orders (Transaction CN45/CN45N)

▸ Networks (Transaction CN46/CN46N)

▸ Activities/Elements (Transaction CN47/CN47N)

▸ Confirmations (Transaction CN48/CN48N)

▸ Relationships (Transaction CN49/CN49N)

▸ Capacity Requirements (Transaction CN50/CN50N)

▸ Production Resources and Tools (Transaction CN51/CN51N)

▸ Material Components (Transaction CN52/CN52N)

▸ Milestones (Transaction CN53/CN53N)

Project Information System: Structures also contains some reports that are only available with the classic interface, such as the following:

▸ Sales Documents (Transaction CNS54)

▸ Sales Document Items (Transaction CNS55)

▸ Change Documents for Project/Network (Transaction CN60)

Contrary to the individual overviews, the partner overview (Transaction CNPAR), which you can use to analyze the partners (see Chapter 1, Section 1.2) for project definitions and WBS elements, is only available as an ALV-based report: compared to the individual overviews, the ALV-based partner overview has an extremely limited range of functions and only a few Customizing options.

Enhanced individual overviews

The way the data is displayed in the enhanced individual overviews is based on the PS info profile and the lower-level profiles. Figure 6.6 shows the evaluation of activities using the enhanced ACTIVITIES/ELEMENTS individual overview. The enhanced individual overviews essentially contain the same functions as in the structure overview (see Section 6.1.1). However, unlike the structure overview, no cost, revenue, budget, or commitment data is shown in the individual overviews; nevertheless, you can branch to the reports of Project Information System: Financials from an individual overview if required.

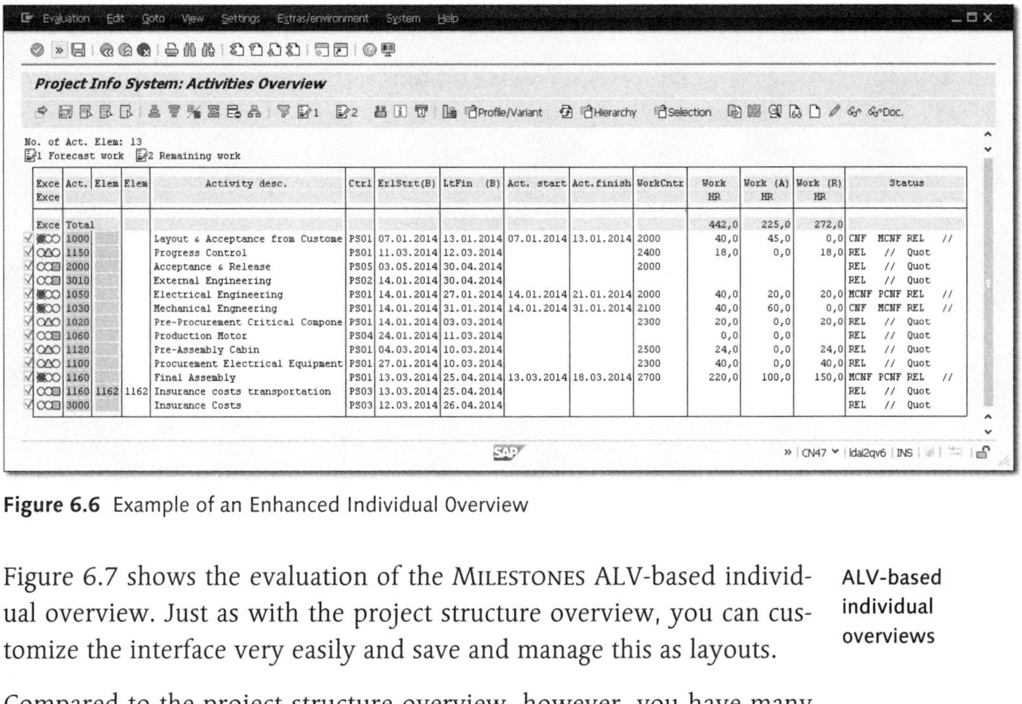

Exce Exce	Act.	Elem	Elem	Activity desc.	Ctrl	ErlStrt(B)	LtFin (B)	Act. start	Act.finish	WorkCntr	Work HR	Work (A) HR	Work (R) HR	Status
Exce	Total										442,0	225,0	272,0	
	1000			Layout & Acceptance from Custome	PS01	07.01.2014	13.01.2014	07.01.2014	13.01.2014	2000	40,0	45,0	0,0	CNF MCNF REL //
	1150			Progress Control	PS01	11.03.2014	12.03.2014			2400	18,0	0,0	18,0	REL // Quot
	2000			Acceptance & Release	PS05	03.05.2014	30.04.2014			2000				REL // Quot
	3010			External Engineering	PS02	14.01.2014	30.04.2014							REL // Quot
	1050			Electrical Engineering	PS01	14.01.2014	27.01.2014	14.01.2014	21.01.2014	2000	40,0	20,0	20,0	MCNF PCNF REL //
	1030			Mechanical Engneering	PS01	14.01.2014	31.01.2014	14.01.2014	31.01.2014	2100	40,0	60,0	0,0	CNF MCNF REL //
	1020			Pre-Procurement Critical Compone	PS01	14.01.2014	03.03.2014			2300	20,0	0,0	20,0	REL // Quot
	1060			Production Motor	PS04	24.01.2014	11.03.2014				0,0	0,0		REL // Quot
	1120			Pre-Assembly Cabin	PS01	04.03.2014	10.03.2014			2500	24,0	0,0	24,0	REL // Quot
	1100			Procurement Electrical Equipment	PS01	27.01.2014	10.03.2014			2300	40,0	0,0	40,0	REL // Quot
	1160			Final Assembly	PS01	13.03.2014	25.04.2014	13.03.2014	18.03.2014	2700	220,0	100,0	150,0	MCNF PCNF REL //
	1160	1162	1162	Insurance costs transportation	PS03	13.03.2014	25.04.2014							REL // Quot
	3000			Insurance Costs	PS03	12.03.2014	26.04.2014							REL // Quot

Figure 6.6 Example of an Enhanced Individual Overview

ALV-based individual overviews

Figure 6.7 shows the evaluation of the MILESTONES ALV-based individual overview. Just as with the project structure overview, you can customize the interface very easily and save and manage this as layouts.

Compared to the project structure overview, however, you have many more Customizing options available with individual overviews. Some of these options include sorting, direct display in Microsoft Excel or Lotus interfaces, different display options (column optimization, striped pattern, and so on), or the formation of totals, subtotals, mean values, or exceptionally high or low values. Similar to the enhanced individual overviews, you can also use filters and exceptions to export data in different file formats, display or change objects, and update the displayed data.

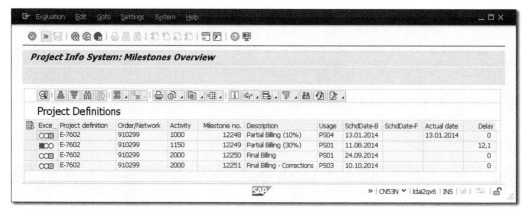

Figure 6.7 Example of an ALV-based Individual Overview

However, ALV-based individual overviews don't offer all of the functions available in enhanced individual overviews. For example, you cannot send the data of these individual overviews to other users by SAP mail; you cannot create any new objects; and from Project Information System: Financials, you can only assign hierarchy reports (drill-down reports), not cost element reports, to the individual overviews. In addition, some settings are deleted when you update the data. The SAP Library and SAP Note 353255 contain detailed information about the functions and restrictions of ALV-based individual overviews.

[◉] | **Project Information System: Structures**

The structure or project structure overview in Project Information System: Structures provides you with a hierarchical overall overview both of the logistical and the financials data of your projects and assigned objects. Individual overviews are used to provide table evaluations of individual object types focusing on master data, status, or logistical information. You can adapt the reports in Project Information System: Structures dynamically and utilize various functions for detailed analysis or for processing objects.

6.2 Project Information System: Financials

You can use reports of Project Information System: Financials to evaluate planned and actual costs, commitments, budget values, and payments. The reports are differentiated by hierarchy, cost element, and line item reports. These three report types each differ in the functions available for displaying and evaluating data, in the data that can be evaluated, and also, in particular, in the level of detail that you can use for your evaluations. The different report types are explained in the following sections.

The common factor for all of the reports of Project Information System: Financials is that (as with the structure reports) you must define the amount of data to be read from the database. You do this in the initial screen using the selection screen, dynamic selection, status selection profiles, and particularly the database profile (see Section 6.1). Depending on the report, however, you can also specify other selection criteria, such as fiscal years, periods, CO versions or cost element intervals, or groups in the initial screen of reports of Project Information System: Financials. You can save selections that are more complex in the form of selection variants that you can use when you call reports at a later stage. When you select large sets of data, you can also execute the reports in the background.

Data selection

6.2.1 Hierarchy Reports

Hierarchy reports are based on drill-down reporting functions in the SAP system and can therefore also be described as *drill-down reports*. The RPSCO project information database, in which you save all project-related CO and payment data summarized as *value categories*, forms the basis for evaluations using hierarchy reports. You must implement some settings in the SAP system before you use hierarchy reports for the first time in SAP Project System.

Prerequisites for Using Hierarchy Reports

Value categories are groupings of cost elements or commitment items (see Section 6.2.4). Value categories are not only required for evaluations

Value categories

461

using hierarchy reports but are also needed for calculating interest on projects (see Chapter 5, Section 5.5). You need to define suitable value categories and assign these categories to all of the relevant cost elements and commitment items even before you perform postings on projects.

You can use Transaction OPI1 to define value categories. In addition to a key and short text, you specify the debit type for each value category—for example, costs and outgoing payments or revenues and incoming payments. You can then use Transactions OPI2 and OPI4 to assign cost element intervals or groups or commitment item intervals to the value categories. You can run a consistency check on your assignments using Transaction CJVC.

Quantity information You can also use value categories to update quantity information in the RPSQT project information database. You can then use this quantity information for evaluations in progress reports of SAP Project Systems, for example (see Chapter 4, Section 4.7.2). To enable quantities to be updated in this database, in addition to the debit type you must also have assigned a unit of measure to the relevant value categories.

Automatic value category Instead of creating value categories manually and assigning all relevant cost elements and commitment items in advance, you can set the AUTOMATIC VALUE CATEGORIES indicator in the update control of the RPSCO project information database. This indicator causes a separate value category with the same name to be created automatically for each newly posted cost element or commitment item; however, you should note that creating value categories automatically can negatively affect performance when you post data (due to the high number of value categories that may be created) and evaluate data.

[+] **Defining Value Categories**

For performance reasons, we recommend that you combine several cost elements or commitment items in value categories; however in this case, you cannot evaluate data at the level of individual cost elements or commitment items using hierarchy reports. If you subsequently change the assignments for value categories, then you must then reconstruct the project information database using Transaction CJEN.

SAP currently delivers different standard hierarchy reports for evaluating costs, budgets, revenues, project results, and forecast data or payments that you can import from client 000 using Customizing Transaction CJEQ if necessary. You can also define your own hierarchy reports depending on your requirements. A customer enhancement is also available for making your own adjustments. Before we explain the different functions that you can use within hierarchy reports for evaluating project data, we will address the technical principles of hierarchy reports first for clarification purposes.

Principles of Hierarchy Reports

You can use two different interfaces (output types) to evaluate data using hierarchy reports: a *graphical report output* and the display as a *classic drill-down report*. Depending on the report definition, the output type is fixed or can be selected manually in the initial screen of the report. You usually use classic drill-down reports if you require high performance for evaluating large datasets. You use the graphical report output especially if you want to display different *list types* simultaneously or if you want to use your own HTML templates for the report header.

Output types

Figure 6.8 shows the graphical report output of the standard PLAN/ACT/ COMMIT/REM.PLAN/ASSIGNED report. The data displayed in a hierarchy report is based on *characteristics* and *key figures*. Characteristics are OBJECT, PERIOD and FISCAL YEAR, VALUE CATEGORY, CURRENCY, RESULTS ANALYSIS CATEGORY (see Chapter 5, Section 5.6), and BUSINESS TRANSACTION. The data of the RPSCO project information database can differ according to the different values of these characteristics. The relevant combinations of characteristic values in the dataset also have specific values. These data values (that is, the planned, budget, commitment, costs, revenue, and financial values and possibly the values calculated from these values in a report using formulas) are called key figures.

Characteristics and key figures

Residual Order Plan Key Figure	[+]

The residual order plan is calculated at the WBS element level when you call the report and results from the total of the apportioned planned values of assigned orders or networks minus their actual and commitment values (however, this value that is calculated for each order is only factored in the total if the value is positive).

Execute Drilldown Report Plan/Actual/Commitment/Rem.Plan/Assigned

Selection date

Plan/Actual/Commitment/Rem.Plan/Assigned   Current data (27.08.2014 10:26:07)

Navigation	Object		Overall CO--...	Actual--...	Commitment-...	RemOrdPlan--...	Assigned--...	Available--...	..
• 🔲 Object	⌄ PRJ E-7602	Elevator Model 1001	180.676	21.341	39.566	55.780	116.687	63.989	
• Val.category	⌄ WBS E-7602	Elevator	180.676	21.341	39.566	55.780	116.687	63.989	
• Period/year	• NWA 910299 2000	Acceptance & Release	8.923	0	6.295	0	6.295	2.628	
• Business Trans.	• NWA 910299 3010	External Engineering	14.884	0	21.000	0	21.000	6.116-	
• Object Currency	⌄ WBS E-7602-1	Engineering / Design	2.673	4.163	0	866	5.029	2.356-	
	> WBS E-7602-1-1	Electrical Engineeri	1.336	470	0	866	1.336	0	
	> WBS E-7602-1-2	Mechanical Engineerin	1.336	3.693	0	0	3.693	2.356-	
	> WBS E-7602-2	Procurement	122.558	0	511	40.240	40.751	81.807	
	> WBS E-7602-3	Assembly	28.678	16.121	11.760	11.023	38.904	10.226-	
	> WBS E-7602-4	Acceptance	1.023	0	0	1.023	1.023	0	
	• Result		180.676	21.341	39.566	55.780	116.687	63.989	

Figure 6.8 Example of the Graphical Report Output of a Hierarchy Report

Form
A *form* and an assigned *report definition* control how the data (that is, characteristics and key figures) is displayed in a hierarchy report. You cannot use ad hoc reports (that is, reports without a form) in SAP Project System. You use a form for the Two Axes (Matrix) form type to control the basic structure of rows and columns in a report. You differentiate between displays in the form of a *detail list* and a *drill-down list* (list types).

Detail and drill-down list
Figure 6.9 shows an example of how a detail list of the 12KST1C standard form is defined. In the detail list of this example, different values of the Fiscal Year characteristic are used as rows and key figures are displayed as columns. A (global) variable is used to define the rows here. Fixed values and values calculated based on formulas are used as key figures. For more details about controlling the values displayed in columns, see Section 6.2.2.

Figure 6.10 shows an example of a drill-down list for the 12KSTC1 form. This drill-down list displays characteristics and their values flexibly as rows, whereas the columns are formed by key figures for different characteristic values of the Fiscal Year characteristic. The fiscal year here is again defined by a variable.

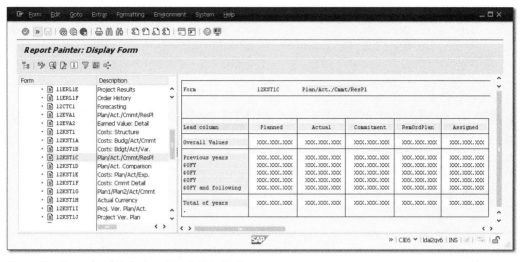

Figure 6.9 Example of Defining a Detail List of a Form

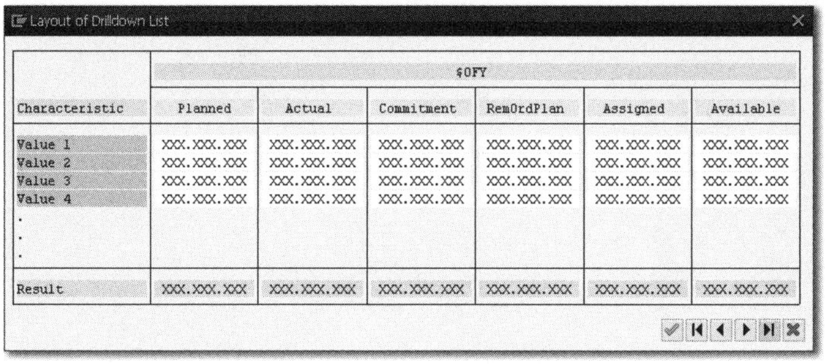

Figure 6.10 Example of Defining a Drill-Down List

| **Evaluating Versions in Hierarchy Reports** | **[+]** |

Note that you can only evaluate data from project or simulation versions in a hierarchy report if you selected the VERSION KEY characteristic in the general selections of the corresponding form.

A form only defines the general structure of the detail and drill-down lists of a hierarchy report; however, the report definition that was created with reference to the form determines its contents. For this reason, the report definition specifies which characteristics can be used for the evaluation (the OBJECT characteristic is always included in this case). You

Report definition

465

can store fixed values in the report definition or make entries in the initial screen of the report for local variables that are used in the form. Settings for the output type and other different display options are also specified in the report definition. Figure 6.11 shows the report definition for the 12KST1C form.

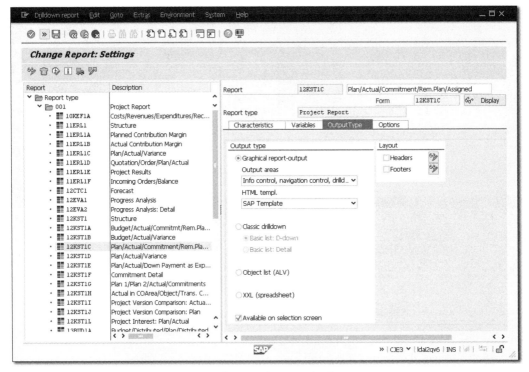

Figure 6.11 Report Definition of a Hierarchy Report

Report-report interfaces Hierarchy reports also allow you to branch to other hierarchy, cost element, or line item reports of SAP Project System for more detailed evaluations. The corresponding report-report interfaces must be set up for this under the REPORT ASSIGNMENT menu path in Customizing of SAP Project System. You can import report-report interfaces for the standard reports from client 000 or define your own report assignments. Note that you can only branch to reports of the same level of detail or to more detailed reports. For example, you cannot branch to a hierarchy report from a line item report.

Creating Your Own Hierarchy Reports

[+]

If you want to create your own hierarchy report, you must first create a suitable form and then a report definition for this form. In this case, we recommend that you use the forms and report definitions delivered as templates in the standard system. If required, you can also set up your own suitable report–report interfaces.

You can use Transactions CJE4, CJE5, and CJE6 to create, change, and display forms. You can edit forms using *Report Painter* functions (see also Section 6.2.2). You can use Transactions CJE1, CJE2, and CJE3 to create, edit, or display report definitions. In Transaction CJE0, you can execute user-defined hierarchy reports directly. You can also integrate your reports into the SAP menu or user menus.

Transactions

Evaluations Using Hierarchy Reports

Figure 6.8 (shown previously) shows the drill-down list of a hierarchy report in which different cost data for the different project objects is displayed in aggregated format. The characteristics assigned to the report definition are displayed in the navigation area. Instead of evaluating the key figures for the OBJECT characteristic, you can also select another characteristic for a drill-down from the navigation area. For example, you can display the distribution of the values to the different value categories or for the period or fiscal year.

When you switch a drill-down, you can either drill-down through all of the values displayed in the report to a different characteristic or you can select a specific characteristic value and only do a drill-down switch (DRILLDOWN) for the values of this characteristic value. We can illustrate this using the example shown in Figure 6.8. Very high (aggregated) planned costs are shown at the level of the PROCUREMENT WBS element. You now only want to evaluate the values of this WBS element further and therefore drill down to the PERIOD/YEAR characteristic for the PROCUREMENT WBS element. You notice that the highest planned costs of the WBS element are shown for period 9. To determine the value categories that the planned costs of the PROCUREMENT WBS element are distributed to in period 9, you drill-down to the VAL.CATEGORY for this period. Figure 6.12 shows the results of this double drill-down.

Drill-down

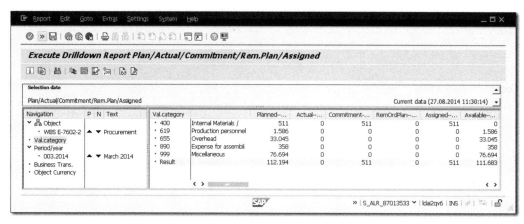

Figure 6.12 Example of a Drill-Down in a Hierarchy Report

Drill-down report   In a classic drill-down report, you can toggle between the drill-down lists and the detail list and call graphics of selected key figures (see Figure 6.13). In the graphical report output, you can simultaneously display drill-down and detail lists and, if required, a graphic display of key figures depending on the settings of the report definition.

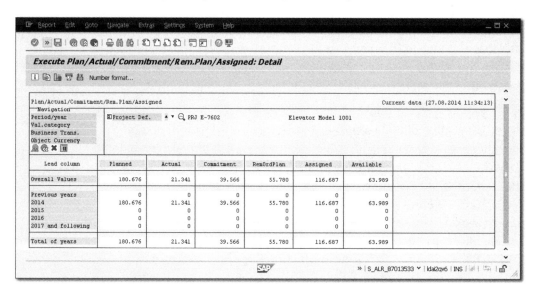

Figure 6.13 Detail View of a Hierarchy Report in the Classical Display

Other functions available in hierarchy reports include the following:

▸ Export and print out data (you can only print report data from the graphical report output on a limited basis, and you do this in the classical display of data, for example)

▸ Convert values into other currencies

▸ Highlight (color) data if values exceed or fall short of threshold values (exceptions)

▸ Sort values in the form of ranking lists and define conditions for displaying values

▸ Maintain and display comments for the report

▸ Branch to the master data display of objects and call other reports

Depending on the output type, hierarchy reports also contain other functions. For example, you can send the data of a classic drill-down report directly to other users via SAP mail. The graphical report output allows you to customize the column display and screen layout much more flexibly for this purpose.

Note that you cannot update data with hierarchy reports. This means that when you make changes to the data after you call a report you must exit the report and call it again to evaluate the current data. You can also save the data of the report before you exit it. The next time you call the report, you can then choose between a new selection of the current data and an evaluation of the report data you saved.

Unlike the reports of Project Information System: Structures, for example, you can only save one dataset in each case for the report data of hierarchy reports. If you save the data again, then the previously saved report data is overwritten. For more information about hierarchy reports, see SAP Note 668240.

6.2.2 Cost Element Report

You can use cost element reports of SAP Project System to evaluate costs, commitments, and revenues of projects and assigned networks or orders. You define cost element reports in the Report Painter; therefore, they are also referred to as *Report Painter* reports. Figure 6.14 shows an example of the evaluation of project data using the standard ACT/COM/ TOTAL/PLAN report in CO area currency.

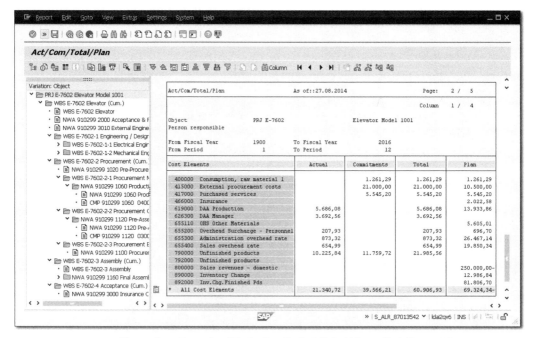

Figure 6.14 Example of Evaluating Project Data Using a Cost Element Report

Prerequisites and Principles of Cost Element Reports

Standard reports Different cost element reports are delivered in the standard system. If required, you can import these reports from client 000 using Customizing Transaction OKSR and then generate them in Transaction OKS7. If, for the sake of clarification, in addition to evaluating data at the level of individual cost elements, you want to evaluate subtotals for individual intervals of cost elements, then you have to create suitable cost element groups in Transaction KAH1. You can arrange cost element groups hierarchically here in the form of nodes, whereby a two-tier structuring of cost element groups will typically suffice. You can then select the cost element group to be evaluated from the initial screen of a cost element report. The report now displays a separate row for each cost element and a node of the cost element group, for which the total of the cost elements contained there is displayed for this node.

Selecting Cost Elements	[+]
Note that the report only displays values for the cost elements that you specified in the initial screen as a cost element group or cost element interval, regardless of whether postings were made for other cost elements. If you leave the selection of the cost element group or cost element interval blank, then all posted cost elements are displayed.	

Evaluations using cost element reports in SAP Project System are based on a logical combination of several database tables (COSP, COSS, COEP, and so on). The tables are combined in SAP Project System by the logical CCSS reporting table stored in Table T804E. You can view the list of combined database tables using the Data Browser (Transaction SE16) by first selecting the T804E table and then the CCSS reporting table. However, the cost element reports use only a subset of, rather than all, characteristics, key figures, and combinations of characteristics and key figures (*basic key figures* or predefined columns) of this CCSS reporting table. This subset is known as the *library*. All Report Painter reports must be assigned to a library and can only use the selected subset on characteristics, key figures, and basic key figures of the assigned library. The cost element reports of SAP Project System are assigned to the 6P3 library by default.

Libraries

You may want to toggle between different cost element reports while evaluating project data. In this case, you can use report groups to avoid having to select data from the database each time. Report groups are collections of reports from one library that access the same data but display it in different ways.

Report groups

[+] **Assigning Cost Element Report to Libraries and Report Groups**

Each cost element report must be assigned to a library and a report group. A report group can also contain several reports; however, these report groups must all use the same library.

If you want to evaluate the data using a cost element report, then you execute the corresponding report group. This simultaneously selects the data from the database for all reports. If several reports are assigned to the report group, you can toggle between the different reports without having to reselect the data each time. The standard Report Painter reports of SAP Project System are assigned to report groups with IDs that begin with 6PP. Cost element reports also exist in SAP Project System for report groups, for example, beginning with 6P0. These are reports that you can only edit with the Report Writer.

Report Painter   You can define reports using the Report Painter. Figure 6.15 shows the definition of a report using an example of the standard ACT/COM/TOTAL/PLAN cost element report in CO area currency. The COST ELEMENT characteristic is used as rows of the report. The columns in this example are formed by basic key figures and key figures calculated using formulas. The display of rows and columns and other display options are controlled by the layout of a report or report section.

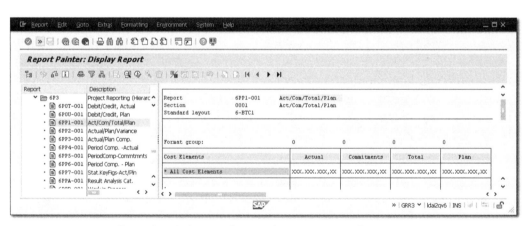

Figure 6.15 Definition of a Cost Element Report in the Report Painter

When you define columns consisting of key figures with characteristics, the specified values of these characteristics determine which values of the key figures you actually want to be selected for the display (see Figure 6.16). For example, you can use the values of the VALUE TYPE characteristic to decide whether planned or actual costs, commitments, or statistical actual costs are to be displayed in a column.

Key figures with characteristics

With the VERSION characteristic, you can determine the CO version from which the data is to be selected and so on. Predefined key figures that contain useful combinations from a basic key figure and one or several characteristics are also delivered in the standard system.

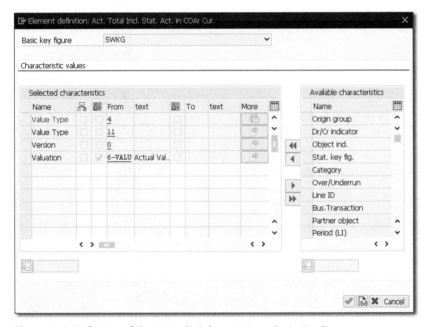

Figure 6.16 Definition of the "Actual" Column Using a Basic Key Figure

In addition to defining rows and columns, the general selections of a report define the characteristics to be used for the selection of data for the report. Figure 6.17 shows an example of general selections.

General selections

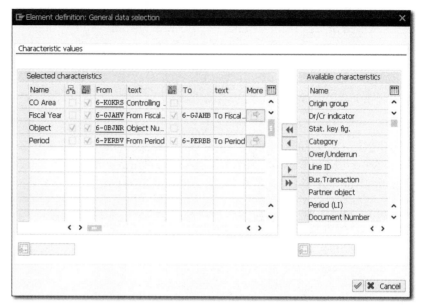

Figure 6.17 Example of Defining General Selections

Variations　You can also use the characteristics of general selections for variations. *Variation* means that you can use the different characteristic values for navigation purposes within the report as part of an evaluation. Depending on which characteristic value or combination of characteristic values you select in the report, only data for these values is displayed.

[+]　**Defining Cost Element Reports**

When you create your own cost element report, you first need to specify the library. You then define the structure of the rows and columns and specify the general selections and, if necessary, any variations. Finally, you must assign the report to a report group. If required, you can also define report-report interfaces for cost element reports.

You can use the default reports in the standard system as templates.

Transactions　You can use Report Painter Transactions GRR1, GRR2, and GRR3 to create, change, and display cost element reports. You can also create cost element reports using the Report Writer via Transaction GR31. In addition, you can use Transaction GR51 to create new report groups with reference to a library. In Transaction GR55, you can execute user-defined report groups directly. You can also integrate your reports into the SAP menu or user menus.

Evaluations Using Cost Element Reports

Figure 6.14 shows the evaluation of project data using the ACT/COM/TOTAL/PLAN report in CO area currency. The variation in the left area, for example, allows you to navigate between the different project objects. Two entries are contained in the variation for some WBS elements. Depending on which entry you select, the system either displays the values that were posted directly on the relevant WBS element or the aggregated values of all lower-level objects and of the WBS element itself. The different values are displayed as totals records for the relevant cost elements. If you used cost element groups for the selection, then subtotals would also be displayed.

The following functions are also available in cost element reports: Functions

▸ Print, export, and send data

▸ Convert values into other currencies

▸ Use threshold values as filters

▸ Sort values

▸ Graphical display of data

▸ Display data using Microsoft Excel or Lotus interfaces

▸ Call other reports

▸ Update data using menu options

Expert Mode	[+]
Note that you can only use some of the preceding functions (in particular, the updating of report data) if you have set the EXPERT MODE indicator in the report options.	

When you exit a cost element report, you can also save the report data as   Extracts
an extract; you can save any number of extracts for a selection. The next time you call the report, you can then decide in the initial screen using

the DATA SOURCE function whether the data is to be selected from the database again or whether you want to use an extract that already exists for your evaluation. You can delete extracts manually or automatically from the system by specifying an expiry date. For more information about cost element reports, see SAP Note 668513.

6.2.3 Line Item Reports

Whereas hierarchy reports only allow you to evaluate project data at the level of value categories and cost element reports only show totals records for cost elements, you can use line item reports to evaluate each business transaction that led to a relevant posting.

Prerequisite for Evaluating Data Using Line Item Reports

Prerequisites To select and evaluate data in line item reports, corresponding line items must first exist. The following prerequisites must be met for writing line items:

- **Plan**
  Plan line items are only supported for certain planning functions (see Chapter 2, Section 2.4). The object status must also explicitly allow plan line items to be written, or integrated planning must be activated.

- **Budget**
  Each budget change is documented by a line item.

- **Commitment**
  If commitment management is activated (see Chapter 4, Section 4.2.1), then all commitments are posted as line items.

- **Actual**
  A line item is written for each actual posting. Line items are also created for results analysis transactions and settlement transactions.

- **Payments**
  Payments line items for payments are only written in SAP Project System for an activated PS Cash Management system (see Section 6.2.4). To write plan line items for the payments, you must also assign the business Transaction FIPA to a number range.

You use the ALV interface for line item reports. A display variant (layout), which you can select from the initial screen of a line item report, defines the way data is displayed. In addition to the display variants delivered by default, you can also define your own layouts in the reports.

Display variants (layouts)

Evaluations Using Line Item Reports

Some of the line item reports available in the standard system include the following:

Standard line item reports

- ▶ Planned Costs/Revenues (Transaction CJI4)
- ▶ Hierarchical Costs/Revenue Planning (Transaction CJI9)
- ▶ Budget (Transaction CJI8)
- ▶ Commitment (Transaction CJI5)
- ▶ Actual Costs/Revenues (Transaction CJI3)
- ▶ Results Analysis (Transaction CJIF)
- ▶ Line Item Settlement (Transaction CJID)
- ▶ Planned Payments (Transaction CJIB)
- ▶ Actual Payments/Payment Commitment (Transaction CJIA)

Figure 6.18 shows the evaluation of line items of a project using the Actual Costs/Revenues report. The line items are displayed as a list that you can flexibly customize using ALV functions (column selection, sorting, filtering, totals and subtotals, exceptionally high or low values, display in Microsoft Excel, and so on). The interface also enables you to print, send, or export the report data by default.

As of EHP 6, you can simultaneously analyze archived and non-archived line items for projects in the Actual Costs/Revenues line item report. This is usually required if you have long-running projects for which you archive line items of past periods before project closure and you still want to access all line items jointly.

The number of line items can become very large in the course of the project and thus impact, for example, the performance of the Actual Costs/Revenues Report report. SAP Note 1687210 and the information contained therein provides a solution that enables you to save the planned and actual line items in an SAP HANA database in parallel and to load and analyze them from this performance-optimized, in-memory database via the new `CJI3N` and `CJI4N` reports (sidecar approach). In contrast to the original reports, these new reports also provide a structure tree to navigate in the selected project structures. SAP Note 1698066 provides additional information on the new reports. With the SAP HANA version of SAP ERP EHP 6, these optimized transactions are available in the SAP system by default. In this case, of course, replicating line items as in a sidecar approach is not necessary.

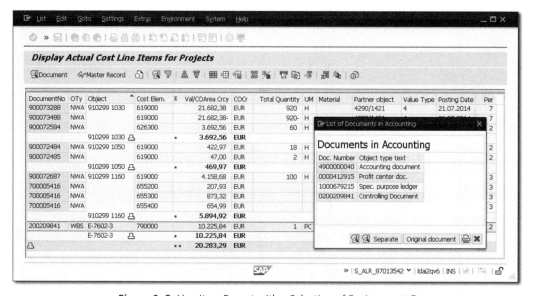

Figure 6.18 Line Item Report with a Selection of Environment Documents

Environment documents A very useful function of line item reports is the ability to branch to the line item environment. You can use this function to branch to the master data of objects and partner object, or to display the source document of a line item—for example, the confirmation that led to costs on an activity. In particular, you can also use the menu options to evaluate all of the cost accounting documents that were created for the relevant business transaction. Depending on the business transaction, these can be cost accounting, Profit Center, or FI documents (see Figure 6.18).

Project Information System: Financials

You can use the reports from Project Information System: Financials to evaluate all project-related accounting data. Depending on the type of reports used, you can use different interfaces, functions, and levels of detail for the evaluation.

The report-report interfaces allow you to branch from less detailed reports to even more specific report types. For example, you can begin the evaluation of project data by using a hierarchy report, evaluate selected data further in a cost element report, branch to a line item report for certain data, and, if necessary, display all relevant environment documents from there.

6.2.4 PS Cash Management

In addition to evaluating project-related data in terms of costs and revenues, the planning and evaluation of payment flows or receipts and expenditures is also germane to very capital-intensive projects to achieve positive cash flow and therefore potential profits from interest. To do this, you can use *PS Cash Management* in SAP Project System. It provides functions you can use both to plan incoming and outgoing payments for your projects and also to evaluate project-related payments and payment obligations. You can update relevant payment data from FI (for example, incoming and outgoing payments, down payments, and down payment requests), from Purchasing (commitments due to purchase requisitions or purchase orders), and from Sales (data from customer quotations, sales orders, billing requests, or billing documents) for projects in PS Cash Management.

Specifics of PS Cash Management

Unlike in Treasury or in Liquidity Planner, for example, in which payments are classified according to vendor and customer groups and payment flows are considered for the entire company, in PS Cash Management payment data is always planned and evaluated on a project-related basis. Therefore, *PS Cash Management* is also known as Project Cash Management. For further information about PS Cash Management, see SAP Note 417511.

Prerequisites for Using PS Cash Management

FM areas

To use PS Cash Management, you must make certain settings in the IMG of the SAP system. From a funds perspective, you first require Financial Management (FM) areas as organizational units for structuring your company. For PS Cash Management, you must then assign company codes to the FM areas. You can assign several company codes to an FM area. Through this assignment, the FM areas are subsequently derived from the relevant company codes of the business transactions. You assign the company codes and define FM areas in general Customizing of the company structure.

Commitment items

You plan and update payment-relevant data in PS Cash Management based on commitment items and their link to G/L accounts. You therefore use commitment items to structure revenues and expenditures. Figure 6.19 shows the editing area of a commitment item in Customizing Transaction FMCIA. The attributes of a commitment item are controlled by the two FINANCIAL TRANS. and COMMITMENT ITEM CAT. fields (attributes). The financial transaction represents business transactions and controls the updating of corresponding payment data.

Figure 6.19 Example of Defining a Commitment Item Manually

[+]

Financial Transaction for PS Cash Management

Note that you can only update data from business transactions for FINANCIAL TRANS. 30 (POST REVENUE, EXPENDITURE, ASSET, INVENTORY STOCK, …) in PS Cash Management.

You can use commitment item categories to differentiate data according to stock, revenues, or expenditures, for example. To update data with reference to commitment items, you must assign the commitment items to one or several relevant G/L accounts.

You can create commitment items manually and assign them to G/L accounts (Transactions FMCIA and FIPOS). You can also create commitment items and assignments automatically (Transaction FIPOS; see Figure 6.20).

Creating commitment items automatically

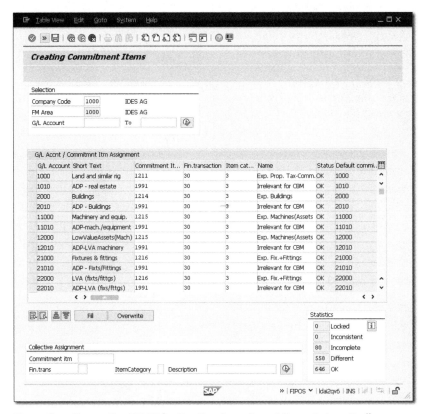

Figure 6.20 Transaction FIPOS for Creating Commitment Items Automatically

481

In this case, the system creates default values for commitment items and their attributes using data from G/L accounts. For example, the name of a commitment item is copied from the name of the G/L account, the attributes of the commitment item are derived from the type of G/L account, and the commitment item is assigned to the G/L account.

Checking assignments

Problems that occur when data is being derived or variances in the default values for commitment items that already exist are highlighted as statuses. Before you copy the default values, you can still change the commitment items manually if necessary. You can use Transaction FM3N to check assignments of commitment items to G/L accounts once again. Here, you can display a list of all commitment items without an assignment or, alternatively, display G/L accounts without a commitment item.

[+]

> **Creating Commitment Items**
>
> If you assigned only one company code to an FM area, then we generally recommend that you create and assign commitment items automatically. Note that you assign a commitment item to all relevant G/L accounts when you set up PS Cash Management. You should also note that other SAP components (for example, Treasury or Funds Management) may also use the same commitment items.

To use hierarchy reports to evaluate payment data, you must assign the commitment items to value categories (see Section 6.2.1). To do this, you can use Transaction OPI4. To update payment data at a later stage, you must assign the KAFM (PAYMENT DATA) activity to a number range. To ensure that line items are written within payment scheduling, you must also have assigned the FIPA activity (PAYMENT SCHEDULING) to a number range. You can make these assignments using Customizing Transaction KANK.

Activating PS Cash Management

After you have implemented all required settings, you must activate PS Cash Management. In Transaction OPI6 in Customizing, you can perform this activation separately for each company code assigned to an FM area.

> **Effects When Activating PS Cash Management** **[!]**
>
> After you activate PS Cash Management for a company code, the system updates all project-related and payment-relevant data from business transactions of this company code into PS Cash Management. Additional documents are created in the SAP system, which may affect the performance of the system.

Payment Scheduling

You can use different options to plan the payment flows of your projects. For example, similar to the detailed planning of costs and revenues (see Chapter 2, Section 2.4.3), you can schedule incoming and outgoing payments manually for commitment items at the level of WBS elements. You can use standard layouts to schedule the payments manually (you may have to import these layouts from client 000 first) or create your own layouts and planner profiles in Customizing. Manual payment scheduling is based on periods, not days.

Manual payment scheduling

Planned payments can also be derived from activity data and invoicing plans, billing plans on WBS elements, or customer quotations or sales orders assigned to a project. These forms of payment scheduling are based on days, for which corresponding terms of payment may also be taken into account. Payment data is only updated for networks if you use activity-assigned networks and asynchronous network costing (Transaction CJ9K) for determining planning data. Chapter 2, Section 2.4.6 and Section 2.5.3 provide more details about costing networks, using invoicing and billing plans, and updating planning data from sales documents.

Automatic payment scheduling

Updating Commitment and Actual Payment Data

Within the implementation phase of projects, if PS Cash Management is activated, then payments and payment obligations from Purchasing and FI are automatically updated into PS Cash Management, provided the corresponding business transactions refer to commitment items for financial Transaction 30 and there is an account assignment to WBS elements, activities, or networks and assigned orders. The following credit and debit business transactions are considered:

Business transactions

- Purchase requisitions and purchase orders
- Down payment requests, down payments, and down payment settlements
- Invoice receipts and incoming payments

The data of the different business transactions is updated among different value types. If PS Cash Management is not activated, then down payments can be evaluated in reports using value type 12. If PS Cash Management is activated, then value type 61 is used. Payment obligations are successively reduced by the corresponding payments. In SAP Project System, you can also perform payment transfers in Transaction FMWA to correct erroneous account assignments.

Note the following special features when updating payment data. As long as you have not transferred any payments (Transaction CJFN), data of settled invoices and partial payments are displayed under value type 54 (INVOICES) but not under value type 57 (PAYMENTS). Cash discount rates of actual payments are only considered after you execute the SAPF181 report in PS Cash Management.

If you subsequently activate PS Cash Management, then you may have to transfer the data from Purchasing first and then the data from FI into PS Cash Management. To do this, you can use Transactions OPH4, OPH5, and OPH6. To display the data correctly, you should then reconstruct the project information database using Transaction CJEN.

Evaluations of Payment Data

Hierarchy reports and line item reports are available by default in SAP Project System for evaluating project-related payment data. Although the line item reports allow you to evaluate the data based on precise days, the evaluation in the hierarchy reports only takes place based on periods. However, you can also go from a hierarchy report to a line item report for selected data and display all relevant environment documents there, if required.

Details about hierarchy and line item reports were already discussed in Section 6.2.1 and Section 6.2.3. Figure 6.21 shows an example of an

evaluation of payment data for a project using the RECEIPTS/EXPENDI-
TURES FOR ALL FISCAL YEARS hierarchy report.

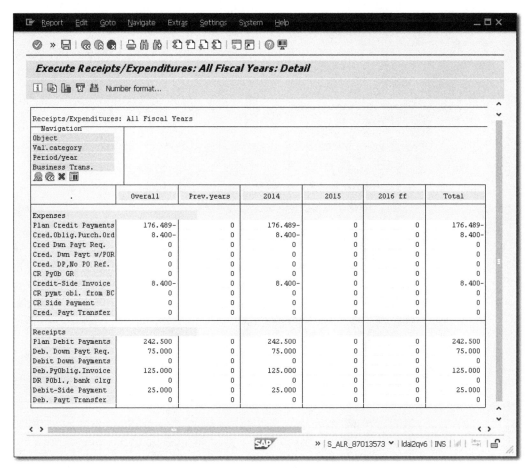

Figure 6.21 Example of Evaluating Revenues and Expenditures Using the Classic
Display of a Hierarchy Report

6.3   Logistical Reports

In Chapter 4, Section 4.5.3 we introduced ProMan, a tool that enables
almost all logistical information for project-related procurements to be
evaluated within a transaction. Project Information System: Structures

(described in Section 6.1) also contains different reports for evaluating logistical data, such as deadline and quantity information or statuses. You can also use progress tracking (see Chapter 4, Section 4.7.3) for evaluating dates of material components.

In this section, we will address all additional reports from Reporting of SAP Project System that you can use to evaluate logistical data of purchasing processes and material procurements. Capacity reports, in particular, are also covered, which you can use to compare the available capacities and capacity requirements of work centers and individual capacities and consequently to evaluate the capacity load utilization.

6.3.1 Purchase Requisitions and Purchase Orders for the Project

Purchasing documents

Transactions ME5J (Purchase Requisitions for Project) and ME2J (Purchase Orders for Project) are specifically available in Reporting of SAP Project System for evaluating project-related Purchasing documents. In the initial screen of these transactions, you first need to determine the selection of the purchase requisitions or purchase orders to be evaluated. You do this by selecting the project objects on which the documents must be assigned, perhaps by a dynamic selection and status selection profiles. You can also use information from Purchasing documents as additional selection criteria. You can save selections that are more complex as variants.

After you execute the report, data from the selected purchase requisitions or purchase orders is displayed in a list that you can also print out if required. Figure 6.22 shows an example of a list of purchase requisitions in Transaction ME5J.

Functions of ME5J report

For more information, you can branch to the display of the relevant Purchasing documents. The following functions are also available in the ME5J report (PURCHASE REQUISITIONS FOR PROJECT):

▸ Branch to the display of material master data, reports for material stock, outline agreements, info records, or vendor evaluations

▸ Designate purchase requisitions for processing inquiries

▶ Assign suppliers manually or automatically

▶ Provide an overview of existing assignments and create purchase orders

▶ Branch to changes in purchase requisitions and the assigned purchase orders

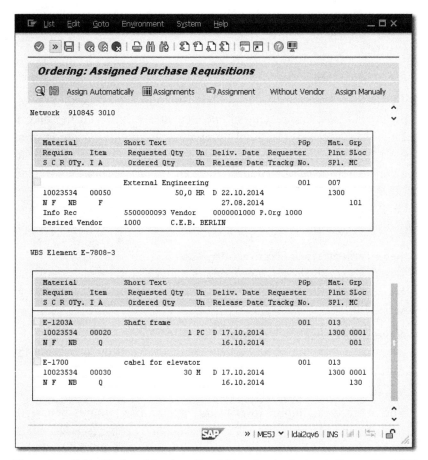

Figure 6.22 Table Display of Purchase Requisitions for the Project in Transaction ME5J

When you use the ME2J report for evaluating purchase orders for your projects, you can use the following functions:

Functions of ME2J report

▸ Branch to purchase order history and changes in purchase orders

▸ Display or maintain schedule lines

▸ Display services in service items

Reporting of SAP Project System also contains Transactions ME5K (Purchase Requisitions for Account Assignment), ME2K (Purchase Orders for Account Assignment), and ME3K (Outline Agreements), which you can use for general evaluations of Purchasing documents.

6.3.2 Material Reports

Overviews Different overviews are already available in Project Information System: Structures for evaluating material-related data (see Section 6.1). You can use the CN52/CN52N (Material Components) individual overviews of Project Information System: Structures to evaluate data for material in networks or in assigned orders. You can use the CN44/CN44N and CN45/CN45N individual overviews to evaluate planned and production orders for projects. The following material reports are also available in SAP Project System:

▸ **Requirement/stock (Transaction MD04)**
This list displays the stock situation of material and requirements and planned activities in the different stock segments (see Chapter 2, Figure 2.47).

▸ **Valuated project stock (Transaction MBBS)**
You can use this report to evaluate material that is managed in valuated project or sales order stocks.

▸ **Missing parts (Transaction CO24)**
You can use this report to evaluate material components that were identified as missing parts within the availability check (see Chapter 2, Section 2.3.3).

▸ **Pegged requirement (Transaction MD09)**
You can use this report for multilevel production processes to determine the original pegged requirement for selected orders or purchase orders.

▶ **Reservations (Transaction MB25)**
You can use this report to display a list of the reservations for selection materials.

▶ **Order report (Transaction MD4C)**
You can use this report to monitor the possible multilevel production of material for projects.

6.3.3 Capacity Reports

You can evaluate planned, actual, and remaining capacity requirements of projects using the *capacity requirements* (CN50/CN50N) individual overviews of Project Information System: Structures (see Section 6.1.2); however, these reports only display the capacity requirements of selected objects. You cannot use these reports to compare capacity requirements with the available capacities.

Reports from the SAP application for capacity requirements planning are used in SAP Project System to evaluate the capacity load utilization of capacities required in projects. We differentiate between simple capacity evaluations and enhanced capacity evaluations for these reports.

Both report types are controlled using *overall profiles* that are defined in Customizing of capacity planning. These overall profiles are only combinations of lower-level profiles that determine the data selection, evaluation interface, and functions of the capacity reports. Different overall profiles are available for evaluation purposes in the standard system and assigned to transactions of the SAP menu. If required, you can make user-specific changes to the assignment of transaction codes for overall profiles using parameters.

Overall profiles

However, for the simple capacity evaluations, you can also select a different overall profile from the menu in the initial screen or specify the overall profile directly when you can call Transaction CM07. You cannot change the overall profile for enhanced capacity evaluations when you call a report. Nevertheless, you can directly select a standard or user-defined profile for the enhanced evaluation when you access Transaction CM25. Table 6.1 lists some transactions and overall profiles assigned by default and parameters that you can use to change this assignment in the user master data.

Transaction (Transaction Code)	Overall Profile	Parameter
Capacity Load (CM01)	SAPX911	CY1
Orders (CM02)	SAPX912	CY2
Pool (CM03)	SAPX913	CY3
Backlog (CM04)	SAPX914	CY4
Overload (CM05)	SAPX915	CY5
Work Center View (CM50)	SAPSFCG020	CY:
Individual Capacity View (CM51)	SAPSFCG022	CY~
Order View (CM52)	SAPSFCG021	CY_
WBS Element/Version (CM53)	SAPPS_G020	CY8
Work Center/Version (CM55)	SAPPS_G021	CY?
Version (CM54)	SAPPS_G022	CY9

Table 6.1 Parameters for Assigning Overall Profiles to Transaction Codes

Capacity Evaluations

Capacity load utilization

In the initial screen of capacity evaluations, you select the work centers and capacity categories that you want to evaluate. The period during which the data is read from the database is fixed in this case by the selection profile stored in the overall profile of the report. Three different overviews that you can toggle among are now available for you to evaluate the capacity load utilization.

Standard overview

Figure 6.23 shows the standard overview of a capacity evaluation. In a standard overview, the capacity requirements on the capacities of the selected work centers are compared in tables periodically (that is, by day, week, and so on depending on the requirements) with the available capacity of these capacities. The difference and the proportion of available capacities and requirements are also displayed in the REMAINING AVAILABLE CAPACITY and CAPACITY LOAD columns. If there is a capacity overload in a period (for example, the requirements exceed the available capacity), then the corresponding row in the report is highlighted.

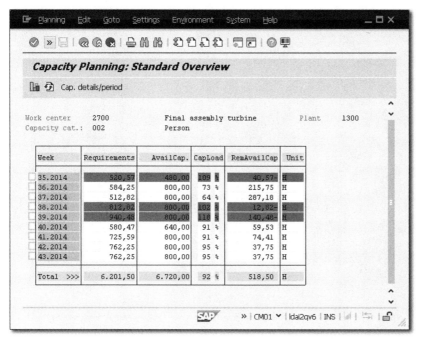

Figure 6.23 Standard Overview of a Capacity Evaluation

To evaluate which objects peg the capacity requirements in the individual periods, you must switch from the standard overview to the CAPACITY DETAILS view. This view lists the pegged requirements of the requirements selected in the standard overview (see Figure 6.24). You can use a field selection to determine what data is to be displayed for the different pegged requirements. You can also compare columns with each other; for example, you can display the difference and the relationship of two columns. You can also create or cancel confirmations for selected pegged requirements from this view if required.

Capacity details

With the exception of the fixed period column, the columns displayed in the variable overview are completely dependent on the settings of the list profile stored in the overall profile. Figure 6.25 shows a variable overview in which the capacity requirements of work orders (for example, of production orders and operative networks) and the requirements due to planned orders are listed separately.

Variable overview

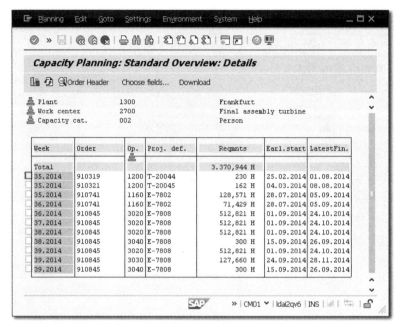

Figure 6.24 Detail View of a Capacity Evaluation

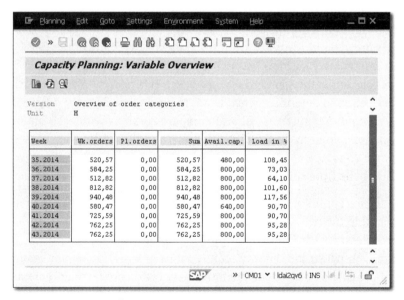

Figure 6.25 Example of the Variable Overview of a Capacity Evaluation

The following functions are available for all views of capacity evaluations:

▶ Print out and export of views

▶ Graphical display of data

▶ Refresh report data

▶ Background processing

▶ Branch to different environment information, depending on the relevant view in work centers, capacities, pegged requirements, and so on

In the simple capacity evaluations, you can change the profiles that
define the attributes of the report, or you can temporarily change the
general settings of the report. Figure 6.26 shows the temporary Customizing options of the report settings.

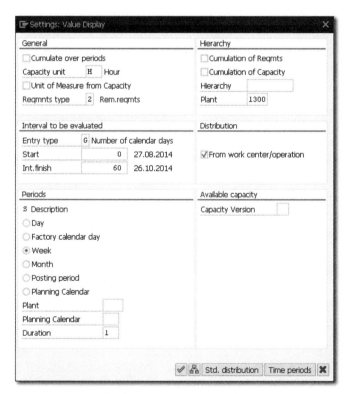

Figure 6.26 Example of the General Settings of a Capacity Evaluation

Note the DISTRIBUTION: FROM WORK CENTER/OPERATION indicator, which specifies that the distribution of the capacity requirements over the duration of the pegged requirements is controlled by the distribution key of the operation or work center (see Chapter 2, Section 2.2.1). If this indicator is not set, then the distribution keys of the report determine the distribution of the capacity requirements.

Restrictions of capacity evaluations

The simple capacity evaluations also contain different restrictions. For example, you cannot evaluate any actual capacity requirements by using these reports. In addition, you cannot evaluate capacity splits of capacity requirements to individual people in work centers, for example; however, you can use enhanced capacity evaluations in SAP Project System to evaluate this capacity data.

Enhanced Capacity Evaluations

You select the capacities to be evaluated in the initial screen of the enhanced capacity evaluations. Figure 6.27 shows the standard initial screen of Transaction CM53 (WBS ELEMENT/VERSION). The capacities are selected here by specifying projects. The system uses this selection to determine all work centers of the project and their capacity requirements. The system also determines the requirements of other projects and orders in the case. The subprofiles of the overall profile control whether the standard available capacity of the work centers or the cumulated available capacity of individual capacities for a capacity category is displayed as the available capacity in the report. In the initial screen, you can temporarily change the settings of periods that are used to read and subsequently display capacity data from the database.

Figure 6.27 Initial Screen of the Enhanced WBS Element/Version Capacity Evaluation

We differentiate between two views in enhanced capacity evaluations. In the *standard overview*, capacity requirements are compared periodically against available capacities. You can use a field selection to decide which columns—for example, which capacity requirements—you want to be displayed. To evaluate the pegged requirements, you must switch to the CAPACITY DETAILS view. You can evaluate the capacity details consecutively for individual periods (CAPA.DETAIL/SINGLE) or simultaneously for several periods (CAPA.DETAIL/COLLECTIVE).

Standard overview and capacity details

You can use the following functions in enhanced capacity evaluations:

Functions of enhanced capacity evaluations

▶ Print out and export data

▶ Field selection

▶ Sort, group, and summarize data

▶ Branch to the display for work center, capacity, and personnel data and, if necessary, pegged requirements

To ensure that you can evaluate actual capacity requirements in enhanced capacity evaluations, the relevant work centers must allow for actual capacity requirements to be determined (see Chapter 2, Section 2.2.1), and the selection profiles of the corresponding overall profiles must permit actual capacity requirements to be evaluated. You can also customize the list profiles of overall profiles in Customizing in such a way that columns for actual capacity requirements are automatically displayed in the reports (see Figure 6.28).

You can also use enhanced capacity evaluations to evaluate split requirements to individual people, for example. The CM51 report (INDIVIDUAL CAPACITY VIEW) and the SAPSFCG022 overall profile are already available by default for this purpose. If requirements were only created on personnel resources due to network activities, then you can also use the CMP9 report (WORKFORCE PLANNING EVALUATION) in SAP Project System (see Figure 2.27 in Chapter 2, Section 2.2.2).

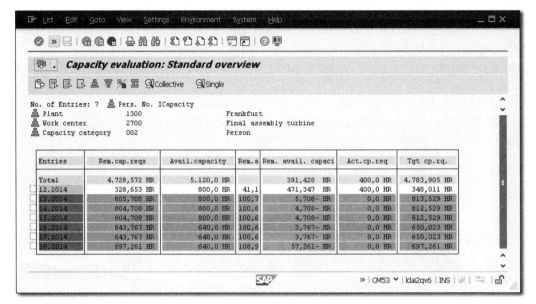

Figure 6.28 Standard Overview of an Enhanced Capacity Evaluation

Restrictions   In contrast to simple capacity evaluations, you cannot refresh the report data of enhanced capacity evaluations. To evaluate each current status of a capacity situation, you must therefore exit these reports first and then select the data again. In addition, unlike simple capacity evaluations, in the enhanced evaluations you cannot select other profiles for evaluating data. Furthermore, you cannot temporarily change report settings for enhanced capacity evaluations. For example, you cannot change the settings of a period split or the summarization using work center hierarchies.

6.4   Project Summarization

You can use the special *project summarization* function in SAP Project System to obtain clear and highly summarized reporting of many projects and orders. When summarizing a project, you need to define your own evaluation or summarization hierarchies consisting of hierarchy nodes, which you can use to evaluate movement data of projects and orders, such as costs, commitments, revenues, or budget values in aggregated format. Figure 6.29 shows an example of the evaluation of summarized project data using the Costs/Revenues/Expenditures/Receipts hierarchy report. In the example shown here, the summarization takes place on the Project Type and Person Responsible hierarchy nodes.

You can use either classification characteristics or master data fields of the objects as hierarchy nodes. In the first case, this is a *project summarization using classifications*, and in the second case, this is a *project summarization using master data*. The type of project summarization (by classification or master data) is controlled by the Project Summarization via Master Data characteristics indicator in the project or network profile. However, when you create a project using a template, the system copies the summarization format from the template. If you summarized the template using a classification and you now want to summarize the new project using master data fields, then you must convert the format of the summarization using the RCJCLMIG report. If, as part of the summarization using a classification, you used characteristics as hierarchy nodes and a master data field doesn't exist for these characteristics, then you can use a customer enhancement to ensure that they are included as additional fields when you perform the summarization using master data.

Summarization by classification/ master data

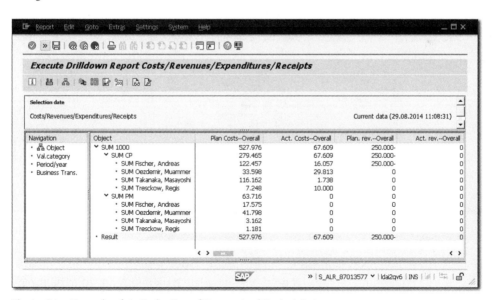

Figure 6.29 Example of an Evaluation of Summarized Project Data

[+]

Recommendation for the Summarization Format

Because a summarization that uses master data fields of objects has several advantages over using the older summarization format (that is, summarization that uses a classification), SAP recommends that you perform project summarizations that use master data. You can use the RCJCLMIG report to convert a summarization that uses classifications to a summarization that uses master data. The following details all relate to project summarization that uses master data.

Summarization hierarchies

Before you can use project summarization, you must first define the hierarchy of the nodes in which you want to evaluate the data. You create summarization hierarchies in Transaction KKRO (see Figure 6.30). For each summarization hierarchy, you first define which object types are to be taken into account for a summarization. You can activate summarizations in each case for internal plant maintenance and service orders, production orders, and projects and sales orders. However, when you summarize projects the assigned additive networks and orders are also automatically summarized. For performance reasons, in the next step you can specify for summarization hierarchies that you want individual totals record tables to be excluded from a summarization.

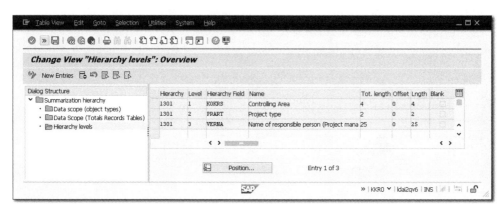

Figure 6.30 Example of Defining a Summarization Hierarchy

Finally, you determine the hierarchy nodes when you define a summarization hierarchy. To do this, you create a maximum of nine hierarchy levels and specify the name of each master data field that you want to be used at this level for summarizing movement data. In the course of the summarization, the system later accumulates the data of objects with the same field values, whereby the objects and field values must first be determined using an *inheritance*.

The CO area is always the highest node of a summarization hierarchy. Therefore, you cannot perform a summarization across CO areas. The list of master data fields that you can use as hierarchy nodes is predefined. Nevertheless, you can also use any additional fields as nodes using a customer enhancement.

You can use inheritance (Transaction CJH1) to determine which objects **Inheritance** are to be included in a summarization and which master data field values for these objects should be used for the summarization. To do this, in the initial screen of Transaction CJH1 (see Figure 6.31), you first need to specify the projects for which data is to be summarized later. When you then perform the inheritance, the system determines from these projects all those WBS elements for which the PROJ. SUMMARIZATION indicator (see Chapter 1, Section 1.2) is set in the master data, and it writes these and the relevant master data field values of these WBS elements into database Table PSERB. At the same time, the system performs a logical inheritance of these field values on all lower-level objects, activities, assigned orders, and WBS elements without the PROJ. SUMMARIZATION indicator and also writes these objects and the inherited field values into database Table PSERB. The actual master data of the objects, however, is not changed by an inheritance.

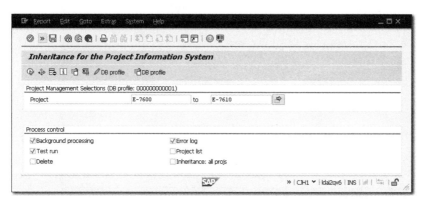

Figure 6.31 Initial Screen of the Inheritance of Project Data

You can perform the inheritance for different projects consecutively and thereby gradually enhance the data of database Table PSERB. If relevant master data changes have emerged, then you must repeat the inheritance to update the table. The objects and field values of database Table PSERB are the basis for subsequent data *summarizations*. You can use Transaction CJH2 to display the results of the inheritance.

Summarization

After you have performed at least one inheritance, you can summarize the data in Transaction KKRC in a second step. In the initial screen of this transaction (see Figure 6.32), you specify the summarization hierarchy or the summarization subhierarchy for which a summarization is to take place. You also specify the period for the summarization. When you execute this transaction, the system determines the summarization objects and their master data field values from database Table PSERB. It also selects their movement data and writes the summarized results on the relevant hierarchy nodes in database Table RPSCO.

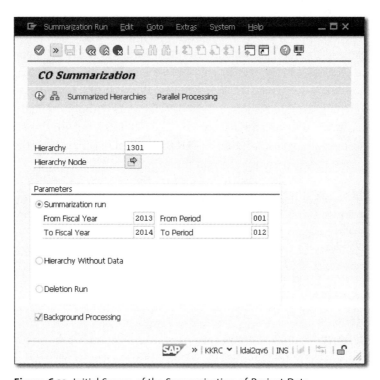

Figure 6.32 Initial Screen of the Summarization of Project Data

Separate hierarchy reports and cost element reports are available in SAP Project System to evaluate summarized accounting data. In the initial screen of these reports, you specify the summarization hierarchy or the summarization subhierarchy that you want to use to display the data. You must have already performed a summarization for this summarization hierarchy. Depending on the report, you need to specify additional selection criteria, such as an evaluation period or the CO version of the data to be evaluated. For more information about project summarization, refer to SAP Notes 313899 and 701076.

Inheritance reports

6.5   SAP HANA-Based Reporting Options

Evaluating project data across longer periods or multiple projects may require high performance levels. In such cases, companies frequently do not evaluate project data in real time and instead generate project reports—for example, using background jobs at night—or use SAP BW for their project reporting.

SAP HANA provides various options to those companies to accelerate the evaluation of large amounts of project data and thus utilize real-time reporting for their projects. On the one hand, the SAP ERP 6.0 version for SAP HANA provides various reporting optimizations, such as a new project line item reporting (see Section 6.2.3), generic accelerations of Report Painter and Report Writer reports, and also optimizations of the CN41N, CN43N, and CN47N reports.

On the other hand, the SAP HANA Live add-on enables the user to leverage the options of an SAP HANA database optimally for reporting purposes and provides a highly flexible reporting across applications.

SAP HANA Live

6.5.1   Virtual Data Model of PS and Project Reporting Using SAP HANA Live

The definition of reports in SAP HANA Live is based on virtual data models of the individual applications. A virtual data model comprises various levels that are represented by different *views*.

Private views The lowest level includes private views, which form an abstraction layer of the physical database tables of the individual applications. Using private views, you can logically summarize different database tables. At the same time, the rather technical denominations of the database fields are converted to meaningful business names so that they can easily be used at the other levels later on.

Reuse views Reuse views form the next level of a virtual data model. Reuse views provide an overview of the private views grouped by business or reporting aspects. The reuse views form the basis for the top level of the virtual data model, the query views.

Query views Query views are defined by individual reporting requirements and can then be consumed by the end users. To use these query views, SAP HANA Live supports various open standards, such as SQL, MDX, or OData. As a result, you can use many different user interfaces for query view-based evaluations—for instance, SAP BusinessObjects Analysis for Microsoft Excel, SAP Lumira, analytical SAP Fiori apps (see Section 6.5.2), other SAP BusinessObjects BI tools, or third-party tools.

In Appendix B, you can find a list of query and reuse views that are currently delivered with the virtual data model of SAP Project System by default. However, you can also define your own reuse and query views. Here, you can combine, for example, logistical and accounting information on projects in a query view. In addition, you can integrate data from other applications, such as Purchasing, Sales, or Stock Management, in the query view. Hence, by means of SAP HANA Live, you can flexibly define project reporting that meets your requirements.

SAP HANA Studio Customer-specific query or reuse views are defined in SAP HANA Studio. In addition to various other tools for managing and monitoring the SAP HANA database, you are provided with different functions for modeling and testing views. Figure 6.33 shows an example of defining a query view for analyzing missing parts in projects using SAP HANA Studio.

Figure 6.34 shows how to use this query view in SAP BusinessObjects Analysis for Microsoft Excel. You can readily drag-and-drop the appropriate attributes and measures that were defined in the query view to columns or rows or use them as filters, for example.

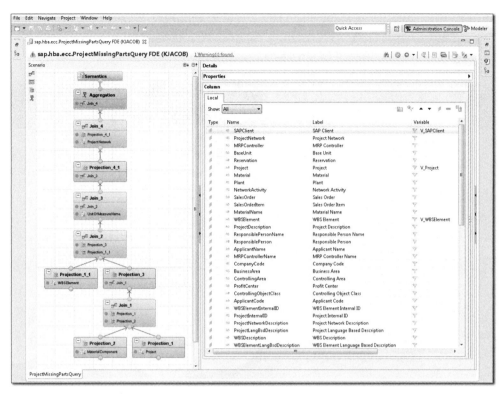

Figure 6.33 Example of a Query View in SAP HANA Studio

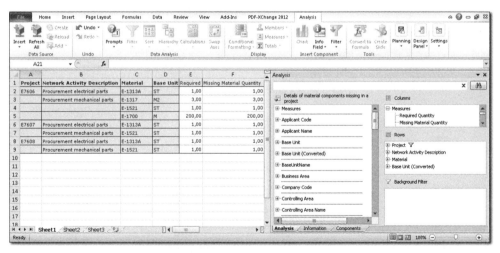

Figure 6.34 Using a Query View in Microsoft Excel

SAP HANA Live Browser

Another tool for displaying, testing, and using views is the SAP HANA Live Browser. Figure 6.35, for example, shows a list of query views that a user marked as favorites.

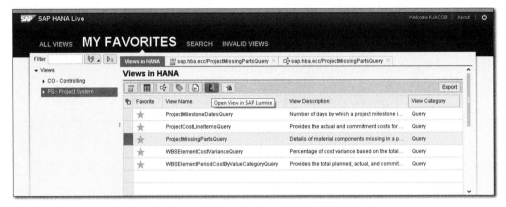

Figure 6.35 Example of a Favorites List in SAP HANA Live Browser

From the list of views, you may navigate to the definition of the view or open a query in SAP BusinessObjects Analysis for Microsoft Office or SAP Lumira (see Figure 6.36).

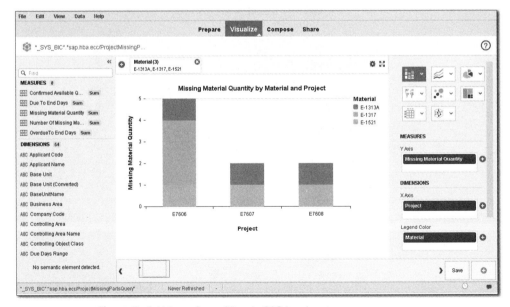

Figure 6.36 Using a Query View in SAP Lumira

6.5.2 Reporting Cockpit: SAP Smart Business for Project Execution

In addition to the SAP Fiori app types *transactional* and *fact sheet*, which are described in Chapter 1, Section 1.7.6, a third type—*analytical apps*—is available. These apps utilize query views defined in SAP HANA Live to provide users with reporting data in the SAP Fiori interface on different end devices and, if required, on mobile devices, such as tablets and smartphones. For SAP Project System, a wide range of such analytical apps is now available so that users can compile their own Reporting Cockpit in SAP Fiori Launchpad (see Figure 1.38 in Chapter 1, Section 1.7.6). Users can combine analytical apps for logistical aspects of projects with apps about project financial data or apps of other applications in order to get a comprehensive overview of their projects and quickly determine critical deviations or imminent risks.

Analytical SAP Fiori apps

Currently, the following analytical apps are available for SAP Project System by default:

- WBS Elements Cost Variance
- WBS Elements Costs at Risk
- WBS Elements Revenue Variance
- WBS Elements Exceeding Work
- WBS Elements Pending Work
- Open Reservations for Project
- Missing Parts for Project
- OVERDUE PROJECT PO ITEMS
- Due Project PO Items
- Overdue Project Milestones
- Due Project Milestones
- Overdue WBS Elements
- Due WBS Elements
- Overdue Network Activities
- Due Network Activities
- POC Projects

- POC WBS Elements

- Project Earned Value

- WBS Elements Earned Value

- Project Report

Example 1— cost variance of WBS elements

Figure 6.37 shows an example of the analytical app for cost variance of WBS elements. On the left hand side, the app displays a list of all WBS elements of selected projects or project parts for which the total of actual cost and commitments exceeds the planned costs. The number of these WBS elements is also highlighted in red in the tile in the Launchpad (see Figure 1.38 in Chapter 1, Section 1.7.6). The list offers some important information, for instance, the volume of cost exceedance (percentage and absolute) and the WBS elements IDENTIFICATION and NAME and the identification of the relevant project. You can adjust and reduce the list using search, filter, or grouping functions.

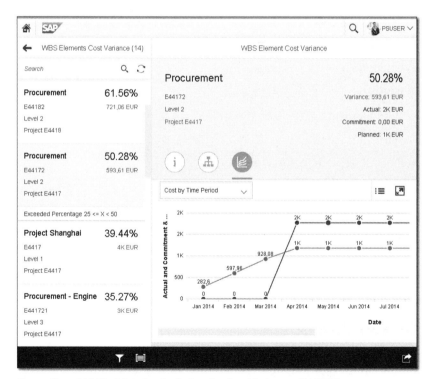

Figure 6.37 SAP Fiori App for Analyzing the Cost Variance of WBS Elements

On the right hand side of the app, you can view the detailed information on the selected WBS element. In the header area, the system displays the information from the list again and the current value for planned and actual costs, commitments, and the resulting variance. In the lower area, you can find additional information that is grouped in tabs. By selecting the appropriate icon below the header area, you can toggle between the tabs. The first tab offers general information on the WBS element and project—for instance, organizational assignment, responsibility, dates, or status. The second tab provides a path to the project definition, starting from the WBS element—that is, the position of the WBS element in the project hierarchy. The third tab that is displayed by default informs you about the chronological development of the total sum of commitment and actual cost compared to the planned cost in the current calendar year (see Figure 6.37). Here, you can select a single period or a period interval to display a list of actual and commitment line items for these periods—for example, to evaluate details on the cause for cost exceedance. If required, you can switch from the graphical display of chronological distribution of costs to a display of costs by value categories.

Additional functions that are available in this app include the following:

▶ Branch to fact sheets—for example, to a project definition or CO line item document

▶ Call transactional apps—for example, to change the WBS element status

▶ Integration with SAP Jam for project collaboration scenarios

▶ Reduction of objects displayed and ability to save as a user-specific variant of the app

Figure 6.38 shows the analytical app for earned values of projects as another example. This app displays the current key figures from the progress analysis for selected projects. If required, you can navigate to a periodic view of planned and actual earned values together with the actual costs or to a view of schedule and cost variances per period of the current year (see Chapter 4, Section 4.7.2). Additional functions enable you to use filters to reduce the projects displayed, to save a user-specific variant of the app if necessary, to switch to a tabular presentation of key

Example 2—project earned value

figures, or to collaborate using SAP Jam. Different from the app for cost variance of WBS elements, this app is only based on a query view and a drill-down configuration in SAP Smart Business.

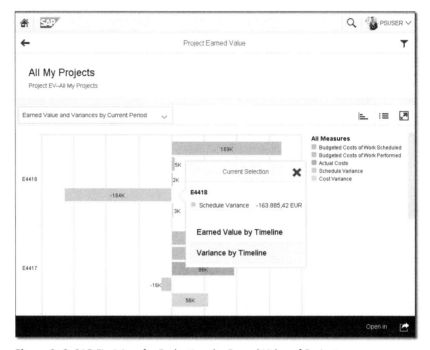

Figure 6.38 SAP Fiori App for Evaluating the Earned Value of Projects

Example 3—
Project Report

The *Project Report* app summarizes various project key figures in one single analytical app. Project managers who are responsible for one or more projects can thus get a quick overview of all current variances and risks of their projects and the current status of costs, revenues, work, and progress. Figure 6.39 shows the initial screen of this app, which displays the planned and actual values of these key figures.

From here, you may navigate to the individual projects and their fact sheets, a periodic display of values, or the relevant line items. The other tabs show the number of critical WBS elements with regard to cost and revenues, schedules, purchase orders, or the work of assigned network activities. From these tabs, you can navigate to the respective analytical app for further analysis.

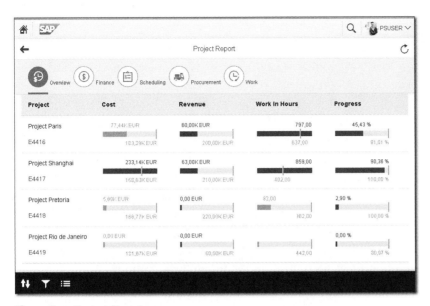

Figure 6.39 Project Report

SAP Smart Business

You define the tiles of the analytical apps of SAP Project System and further details of the app using *SAP Smart Business*. The analytical apps of SAP Project System are therefore summarized under the term *SAP Smart Business for Project Execution*. SAP Smart Business is a tool that you can use—for example, starting from SAP HANA Live query views—to define key figures (key performance indicators, KPIs) that are relevant for your business processes. Later on, you can evaluate these KPIs in the SAP Fiori user interface, for example.

You define tiles and various configurations of the app in SAP Smart Business using special modeling apps. To enable users to add and use tiles in their Launchpads, you must first create and activate a corresponding KPI. In addition to the identification and name, the definition of the KPI also comprises the identification of which OData service and which entity set—that is, which query—is to be used. Here, you also define which key figure the KPI represents and whether this key figure is to be as high or low as possible or has to have a specific target value. For the analytical app shown in the first example, this key figure is the number

KPI modeling

of WBS elements with a cost variance of which the value is to be as low as possible.

Evaluation

For each KPI, you must create and activate at least one *evaluation*. This evaluation contains another setting for displaying the key figure in the tile—for instance, scaling, unit of measure, and target or threshold value. But you also use the evaluation to assign users or user roles to the KPI and thus specify the authorizations for using the KPI. In addition, you can use the filter information in an evaluation to define which objects are incorporated in the calculation and display of the KPI. For KPIs in SAP Project System, you thus determine which users can evaluate which projects or project parts using the KPI and the corresponding evaluation. A user of the KPI—for example, a project manager—can specify additional filters in the appropriate app or further restrict the selection of projects. He can then save these settings as a user-specific variant of the KPI or the evaluation.

Visualization and drill-down configurations

Finally, you must also create a visualization for the evaluation. If you want to use the generic drill-down functions of SAP Smart Business—such as the earned value display of the second example—for a KPI, then you must create a drill-down configuration for a visualization. The visualization also defines the presentation of a key figure in the corresponding tile in the Launchpad. The following tile formats are available:

▸ **Numeric**
The key figure is displayed as a numeric value (see Example 1).

▸ **Deviation**
The key figure is graphically displayed as a bullet chart together with the target value and threshold values.

▸ **Trend**
The chronological development of the key figure is displayed as a curve.

▸ **Comparison**
The key figure is displayed for three elements in the form of comparing bars—for example, the system can display the earned values of the three projects with the lowest earned values (see Example 2).

By means of the drill-down configuration of a visualization, you define the views that are available for selection when opening a tile or that can be used as a drill down; with this configuration you also specify whether user-specific filtering is to be possible and which filter dimensions are provided. When defining a view, you specify the name of the view and whether the data is to be displayed graphically or in a tabular format. You can also decide whether the view supports both presentation forms and whether the users can toggle between them. Furthermore, you determine the sorting and which measures and which dimensions are used for display. For graphical presentations, you additionally need to define the type of graphic, such as bar chart, lines, or column diagram.

> **Role Assignment** [+]
>
> To use KPIs and the corresponding tiles (as well as to use fact sheets and transactional apps), you need to assign different roles to the users. You can find the required roles and further implementation details in the documentation on SAP Fiori and the individual apps.

6.6 Summary

Different reports are available in SAP Project System for real-time reporting of all project data. Depending on what data you want to evaluate, you use reports from the different information systems for structures, hierarchy, cost elements, and line item reports from Project Information System: financials, or logistical reports, such as material or capacity evaluations. You can use project summarization to clearly evaluate the data of many projects based on user-defined summarization criteria. The virtual data model of SAP Project System in SAP HANA Live and SAP Smart Business for Project Execution provides you with SAP HANA-optimized and mobile reporting options.

In many enterprises, projects and project portfolios are managed using a variety of programs. This chapter looks at some typical scenarios that illustrate how SAP Project System can be integrated with other programs.

7 Integration Scenarios with Other Project Management Tools

The *External Project Software* (EPS interface) interface and—as of EHP 3—services of SAP's service-oriented architecture (SOA) can be used for bidirectional data exchange with other project management tools or generic external programs from within SAP Project System.

The purpose of SOA is to enable companies to design their IT-based business processes in a more flexible manner. The core element of SOA is the Enterprise Services. From a business point of view, an Enterprise Service represents an executable business function within a business process. From a technical point of view, an Enterprise Service is an encapsulated function of an SAP or non-SAP application that can be accessed through well-defined interfaces. If you couple the Enterprise Services of different applications, you can easily map business processes across different systems and enhance them at a later stage, if necessary. As of EHP 3, SAP Project System provides more than 50 Enterprise Services.

Enterprise services

Typical uses of the EPS interface include exporting project data for presentation purposes, initial data transfer from legacy systems to SAP Project System, and integrating special tools that are often developed in-house and deal with individual aspects of project management (that is, creating materials lists, scheduling, and offline object processing). The EPS interface is based on business object types and BAPIs.

EPS interface

Business objects Business object types are used to structure data from the SAP system into individual components, in accordance with business criteria. SAP Project System has the business object types *Project Definition*, *Work-BreakDownStruc*, and *Network*, among others, which are used to encapsulate data for project definitions, work breakdown structures, and networks. Each business object type provides clearly defined methods for communicating with external programs. These methods are referred to as *BAPIs*. Data exchange that is based on BAPIs between the external programs and a business object can flow in either direction.

BAPIs The data in business objects is only visible to the outside world via BAPIs. This separation of data and access methods enables you, with the help of BAPIs, to read, modify, and create business objects without having to know all of the SAP-specific implementation details of the relevant business object type. You can use the BAPI transaction to view a list of the business object types, the BAPIs available in each case, and detailed documentation for every BAPI in the SAP system. For a list of the BAPIs for the three business object types in SAP Project System, see Appendix A.

The EPS interface enables access to the data in SAP Project System; however, to exchange this data with other programs an additional interface is required that maps SAP Project System data to data fields in the external software and vice versa. You can develop this interface, if you like, but there already exists an entire range of such interfaces for a variety of standard programs, such as Microsoft Project and Oracle Primavera P6. You can purchase these interfaces from SAP partners or other providers. SAP provides its customers and partners with a free interface for data exchange between SAP Project System (SAP PS) and Microsoft Project Client. This interface, known as the *Open PS interface for Microsoft Project*, is discussed in more detail in the following sections. The SAP Enterprise Project Connection interface can be used for the integration with other project management tools and, in particular, Primavera (introduced in Section 7.2). Finally, this chapter describes integration scenarios for SAP Portfolio and Project Management, and SAP Commercial Project Management which you can use to supplement SAP Project System with additional processes and functions.

7.1   Open PS for Microsoft Project

You can use the Open PS for Microsoft Project interface to download   Uses
projects from SAP Project System to the Microsoft Project Client. You
can also use this interface to roll up project data to SAP Project System to
create new projects or modify existing ones. The ability to download
projects in Microsoft Project is particularly important for project team
members who need access to offline project data—for customer presentations, for example. You can download projects as often as you like.
When doing so, you can either create a new project each time in Microsoft Project or update a previously downloaded project.

If necessary, you can also modify projects that you downloaded in
Microsoft Project—for on-site scheduling arrangements with business
partners, for example—and then transfer your modifications back to the
SAP system or create new projects in Microsoft Project and then use the
rollup function to create new projects in SAP Project System. To roll up
modified or newly created projects in the SAP system, you must explicitly assign the SAP_PS_EPS role to users. You first have to create this
role in the SAP system using Transaction PFCG. This is the only action
you need to take for this role.

The Open PS interface is used mainly to exchange data regarding struc-   Data exchange
ture, scheduling, and resources between SAP PS and Microsoft Project.
However, for information purposes planned costs and actual costs of
activities can also be downloaded to Microsoft Project. Furthermore, to
carry out resource planning at the personnel level in Microsoft Project
you can download personnel data from the HR module in the SAP system to Microsoft Project.

Because Microsoft Project and SAP Project System use different project
structures and data fields, Open PS must have a suitable means of mapping these structures and this data. For example, in Microsoft Project,
activities are mapped as individual tasks, whereas WBS elements, if
activities are assigned to them, are mapped as summary tasks; otherwise, they are also mapped as individual tasks. One characteristic of
material components is that they cannot be downloaded. The Open PS
interface documentation contains a detailed explanation of how the

various structure objects are mapped; in particular, it provides information on which PS object fields are mapped to which Microsoft Project fields.

Because Microsoft Project and SAP Project System also use different scheduling logics, differences can occur with regard to the project dates in those two project management tools. To avoid that, Open PS allows you to disable the automatic recalculation of project dates in Microsoft Project after the import of project data. This option also imports buffer times from the SAP system, which are then used to highlight time-critical activities in Microsoft Project. However, note that this option does not allow for importing additional resources and that you cannot roll up changes at a later point in time.

[!] | **Data Consistency in Microsoft Project and SAP Project System**

Due to the different handling—for example, of work, duration, or date restrictions—in Microsoft Project and SAP Project System, the dates and other data are not always fully consistent. Ensure that you use appropriate settings in the projects in SAP Project System and Microsoft Project to avoid inconsistencies. The Open PS documentation and SAP Note 1332046 provide further information on the appropriate settings.

Open PS installation
You must download the documentation and the Open PS interface using SAP's Software Distribution Center. To use the Open PS interface, you have to install it on the same local computer on which the Microsoft Project client is installed. If you then start Open PS, Microsoft Project, with an additional Open PS toolbar, is also started automatically. To create a link to SAP Project System, you then have to manually enter information about the SAP user and the SAP system, which you should save so that you don't have to enter it each time.

Open PS settings
In the Open PS settings, select the object types that you want to be exchanged between SAP Project System and Microsoft Project (see Figure 7.1). If you also want to exchange PS user field data with Microsoft Project, then you have to specify the assignments of user fields to Microsoft Project fields in the settings. The other settings are predefined and usually don't require modification.

Select Objects for Transfer

Select object type
- ☑ WBS milestones
- ☑ Activities
- ☑ Activity milestones
- ☑ Relationships
- ☑ Resources / Work center

- ☑ Transfer scheduling information
- ☑ Switch off MSP Calculation

When downloading project
- ☑ Download actuals
- ☑ Download Networks with status 'Locked'

If server supports download of cost information
- ⦿ Always download costs
- ○ Never download costs
- ○ Always ask before downloading

Set indicators when creating networks
- ☐ Schedule automatically
- ☐ Calculate costs automatically

[OK]   [Cancel]

Figure 7.1 Open PS Data Transfer Settings

In the remainder of this section, a simple example scenario is described to illustrate how Open PS can be used. After setting up and starting the interface, you can establish a connection to an SAP system. First, log on to the SAP system with an SAP user. Once you have done this, you have access to more functions in the Open PS toolbar. For example, you can download a project from SAP Project System by selecting the project you want to download in the appropriate dialog box (see Figure 7.2); note that you cannot download multiple projects simultaneously. If necessary, you can automatically lock networks belonging to this project while editing in Microsoft Project. Once the download process is completed, you can view details of the process in a log file.

Using the Open PS interface

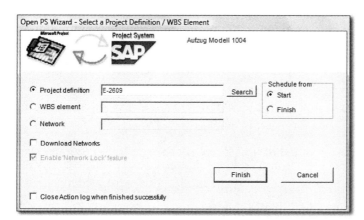

Figure 7.2 Open PS Dialog Box for Downloading Projects to Microsoft Project

The downloaded project is then displayed in the Open PS screen in
Microsoft Project (see Figure 7.3). The work centers of the activities can
also be downloaded to Microsoft Project as resources, along with structure and scheduling data, and can then be analyzed there in the
RESOURCES screen. If you want to use additional work centers and personnel resources from the SAP system for resource planning in Microsoft Project, then you should use Open PS to search for the appropriate
resources in the SAP system and to download these as well.

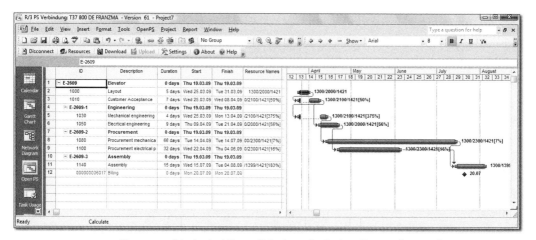

Figure 7.3 Display in Microsoft Project of a Project Exported Using the Open
PSInterface

You can now analyze and, if necessary, modify the project in Microsoft
Project. For example, you can modify the time scheduling, add new
tasks, create relationships, or assign resources to tasks. If you assign
more than one resource to a task, especially personnel resources, these
are mapped in SAP Project System as activity elements after they are
rolled up. For new tasks, you can use an indicator to control whether
these tasks can be uploaded to SAP Project System later or whether they
are only to be used for planning in Microsoft Project.

To transfer the modified project data back to SAP Project System, start
the project rollup process. If you locked certain networks during the
download process, then you have to unlock these networks before
uploading. Open PS now compares the project in Microsoft Project with
the project in SAP Project System and displays a list of updates. You can

now choose whether to transfer all of the updates or just a select number of updates. As before, a log file is created that contains all of the details of the upload process.

7.2 SAP Enterprise Project Connection

Through SAP Enterprise Project Connection (EPC), SAP provides an interface specifically for the integration of data from SAP Project System and Plant Maintenance with other project management and scheduling tools. In the standard version, EPC can be used to exchange data with Oracle Primavera P6 and, as of EPC 2.0, with Microsoft Project Server. SAP EPC consists of the following components:

- **Integrated Services**   Components
  This component comprises services that can be called via the SAP EPC user interface and ensure data transfer.

- **Central Technical Configuration**
  This is a Java component that allows for configuration of the system connections and other control functions.

- **SAP ERP add-on component**
  The SAP ERP add-on component includes BAPIs and transactions for the execution and evaluation of data transfers in the SAP ERP system.

- **Sample content for integration**
  The sample content contains details regarding the mapping of SAP ERP data to data and objects in Primavera or Microsoft Project Server.

The *Integrated Services* and *Central Technical Configuration* components are installed on SAP NetWeaver Application Server and are used for interface administration only.

Users can transfer data with the SAP ERP add-on component by using   Data exchange
the transactions provided therein. The following transactions are available for SAP EPC, for example, for data exchange:

- TRANSFER PROJECTS
- TRANSFER PM ORDERS
- DISPLAY TRANSFER RESULTS

The TRANSFER PROJECTS transaction allows for data exchange between projects in SAP Project System and Oracle Primavera P6 or Microsoft Project Server (see Figure 7.4). In the initial screen of this transaction, you select the projects whose data you want to exchange as well as a transfer mode and a transfer type. The AUTOMATIC TRANSFER mode directly triggers the data transfer of the selected projects upon execution; the INTERACTIVE SELECTION mode enables you to check the scope of the selection again. The transfer type defines the direction of the data exchange—that is, from the SAP system to Primavera/Microsoft Project or vice versa. A separate transfer type is available for the export of actual costs. If required, you can also save your selection as a variant and schedule it as a background job. You can find more details on the data transfer, on the mapping of objects and fields, and on the mapping rules used in the SAP Library and in SAP Notes 1887361 and 1842546.

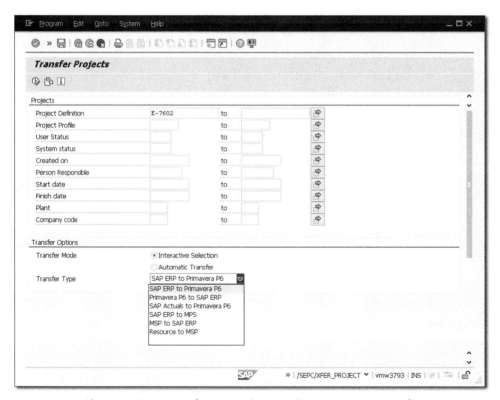

Figure 7.4 Transaction for Data Exchange with Primavera or Microsoft Project Server

After the data transfer, you can view the transfer result. Status information and the respective traffic lights indicate warning messages or transfer errors. You can view detailed information that helps you to eliminate errors or post-process exchanged data.

The DISPLAY TRANSFER RESULTS transaction allows you to obtain a central overview of the data transfer result.

7.3 SAP Portfolio and Project Management

SAP Portfolio and Project Management (PPM) consists of the closely integrated components *PPM Portfolio Management* and *PPM Project Management*. Portfolio Management provides functions for company-wide management, for example, of IT projects, innovation projects, or investment projects. The Project Management component is another SAP tool for operational project management. SAP PPM is the successor of cProjects and SAP Resource and Portfolio Management and combines the two solutions in one product with a harmonized user interface and an extended functional scope. The following information deals with the Portfolio Management and Project Management components and SAP Project System integration scenarios in particular.

7.3.1 PPM Project Management

PPM Project Management's design and functional scope make it particularly suitable for IT, development, and service projects. You can use PPM Project Management independent of or in combination with SAP Project System. In this context, different integration scenarios are available. On the one hand, you can use a project in SAP Project System for project accounting of a PPM Project Management project linked to it, and on the other hand you can use projects simultaneously in SAP Project System and in PPM Project Management to implement different project views for different user groups.

Usage

PPM Project Management includes functions for phase-based and task-based structuring of projects (see Figure 7.5), time scheduling, and various document management options. Resource planning in PPM Project

Functional scope

Management is based on roles, which describe the resource requirements of a project, and business partners, who are used as resources for role assignment. Resources can be assigned to these project roles in SAP PPM in different ways: in addition to the direct staffing of roles in a project (for example, by the project manager), you can also use advanced, cross-project staffing scenarios. In these processes, depending on the status of the role, resource managers are responsible for the role assignment. For this purpose, PPM provides two fast-entry screens: RESOURCES and ASSIGNMENT OVERVIEW.

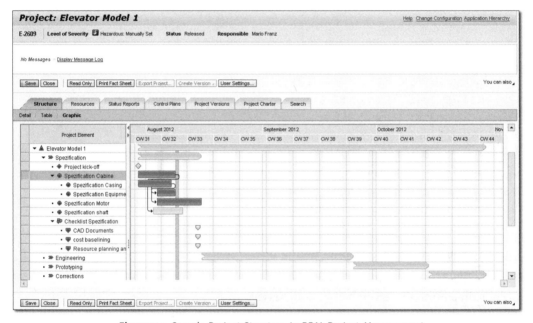

Figure 7.5 Sample Project Structure in PPM Project Management

Project templates   To simplify the project creation process, you can use PPM Project Management to define project templates and use these to copy operative projects. You can also use it in the project execution process to incorporate simulation versions for what-if scenario analyses. The structure objects of a project in PPM Project Management can have a status, which you can use to control the lifecycle of the structure objects. The transition from one phase of a project to the next is usually controlled in PPM Project Management via special approval processes. In these processes, you can use *checklists* to ensure that all of the mandatory conditions for a particular phase of the project are fulfilled. You can also use project status reports and versions to document the progress of a project in PPM Project Management.

In PPM Project Management, an authorization concept, which is based on Access Control Lists (ACLs), enables you to easily assign authorizations at the object level, down to the level of individual documents. Different options to link PPM Project Management projects with each other and the use of a *multiproject monitor* in PPM also enables you to perform multiproject management in PPM Project Management. Special project evaluations, predefined Business Content for SAP BW, and a function for connecting PPM Project Management to SAP Alert Management allow you to effectively monitor all your PPM Project Management projects. PPM Project Management provides additional integration scenarios for the following, among other things: SAP Supplier Relationship Management (SRM), for procuring external project resources, for example; the CATS, for recording time spent on tasks in PPM Project Management projects; and PPM Portfolio Management in particular. Also, *object links* can be used to connect almost all of the structure objects of SAP PPM projects with objects of an SAP ERP system.

Authorization concept

Object links enable you to create links, such as a link between a PPM Project Management phase and a PS network. This means that in PPM Project Management evaluations you can analyze network data together with the phase data, for example. Moreover, in PPM Project Management, you then can use network data to identify *threshold value violations* and therefore to trigger automatic alert messages. Object links also enable you to analyze network data directly in the specific phase (see Figure 7.6) and, if necessary, to go directly from PPM Project Management to the detailed display or to processing transactions for the network.

Object links

Customizing of PPM Project Management is where you define the object links and the Remote Function Call (RFC) connection to the SAP ERP system. The standard version already contains various object links for PPM Project Management. Figure 7.7 shows an example of an object link definition for networks in SAP Project System.

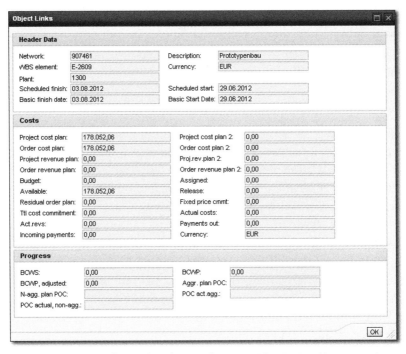

Figure 7.6 Example of a Display of Network Data in PPM Project Management

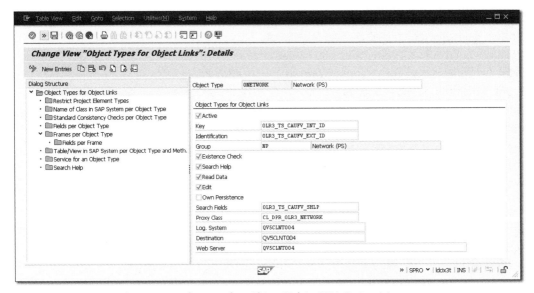

Figure 7.7 Definition of an Object Link in PPM Customizing

Integrating Financials Functions

Special integration scenarios between SAP Project System and PPM Project Management can be used to exchange CO data. Because PPM Project Management does not provide any Financials functions (apart from a rudimentary cost and revenue planning function that is based on planned resource requirements), you can run projects in SAP Project System parallel to your projects in PPM Project Management, which hierarchically map all financial aspects of project planning and execution. Specific information on planned activities and their costs and revenue rates can be transferred from PPM Project Management to SAP Project System for this purpose, and, if necessary, additional cost, revenue, and budget data can be added here.

Controlling methods

There are various ways, or *CO methods*, of linking a PPM Project Management project to a PS project:

▶ **Hierarchical CO (structure element, manually)**
Manually create a work breakdown structure in SAP Project System and then assign phases, tasks, and subtasks of a PPM Project Management project to the WBS elements.

▶ **Hierarchical CO (project role, manually)**
Likewise, create a work breakdown structure in SAP Project System and then assign roles to the various WBS elements in PPM Project Management.

▶ **Hierarchical CO (structure element, automatically)**
To define a PPM Project Management project, the system automatically creates a project definition and a billing element in SAP Project System. In accordance with the structure of the SAP PPM Project Management project, subordinate WBS elements are created for phases, tasks, and subtasks and linked to these. You can define the maximum number of levels by defining a CO level. All subordinate structure elements of the SAP PPM Project Management project are then assigned to the WBS elements at the lowest level.

▶ **Hierarchical CO (project role, automatically)**
A project definition and a billing element are automatically created at the highest level in SAP Project System. Additional WBS elements are created for every role in the SAP PPM Project Management project.

You can also use additional CO methods if you don't require hierarchical CO for an SAP PPM Project Management project and instead want to use internal orders rather than WBS elements as the CO elements in the SAP ERP system for integrating Financials functions.

[+] **Manual Changes of Automatically Created Assignments**

If necessary, before a project is released in PPM Project Management, you can make manual changes to the assignments that were created using automatic CO methods. If you do this, however, you cannot revert to the automatic CO method. From here on, this means that you will have to create links manually for project elements that were retroactively created in PPM Project Management.

Project elements and WBS elements

A project element in PPM Project Management can be assigned to a maximum of one WBS element. However, a WBS element can be linked to multiple elements in PPM Project Management, provided that these elements all belong to the same SAP PPM project. Also, note that you cannot assign the project elements of a project in SAP PPM to WBS elements belonging to different projects in SAP Project System; however, different WBS elements can be assigned to project elements of different projects in SAP PPM.

You determine the CO method, the CO level, and a CO scenario (such as one that contains data on the costing sheet or the settlement profile of the CO objects in the SAP ERP system) based on the project type in SAP PPM specified in the Customizing section of the SAP ERP system under the menu item INTEGRATION WITH OTHER SAP COMPONENTS • COLLABORATION PROJECTS (see Figure 7.8). The Customizing section also contains documentation on the various BAdIs available to you for making customer-specific adaptations in the process of integrating Financials functions.

Transfer

In the Customizing section of PPM Project Management, you also need to specify when projects and WBS elements should be automatically created and when the cost-relevant data of a project in SAP PPM should be transferred to SAP Project System in accordance with the project type. This process, known as *transfer*, can take place independent of the status of the project in SAP PPM every time the project is saved, automatically every time the project is saved if the FLAGGED FOR TRANSFER status is set, or if the RELEASED status is set.

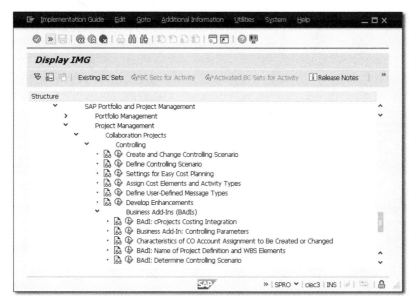

Figure 7.8 Settings for Financials Integration in the SAP System of the Project System

The technical process of integrating Financials functions is also based on object links. In the standard version, PPM Project Management comes with the object type 0FIN_INT_ERP_PS. In this object type, you only have to create the RFC connection to the SAP ERP system of SAP Project System to use the RFC for object links. As soon as an object link is created between a project element in PPM Project Management and a WBS element, you can display various data of the WBS element directly in the project element in SAP PPM or call various Internet services for the WBS element in PPM Project Management.

7.3.2 PPM Portfolio Management

Although SAP Project System and PPM Project Management can be used for the detailed planning and operational management of projects, PPM Portfolio Management is used for the strategic analysis and control of entire project portfolios and, in particular, for planning and approving project ideas at an early stage.

Portfolio structuring

To manage project portfolios, you can define various *portfolios* in SAP PPM and hierarchically subdivide these portfolios into *portfolio buckets* (see Figure 7.9). At the portfolio bucket level, you can already plan costs, budgets, or capacity data, for example. You can then assign *portfolio items* to the portfolio buckets at the lowest level. At an early stage, portfolio items can be used to define project proposals and ideas in SAP PPM and to support selection and approval processes later on. At this stage, created projects and detailed planning are usually not available yet. You can then manually or automatically generate projects in PPM Project Management or SAP Project System and link them to a portfolio item at a later stage—for example, after the respective approval processes. Synchronization scenarios serve to automatically exchange data between the portfolio item and the linked project. This enables you to monitor and analyze project data in Portfolio Management using various dashboards, reports, and metrics.

Figure 7.9 Sample Portfolio Structure in SAP PPM

> **Classification Hierarchies**
>
> For valuation purposes, you can define several alternative portfolio hierarchies, so-called *classification hierarchies*. Portfolio items can then simultaneously be assigned to different portfolio buckets of the classification hierarchies. The percentage distribution that you specify for assignments determines the details of the data aggregation in the classification hierarchies. Typical portfolio structuring options include, for example, structuring by region or by functional or organizational aspects.

Now we will describe the usage of portfolio items and the integration with projects in SAP Project System via an example of the construction of a new office building.

In your enterprise, several structural measures are supposed to be implemented as investments. One of the investment proposals includes the construction of a new office building. To evaluate this proposal, you first enter a portfolio item in an appropriate portfolio bucket (see Figure 7.10).

Portfolio item

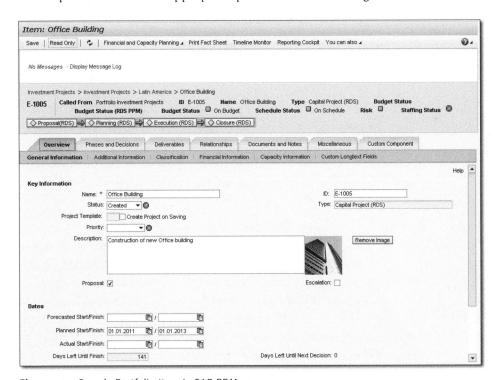

Figure 7.10 Sample Portfolio Item in SAP PPM

Entering key figures
In addition to general data for the description and scheduling of this proposal, you also enter various key figures—for example, those to do with risk, feasibility, or the economic benefits of this plan. These key figures were defined for the portfolio as a common basis for later approval processes in your enterprise in advance. *Questionnaires* and *evaluation models* can be used to simplify the definition of the key figures and make it more transparent or to automatically derive key figure values from other field values. In addition to various standard key figures, you can also define custom key figure fields and integrate them with SAP PPM. If there are relationships with other objects, then you can define them as dependencies with other portfolio items or by means of object links and documents in the portfolio item.

[+] **Initiatives and Collections**

Initiatives can be used in SAP PPM to group and manage various portfolio items and projects. Initiatives are usually used for innovation plans in which the development of new products and their introduction to the market are supposed to be managed together.

An alternative, less strict form of portfolio item groups in SAP PPM is *collections*. Collections merely serve to monitor several portfolio items of different buckets together.

Decision points
The lifecycle of a portfolio item can be divided into different phases, so-called *decision points*. You schedule the start and end dates and the decision dates for the individual phases of the office building project. Statuses control the process of the individual phases. At the portfolio item level, you can view information on the current decision point at any time.

Financial and capacity planning
In a next step, you perform first rough financial and capacity planning for the office building project at the portfolio item level (see Figure 7.11). Depending on the settings, planning can be implemented for fiscal years or individual periods, for example. You can define the financial and capacity planning structure freely in SAP PPM Customizing using *views*, *types*, and *groups*. If required, you can also upload (rollup) certain financial and capacity data to the parent portfolio buckets in order to compare it to the corresponding higher-level planning data.

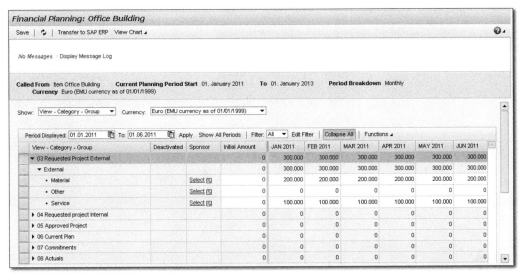

Figure 7.11 Sample Financial Planning at the Portfolio Item Level

After completing the definition of the portfolio item data, the corresponding approval processes can be implemented. PPM supports these approval processes—for example, with status management and workflow and with *portfolio reviews* and *scoreboards*. Portfolio reviews are used for approval—but also for portfolio item monitoring—and can be carried out periodically (for example, annually) or ad hoc. After creating a review in SAP PPM, you can assign this review the portfolio item that you want to evaluate. A *reporting cockpit* provides an overview of the essential key figures and planning data of the review items in tables and diagrams. The scoreboard function allows you to have the system create ranking lists of the review portfolio items automatically, based on the different evaluation models. Evaluation models are defined in SAP PPM Customizing and are based on a weighted valuation of the portfolio item key figures.

Reviews and scoreboards

What-if scenarios within reviews can be used to simulate different key figures, financial data, and capacity data for all or a part of the review items. For what-if scenarios, separate reporting cockpits and dashboards are available with which you can compare the simulated key figures and planning data to the original data.

What-if scenarios

Links to projects

After the office building project has been approved in a portfolio review, you change the status of the portfolio item or of the last decision point accordingly. You create a new operational project in SAP Project System automatically using a customer enhancement or by setting the CREATE PROJECT ON SAVING indicator and selecting an appropriate project template in the portfolio item overview. You can now have the system automatically create various object links between the project and the portfolio item as well as between the decision points and the project elements, which allows for data exchange—for example, of date information, system status, financial data, or capacity data. The following object links are available:

- Portfolio item ↔ Project
- Decision point ↔ WBS elements or activities
- Object link to Financials integration

The exchange of the data or status information can be *bidirectional, synchronous,* or *asynchronous.* This enables you, for example, to transfer forecast dates from the portfolio item to the project as well as planned and actual dates from the project to the portfolio item.

[+] **Manually Creating Projects and Linking Objects**

As an alternative to creating and linking projects from portfolio items automatically, you can also manually create a project in SAP Project System and link project definition, WBS elements, or activities in SAP PPM to the portfolio item or the decision points.

Financials integration

If an object link to the Financials integration between the portfolio item and project exists, then you can exchange financial data between the two objects. To upload accounting data from SAP Project System, use the /RPM/FICO_INT_PLANNING program, which you can schedule in SAP PPM as a regular background job, for example (see Figure 7.12). The data transferred from the project to financial planning of the portfolio item can also be automatically uploaded within the portfolio structure so that it is available in the parent portfolio buckets for valuation purposes.

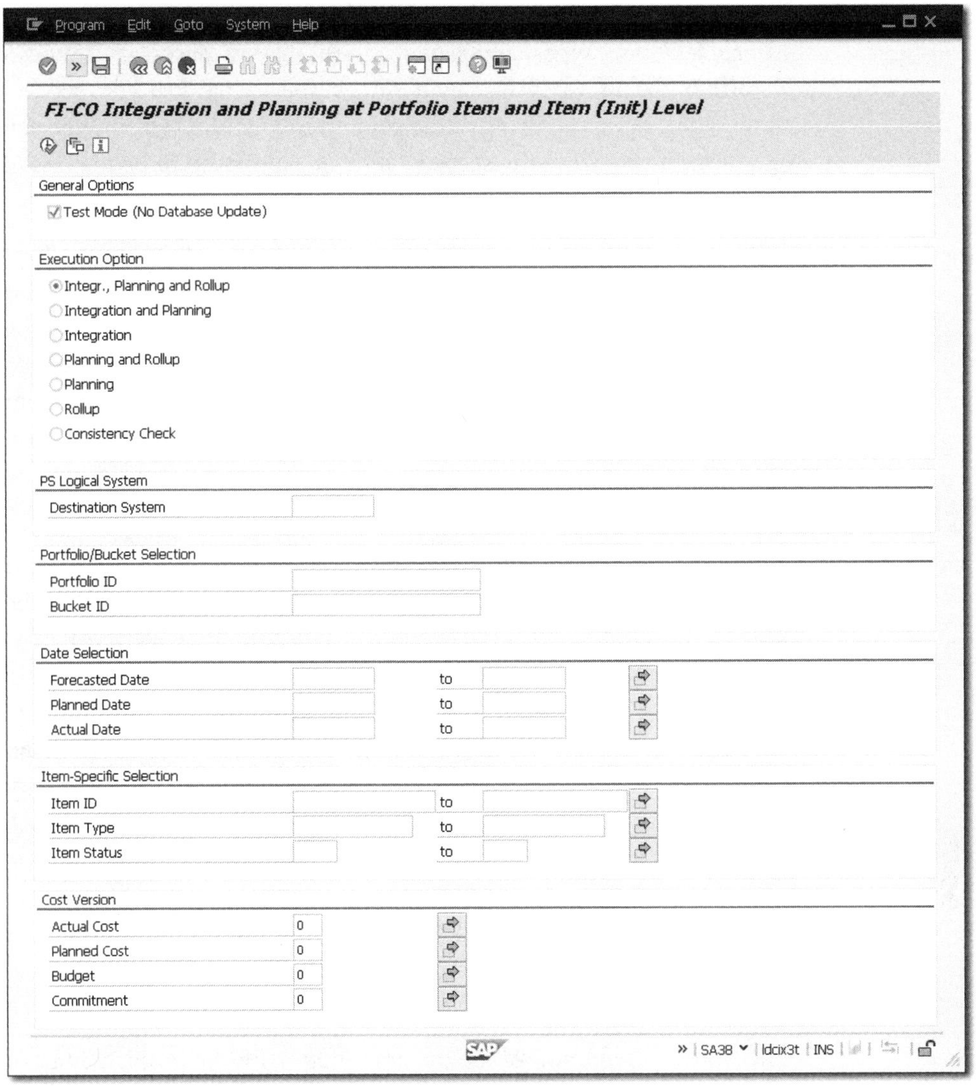

Figure 7.12 Program for the Integration of Accounting Data

You can implement detailed settings for the Financials integration in the Customizing of SAP PPM and of the SAP ERP system. In SAP PPM, besides the technical details of the object link, you define, for example, how data of hierarchically subordinate objects in the project and of assigned orders is supposed to be processed. In particular, you define

Detailed setting

the assignment of the cost and revenue elements in the SAP ERP system for financial views, types, and groups in SAP PPM. If necessary, you can add further details to this assignment by specifying cost centers and activity types. In Customizing of the connected SAP ERP system, you can also determine how already settled values are supposed to be processed in the context of the integration with SAP PPM.

Budget transfer

In addition to loading accounting data from SAP Project System to Portfolio Management, you can also transfer financial data from portfolio items as hierarchically structured planned costs or budgets to the assigned projects. In this way, you can transfer the budget assigned to the construction of the new office building in Portfolio Management from financials planning of the portfolio item to the project. The person responsible for the project can then distribute this budget within the project structure (see Chapter 3, Section 3.1).

Integration of capacity data

In additional to the financial data, you can also upload capacity data from SAP Project System in Portfolio Management and compare it to the planned values in SAP PPM. To derive capacity data, however, SAP PPM does not directly use the capacity data of projects in SAP Project System (see Chapter 2, Section 2.2.1) but derives the corresponding values from the transferred accounting data. In SAP PPM Customizing, you assign cost elements, activity types, and cost centers to the respective capacity views, types, and groups. When uploading accounting data from SAP Project System using the /RPM/FICO_INT_PLANNING program, the system automatically transfers the quantity data from the CO records to the assigned capacity records in SAP PPM. In contrast to the Financials integration, you cannot download capacity data from portfolio items to the assigned projects in SAP Project System.

Thanks to the integration of the portfolio item with the project, you can now also monitor aggregated project details in Portfolio Management. If required, you can also directly navigate from a portfolio item to the SAP Project System processing or reporting transactions to view further details. Numerous reporting options, such as various dashboards, the reporting cockpit, metrics management, predefined BI content and reports, and integration scenarios for SAP BusinessObjects BI, support you in monitoring and controlling your project portfolios in SAP PPM.

7.4   SAP Commercial Project Management

SAP Commercial Project Management (SAP CPM) is an add-on of the SAP ERP system, which complements Project System and also SAP PPM Project Management and other SAP applications with various functions for optimizing business processes. SAP CPM was specifically developed for handling customer projects that are focused on professional-service scenarios or construction projects. Various functions of SAP CPM, however, can also be used for other project types and industries. SAP CPM comprises three components that are described in more detail in the following sections.

7.4.1   Project Cost and Revenue Planning

The *Project Cost and Revenue Planning* component offers another option for financial planning of projects. In contrast to the options outlined in Chapter 2, you can use the financial plan of Project Cost and Revenue Planning also in the quotation phase of a customer project for which a project structure for planning may not exist yet. A financial plan of SAP CPM enables you to define your own quotation structure, which can then be used for structured financial planning. If a project structure exists later on, then you can assign the quotation structure to the project structure and transfer the planned values to it. Of course, you can also use a project structure directly for financial planning if it already exists at the time of planning.

Project Cost and Revenue Planning

Further advantages of SAP CPM Project Cost and Revenue Planning include, for example:

▶ Use of SAP BusinessObjects Analysis and Microsoft Excel as a planning interface to allow you to define your own workbooks and to integrate analysis functions with planning

▶ A uniform planning tool across all project phases, starting from cost estimations, to detailed project calculations and planning of variance costs, to special functions and workbooks for cost forecast

▶ Collective planning of quantities, costs, and revenues in one planning interface with embedded analysis functions

▸ The option to plan based on months, weeks, or days

▸ Enhanced functions for copying and versioning financial planning data as well as for comparing planned/actual and version values

Figure 7.13 shows an example of Project Cost and Revenue Planning using SAP CPM. From the technical perspective, Project Cost and Revenue Planning of SAP CPM uses SAP BW Integrated Planning. Different from the planning described in Chapter 2, Section 2.4.5, in SAP CPM the financial planning data is not directly written to the planning tables of SAP ERP but stored in real-time InfoCubes of SAP BW. If required, you can transfer the planning data to the SAP ERP system for follow-up processes later on—for example, in the form of a cost or revenue planning, for quantity or material component updates in networks, or for resource staffing processes to MRS. Thanks to this flexible technical framework, Project Cost and Revenue Planning of SAP CPM provides you with many adaption and enhancement options.

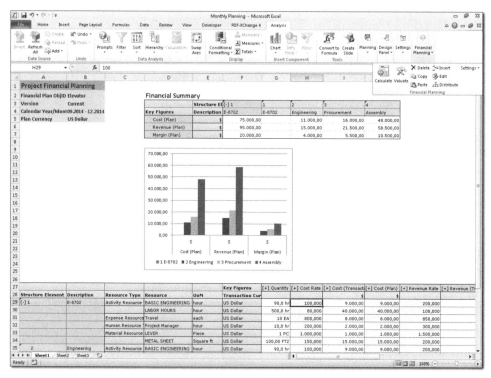

Figure 7.13 Example of Project Cost and Revenue Planning Using SAP CPM

7.4.2 Project Issue and Change Management

The *Project Issue and Change Management* component of SAP CPM constitutes a modern, Web Dynpro-based alternative to the Claim Management discussed in Chapter 4, Section 4.8. The two essential business processes that are supported by this component involve the entry and processing of issues within project processing and the handling and approval of project-related change requests. These two processes, which are often linked with one another, are described in more detail in the following sections.

Project Issue and Change Management

Entering and Processing Issues

To document and possibly solve difficulties within the flow of a project, you can use *issues* in SAP CPM (see Figure 7.14). The information that you can store for an issue includes the following:

Issues

▸ General issue details, such as identification, title, description, type, and priority of the issue as well as employee responsible and processing status

▸ Measures for further processing of the issue, up to solution and completion

▸ Information on relevant internal or external business partners and their roles

▸ Reference objects referring to the issue—for instance, project item or purchasing or sales documents—which you want to display or process from the issue

▸ Documents of document management, attachments, or links in the form of URLs

▸ Information on the possible effects of the issue—for example, estimated variance costs or estimated scheduling delay—as well as expected date of solution and a solution proposal itself

▸ A document history enables you to track subsequent changes to the issue

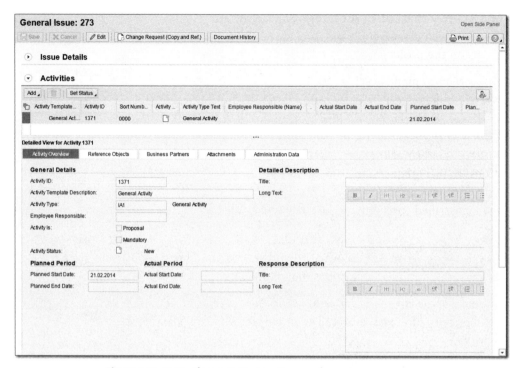

Figure 7.14 Entry of an Activity as a Measure for an Issue

Activities
Figure 7.14 shows an example of entering an issue and the corresponding measures in SAP CPM. Measures are defined via *activities*. Activities can be created manually, using templates, or automatically. If you assign partners to activities, then you can also use activities to send corresponding notifications via email or define approval processes in the form of workflows, for example.

[+] **BRFplus**

The rules for automatically creating activities and sending workflows and emails can be configured very flexibly using Business Rule Framework plus (BRFplus).

Change Management

Within the scope of a project, issues or change requests of customers may require changes to a project that can impact the schedule, the resources required, costs, or revenues. By means of Change Management, you can document these requirements, estimate and evaluate impacts on the project plan, and define approval processes.

Change Management occurs with reference to a *change request* in SAP CPM. You can create a change request directly, copy it, or create it based on an issue. In the latter case, you can then copy the data from the issue to the change request and transfer the issue as a reference object. If required, you can also create a collective change request by grouping various change requests in order to optimize further processing. A change request provides functions and fields that are similar to the issues described previously—for example, assignment of partners, attachments, and reference objects and the use of activities to define measures and approval processes. In a change request, you can also enter cost estimation alternatives.

Change requests

Cost estimation alternatives in combination with the appropriate workbooks of Project Cost and Revenue Planning of SAP CPM enable you to plan changes to the financial planning of your projects or project parts and link them with the change request. In this context, you can also enter multiple cost estimation alternatives for a change request. Later on, you can mark an alternative as ready for approval by setting a status. When a cost estimation alternative is approved, its values can be evaluated together with the other financial planning values in the project cost status reporting of SAP CPM. The approval process is performed via the appropriate activities and BRFplus.

Cost estimation alternatives

7.4.3   Project Workspace

Many business objects and documents from different applications or systems play a role during the various phases of a customer project. These include, for example, opportunities of SAP Customer Relationship Management (SAP CRM), quotations, orders from sales and distribution, financial plans, projects, issues and change requests, purchase requisitions, orders, and so on. Furthermore, employees with different roles are involved depending on the phase, such as sales employees, project managers, controllers, or (project) purchasers. The third component of SAP CPM, *Project Workspace*, constitutes a user-friendly

Project Workspace

working environment for all project participants, in which users are provided with information on all relevant objects and documents in an integrated manner. The information a user can view depends on his or her role.

Figure 7.15 shows the initial screen of SAP CPM Project Workspace, in which various key figures and information for different projects are displayed in a clear overview. Before we discuss Project Workspace and its cross-project and project-specific views in more detail, we will first take a look at the integration and display of relevant data from SAP CRM, SAP ERP, or SAP PPM using *master projects*.

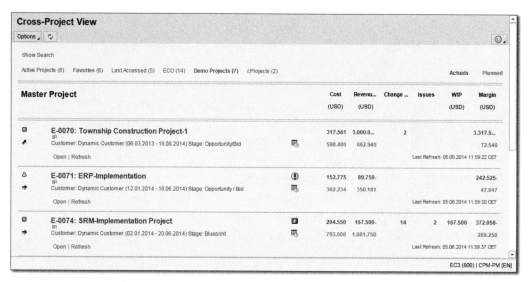

Figure 7.15 Cross-Project View of the Project Workspace in SAP CPM

Master projects A master project in SAP CPM serves as the link for all business objects that are relevant for a customer project and originate from SAP or non-SAP systems. The master project is thus the leading object in SAP CPM. Besides the type of the master project, a description, and an ID, you can allocate additional information to a master project, such as details of the organizational assignment, start and end dates, the current project phase, or reporting attributes that can be configured freely in CPM Customizing. By means of BAdIs, you can synchronize various pieces of information with the business objects assigned to the master project.

For example, you may automatically synchronize the start and end date with the dates of a project definition in SAP Project System or transfer reporting attributes to the customer fields of assigned SAP objects.

The structure of a master project is defined by the assigned business objects. The assignment of business objects can be made manually or partly automated. For example, if you assign a project definition to a master project, then the subordinate project items or linked sales documents can be assigned automatically to the master project. In SAP CPM, you can add further information and attributes to the assigned business objects as required. In addition, in SAP CPM you can define different *views* of the master project structure. With this structure, you specify the business objects to be displayed and how their hierarchical structure is to be presented. This allows for different Project Workspace views for the sales employees and project managers, for example.

Master project structure

For master projects, the SAP CPM Project Workspace provides you with additional functions. These include the following:

▶ Definition of teams and roles for the documentation of all relevant project members and their responsibilities. By assigning roles to the team members, you can influence their views and authorizations in SAP CPM Project Workspace.

▶ The Rate Card Editor to specify master project-specific prices, which are taken into account during pricing of the assigned sales documents.

▶ The Billing Plan Manager for advanced planning and control of billing events (for instance, collective planning of fixed price and resource-related billing events or usage of delta data records when changes are made to the quantity or amounts of billing-relevant events).

▶ Status Management, with the option to enter descriptive texts and trends on the current status of individual, freely configurable aspects (for example, overall status, quality, budget, and so on). You can track the development of the project status via change logs, status reports, and functions for checking or reviewing the status.

▶ The Alerts Framework for the flexible definition of exceptional situations that are to be displayed directly in Project Workspace. Examples of alerts that are available to you by default include variances of planned and actual costs, open invoices or overdue customer payments, number of issues or change requests, and so on.

Cross-project view The cross-project view of Project Workspace (see Figure 7.15) provides an overview of critical key figures of your projects, the current status trends, and relevant alerts and important key dates. Many settings of this view can be adapted in a user-specific manner—for instance, the order in which the master projects are displayed, their grouping in categories, the selection of key figures, or alerts settings.

Master project workspace From the cross-project view, you can now navigate to the master project workspace. Depending on your role and the authorizations in the project, the system displays different views in the master project workspace. Figure 7.16 shows the overview of the master project workspace as an example.

Figure 7.16 Overview of a Project in the Master Project Workspace of SAP CPM

On the left hand side, you can view the structure of the master project with the various business objects. From here, you can navigate within the master project structure, view important information on an object, or directly go to the transactions for displaying or processing objects. On the right hand side, you can find analysis functions that are integrated with the workspace. You are provided with current information on different aspects of the object selected, such as costs, work in process, or project progress (in a tabular or graphical form).

The master project workspace provides the following default views:

▶ Commercial View for analyzing assigned sales documents and navigating to their processing area

▶ Procurement View for providing an overview of the information on the purchasing history, including purchase orders, open purchase requisitions, service entry sheets and invoices, for calling the corresponding transactions

▶ Team overview

▶ View for analyzing and creating financial plans (see Section 7.4.1)

▶ Overview of all issues and change requests for the master project (see Section 7.4.2)

▶ Documents for viewing and assigning documents and attachments

The use of Floorplan Manager (FPM) and the embedded analysis functions as well as various customer enhancement options of SAP CPM allow for many different customer-specific and partially user-specific Customizing options of the workspace.

7.5 Summary

SAP Project System provides a range of BAPIs and Enterprise Services for data exchange with external programs. These BAPIs and services of the service-oriented architecture can be used to export project data from SAP Project System, modify projects, or create new project objects. SAP provides special interfaces for data exchange with Microsoft Project and Oracle Primavera. Projects in PPM Project Management can use SAP

Project System integration scenarios—for example, for Financials integration with the SAP ERP system. The integration of SAP Project System with PPM Portfolio Management can be used to define, approve, control, and monitor entire project portfolios. SAP Commercial Project Management complements SAP Project System with various functions and processes, specifically for customer project handling.

Appendices

A BAPIs in SAP Project System

Table A.1 through Table A.3 provide an overview of Business Application Programming Interfaces (BAPIs) in SAP Project System for the object types: ProjectDefinition, WorkBreakdownStruct, and Network.

BAPI	Description
ExistenceCheck	Enables you to check whether a project definition already exists.
Getlist	Returns a list of project definitions based on selection criteria.
Getdetail	Enables you to display the detailed information on the project definition.
CreateFromData	Enables you to create a project definition.
Update	Enables you to modify a project definition.

Table A.1 BAPIs for the ProjectDefinition Business Object Type

BAPI	Description
ExistenceCheck	Enables you to check whether a WBS element already exists.
Getinfo	Enables you to display the detailed information on the project definition and WBS elements, and assigned milestones and activities.
SaveReplica	Used internally only as part of Application Link and Enabling (ALE) business processes provided by SAP for work breakdown structures.
Maintain	Enables you to edit the project definition, its WBS elements, hierarchical relationships, and WBS element milestones. It also provides you with the entire functionality of the Maintain BAPI of Business Object Type NETWORK, which in turn enables you to edit networks (see Table A.3).

Table A.2 BAPIs for the WorkBreakdownStruct Business Object Type

BAPI	Description
ExistenceCheck	Enables you to check whether a network already exists.
GetList	Returns a list of networks based on selection criteria.
Getdetail GetInfo	These methods enable you to display the detailed information for a network, including all network objects in the system.
Maintain	Enables you to edit data in network headers, assigned activities and their relationships, and activity elements and milestones.
GetListComponent	Returns a list of material components for selected activities.
GetDetailComponent	Returns detailed information on material components of selected activities.
AddComponent	Enables you to assign a material component to network activities, or to assign multiple material components simultaneously to network activities.
ChangeComponent	Enables you to modify material components of a network. However, you cannot modify the procurement type.
RemoveComponent	Enables you to remove material components of a network.
GetListConfirmation	Returns a list of all confirmations for an activity or activity element.
GetDetailConfirmation	Returns detailed information on a confirmation of an activity or activity element.
GetProposalConfirmation	Returns default values for creating a confirmation.
AddConfirmation	Enables you to record confirmations for network activities, activity elements, or activity splits.
CancelConfirmation	Enables you to cancel a network confirmation that has already been posted.

Table A.3 BAPIs for the Network Business Object Type

B Query and Reuse Views of SAP Project System in SAP HANA Live

Table B.1 provides you with an overview of the query views that are currently available in the standard SAP system. Table B.2 lists the reuse views of SAP Project System in SAP HANA Live. You can use these views for the definition of a project reporting.

View Name	Description
NetworkActivityConfirmation-Query	Details on activity confirmations
NetworkActivityDatesQuery	Activity details on schedule variances (today vs. latest dates)
NetworkActivityRelationsQuery	Predecessor/successor details of activities
NetworkActivityStatusQuery	Activity status details
NetworkActivityWorkDeviation-Query	Deviations of planned work of activities
PlantSalesOrderStockQuery	Plant/sales order stocks
ProjectCompletionPercentQuery	Planned and actual progress of projects in the current and previous year
ProjectCostLinetemsQuery	Commitment and actual cost line items
ProjectEarnedValueQuery	Aggregated earned values of projects
ProjectHierarchyQueryView	Hierarchy information
ProjectMaterialStockQuery	Project stocks
ProjectMaterialWarehouse-StockQuery	Stocks across all stock segments
ProjectMilestoneDatesQuery	Milestone details on schedule variances
ProjectMilestoneTrendAnalysis-Query	Information on milestone trend analysis

Table B.1 Default Query Views of Project System in SAP HANA Live

View Name	Description
`ProjectMilestoneTrend-StatisticsQuery`	Number of milestones for milestone trends
`ProjectMissingPartsQuery`	Material missing parts for projects
`ProjectNetworkDatesQuery`	Network details on schedule variances (today vs. latest dates)
`ProjectNetworkStatusQuery`	Network status details
`ProjectOpenReservationQuery`	Details on open reservations in projects
`ProjectPurchaseOrderItemDates-Query`	Due and overdue PO items for projects
`ProjectPurchasingDocSchedule-LineQuery`	Schedule line details of PO items for projects
`ProjectPurOrdItemVndr-ConfirmationQuery`	Vendor confirmations of PO items for projects
`ProjectRevenueLineItemsQuery`	Revenue line items of WBS elements
`ProjectStatusQuery`	Project status details
`ProjVndrMatlReliability-BsdOnDlvDteQuery`	Vendor reliability for material deliveries
`ProjVndrReliabiltiyBsdOn-DeliveryDteQuery`	General vendor reliability
`WBSElementCompletion-PercentQuery`	Planned and actual percentage of completion of WBS elements in the current and previous year
`WBSElementCostVarianceQuery`	Comparison of total planned costs with commitments and actual costs at the WBS element level
`WBSElementDatesQuery`	WBS element details on schedule variances (today vs. latest dates)
`WBSElementEarnedValueQuery`	Aggregated earned values and actual costs for WBS elements
`WBSElementPeriodCostByValue-CategoryQuery`	Cost information sorted by value categories at the WBS element level
`WBSElementPeriodCostBy-YearQuery`	Chronological distribution of costs at the WBS element level

Table B.1 Default Query Views of Project System in SAP HANA Live (Cont.)

View Name	Description
WBSElementPeriodCostVariance-Query	Comparison of planned costs with commitments and actual costs at the WBS element level for a specific period of time
WBSElementPeriodRevenue-ByYearQuery	Chronological distribution of planned and actual revenues at the WBS element level
WBSElementPeriodRevenue-VarianceQuery	WBS elements with revenue variance for a specific period of time
WBSElementRevenueVarianceQuery	WBS elements with revenue variance
WBSElementStatusQuery	WBS element status details
WBSElementWorkDeviationQuery	Deviations of planned work, aggregated at WBS element level

Table B.1 Default Query Views of Project System in SAP HANA Live (Cont.)

View Name	Description
ControllingValType	Name of value types
MaterialComponent	Details on the material components
NetworkActivity	Details on network activities
NetworkActivityConfirmation	Details on activity confirmations
NetworkActivityRelations	Details on relationships and predecessors/successors
Project	Details on project definitions and their statuses
ProjectCostItems	Cost information from RPSCO
ProjectCostLineItems	Line item details from COEP and COOI (costs and commitments)
ProjectCumltvEarnedValue	Cumulative earned values and actual costs of projects
ProjectCumulativeCompletion-Percent	Cumulative planned and actual percentage of completion for projects
ProjectLedgerNumber	Account information on projects
ProjectMilestone	Details on milestones

Table B.2 Default Reuse Views of Project System in SAP HANA Live

View Name	Description
ProjectNetwork	Network details
ProjectPeriodCostItems	Cost information per period
ProjectPeriodRevenueItems	Revenue information per period
ProjectPurOrdItemVndr-Confirmation	Details on vendor confirmations of PO items for projects
ProjectRevenueItems	Revenue information from RPSCO
ProjectRevenueLineItems	Revenue line item details from COEP
ProjVndrMatlReliabilityBsd-OnDeliveryDte	Details on vendor reliability per material
ProjVndrReliabiltiyBasedOn-DeliveryDate	Details on general vendor reliability
WBSEarnedValueAndActlCosts	Aggregated earned values and actual costs for WBS elements
WBSElement	Details on WBS elements, including dates and statuses
WBSElementCompletionPercent	Planned and actual percentage of completion for WBS elements and periods
WBSElementCumltvEarnedValue	Cumulative earned values and actual costs for WBS elements
WBSElementCumulative-CompletionPercent	Cumulative planned and actual percentage of completion for WBS elements
WBSElementEarnedValue	Earned values and actual costs of WBS elements and periods

Table B.2 Default Reuse Views of Project System in SAP HANA Live (Cont.)

C Selected Project System Database Tables

Table C.1 and Table C.2 provide you with the most critical database tables of SAP Project System.

Table Name	Short Description
PROJ	Project definition
PRPS	WBS elements
PRTE	Dates for WBS elements
PRHI	WBS hierarchy
AUFK/AFKO	Orders and networks
AFVC/AFVU/AFVV	Network activities
RESB	Material components
MLST	Milestones
VS<Table_name>_CN	Version master data

Table C.1 Database Tables for Project System Master Data

Identification	Short Description
RPSCO	Project info database (costs, revenues, etc.)
RPSQT	Project info database (quantities, statistical key figures, etc.)
COSP	Primary costs (totals records)
COSS	Secondary costs (totals records)
COSB	Variances/accrual (totals records)
COEP	Actual costs (line items)
COOI	Commitments (line items)
COEJ	Planned costs (line items)
BPGE	Overall budget, overall planned costs
BPJA	Fiscal year budget, fiscal year plan values

Table C.2 Database Tables for Project System Transaction Data

Identification	Short Description
QBEW	Project stock evaluation
MSPR	Evaluated and unevaluated project stock

Table C.2 Database Tables for Project System Transaction Data (Cont.)

D Transactions and Menu Paths

You can access the Project System menu in the SAP standard menu via the LOGISTICS menu or the FINANCIALS menu.

To access the SAP Customizing Implementation Guide (IMG), either enter Transaction SPRO or choose the following menu path: TOOLS · CUSTOMIZING · IMG · WORK ON PROJECT.

D.1 Structures and Master Data

This section offers you an overview of transactions, Customizing activities, and menu paths for creating and editing project structures and their master data.

D.1.1 Transactions in the SAP Menu

The relevant transactions in the SAP menu are listed first.

Operative Structures

Project Builder [CJ20N]: PROJECT SYSTEM · PROJECT · PROJECT BUILDER

Project Planning Board [CJ27/CJ2B/CJ2C]: PROJECT SYSTEM · PROJECT · PROJECT PLANNING BOARD · CREATE PROJECT/CHANGE PROJECT/DISPLAY PROJECT

Structure Planning [CJ2D/CJ20/CJ2A]: PROJECT SYSTEM · PROJECT · SPECIAL MAINTENANCE FUNCTIONS · STRUCTURE PLANNING · CREATE PROJECT/CHANGE PROJECT/DISPLAY PROJECT

Work Breakdown Structure [CJ01/CJ02/CJ03]: PROJECT SYSTEM · PROJECT · SPECIAL MAINTENANCE FUNCTIONS · WORK BREAKDOWN STRUCTURE (WBS) · CREATE/CHANGE/DISPLAY

Project Definition [CJ06/CJ07/CJ08]: PROJECT SYSTEM · PROJECT · SPECIAL MAINTENANCE FUNCTIONS · WORK BREAKDOWN STRUCTURE (WBS) · PROJECT DEFINITION · CREATE/CHANGE/DISPLAY

Single Element [CJ11/CJ12/CJ13]: Project System • Project • Special Maintenance Functions • Work Breakdown Structure (WBS) • Single Element • Create/Change/Display

Network [CN21/CN22/CN23]: Project System • Project • Special Maintenance Functions • Network • Create/Change/Display

Edit Large Projects [PSHLP10/PSHLP20/PSHLP30/PSHLP90]: Project System • Project • Edit Large Projects • Project Worklist/Project Editor/Design Workbench/Administrator Workbench

Mass Change [CNMASS]: Project System • Basic Data • Tools • Mass Change

Archive Project Structures [CN80]: Project System • Basic Data • Tools • Archiving • Project Structures

Standard Structures and Versions

Standard WBS [CJ91/CJ92/CJ93]: Project System • Basic Data • Templates • Standard WBS • Create/Change/Display

Standard Network [CN01/CN02/CN03/CN98]: Project System • Basic Data • Templates • Standard Network • Create/Change/Display/Delete

Standard Milestone [CN11/CN12/CN13]: Project System • Basic Data • Templates • Standard Milestone • Create/Change/Display

Simulation [CJV1/CJV2/CJV3/CJV5]: Project System • Project • Simulation • Create/Change/Display/Delete

Transfer Project [CJV4]: Project System • Project • Simulation • Transfer Project

Project Version [CN72]: Project System • Project • Project Version • Create

D.1.2 Customizing Activities

The following provides an overview of relevant Customizing activities for creating project structures and their master data.

Operative Structures

Create Project Profile [OPSA]: SAP Customizing Implementation Guide • Project System • Structures • Operative Structures • Work Breakdown Structure (WBS) • Create Project Profile

Define Special Characters for Project [OPSK]: SAP Customizing Implementation Guide • Project System • Structures • Operative Structures • Work Breakdown Structure (WBS) • Project Coding Mask • Define Special Characters for Projects

Define Project Coding Mask [OPSJ]: SAP Customizing Implementation Guide • Project System • Structures • Operative Structures • Work Breakdown Structure (WBS) • Project Coding Mask • Define Project Coding Mask

Specify Persons Responsible for WBS Elements [OPS6]: Customizing Implementation Guide • Project System • Structures • Operative Structures • Work Breakdown Structure (WBS) • Specify Persons Responsible for WBS Elements

Create Status Profile [OK02]: Customizing Implementation Guide • Project System • Structures • Operative Structures • Work Breakdown Structure (WBS) • WBS User Status • Create Status Profile

Edit Status Combination Codes: Customizing Implementation Guide • Project System • Structures • Operative Structures • Work Breakdown Structure (WBS) • Edit Status Combination Code

Maintain Validations [OPSI]: Customizing Implementation Guide • Project System • Structures • Operative Structures • Work Breakdown Structure (WBS) • Maintain Validations

Maintain Substitutions [OPSN]: Customizing Implementation Guide • Project System • Structures • Operative Structures • Work Breakdown Structure (WBS) • Maintain Substitutions

Set Up Number Ranges for Network [CO82]: Customizing Implementation Guide • Project System • Structures • Operative Structures • Network • Settings for Networks • Set Up Number Ranges for Network

Maintain Network Types [OPSC]: CUSTOMIZING IMPLEMENTATION GUIDE • PROJECT SYSTEM • STRUCTURES • OPERATIVE STRUCTURES • NETWORK • SETTINGS FOR NETWORKS • MAINTAIN NETWORK TYPES

Specify Parameters for Network Type [OPUV]: CUSTOMIZING IMPLEMENTATION GUIDE • PROJECT SYSTEM • STRUCTURES • OPERATIVE STRUCTURES • NETWORK • SETTINGS FOR NETWORKS • SPECIFY PARAMETERS FOR NETWORK TYPE

Maintain Network Profiles [OPUU]: CUSTOMIZING IMPLEMENTATION GUIDE • PROJECT SYSTEM • STRUCTURES • OPERATIVE STRUCTURES • NETWORK • SETTINGS FOR NETWORKS • MAINTAIN NETWORK PROFILES

Define Control Key [OPSU]: CUSTOMIZING IMPLEMENTATION GUIDE • PROJECT SYSTEM • STRUCTURES • OPERATIVE STRUCTURES • NETWORK • SETTINGS FOR NETWORK ACTIVITIES • DEFINE CONTROL KEY

Define Parameters for Subnetworks [OPTP]: CUSTOMIZING IMPLEMENTATION GUIDE • PROJECT SYSTEM • STRUCTURES • OPERATIVE STRUCTURES • NETWORK • DEFINE PARAMETERS FOR SUBNETWORKS

Define Milestone Usage: CUSTOMIZING IMPLEMENTATION GUIDE • PROJECT SYSTEM • STRUCTURES • OPERATIVE STRUCTURES • MILESTONES • DEFINE MILESTONE USAGE

Define Profiles for the Project Planning Board [OPT7] : CUSTOMIZING IMPLEMENTATION GUIDE • PROJECT SYSTEM • STRUCTURES • PROJECT PLANNING BOARD • DEFINE PROFILES FOR THE PROJECT PLANNING BOARD

Standard Structures and Versions

Set Up Number Ranges for Standard Networks [CNN1]: CUSTOMIZING IMPLEMENTATION GUIDE • PROJECT SYSTEM • STRUCTURES • TEMPLATES • STANDARD NETWORK • SET UP NUMBER RANGES FOR STANDARD NETWORKS

Define Parameters for Standard Network [OP8B]: CUSTOMIZING IMPLEMENTATION GUIDE • PROJECT SYSTEM • STRUCTURES • TEMPLATES • STANDARD NETWORK • DEFINE PARAMETERS FOR STANDARD NETWORK

Maintain Standard Network Profiles [OPS5]: CUSTOMIZING IMPLEMENTATION GUIDE • PROJECT SYSTEM • STRUCTURES • TEMPLATES • STANDARD NETWORK • MAINTAIN STANDARD NETWORK PROFILES

Define Status for Standard Networks [OPUW]: CUSTOMIZING IMPLEMENTATION GUIDE • PROJECT SYSTEM • STRUCTURES • TEMPLATES • STANDARD NETWORK • DEFINE STATUS FOR STANDARD NETWORKS

Define Milestone Groups for Standard Milestones [OPT6]: CUSTOMIZING IMPLEMENTATION GUIDE • PROJECT SYSTEM • STRUCTURES • TEMPLATES • STANDARD MILESTONE • DEFINE MILESTONE GROUPS FOR STANDARD MILESTONES

Stipulate Version Keys for the Simulation [OPUS]: CUSTOMIZING IMPLEMENTATION GUIDE • PROJECT SYSTEM • SIMULATION • STIPULATE VERSION KEYS FOR THE SIMULATION

Stipulate Simulation Profiles: CUSTOMIZING IMPLEMENTATION GUIDE • PROJECT SYSTEM • SIMULATION • STIPULATE SIMULATION PROFILES

Create Profile for Project Version [OPTS]: CUSTOMIZING IMPLEMENTATION GUIDE • PROJECT SYSTEM • PROJECT VERSIONS • CREATE PROFILE FOR PROJECT VERSION

D.2   Planning Functions

The following functions and their Customizing settings are primarily used for project planning in SAP Project System.

D.2.1   Transactions in the SAP Menu

This section first provides an overview of transactions that can be used for planning.

Date Planning

Basic Dates [CJ21/CJ22]: PROJECT SYSTEM • DATES • CHANGE/DISPLAY BASIC DATES

Forecast Dates [CJ23/CJ24]: PROJECT SYSTEM • DATES • CHANGE/DISPLAY FORECAST DATES

Project Scheduling [CJ29]: PROJECT SYSTEM • DATES • PROJECT SCHEDULING

Overall Network Scheduling [CJ24]: PROJECT SYSTEM • DATES • OVERALL NETWORK SCHEDULING

Overall Network Scheduling (New) [CJ24N]: PROJECT SYSTEM • DATES • OVERALL NETWORK SCHEDULING (NEW)

Resource Planning

(Project) Work Center [CNR1/CNR2/CNR3]: PROJECT SYSTEM • BASIC DATA • MASTER DATA • WORK CENTER • MASTER RECORD • CREATE/CHANGE/DISPLAY

Workforce Planning for Personnel Resources [CMP2/CMP3/CMP9]: PROJECT SYSTEM • RESOURCES • WORKFORCE PLANNING • PROJECT VIEW/WORK CENTER VIEW/EVALUATION

Capacity Leveling [CM32/CM26]: PROJECT SYSTEM • RESOURCES • CAPACITY REQUIREMENTS PLANNING • LEVELING • PROJECT VIEW • PLANNING TABLE (GRAPHICAL)/(TABULAR)

Material Planning

Single-Level Project Bill of Material [CS71/CS72/CS73]: LOGISTICS • PRODUCTION • MASTER DATA • BILLS OF MATERIAL • BILL OF MATERIAL • WBS BOM • SINGLE-LEVEL • CREATE/CHANGE/DISPLAY

Multi-Level Project Bill of Material [CS74/CS75/CS76/CSPB]: LOGISTICS • PRODUCTION • MASTER DATA • BILLS OF MATERIAL • BILL OF MATERIAL • WBS BOM • MULTILEVEL • CREATE/CHANGE/DISPLAY/PROJECT BROWSER

Bill of Material Transfer [CN33]: PROJECT SYSTEM • MATERIAL • PLANNING • BILL OF MATERIAL TRANSFER

iPPE Product Designer [PDN]: LOGISTICS • PRODUCTION • MASTER DATA • INTEGRATED PRODUCT ENGINEERING • PRODUCT DESIGNER

Assign WBS Elements for Requirements Grouping [GRM4/GRM3]:
Project System • Material • Planning • Requirements Grouping •
Assign WBS Elements Individually/Using List

Assign MRP Groups [GRM5]: Project System • Material • Planning •
Requirements Grouping • Assign MRP Groups

Costs and Revenue Planning

Overall Planning [CJ40/CJ41]: Project System • Financials • Planning • Costs in WBS • Overall values • Change/Display

Cost and Activity Inputs [CJR2/CJR3]: Project System • Financials • Planning • Costs in WBS • Cost and Activity Inputs • Change/Display

Models for Easy Cost Planning [CKCM]: Project System • Basic Data • Templates • Models for Easy Cost Planning

(Asynchronous) Network Costing [CJ9K]: Project System • Financials • Planning • Network Costing

Payments in WBS [CJ48/CJ49]: Project System • Financials • Planning • Payments in WBS • Change/Display

Revenues in WBS [CJ42/CJ43]: Project System • Financials • Planning • Revenues in WBS • Change/Display

Sales Pricing [DP81/DP82]: Project System • Financials • Planning • Sales Pricing/Sales Pricing for Project

Copy Costs and Revenues (Indiv.) [CJ9BS/CJ9CS/CJ9FS]: Project System • Financials • Planning • Copy Costs and Revenues • Copy WBS Plan to Plan/Copy WBS Actual to Plan/Copy Project Costing (Indiv.)

Copy Costs and Revenues (Collective) [CJ9B/CJ9C/CJ9F]: Project System • Financials • Planning • Copy Costs and Revenues • Copy WBS Plan to Plan/Copy WBS Actual to Plan/Copy Project Costing (Collective)

Roles [PFCG]: Tools • Administration • User Maintenance • Role Administration • Roles

D.2.2 Customizing Activities

The following Customizing activities are available in SAP Project System for planning functions.

Date Planning

Define Scheduling Type [OPJN]: Customizing Implementation Guide • Project System • Dates • Scheduling • Define Scheduling Types

Specify Parameters for Network Scheduling [OPU6]: Customizing Implementation Guide • Project System • Dates • Scheduling • Specify Parameters for Network Scheduling

Define Parameters for WBS Scheduling: Customizing Implementation Guide • Project System • Dates • Date Planning in WBS • Define Parameters for WBS Scheduling

Resource Planning

Specify Work Center Categories [OP40]: Customizing Implementation Guide • Project System • Resources • Work Center • Specify Work Center Categories

Define Capacity Categories: Customizing Implementation Guide • Project System • Resources • Define Capacity Categories

Define Profiles for Workforce Planning [CMPC]: Customizing Implementation Guide • Project System • Resources • Define Profiles for Workforce Planning

Account Assignment Categories and Document Types for Purchase Requisitions [OPTT]: Customizing Implementation Guide • Project System • Structures • Operative Structures • Network • Settings for Network Activities • Account Assignment Categories and Document Types for Purchase Requisitions

Material Planning

Define Procurement Indicators for Material Components [OPS8]: Customizing Implementation Guide • Project System • Material • Procurement • Define Procurement Indicators for Material Components

Catalogs (OCI interface): Customizing Implementation Guide • Project System • Material • Interface for Procurement Using Catalogs (OCI)

iPPE Reference Points: Customizing Implementation Guide • Project System • Material • Integration of the Project System with iPPE • Define Reference Point for the Integration of the Project System with iPPE

Define Reference Points for BOM Transfer: Customizing Implementation Guide • Project System • Material • Bill of Material Transfer • Define Reference Points for BOM Transfer

Define Fields in BOM and Activity as Reference Point [CN38]: Customizing Implementation Guide • Project System • Material • Bill of Material Transfer • Define Fields in BOM and Activity as Reference Point

Define Profiles for BOM Transfer: Customizing Implementation Guide • Project System • Material • Bill of Material Transfer • Define Profiles for Bill of Material Transfer

Activate MRP Groups for Requirements Grouping: Customizing Implementation Guide • Project System • Material • Procurement • Activate MRP Groups for Requirements Grouping

Define Checking Control [OPJK]: Customizing Implementation Guide • Project System • Material • Availability Check • Define Checking Control

Costs and Revenue Planning

Create CO Versions: Customizing Implementation Guide • Project System • Costs • Create CO Versions

Create/Change Planning Profile [OPSB]: Customizing Implementation Guide • Project System • Costs • Planned Costs • Manual Cost Planning in WBS • Hierarchical Cost Planning • Create/Change Planning Profile

Create Costing Variant for Unit Costing [OKKT]: Customizing Implementation Guide • Project System • Costs • Planned Costs • Manual Cost Planning in WBS • Unit Costing • Create Costing Variant

Easy Cost Planning: Customizing Implementation Guide • Project System • Costs • Planned Costs • Easy Cost Planning and Execution Services • Easy Cost Planning

Define Costing Variants for Network Costing [OPL1]: Customizing Implementation Guide •Project System • Costs • Planned Costs • Automatic Costing in Networks/Activities • Costing • Define Costing Variants

Define Order Value Updating for Orders for Projects [OPSV]: Customizing Implementation Guide • Project System • Costs • Planned Costs • Define Order Value Updating for Orders for Projects

DPP Profile [ODP1]: Customizing Implementation Guide • Project System • Revenues and Earnings • Integration with SD Documents • Creating Quotations and Project Billing • Maintain Profiles for Quotations and Billing

Operational Data Provisioning for Operational Analytics: SAP NetWeaver • Search and Operational Analytics • Operational Data Provisioning for Operational Analytics • Basic Configuration for Operational Analytics/Define Client for Modeling

Activate BI Content Bundle for Planning: Controlling • Controlling General • Roles for NetWeaver Business Client • Project Planner and Calculator • Activate BI Content Bundle for Planning

D.3 Budget

For budgeting projects, you can specifically call the transactions, Customizing activities, and menu paths listed here.

D.3.1 Transactions in the SAP Menu

The transactions listed in this section play an important role for budgeting.

Budgeting in Project System

Original Budget [CJ30/CJ31]: PROJECT SYSTEM • FINANCIALS • BUDGETING • ORIGINAL BUDGET • CHANGE/DISPLAY

Supplement [CJ37/CJ36]: PROJECT SYSTEM • FINANCIALS • BUDGETING • SUPPLEMENT • IN PROJECT/TO PROJECT

Return [CJ38/CJ35]: PROJECT SYSTEM • FINANCIALS • BUDGETING • RETURN • IN PROJECT/FROM PROJECT

Transfer [CJ34]: PROJECT SYSTEM • FINANCIALS • BUDGETING • TRANSFER

Release [CJ32/CJ33]: PROJECT SYSTEM • FINANCIALS • BUDGETING • RELEASE • CHANGE/DISPLAY

Mass Release of Budget for Projects [IMCBR3]: PROJECT SYSTEM • FINANCIALS • BUDGETING • TOOLS • MASS RELEASE OF BUDGET FOR PROJECTS

Availability Control [CJBV/CVBW]: PROJECT SYSTEM • FINANCIALS • BUDGETING • TOOLS • ACTIVATE/DEACTIVATE AVAILABILITY CONTROL

Transfer Plan to Project Budget [IMCCP3]: PROJECT SYSTEM • FINANCIALS • BUDGETING •TOOLS • TRANSFER PLAN TO PROJECT BUDGET

Budget Carryforward [CJCO]: PROJECT SYSTEM • FINANCIALS • YEAR-END CLOSING • BUDGET CARRYFORWARD

Integration for Investment Management

Plan Proposal [IM34]: FINANCIALS • INVESTMENT MANAGEMENT • PROGRAMS • PROGRAM PLANNING • PLAN PROPOSAL

Budget Distribution [IM52/IM53]: FINANCIALS • INVESTMENT MANAGEMENT • PROGRAMS • BUDGETING • BUDGET DISTRIBUTION • EDIT/DISPLAY

D.3.2 Customizing Activities

The following settings can be made in Customizing for budget management.

Budgeting in Project System

Maintain Budget Profiles [OPS9]: Customizing Implementation Guide • Project System • Costs • Budget • Maintain Budget Profiles

Define Tolerance Limits: Customizing Implementation Guide • Project System • Costs • Budget • Define Tolerance Limits

Specify Exempt Cost Elements [OPTK]: Customizing Implementation Guide • Project System • Costs • Budget • Specify Exempt Cost Elements

Reconstruct Availability Control [CJBN]: Customizing Implementation Guide • Project System • Costs •Budget • Reconstruct Availability Control

Integration for Investment Management

Define Program Types: Customizing Implementation Guide • Investment Management • Investment Programs • Master Data • Define Program Types

D.4 Project Execution Processes

The transactions and menu paths listed in this section are available during the execution phase of projects.

D.4.1 Transactions in the SAP Menu

In this section, you can find a selection of transactions that are relevant for project execution.

Account Assignment of Documents, Confirmations, and Procurement Processes

Purchase Requisitions [ME51N/ME52N/ME53N]: Logistics • Materials Management • Purchasing • Purchase Requisition • Create/Change/Display

Create Purchase Order [ME21N/ME25/ME58/ME59]: Logistics • Materials Management • Purchasing • Purchase Order • Create • Vendor/Supplying Plant Known/Vendor Unknown/Via Requisition Assignment List/Automatically via Purchase Requisitions

Goods Receipt [MIGO]: Logistics • Materials Management • Purchasing • Purchase Order • Follow-On Functions • Goods Receipt

Entry of Services [ML81N]: Logistics • Materials Management • Purchasing • Purchase Order • Follow-On Functions • Service Entry Sheet • Maintain

Activity Allocations [KB21N/KB23N/KB24N]: Project System • Financials • Actual Postings • Activity Allocation • Enter/Display/Cancel

Individual Confirmation [CN25/CN28/CN29]: Project System • Progress • Confirmation • Individual Confirmation • Enter/Display/Cancel/reverse

Collective Confirmation [CN27]: Project System • Progress • Confirmation • Collective Confirmation

CATS Classic [CAT2/CAT3]: Project System • Progress • Confirmation • Time Sheet • CATS Classic • Record/Display Working Times

CATS for Service Providers [CATSXT/CATSXT_ADMIN]: Project System • Progress • Confirmation • Time Sheet • CATS for Service Providers • Record Own Working Times/Record Working Times

Transfer [CATA/CAT7/CAT6/CATM/CAT9/CAT5]: Project System • Progress • Confirmation • Time Sheet • Transfer • All Component/Accounting/Human Resources/External Services/Plant Maintenance/Customer Service/Project System

MRP Run Project Stock [MD51]: PROJECT SYSTEM • MATERIAL • PLANNING • MRP PROJECT

Delivery from Project [CNS0]: PROJECT SYSTEM • MATERIAL • EXECUTION • DELIVERY FROM PROJECT

ProMan [CNMM]: PROJECT SYSTEM • MATERIAL • EXECUTION • PROJECT-ORIENTED PROCUREMENT (PROMAN)

Billing, Project Progress, and Claim Management

Invoice [VF01/VF02/VF03/VF04/VF11]: LOGISTICS • SALES • BILLING • INVOICE • CREATE/MODIFY/DISPLAY/EDIT BILLING DUE LIST/CANCEL

Resource-Related Billing [DP91/DP96/DP93]: LOGISTICS • SALES AND DISTRIBUTION • SALES • ORDER • SUBSEQUENT FUNCTIONS • RESOURCE-RELATED BILLING DOCUMENT/RESOURCE-RELATED BILLING DOCUMENT (COLLECTIVE PROCESSING)/BILLING BETWEEN COMPANY CODES

Milestone Trend Analysis [CNMT]: PROJECT SYSTEM • INFORMATION SYSTEM • PROGRESS • MILESTONE TREND ANALYSIS

Progress Determination [CNE1/CNE2]: PROJECT SYSTEM • PROGRESS • PROGRESS DETERMINATION • INDIVIDUAL PROCESSING/COLLECTIVE PROCESSING

Progress Analysis Workbench [CNPAWB]: PROJECT SYSTEM • PROGRESS • PROGRESS ANALYSIS WORKBENCH

Progress Tracking [COMPXPD/WBSXPD/NTWXPD]: PROJECT SYSTEM • PROGRESS • PROGRESS TRACKING/PROGRESS TRACKING FOR WORK BREAKDOWN STRUCTURES/PROGRESS TRACKING FOR NETWORKS

Claim [CLM1/CLM2/CLM3]: PROJECT SYSTEM • NOTIFICATIONS • CLAIM • CREATE/CHANGE/DISPLAY

Claim Analyses [CLM10/CLM11]: PROJECT SYSTEM • INFORMATION SYSTEM • CLAIM • OVERVIEW/HIERARCHY

D.4.2   Customizing Activities

In Customizing of SAP Project System, you can make the following settings with regard to project execution.

Account Assignment of Documents, Confirmations, and Procurement Processes

Execution Services: CUSTOMIZING IMPLEMENTATION GUIDE • PROJECT SYSTEM • COSTS • PLANNED COSTS • EASY COST PLANNING AND EXECUTION SERVICES • EXECUTION SERVICES

Define Confirmation Parameters [OPST]: CUSTOMIZING IMPLEMENTATION GUIDE • PROJECT SYSTEM • CONFIRMATION • DEFINE CONFIRMATION PARAMETERS

CATS Time Sheet: CUSTOMIZING IMPLEMENTATION GUIDE • CROSS-APPLICATION COMPONENTS • TIME SHEET

ProMan Profiles: CUSTOMIZING IMPLEMENTATION GUIDE • PROJECT SYSTEM • MATERIAL • PROJECT-ORIENTED PROCUREMENT (PROMAN)

Project Progress and Claim Management

Progress Analysis: CUSTOMIZING IMPLEMENTATION GUIDE • PROJECT SYSTEM • PROGRESS • PROGRESS ANALYSIS

Progress Tracking: CUSTOMIZING IMPLEMENTATION GUIDE • PROJECT SYSTEM • PROGRESS • PROGRESS TRACKING

Claim Management: CUSTOMIZING IMPLEMENTATION GUIDE • PROJECT SYSTEM • CLAIM

D.5   Period-End Closing

The following transactions and Customizing activities are used for period-end closing.

D.5.1 Transactions in the SAP Menu

You can first view a list of transactions that are important for period-end closing.

Schedule Manager [SCMA]: Project System • Financials • Period-End Closing • Schedule Manager

Revaluation at Actual Prices [CJN1/CJN2]: Project System • Financials • Period-End Closing • Single Functions • Revaluation at Actual Prices • Individual Processing/Collective Processing

Overhead Calculation Commitments and Actual [CJO8/CJO9/CJ44/CJ45]: Project System • Financials • Period-End Closing • Single Functions • Applied Overhead • Commitments: Individual Processing/Commitments: Collective Processing/Individual Processing, Actual/Collective Processing, Actual

Plan Overhead Calculation [CJ46/CJ47]: Project System • Financials • Planning • Allocations • Overhead • Individual Processing/Collective Processing

Actual Template Allocation [CPTK/CPTL]: Project System • Financials • Period-End Closing • Single Functions • Template Allocation • Individual Processing/Collective Processing

Plan Template Allocation [CPUK/CPUL]: Project System • Financials • Planning • Allocations • Template Allocation • Individual Processing/Collective Processing

Actual Interest Calculation [CJZ2/CJZ1]: Project System • Financials • Period-End Closing • Single Functions • Interest Calculation • Individual Processing/Collective Processing

Plan Interest Calculation [CJZ3/CJZ5]: Project System • Financials • Planning • Allocations • Interest Calculation • Individual Processing/Collective Processing

Actual Results Analysis [KKA2/KKAJ]: Project System • Financials • Period-End Closing • Single Functions • Results Analysis • Proceed • Individual Processing/Collective Processing

Plan Results Analysis [KKA2P/KKAJP]: Project System • Financials • Planning • Allocations • Results Analysis • Proceed • Individual Processing/Collective Processing

Project-Based Incoming Orders [CJA2/CJA1]: Project System • Financials • Period-End Closing • Single Functions • Incoming Orders • Individual Processing/Collective Processing

Cost Forecast [CJ9L/CJ9M]: Project System • Financials • Period-End Closing • Single Functions • Cost Forecast • Individual Processing/ Collective Processing/Forecast Workbench

Settlement Rule [CJB2/CJB1]: Project System • Financials • Period-End Closing • Single Functions • Settlement Rule • Individual Processing/Collective Processing

Actual Settlement [CJ88/CJ8G/CJIC]: Project System • Financials • Period-End Closing • Single Functions • Settlement • Individual Processing/Collective Processing/Line Item Apportionment

Plan Settlement [CJ9E/CJ9G]: Project System • Financials • Planning • Allocations • Settlement • Individual Processing/Collective Processing

D.5.2 Customizing Activities

The following adaption options are available in Customizing of SAP Project System for period-end closing.

Overhead Calculation: Customizing Implementation Guide • Project System • Costs • Automatic and Periodic Allocations • Overhead

Template Allocation: Customizing Implementation Guide • Project System • Costs • Automatic and Periodic Allocations • Template – Allocation of Overhead

Interest Calculation: Customizing Implementation Guide • Project System • Costs • Automatic and Periodic Allocations • Interest Calculation

Results Analysis: Customizing Implementation Guide • Project System • Revenues and Earnings • Automatic and Periodic Allocations • Results Analysis

Project-Based Incoming Orders: Customizing Implementation Guide • Project System • Revenues and Earnings • Automatic and Periodic Allocations • Incoming Orders

Forecast Workbench: Customizing Implementation Guide • Project System • Costs • Actual Costs and Expectation • Specify Settings for Forecast Workbench

Settlement: Customizing Implementation Guide • Project System • Costs • Automatic and Periodic Allocations • Settlement

D.6 Reporting

Finally, the following lists the basic transactions, Customizing activities, and menu paths that are available in Reporting.

D.6.1 Transactions in the SAP Menu

You can call the transactions listed here in Project Information System: Structures, Project Information System: Financials, and for logistical reports.

Info System Structures

(Project) Structure Overview [CN41N/CN41]: Project System • Information System • Structures • Project Structure Overview/Structure Overview

Individual Overviews: Project System • Information System • Structures • Individual Overviews

Enhanced Individual Overviews: Project System • Information System • Structures • Enhanced Individual Overviews

Change Documents [CN60/CJCS/CN61]: Project System • Information System • Structures • Change Documents • For Project/Network/For Standard WBS/For Standard Network

Info System Controlling and Summarization

Form [CJE4/CJE5/CJE6]: Project System • Information System • Tools • Hierarchy Reports • Form • Create/Change/Display

(Hierarchy) Report [CJE1/CJE2/CJE3/CJE0]: Project System • Information System • Tools • Hierarchy Reports • Report • Create/Change/Display/Execute

Plan-Based Standard Hierarchy Reports: Project System • Information System • Financials • Costs • Plan-Based • Hierarchical

Budget-Related Standard Hierarchy Reports: Project System • Information System • Financials • Costs • Budget-Related

Revenues/Results-Based Standard Hierarchy Reports: Project System • Information System • Financials • Revenues and Earnings • Hierarchical

Report Group [GR51/GR52/GR53/GR54/GR55]: Project System • Information System • Tools • Cost Element Reports • Define • Report Writer • Report Group • Create/Change/Display/Delete/Execute

Cost Element Report [GRR1/GRR2/GRR3/GR34]: Project System • Information System • Tools • Cost Element Reports • Define • Report • Create/Change/Display/Delete

Plan-Based Standard Cost Element Reports: Project System • Information System • Financials • Costs • Plan-Based • By Cost Element

Revenues/Earnings-Based Standard Cost Element Reports: Project System • Information System • Financials • Revenues and Earnings • By Cost Element

Line Items Reports: Project System • Information System • Financials • Line Items

Standard Payment Reports: PROJECT SYSTEM • INFORMATION SYSTEM • FINANCIALS • PAYMENTS

Summarization [CJH1/CJH2/KKRC]: PROJECT SYSTEM • INFORMATION SYSTEM • TOOLS • SUMMARIZATION • INHERITANCE/INHERITANCE EVALUATION/SUMMARIZATION

Summarization Standard Reports: PROJECT SYSTEM • INFORMATION SYSTEM • FINANCIALS • SUMMARIZATION

Logistical Reports

Orders for Project [ME5J/ME5K]: PROJECT SYSTEM • INFORMATION SYSTEM • MATERIAL • PURCHASE REQUISITIONS • FOR PROJECT/FOR ACCOUNT ASSIGNMENT

Orders for Project [ME5J/ME5K]: PROJECT SYSTEM • INFORMATION SYSTEM • MATERIAL • PURCHASE ORDERS • FOR PROJECT/FOR ACCOUNT ASSIGNMENT

Material Reports [CN52N/MD04/CO24/MB25/MD4C/MBBS]: PROJECT SYSTEM • INFORMATION SYSTEM • MATERIAL • MATERIAL COMPONENTS/STOCK/REQUIREMENTS/MISSING PARTS/RESERVATIONS/ORDER REPORT/VALUATED PROJECT STOCK

Capacity Evaluation Work Center View [CM01/CM02/CM03/CM04/CM05]: PROJECT SYSTEM • RESOURCES • CAPACITY REQUIREMENTS PLANNING • EVALUATION • WORK CENTER VIEW • LOAD/ORDERS/POOL/BACKLOG/OVERLOAD

Extended Evaluation [CM50/CM51/CM52]: PROJECT SYSTEM • RESOURCES • CAPACITY REQUIREMENTS PLANNING • EVALUATION • EXTENDED EVALUATION • WORK CENTER VIEW/INDIVIDUAL CAPACITY VIEW/ORDER VIEW

Extended Evaluation Project View [CM53/CM54/CM55]: PROJECT SYSTEM • RESOURCES • CAPACITY REQUIREMENTS PLANNING • EVALUATION • EXTENDED EVALUATION • PROJECT VIEW • WBS ELEMENT/VERSION/VERSION/WORK CENTER/VERSION

D.6.2 Customizing Activities

You can run the following Customizing activities for Reporting.

Selection

Database Profile [OPTX]: Customizing Implementation Guide • Project System • Information System • Selection • Define Database Selection Profile

Project View for Information System [OPUR]: Customizing Implementation Guide • Project System • Information System • Selection • Define Project View for Information System

Status Selection Profile [BS42]: Customizing Implementation Guide • Project System • Information System • Selection • Define Selection Profiles for Information System

Info System Structures

PS Info Profile [OPSM]: Customizing Implementation Guide • Project System • Information System • Technical Project Reports • Define Overall Profiles for Information System

Define Profiles for Calling Overviews [OPSL]: Customizing Implementation Guide • Project System • Information System • Technical Project Reports • Define Profiles for Calling Overviews

Info System Controlling and Summarization

Value Categories: Customizing Implementation Guide • Project System • Costs • Value Categories

Commitment Items: Customizing Implementation Guide • Project System • Payments • Commitment Items

Activate Project Cash Management [OPI6]: Customizing Implementation Guide • Project System • Payments • Activate Project Cash Management in Company Code

Import Hierarchy Reports [CJEQ]: CUSTOMIZING IMPLEMENTATION GUIDE • PROJECT SYSTEM • INFORMATION SYSTEM • COSTS/REVENUES INFORMATION SYSTEM • HIERARCHY REPORT • IMPORT REPORTS

Import Cost Element Reports [OKSR]: CUSTOMIZING IMPLEMENTATION GUIDE • PROJECT SYSTEM • INFORMATION SYSTEM • COSTS/REVENUES INFORMATION SYSTEM • COST ELEMENT ANALYSIS • STANDARD REPORTS • IMPORT REPORTS

Rebuild Project Information Database [CJEN]: CUSTOMIZING IMPLEMENTATION GUIDE • PROJECT SYSTEM • INFORMATION SYSTEM • COSTS/REVENUES INFORMATION SYSTEM • PROJECT INFO DATABASE (COSTS, REVENUES, FINANCES) • REBUILD PROJECT INFORMATION DATABASE

Maintain Summarization Hierarchy [KKR0]: CUSTOMIZING IMPLEMENTATION GUIDE • PROJECT SYSTEM • INFORMATION SYSTEM • RESPONSIBILITY ACCOUNTING • PROJECT SUMMARIZATION • MAINTAIN SUMMARIZATION HIERARCHY

Logistical Reports

Profiles for Capacity Evaluation [OPA2 – OPA6]: CUSTOMIZING IMPLEMENTATION GUIDE • PRODUCTION • CAPACITY REQUIREMENTS PLANNING • EVALUATION • PROFILES • DEFINE SELECTION PROFILES/OPTIONS PROFILES/LIST PROFILES/GRAPHIC PROFILES/OVERALL PROFILES

Profiles for Enhanced Evaluation [OPD0 – OPD4]: CUSTOMIZING IMPLEMENTATION GUIDE • PRODUCTION • CAPACITY REQUIREMENTS PLANNING • CAPACITY LEVELING AND EXTENDED EVALUATION • DEFINE OVERALL PROFILE/SELECTION PROFILE/TIME PROFILE/EVALUATION PROFILE/PERIOD PROFILE

E   The Author

Dr. Mario Franz currently assumes responsibility for SAP Project System at SAP's development department. Previously, he held various roles at SAP taking care of Enterprise Portfolio and Project Management. In particular, he ran SAP courses on this topic for several years and has trained SAP Project System consultants.

Index